CliffsNotes®

Police Officer Exam

CRAM PLAN™

Northeast Editing, Inc.

WILEY

Wiley Publishing, Inc.

CliffsNotes® Police Officer Exam Cram Plan™

Published by:
Wiley Publishing, Inc.
111 River Street
Hoboken, NJ 07030-5774
www.wiley.com

Published simultaneously in Canada

Library of Congress Control Number: 2011922788
ISBN: 978-0-470-87812-5 (pbk)
ISBN: 978-1-118-03364-7 (ebk)

10 9 8 7 6 5 4 3

About the Authors

Northeast Editing, Inc., has been developing electronic and print products for educational publishers since 1992. Founded by Tracey Vasil Biscontini, the company works with clients to create high-quality, socially sensitive test-preparation and library-reference products, textbooks, teacher guides, and trade books for students of all ages. Located in a former rectory in Jenkins Township, nestled between Wilkes-Barre and Scranton in northeastern Pennsylvania, the company employs nine full-time editors, several part-time employees, and a large pool of local freelance authors and editors. The staff enjoys a relaxed work environment that feels like a home away from home. When they're not hard at work, the editors and writers at Northeast Editing, Inc., enjoy breaks in a large backyard and take time to scratch the bellies of the three rescued cats that live at the office.

Acknowledgements

Northeast Editing would like to extend special thanks to Greg Tubach, our acquisitions editor, and Elizabeth Kuball, our project editor, for their advice and patience during every step of this project.

Editorial

Acquisition Editor: Greg Tubach

Project Editor: Elizabeth Kuball

Copy Editor: Elizabeth Kuball

Technical Editors: Jane Burstein, Michael McAsey, Mary Jane Sterling

Composition

Proofreader: Laura Bowman

Wiley Publishing, Inc., Composition Services

Table of Contents

Introduction

Twenty-four hours a day, seven days a week, police officers are on the street, working diligently to fight crime, maintain order, and keep our cities and towns safe. These officers dedicate their lives to serving and protecting the public.

Police officers face many dangers every day. However, the risks of the job are outweighed by the gratification they receive from upholding the law and protecting their communities.

Because of the dangers and difficulties of the job, police officers must be capable of thinking quickly, acting with authority, and maintaining their composure in stressful and potentially dangerous situations. Officers must also work well with others, because their lives often depend on their ability to think and act as a team.

Due to these requirements, prospective police officers must pass a rigorous screening process before earning the right to wear a badge. Candidates endure a series of challenges, including written exams, physical ability tests, medical and psychological evaluations, background investigations, and interviews.

If you're holding this book, you know that a prospective police officer must be organized and diligent to meet the high standards expected of all law-enforcement officials. Think of this book as another tool in your arsenal as you continue your journey to becoming a police officer. This book will prepare you for the written exam in an organized and timely manner and provide you with additional information about the application requirements, physical abilities test, and personal history statement.

Police Officer Career Opportunities

If you're thinking about becoming a police officer, there are a wide range of career opportunities available to you. Police officers serve their communities in many capacities, all of which include unique duties and responsibilities. Here is a brief description of some of the possible career opportunities for a police officer, which may vary from location to location:

- **Patrol officer:** Patrol officers are the most common type of police officers. These officers are responsible for patrolling designated areas and watching for criminal activity or other suspicious behavior. Patrol officers must use their knowledge and their senses to recognize criminal activity, apprehend suspects, and prevent crime. Although many patrol officers perform their duties on foot, others use automobiles, motorcycles, bicycles, horses, boats, or aircrafts to monitor their communities.
- **Traffic officer:** Traffic officers are responsible for enforcing traffic regulations and investigating traffic accidents. Traffic officers also may be required to use their knowledge of traffic laws and patterns to note and report the need for any changes to the current traffic regulations.
- **Juvenile officer:** Juvenile officers are responsible for addressing issues concerning underage offenders and juvenile crime. These officers must have expertise in juvenile criminal laws and procedures. They also must be skilled at working with adolescents and children.
- **Canine officer:** Canine officers are specifically trained to carry out responsibilities that involve the use of trained police dogs. These officers, who are frequently called upon in situations that require the keen senses and physical abilities of police dogs, must demonstrate the desire and ability to work with canine partners.

- **Crime scene investigator:** Police officers who serve as crime scene investigators are responsible for gathering evidence at crime scenes and assisting police detectives with ongoing investigations. These officers usually hold degrees in criminal justice, forensics, or other similar fields.
- **Crime prevention officer:** These officers work to prevent crime in their communities by educating the public on crime and crime prevention. Crime prevention officers often serve as public speakers, security surveyors, and crime prevention strategists.
- **Community policing officer:** Like crime prevention officers, community policing officers help fight crime by taking a more active role in their communities. These officers work on special beats where they're expected to interact with community members and take part in public events. These officers must recognize community problems and create, identify, and evaluate solutions.
- **Warrant officer:** Warrant officers are responsible for serving various types of warrants. These may include arrest, search, and bench warrants.
- **Other officers:** Some police officers may serve as members of hostage negotiation teams, SWAT teams, or bomb squads. Officers also may serve as part of a specific department, such as major crimes, special victims, or property crimes.

Becoming a Police Officer

To become a police officer, you must pass a strict screening process. This process determines whether you're truly qualified for a life in law enforcement. This section provides a brief overview of the various steps in the selection process. The order of the steps may vary.

Application

The selection process begins when you fill out an application. Depending on the size and finances of the department you want to join, applications may be distributed at regular intervals or when new positions become available. Applicants must satisfy a number of important requirements before they can fill out an application. Applicants must:

- Show proof of high school graduation or completion of a high school equivalency test, such as the GED
- Meet a minimum age requirement (usually 21 years of age)
- Show proof of citizenship
- Have a valid driver's license and an acceptable driving record
- Not have any felony convictions or dishonorable discharges from the military
- Have natural or corrected 20/20 vision and normal color vision
- Meet the minimum medical standards established by civil service personnel
- Not have a history of any drug or alcohol abuse

These requirements may vary from department to department. Check with your local department to learn about its specific requirements before you fill out an application.

Written Exam

Since you're already reading this book, you probably know that you'll have to pass a written exam to become a police officer. The police officer written exam is a general aptitude test designed to assess your critical-thinking abilities. For more information on the written exam, see "About the Test," later in this introduction.

Physical Ability Test

Because police work can be physically demanding, you'll need to pass a physical ability test. This test is designed to assess your stamina and overall physical fitness. The various components of the physical ability test will demonstrate your muscular strength, flexibility, endurance, and aerobic conditioning. Here are some of the activities that you may be asked to complete during this test:

- Simulated victim carry with a 165-pound dummy
- Push-up, pull-up, and sit-up repetitions
- Obstacle course
- Stair climbing
- Weight-training test, which can include curling, squatting, and bench-pressing using different weights and equipment

Again, as with all stages of the selection process, the exact nature of the physical ability test may vary. Check with your local department to find out what your requirements will be.

Medical and Psychological Evaluation

Clearly, a police officer needs to be healthy, both mentally and physically. As part of the selection process, you'll have to submit to medical and psychological examinations that evaluate your overall health. The medical evaluation is designed both to assess your physical health and to determine whether you have any preexisting conditions that may inhibit your ability to perform the duties of a police officer.

The psychological evaluation is designed to evaluate your mental health. This assessment helps the department to assess your judgment and common sense, qualities that are of vital importance to a police officer. It also can help to demonstrate any mental-health conditions that may affect your ability to work as a police officer. The psychological evaluation may be performed by a professional psychologist, or it may be given as a written assessment.

The medical and psychological evaluations are critical because, due to the dangers involved in police work, all officers must be physically and mentally fit. Officers with any physical or mental deficiencies may present a danger to themselves and their co-workers.

Background Investigation

Police departments routinely research candidates' personal backgrounds to ensure that the information in their applications and personal history statements is accurate. If you reach this stage of the selection process, a detective or other qualified investigator will conduct a thorough background check. The detective will investigate your past by reviewing personal information, such as your educational accomplishments, employment history, criminal record, driving record, and military service, if applicable. In many cases, the detective also will interview people who know you, including acquaintances, neighbors, teachers, and co-workers. This investigation helps the department construct a clear picture of your character.

You also may be required to take a polygraph or "lie detector" test as a part of this investigation. A qualified polygraph operator will administer the test, asking you a series of basic questions about your background. Then the results of this test will be forwarded to investigators and used as part of your background investigation. During this test, it's very important to answer all questions truthfully. Don't try to cover up any previous indiscretions. Many past mistakes can be overlooked easily, but lies cannot. Remember that truthfulness is a key factor throughout the selection process, and any dishonesty on your part will only hurt your chances of becoming a police officer.

Oral Board Interview

When a police department is hiring new officers, those candidates who score the highest on the various qualifying exams are often asked to appear before an oral board and participate in a formal interview. During this interview, the candidates are questioned by a panel of about three to five interviewers who ask them questions about their background and their ability to perform a police officer's duties. Some common questions include

- What do you think makes you more qualified than other candidates?
- Would you be able to use deadly force against another person?
- What are your strengths and weaknesses?

Your answers will allow the panelists to develop a sense of your personal character, situational abilities, and communication skills. You must attain board approval to be considered for a position with the police department.

About the Test

One of most important steps in becoming a police officer is passing the police officer exam. This written exam is specially designed to test your competency in several critical subject areas.

Although the length and time limit of the police officer exam may vary according to standards set by individual states or departments, most exams require candidates to answer approximately 75 to 150 multiple-choice questions in one and a half to three hours.

The following are the basic question types you're likely to find on the police officer exam:

- **Verbal (see Chapter V):** Verbal questions on the police officer exam test your reading and writing skills. You may be required to answer questions based on reading passages, demonstrate your ability to recognize and use proper grammar, and identify the correct spelling of words.

- **Memorization and visualization (see Chapter VI):** These questions test your ability to remember important details in various situations. In some instances, you may be presented with an image that you'll study for a certain amount of time. After that time is up, you'll be asked to answer several questions about the image. You won't be allowed to look at the image as you answer the questions. Other memorization and visualization questions may require you to interpret a map, recognize a row of houses from behind, or determine in which direction a suspect was seen fleeing.

- **Mathematics questions (see Chapter VII):** The police officer exam also assesses your mathematical abilities. The questions on the mathematics portion of the exam are designed to test your knowledge of simple addition, subtraction, multiplication, and division. Some questions also may involve basic concepts like decimals, percentages, ratios, fractions, circumference, area, and time. In addition, you'll likely encounter various word problems and scenario-based questions.

- **Judgment and problem solving (see Chapter VIII):** Judgment and problem-solving questions test your ability to use sound reasoning and common sense to make critical decisions in various situations. Some of these questions may present you with a scenario and ask you to identify the best course of action. Others may require you to arrange the lines of a police report in the proper order. Although many of these questions involve specific police procedures and policies, remember that you're being tested on your judgment and reasoning skills, not on your knowledge of department protocols.

After you've completed the exam, your score will determine if you'll continue through the selection process. For most tests, a score of 70 or better is considered passing. Some departments consider only those applicants who score in the top 20% to 25%.

About This Book

As you begin to prepare for the police officer exam, your first step should be to choose the appropriate cram plan. Depending on how much time you have to study for the test, you may select the two-month plan (Chapter II), the one-month plan (Chapter III), or the one-week plan (Chapter IV). Each plan includes a study schedule for you to follow and describes how much time you'll need to complete each task.

You should get started by taking the Diagnostic Test (Chapter I). Your errors on this test will pinpoint your weaknesses and help you discover the areas that require additional attention. In Chapters V through VIII, you'll find practice exercises that will help sharpen your skills in different subject areas. Taking the Full-Length Practice Test (Chapter IX) will provide you with an opportunity to preview your possible performance on the police officer exam.

I. Diagnostic Test

Answer Sheet

Section 1

1 Ⓐ Ⓑ Ⓒ	21 Ⓐ Ⓑ Ⓒ Ⓓ
2 Ⓐ Ⓑ Ⓒ	22 Ⓐ Ⓑ Ⓒ Ⓓ
3 Ⓐ Ⓑ Ⓒ	23 Ⓐ Ⓑ Ⓒ Ⓓ
4 Ⓐ Ⓑ Ⓒ	24 Ⓐ Ⓑ Ⓒ Ⓓ
5 Ⓐ Ⓑ Ⓒ	25 Ⓐ Ⓑ Ⓒ Ⓓ
6 Ⓐ Ⓑ Ⓒ	26 Ⓐ Ⓑ Ⓒ Ⓓ
7 Ⓐ Ⓑ Ⓒ	27 Ⓐ Ⓑ Ⓒ Ⓓ
8 Ⓐ Ⓑ Ⓒ	28 Ⓐ Ⓑ Ⓒ Ⓓ
9 Ⓐ Ⓑ Ⓒ	29 Ⓐ Ⓑ Ⓒ Ⓓ
10 Ⓐ Ⓑ Ⓒ	30 Ⓐ Ⓑ Ⓒ Ⓓ
11 Ⓐ Ⓑ Ⓒ Ⓓ	31 Ⓐ Ⓑ Ⓒ Ⓓ
12 Ⓐ Ⓑ Ⓒ Ⓓ	32 Ⓐ Ⓑ Ⓒ Ⓓ
13 Ⓐ Ⓑ Ⓒ Ⓓ	33 Ⓐ Ⓑ Ⓒ Ⓓ
14 Ⓐ Ⓑ Ⓒ Ⓓ	34 Ⓐ Ⓑ
15 Ⓐ Ⓑ	35 Ⓐ Ⓑ Ⓒ Ⓓ
16 Ⓐ Ⓑ	36 Ⓐ Ⓑ Ⓒ Ⓓ
17 Ⓐ Ⓑ	37 Ⓐ Ⓑ Ⓒ Ⓓ
18 Ⓐ Ⓑ	38 Ⓐ Ⓑ Ⓒ Ⓓ
19 Ⓐ Ⓑ	39 Ⓐ Ⓑ Ⓒ Ⓓ
20 Ⓐ Ⓑ	40 Ⓐ Ⓑ Ⓒ Ⓓ

41. _____
42. _____
43. _____
44. _____
45. _____

46. _____
47. _____
48. _____
49. _____
50. _____

Section 2

1 Ⓐ Ⓑ Ⓒ Ⓓ	26 Ⓐ Ⓑ Ⓒ Ⓓ
2 Ⓐ Ⓑ Ⓒ Ⓓ	27 Ⓐ Ⓑ Ⓒ Ⓓ
3 Ⓐ Ⓑ Ⓒ Ⓓ	28 Ⓐ Ⓑ Ⓒ Ⓓ
4 Ⓐ Ⓑ Ⓒ Ⓓ	29 Ⓐ Ⓑ Ⓒ Ⓓ
5 Ⓐ Ⓑ Ⓒ Ⓓ	30 Ⓐ Ⓑ Ⓒ Ⓓ
6 Ⓐ Ⓑ Ⓒ Ⓓ	31 Ⓐ Ⓑ Ⓒ Ⓓ
7 Ⓐ Ⓑ Ⓒ Ⓓ	32 Ⓐ Ⓑ Ⓒ Ⓓ
8 Ⓐ Ⓑ Ⓒ Ⓓ	33 Ⓐ Ⓑ Ⓒ Ⓓ
9 Ⓐ Ⓑ Ⓒ Ⓓ	34 Ⓐ Ⓑ Ⓒ Ⓓ
10 Ⓐ Ⓑ Ⓒ Ⓓ	35 Ⓐ Ⓑ Ⓒ Ⓓ
11 Ⓐ Ⓑ Ⓒ Ⓓ	36 Ⓐ Ⓑ Ⓒ Ⓓ
12 Ⓐ Ⓑ Ⓒ Ⓓ	37 Ⓐ Ⓑ Ⓒ Ⓓ
13 Ⓐ Ⓑ Ⓒ Ⓓ	38 Ⓐ Ⓑ Ⓒ Ⓓ
14 Ⓐ Ⓑ Ⓒ Ⓓ	39 Ⓐ Ⓑ Ⓒ Ⓓ
15 Ⓐ Ⓑ Ⓒ Ⓓ	40 Ⓐ Ⓑ Ⓒ Ⓓ
16 Ⓐ Ⓑ Ⓒ Ⓓ	41 Ⓐ Ⓑ Ⓒ Ⓓ
17 Ⓐ Ⓑ Ⓒ Ⓓ	42 Ⓐ Ⓑ Ⓒ Ⓓ
18 Ⓐ Ⓑ Ⓒ Ⓓ	43 Ⓐ Ⓑ Ⓒ Ⓓ
19 Ⓐ Ⓑ Ⓒ Ⓓ	44 Ⓐ Ⓑ Ⓒ Ⓓ
20 Ⓐ Ⓑ Ⓒ Ⓓ	45 Ⓐ Ⓑ Ⓒ Ⓓ
21 Ⓐ Ⓑ Ⓒ Ⓓ	46 Ⓐ Ⓑ Ⓒ Ⓓ
22 Ⓐ Ⓑ Ⓒ Ⓓ	47 Ⓐ Ⓑ Ⓒ Ⓓ
23 Ⓐ Ⓑ Ⓒ Ⓓ	48 Ⓐ Ⓑ Ⓒ Ⓓ
24 Ⓐ Ⓑ Ⓒ Ⓓ	49 Ⓐ Ⓑ Ⓒ Ⓓ
25 Ⓐ Ⓑ Ⓒ Ⓓ	50 Ⓐ Ⓑ Ⓒ Ⓓ

CUT HERE

Section 3

1 Ⓐ Ⓑ Ⓒ Ⓓ	26 Ⓐ Ⓑ Ⓒ Ⓓ
2 Ⓐ Ⓑ Ⓒ Ⓓ	27 Ⓐ Ⓑ Ⓒ Ⓓ
3 Ⓐ Ⓑ Ⓒ Ⓓ	28 Ⓐ Ⓑ Ⓒ Ⓓ
4 Ⓐ Ⓑ Ⓒ Ⓓ	29 Ⓐ Ⓑ Ⓒ Ⓓ
5 Ⓐ Ⓑ Ⓒ Ⓓ	30 Ⓐ Ⓑ Ⓒ Ⓓ
6 Ⓐ Ⓑ Ⓒ Ⓓ	31 Ⓐ Ⓑ Ⓒ Ⓓ
7 Ⓐ Ⓑ Ⓒ Ⓓ	32 Ⓐ Ⓑ Ⓒ Ⓓ
8 Ⓐ Ⓑ Ⓒ Ⓓ	33 Ⓐ Ⓑ Ⓒ Ⓓ
9 Ⓐ Ⓑ Ⓒ Ⓓ	34 Ⓐ Ⓑ Ⓒ Ⓓ
10 Ⓐ Ⓑ Ⓒ Ⓓ	35 Ⓐ Ⓑ Ⓒ Ⓓ
11 Ⓐ Ⓑ Ⓒ Ⓓ	36 Ⓐ Ⓑ Ⓒ Ⓓ
12 Ⓐ Ⓑ Ⓒ Ⓓ	37 Ⓐ Ⓑ Ⓒ Ⓓ
13 Ⓐ Ⓑ Ⓒ Ⓓ	38 Ⓐ Ⓑ Ⓒ Ⓓ
14 Ⓐ Ⓑ Ⓒ Ⓓ	39 Ⓐ Ⓑ Ⓒ Ⓓ
15 Ⓐ Ⓑ Ⓒ Ⓓ	40 Ⓐ Ⓑ Ⓒ Ⓓ
16 Ⓐ Ⓑ Ⓒ Ⓓ	41 Ⓐ Ⓑ Ⓒ Ⓓ
17 Ⓐ Ⓑ Ⓒ Ⓓ	42 Ⓐ Ⓑ Ⓒ Ⓓ
18 Ⓐ Ⓑ Ⓒ Ⓓ	43 Ⓐ Ⓑ Ⓒ Ⓓ
19 Ⓐ Ⓑ Ⓒ Ⓓ	44 Ⓐ Ⓑ Ⓒ Ⓓ
20 Ⓐ Ⓑ Ⓒ Ⓓ	45 Ⓐ Ⓑ Ⓒ Ⓓ
21 Ⓐ Ⓑ Ⓒ Ⓓ	46 Ⓐ Ⓑ Ⓒ Ⓓ
22 Ⓐ Ⓑ Ⓒ Ⓓ	47 Ⓐ Ⓑ Ⓒ Ⓓ
23 Ⓐ Ⓑ Ⓒ Ⓓ	48 Ⓐ Ⓑ Ⓒ Ⓓ
24 Ⓐ Ⓑ Ⓒ Ⓓ	49 Ⓐ Ⓑ Ⓒ Ⓓ
25 Ⓐ Ⓑ Ⓒ Ⓓ	50 Ⓐ Ⓑ Ⓒ Ⓓ

CUT HERE

Section 4

1	Ⓐ Ⓑ Ⓒ Ⓓ	26	Ⓐ Ⓑ Ⓒ Ⓓ
2	Ⓐ Ⓑ Ⓒ Ⓓ	27	Ⓐ Ⓑ Ⓒ Ⓓ
3	Ⓐ Ⓑ Ⓒ Ⓓ	28	Ⓐ Ⓑ Ⓒ Ⓓ
4	Ⓐ Ⓑ Ⓒ Ⓓ	29	Ⓐ Ⓑ Ⓒ Ⓓ
5	Ⓐ Ⓑ Ⓒ Ⓓ	30	Ⓐ Ⓑ Ⓒ Ⓓ
6	Ⓐ Ⓑ Ⓒ Ⓓ	31	Ⓐ Ⓑ Ⓒ Ⓓ
7	Ⓐ Ⓑ Ⓒ Ⓓ	32	Ⓐ Ⓑ Ⓒ Ⓓ
8	Ⓐ Ⓑ Ⓒ Ⓓ	33	Ⓐ Ⓑ Ⓒ Ⓓ
9	Ⓐ Ⓑ Ⓒ Ⓓ	34	Ⓐ Ⓑ Ⓒ Ⓓ
10	Ⓐ Ⓑ Ⓒ Ⓓ	35	Ⓐ Ⓑ Ⓒ Ⓓ
11	Ⓐ Ⓑ Ⓒ Ⓓ	36	Ⓐ Ⓑ Ⓒ Ⓓ
12	Ⓐ Ⓑ Ⓒ Ⓓ	37	Ⓐ Ⓑ Ⓒ Ⓓ
13	Ⓐ Ⓑ Ⓒ Ⓓ	38	Ⓐ Ⓑ Ⓒ Ⓓ
14	Ⓐ Ⓑ Ⓒ Ⓓ	39	Ⓐ Ⓑ Ⓒ Ⓓ
15	Ⓐ Ⓑ Ⓒ Ⓓ	40	Ⓐ Ⓑ Ⓒ Ⓓ
16	Ⓐ Ⓑ Ⓒ Ⓓ	41	Ⓐ Ⓑ Ⓒ Ⓓ
17	Ⓐ Ⓑ Ⓒ Ⓓ	42	Ⓐ Ⓑ Ⓒ Ⓓ
18	Ⓐ Ⓑ Ⓒ Ⓓ	43	Ⓐ Ⓑ Ⓒ Ⓓ
19	Ⓐ Ⓑ Ⓒ Ⓓ	44	Ⓐ Ⓑ Ⓒ Ⓓ
20	Ⓐ Ⓑ Ⓒ Ⓓ	45	Ⓐ Ⓑ Ⓒ Ⓓ
21	Ⓐ Ⓑ Ⓒ Ⓓ	46	Ⓐ Ⓑ Ⓒ Ⓓ
22	Ⓐ Ⓑ Ⓒ Ⓓ	47	Ⓐ Ⓑ Ⓒ Ⓓ
23	Ⓐ Ⓑ Ⓒ Ⓓ	48	Ⓐ Ⓑ Ⓒ Ⓓ
24	Ⓐ Ⓑ Ⓒ Ⓓ	49	Ⓐ Ⓑ Ⓒ Ⓓ
25	Ⓐ Ⓑ Ⓒ Ⓓ	50	Ⓐ Ⓑ Ⓒ Ⓓ

CUT HERE

Section 1: Verbal

Time: 50 minutes

50 questions

Directions (1–10): Select the best answer choice to complete each sentence.

1. The suspects lined up in a single row with _____ arms in the air.

   A. there
   B. their
   C. they're

2. Within a span of ten minutes, the police unit responded to the scenes of two separate _____ in the same neighborhood.

   A. incidents
   B. incidents'
   C. incident's

3. The neighbor informed the _____ parents that she would call the police if he didn't stay off her property.

   A. teenagers'
   B. teenagers
   C. teenager's

4. After speaking with the victim of the home invasion, the officer had the _____ name, his physical description, and the description of his weapon.

   A. suspects
   B. suspect's
   C. suspects'

5. While training in the police academy, superiors often use mock wanted _____ to test their recruits' memorization skills.

   A. posters
   B. poster's
   C. posters'

6. Identity theft is a serious crime that often ruins _____ financial and personal lives.

   A. victims
   B. victim's
   C. victims'

7. When the suspect walked out of the bank, the officer yelled, "Drop the gun and put _____ hands in the air!"

   A. you're
   B. you are
   C. your

8. The police will search the suspect's house and his girlfriend's house as soon as the judge approves _____ separate warrants.

   A. to
   B. too
   C. two

9. The officers took turns patrolling the area _____ the suspect was last seen.

   A. wear
   B. where
   C. ware

10. The vehicle accumulated multiple parking violations before the officers _____ it.

    A. toad
    B. towed
    C. toed

Directions (11–12): Choose the answer that reflects the error(s) in capitalization.

11. Officers Landers and Torres turned right onto 145 Pine street, where they saw the suspect fleeing on foot.

    A. Officers
    B. Pine
    C. street
    D. suspect

12. The city increased Police Presence from Friday through Sunday because of the expected crowds from the New Year's Eve celebrations.

    A. Police Presence
    B. Friday
    C. Sunday
    D. New Year's Eve

Directions (13–14): Choose the sentence that corrects the error(s) in punctuation.

13. The victim who lives at 65 Dover Avenue reported that his wallet and sunglasses were stolen.

    A. The victim who lives at 65 Dover Avenue reported that his wallet and sunglasses were stolen.
    B. The victim, who lives at 65, Dover Avenue, reported that his wallet and sunglasses were stolen.
    C. The victim, who lives at 65 Dover Avenue reported that his wallet and sunglasses were stolen.
    D. The victim, who lives at 65 Dover Avenue, reported that his wallet and sunglasses were stolen.

14. The officer called in her location she then waited in the parking lot for backup.

    A. The officer called in her location, she then waited in the parking lot for backup.
    B. The officer called in her location; she then waited in the parking lot for backup.
    C. The officer called in her location she then waited; in the parking lot for backup.
    D. The officer, called in her location, she then waited in the parking lot for backup.

Directions (15–20): Answer the questions solely on the basis of the following incident report.

INCIDENT REPORT – POLICE DEPARTMENT			
1. ADDRESS OF INCIDENT	2. OFFENSE	3. CODE	4. DATE
5. NAME OF VICTIM: INDIVIDUAL OR BUSINESS	6. ADDRESS	PHONE	
7. ASSIGNED OFFICERS/BADGE NUMBERS	8. AGE OF VICTIM	9. RACE OF VICTIM	10. VICTIM'S DATE OF BIRTH
11. NAME OF SUSPECT	12. ADDRESS		
13. AGE	14. RACE	15. SEX	16. DATE OF BIRTH	17. HEIGHT	18. WEIGHT
19. HAIR	20. EYES	21. PHYSICAL DESCRIPTION	
22. CHARGES			
23. ITEM	24. BRAND	25. SERIAL NUMBER	26. VALUE
27. ITEM	28. BRAND	29. SERIAL NUMBER	30. VALUE
31. ITEM	32. BRAND	33. SERIAL NUMBER	34. VALUE
35. _____			
SIGNATURE OF OFFICER/BADGE NUMBER			

Max Bernard, owner of a house located on 313 Blackwell Dr., called police headquarters at 7:15 p.m. on Friday, June 6, to report that his house had been broken into sometime during the day while he was at work. Officers Francine Meyers and Bobbi Jean Thurmond arrived at the house at 7:20 p.m. to investigate the incident. Mr. Bernard reported that his watch was missing and that more than $4,000 in cash was taken from his bedroom safe.

15. Section 11 of the incident report can be fully completed based on the information in the paragraph.

A. True
 B. False

16. The incident took place at 313 Blackwell Dr.

    A. True
    B. False

Brenda Moore, 65, of 235 Columbus Dr., called police headquarters at 10:05 p.m. on Wednesday, March 20, to report that her purse had been stolen while she was walking southward near the 100 block of Washington Boulevard at approximately 9:55 p.m. Officers Monique Patton (badge number 452) and Anthony Edwards (badge number 374) arrived at 105 Washington Blvd. at 10:15 p.m. to investigate the incident. Ms. Moore reported that her purse contained her wallet, keys, cellphone, approximately $27 in cash, and three credit cards.

17. The incident report can be fully completed based on the information in the paragraph.

    A. True
    B. False

18. Ms. Moore's purse contained four credit cards.

    A. True
    B. False

José Roberts, 47, of 235 Ocean View Ave., called police headquarters at 5:30 p.m. on Thursday, February 8, to report trespassing at his residence. Officers Inez Sanchez (badge number 78) and Maggie Rowe (badge number 154) arrived at the residence at 5:47 p.m. to investigate the incident. Mr. Roberts reported that his neighbor, Shawn Ferguson, trespassed onto his property and refused to leave at Mr. Roberts's request.

19. Sections 4 and 5 of the incident report can be fully completed based on the information in the paragraph.

    A. True
    B. False

20. The victim's name is José Sanchez.

    A. True
    B. False

Directions (21–27): Select the word that is spelled incorrectly in each sentence.

21. The confidential informent provided the undercover police officer with enough information to arrest the suspect.

    A. confidential
    B. informent
    C. undercover
    D. officer

22. The emergency response unit was the first to arrive on the scene of an apparant homicide.

    A. emergency
    B. response
    C. apparant
    D. homicide

23. Officer Juarez picked up the weapon and put it in an appropriately marked avidence container.

   A. Officer
   B. weapon
   C. appropriately
   D. avidence

24. When responding to the scene of a motor-vehicle collision, police officers should always position their patrol cars behind disaibled vehicles.

   A. collision
   B. position
   C. disaibled
   D. vehicles

25. Officer Rawls would like to voluntear at a cultural organization where he could work with elderly individuals.

   A. voluntear
   B. cultural
   C. organization
   D. individuals

26. Police officers do not usually exert force to overcome a suspect's resistance or to gain coroperation and compliance.

   A. usually
   B. exert
   C. resistance
   D. coroperation

27. The officers are being trained to use the latest equipment and technology, which will undoubtedly make paperwork more effecient.

   A. equipment
   B. technology
   C. undoubtedly
   D. effecient

Directions (28–33): Select the answer choice that best describes the sentences.

Question 28 refers to the following.

Officer Johnson fills out an accident report after responding to the scene. She reads through the report, which contains the following two sentences:

   I. The driver of vehicle A failed to stop at the stop sign and hit the front passenger side of vehicle B as it was passing through the intersection.
   II. The witness said she see the driver of vehicle A pass through the intersection without stopping.

28. Which of the following best describes the preceding sentences?

   A. Only sentence I is grammatically correct.
   B. Only sentence II is grammatically correct.
   C. Neither sentence I nor sentence II is grammatically correct.
   D. Both sentence I and sentence II are grammatically correct.

Question 29 refers to the following.

Lieutenant O'Malley is filling out an incident report, which contains the following two sentences:

I. José Sanchez, owner of Sanchez's Food Mart, described the robbery suspect as a juvenile he was wearing a black sweatshirt and blue jeans.

II. The suspect removed items valued at more than $200 from the meat section of the grocery store.

29. Which of the following best describes the preceding sentences?

A. Only sentence I is grammatically correct.
B. Only sentence II is grammatically correct.
C. Neither sentence I nor sentence II is grammatically correct.
D. Both sentence I and sentence II are grammatically correct.

Question 30 refers to the following.

A recruit officer is preparing a statement for her commanding officer. The statement contains the following two sentences:

I. Officer Juarez and I were called to investigate a fight among a group of teenagers at 41 Main St. around 11:30 p.m. on Friday.

II. After arriving at the scene, Officer Juarez and I discovered that the fight had broken up and the crowd had dispersed.

30. Which of the following best describes the preceding sentences?

A. Only sentence I is grammatically correct.
B. Only sentence II is grammatically correct.
C. Neither sentence I nor sentence II is grammatically correct.
D. Both sentence I and sentence II are grammatically correct.

Question 31 refers to the following.

An officer fills out an incident report after responding to a call. He reads through the report, which contains the following two sentences:

I. The victim's 10-year-old daughter called 911 after seeing her father strike our mother in the face during an argument.

II. The suspect told police that his daughter call 911 by mistake.

31. Which of the following best describes the preceding sentences?

A. Only sentence I is grammatically correct.
B. Only sentence II is grammatically correct.
C. Neither sentence I nor sentence II is grammatically correct.
D. Both sentence I and sentence II are grammatically correct.

Question 32 refers to the following.

After responding to a motor-vehicle accident, Officer Montgomery fills out an incident report. It contains the following two sentences:

I. After turning left onto Samson Street, Mr. Davis drove over a patch of ice and lost control of the vehicle.

II. The driver sustained only minor injuries and was treated at the scene by emergency services.

32. Which of the following best describes the preceding sentences?

A. Only sentence I is grammatically correct.
B. Only sentence II is grammatically correct.
C. Neither sentence I nor sentence II is grammatically correct.
D. Both sentence I and sentence II are grammatically correct.

Question 33 refers to the following.

Officer Lewis filled out an incident report at the end of her shift. The report contains the following two sentences:

I. The unidentified suspect, who wore red shorts and a white shirt, fled the residence when the occupants returned home.

II. After the suspect fled and the residents called police headquarters.

33. Which of the following best describes the preceding sentences?

A. Only sentence I is grammatically correct.

B. Only sentence II is grammatically correct.

C. Neither sentence I nor sentence II is grammatically correct.

D. Both sentence I and sentence II are grammatically correct.

Directions (34–40): Answer the questions solely on the basis of the corresponding passage.

Questions 34 through 37 refer to the following passage.

Officers Franco and Hill responded to a home invasion report at 14 Pine St. at 4:16 a.m. on June 19. When the officers arrived at the residence, the owner, Jennifer Janoski,
(5) reported that someone broke into her home while she slept. Mrs. Janoski explained that she woke up when she heard a noise and saw someone standing in her bedroom. Mrs. Janoski screamed, and the suspect fled from
(10) the room and out of the house. Then Mrs. Janoski called the police and waited in her bathroom. She was the only person at home at the time because her husband was out of town visiting their son.
(15) When officers Franco and Hill inspected the scene, they noticed overturned drawers in the bedroom, den, and kitchen. The contents of the drawers were strewn around the rooms. After making a careful inspection, Mrs.
(20) Janoski reported that her Gucci purse was stolen. It contained an empty wallet and other personal items. She also reported that a small jewelry box containing her wedding band, a diamond ring, a sapphire ring, two pairs of
(25) diamond earrings, a man's watch, and an old handkerchief with the initials J. J. also were stolen.

While Officer Hills interviewed Mrs. Janoski, Officer Franco searched the property
(30) and spoke with neighbors. Mr. Tom Williams, resident of 13 Pine St., told Officer Franco that he was getting a glass of water around 4:15 a.m. when he heard a scream. Mr. Williams opened his front door to determine
(35) where the scream came from, and he saw a man running down the street. Mr. Williams did not see much because the street was dark, but he described the suspect as wearing black clothing and white sneakers. Mr. Williams
(40) said that the suspect headed north toward the town park. Officer Franco determined that none of the other neighbors noticed anything unusual. Officer Franco headed toward the park on foot and called another police unit to
(45) check the perimeter of the park.

Officer Franco returned a short time later with no leads. He and Officer Hills returned to the park to search one more time before heading back to the station to complete their crime
(50) report at 6:25 a.m.

34. Mrs. Janoski's initials are sewn onto the handkerchief.

A. True

B. False

35. Which of these words could best replace the word *strewn* on line 18 of the passage?

    A. littered
    B. cleaned
    C. strained
    D. folded

36. Where was Mrs. Janoski's husband at the time of the incident?

    A. Sleeping in his bed
    B. Reading in their study
    C. Out of town visiting their son
    D. Working at his office

37. Which of these did Mrs. Janoski *not* report missing after the incident?

    A. A purse
    B. A wallet
    C. A necklace
    D. A watch

Questions 38 through 40 refer to the following passage.

On August 17, officers Kelly and Vasquez arrived at 37 Main St., Apt. 2B, at 4:35 p.m., in response to a burglary reported by a Mr. Robert Loucks. When the officers arrived at the scene, Mr. Loucks reported that he had left for work at the local community college at 7:30 a.m. and that his wife, Mrs. Laura Loucks, had left for her job as a personal trainer at 9 a.m. Because Mrs. Loucks walks to work, Mr. Loucks picked her up on his way home. They returned to their apartment around 4:20 p.m. When Mrs. Loucks entered the master bedroom, she noticed that her jewelry box was on the floor, face down and empty. The safe in the closet was open and empty, too. Her husband called the police while she checked the rest of the apartment. While waiting for the police, they discovered that Mr. Loucks's stamp collection also had been stolen from his office.

Officer Vasquez talked with Mrs. Olivia White, age 32, who lives in apartment 2D. She told Officer Vasquez that she heard unfamiliar voices in the hallway outside her apartment door at 1:30 p.m. When she looked into the hallway, she saw a young man and a young woman standing by the stairwell. The male was slightly taller than the female. The male was white, about 18 or 19 years old, and had a blond crew cut. He was wearing glasses and carrying a black backpack. The female was approximately 16 years old and had curly black hair. Both teens wore khaki pants and polo shirts. The male's shirt was green, while the female's shirt was pink.

Officers Vasquez and Kelly finished their interviews and departed from the scene at approximately 5:25 p.m. Then the officers returned to the station to complete their crime report.

38. Which of the following is true of the female Mrs. White saw in the hallway?

    A. She was wearing a pink polo shirt.
    B. She was wearing glasses.
    C. She was carrying a black bag.
    D. She had short, blond hair.

39. Where is Mr. and Mrs. Loucks's safe located?

    A. In the living room
    B. In the master bedroom
    C. In the spare bedroom
    D. In the office

40. Which apartment do the Loucks live in?

    A. 2A
    B. 2B
    C. 2C
    D. 2D

Directions (41–50): Answer the questions solely on the basis of the corresponding incident reports.

Questions 41 through 45 refer to the following incident report.

INCIDENT REPORT – POLICE DEPARTMENT

1. ADDRESS OF INCIDENT	2. OFFENSE	3. CODE	4. DATE
56 Beech St.	Assault		

5. NAME OF VICTIM: INDIVIDUAL OR BUSINESS	6. ADDRESS PHONE
Amelia Martinez	56 Beech St.

7. ASSIGNED OFFICERS/BADGE NUMBERS	8. AGE OF VICTIM	9. RACE OF VICTIM	10. VICTIM'S DATE OF BIRTH
Matthew Palmer #235	25	Hispanic	November 18

11. NAME OF SUSPECT	12. ADDRESS
Oscar Bishop	15 Maddox St.

13. AGE	14. RACE	15. SEX	16. DATE OF BIRTH	17. HEIGHT	18. WEIGHT
30	Hispanic	Male	April 26	5'9"	175

19. HAIR	20. EYES	21. PHYSICAL DESCRIPTION
Brown	Brown	Blue jeans, black sweatshirt, black baseball cap

22. CHARGES

23. ITEM	24. BRAND	25. SERIAL NUMBER	26. VALUE

27. ITEM	28. BRAND	29. SERIAL NUMBER	30. VALUE

31. ITEM	32. BRAND	33. SERIAL NUMBER	34. VALUE

35. _____*Matthew Palmer #235*_____
SIGNATURE OF OFFICER/BADGE NUMBER

---

41. What is the name of the victim?

42. What is the badge number of the responding officer?

43. What is the suspect's address?

44. What is the victim's birth date?

45. What is the suspect's hair color?

Questions 46 through 50 refer to the following incident report.

INCIDENT REPORT – POLICE DEPARTMENT

1. ADDRESS OF INCIDENT	2. OFFENSE	3. CODE	4. DATE
3265 Lake St.	Theft		September 30

5. NAME OF VICTIM:INDIVIDUAL OR BUSINESS	6. ADDRESS PHONE		
Jerome McCoy	60 Fern Dr. 596-2392		

7. ASSIGNED OFFICERS/BADGE NUMBERS	8. AGE OF VICTIM	9. RACE OF VICTIM	10. VICTIM'S DATE OF BIRTH
Miguel Castillo #951 Lynda Yates #365	41	Black	

11. NAME OF SUSPECT	12. ADDRESS
Steven Campbell	41 Maple St.

13. AGE	14. RACE	15. SEX	16. DATE OF BIRTH	17. HEIGHT	18. WEIGHT
35	White	Male		6'1"	190

19. HAIR	20. EYES	21. PHYSICAL DESCRIPTION
Brown	Hazel	Skull tattoo on left wrist, wearing a red jacket and white pants

22. CHARGES

23. ITEM	24. BRAND	25. SERIAL NUMBER	26. VALUE
MP3 player	Muzic, Inc.	2155426552	$85

27. ITEM	28. BRAND	29. SERIAL NUMBER	30. VALUE

31. ITEM	32. BRAND	33. SERIAL NUMBER	34. VALUE

35. <u>Miguel Castillo #951, Lynda Yates #365</u>
SIGNATURE OF OFFICER/BADGE NUMBER

46. What is the value of the stolen item?

47. How old is the suspect?

48. Where did the incident take place?

49. What color pants is the suspect wearing?

50. What item did the suspect steal from the victim?

IF YOU FINISH BEFORE TIME IS CALLED, CHECK YOUR WORK ON THIS SECTION ONLY. DO NOT WORK ON ANY OTHER SECTION IN THE TEST.

Section 2: Memorization and Visualization

Time: 90 minutes

50 questions

Directions (1–50): Answer the questions solely on the basis of the information provided.

1. You're traveling north while pursuing a suspect on foot. You follow as the suspect makes two right-hand turns, a left-hand turn, and two more right-hand turns.

   In which direction are you traveling now?

   A. North
   B. South
   C. East
   D. West

2. Officer Williams responds to the scene of a motor-vehicle accident on Monroe Street and Flagg Lane. The man driving vehicle 1 tells the officer that he was traveling west on Monroe Street when vehicle 2, traveling north on Flagg Lane, failed to stop at a stop sign and continued straight through the intersection. Vehicle 2 hit vehicle 1 in the intersection. Vehicle 1 was then struck from behind by vehicle 3.

   Which diagram is most consistent with the driver's statement?

A.

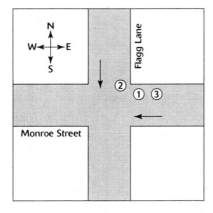

B.

C.

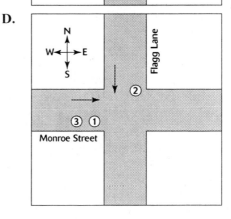

D.

3. Officer McMichaels responds to the scene of a motor-vehicle accident on Loveland Lane and Montgomery Street. The woman driving vehicle 1 tells the officer that she was traveling south on Loveland Lane when vehicle 2, traveling west on Montgomery Street, failed to stop at a stop sign and continued through the intersection. Vehicle 2 hit vehicle 1 in the intersection. Vehicle 1 was then struck from behind by vehicle 3.

Which diagram is most consistent with the driver's statement?

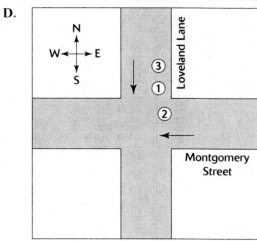

A.

B.

C.

D.

Questions 4 through 7 refer to the following map. The flow of traffic is indicated by the arrows. You must follow the flow of traffic.

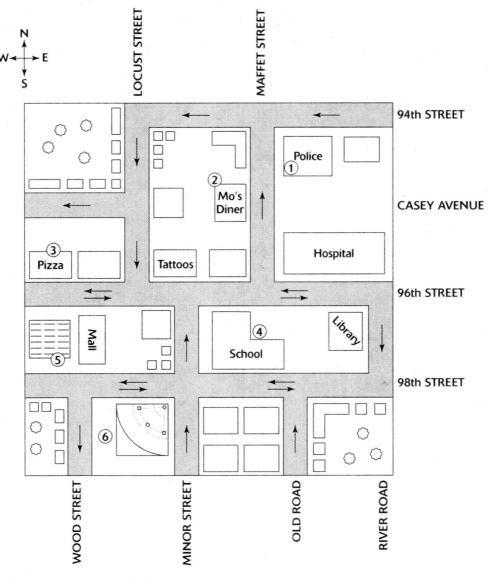

4. If you're located on 98th Street and travel north on Minor Street and then turn east on 96th Street and north on Maffet Street, which of the following will you be closest to?

A. the police station
B. the pizza shop
C. the school
D. the baseball field

5. While patrolling the area around the library on River Road, you receive instructions to respond to an emergency that has taken place in the neighborhood of Locust and 94th streets. Which of the following is the most direct route for you to take in your patrol car, making sure to obey all traffic regulations?

   A. north on River Road, west on 96th Street, north on Locust Street
   B. south on River Road, west on 98th Street, north on Minor Street, east on 96th Street, north on Maffet Street, west on 94th Street
   C. south on River Road, west on 98th Street, north on Minor Street, west on 96th Street, north on Locust Street
   D. north on River Road, east on 96th Street, north on Maffet Street, west on 94th Street

6. If you're located at point 2 and travel north and then turn west onto 94th Street and south on Locust Street, which of the following points will you be closest to?

   A. 1
   B. 2
   C. 3
   D. 4

7. You are to respond to a call of a carjacking in the south entrance of the mall's parking lot. You're leaving from the police station in your police cruiser. Which of the following is the most direct route to the south entrance of the mall's parking?

   A. west on 94th Street, south on Locust Street, east on 96th Street
   B. west on 94th Street, south on Maffet Street, east on 96th Street
   C. west on 94th Street, south on Maffet Street, west on 96th Street, south on Minor Street, west on 98th Street
   D. west on 94th Street, south on Locust Street, east on 96th Street, south on River Road, west on 98th Street

8. While speaking with the owner of a convenience store that has just been robbed, you're told that the suspect left the store with a black backpack full of cash. The suspect, a white male, headed south for two blocks and then turned left.

   According to the information you received, you would be most correct if you reported that the suspect was last seen traveling:

   A. north
   B. south
   C. east
   D. west

9. While questioning a witness to a robbery, you're told that the suspect shoved the victim to the ground, took her packages, and then ran down the street, heading south. He ran three more blocks, turned left, and then turned right before disappearing around the corner of a building.

   According to the information you received, you would be most correct if you reported that the suspect was last seen traveling:

   A. north
   B. south
   C. east
   D. west

10. You're on a routine patrol when you walk past these buildings:

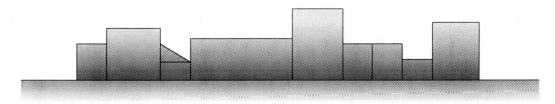

Your view of the buildings changes as you turn the corner. Which of the following most accurately represents your view from the back of the buildings?

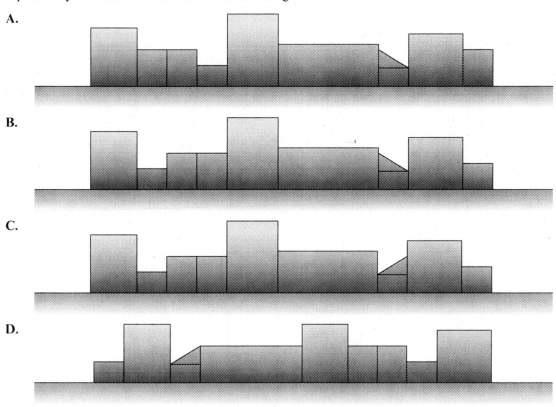

A.

B.

C.

D.

11. You're gathering statements from witnesses of a bank robbery. Each witness tells you that the suspect burst out of the building wearing a ski mask, a green sweatshirt, and jeans. He ran north for a block or two and then turned right. The owner of a bakery on the next block tells you that the suspect then got in a white Toyota that turned left.

According to the information you received, you would be most accurate if you reported that the suspect was last seen traveling:

A. north
B. south
C. east
D. west

Questions 12 through 15 refer to the following photograph. Study the photograph for ten minutes; then cover the photograph and answer the questions based on your memory.

12. How many bags is the man standing to the immediate left of the ticket booth carrying?

    A. 1
    B. 2
    C. 3
    D. 4

13. The sign hanging on the fence outside the carousel says:

    A. DO NOT ENTER
    B. CHILDREN ONLY
    C. WET PAINT
    D. OUT OF ORDER

14. Which of the following objects is *not* featured in the carousel's design?

    A. butterflies
    B. angels
    C. clouds
    D. birds

15. In which direction do the lines run on the bottom of the ticket stand?

    A. horizontally
    B. vertically
    C. diagonally
    D. horizontally and vertically

Questions 16 through 18 refer to the following photograph. Study the photograph for ten minutes; then cover the photograph and answer the questions based on your memory.

Photo credit: National Park Service

16. How many people are standing outside the cabin?

    A. 5
    B. 6
    C. 7
    D. 8

17. What is hanging above the doorway of the cabin?

    A. antlers
    B. horseshoes
    C. a sign
    D. a spotlight

18. What does the sign on the left say?

    A. THEODORE ROOSEVELT'S HUNTING CABIN
    B. THEODORE ROOSEVELT'S MALTESE CROSS CABIN
    C. THEODORE ROOSEVELT'S CHILDHOOD HOME
    D. THEODORE ROOSEVELT'S MOUNTAIN VACATION HOME

19. You're on a routine patrol when you walk past these buildings:

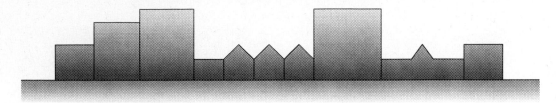

Your view of the buildings changes as you turn the corner. Which of the following most accurately represents your view from the back of the buildings?

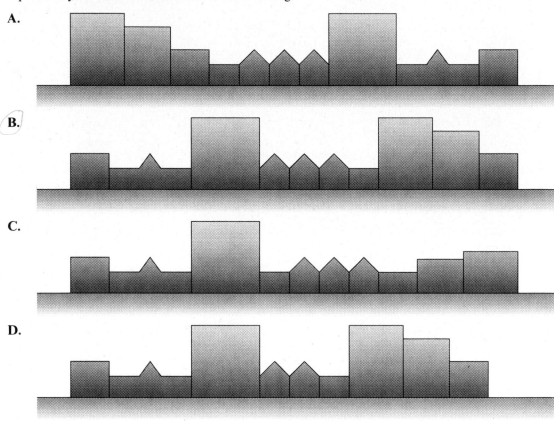

A.

B.

C.

D.

Questions 20 through 24 refer to the following photograph. Study the photograph for ten minutes; then cover the photograph and answer the questions based on your memory.

20. How many animals are in the photograph?

    A. 1
    B. 2
    C. 3
    D. 4

21. What is hanging on the clothesline in the foreground of the photograph?

    A. socks
    B. sheets
    C. pants
    D. coats

22. How many windows are visible on the first house to the right?

    A. 2
    B. 3
    C. 4
    D. 6

23. What items are propped up against the side of each house?

    A. firewood
    B. lawn furniture
    C. barrels
    D. shingles

24. How many vehicles are in the photograph?

    A. 1
    B. 2
    C. 3
    D. 4

Questions 25 through 27 refer to the following map. The flow of traffic is indicated by the arrows. You must follow the flow of traffic.

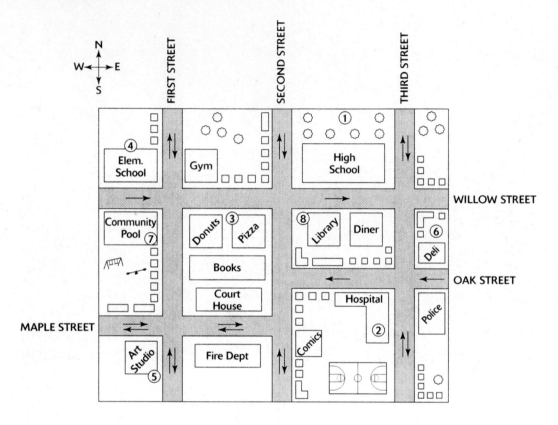

25. From the police station, which of the following is the quickest route to get to the library, making sure to obey all traffic regulations?

   A. north on Third Street, west on Willow Street

   B. west on Oak Street, north on Second Street, east on Willow Street

   C. east on Oak Street, north on Second Street, east on Willow Street

   D. west on Oak Street, south on Second Street, west on Maple Street, north on First Street, east on Willow Street

26. Starting at point 5, which of the following is the quickest route to point 6?

   A. north on First Street, east on Willow Street, south on Third Street

   B. north on First Street, east on Maple Street, north on Second Street, east on Oak Street

   C. north on First Street, east on Willow Street, south on Second Street

   D. north on First Street, west on Maple Street, north on Second Street, east on Willow Street

27. After patrolling the park, Officer Bean decides to patrol the surrounding area. He gets in his patrol car and travels south on Second Street. He then makes a right on Maple Street and another right on First Street. He turns east on Willow Street and follows the road for a bit, before traveling south on Third Street and making a right. At the next intersection, which building should Officer Bean see directly in front of him?

A. the hospital
B. the deli
C. the bookstore
D. the community pool

Questions 28 through 31 refer to the following map. The flow of traffic is indicated by the arrows. You must follow the flow of traffic.

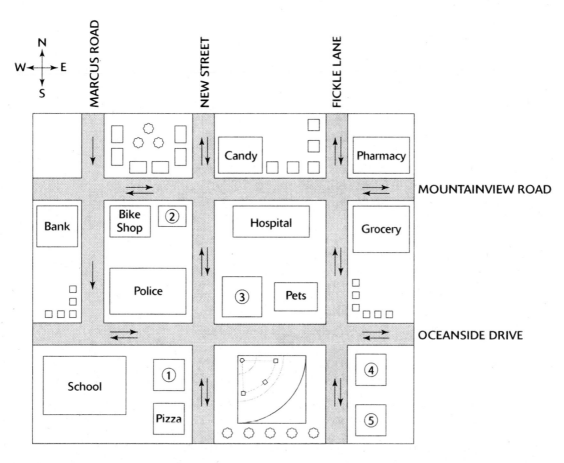

28. If you are located on Oceanside Drive and travel north on New Street and then turn east on Mountain View Road and south on Fickle Lane, which of the following will you be closest to?

A. the police station
B. the bank
C. the pizza shop
D. the pet store

29. While patrolling the area around the bank on Marcus Road, you receive instructions to respond to an emergency that has taken place in the neighborhood of Mountain View Road and Fickle Lane. Which of the following is the most direct route for you to take in your patrol car, making sure to obey all traffic regulations?

A. north on Marcus Road, east on Mountain View Road, north on Fickle Lane
B. south on Marcus Road, east on Oceanside Drive, north on Fickle Lane
C. south on Marcus Road, east on Oceanside Drive, north on New Street, east on Mountain View Road, north on Fickle Lane
D. south on Marcus Road, west on Oceanside Drive, north on New Street, east on Mountain View Road, north on Fickle Lane

30. If you are located at point 5 and travel north, then turn west onto Mountain View Road and south on Marcus Road, which point will you be closest to?

A. 1
B. 2
C. 3
D. 4

31. You are to respond to a call of a robbery at gunpoint at the eastern entrance of the baseball field. You get in your patrol car, which is parked at the northernmost point of Marcus Road. Which of the following is your most direct route to the east entrance of the baseball field?

A. east on Mountain View Road, south on Fickle Lane
B. east on Mountain View Road, south on New Street
C. south on Marcus Road, east on Oceanside Drive, south on New Street
D. south on Marcus Road, east on Oceanside Drive, south on Fickle Lane

Questions 32 through 35 refer to the following map. The flow of traffic is indicated by the arrows. You must follow the flow of traffic.

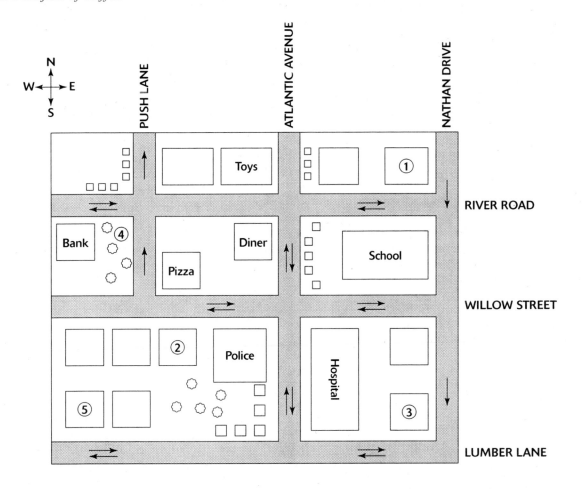

32. If you're at point 5, in which direction must you first travel to reach point 4?

A. north
B. south
C. east
D. west

33. While at the bank, you're instructed to respond to an emergency at the pizza shop. Which of the following is the quickest route from the bank to the pizza shop, making sure to obey all traffic regulations?

A. west on River Road, south on Push Lane, west on Willow Street
B. east on River Road, south on Push Lane, east on Willow Street
C. east on River Road, south on Atlantic Avenue, west on Willow Street
D. west on River Road, south on Atlantic Avenue, west on Willow Street

34. After patrolling the park at point 4 on foot, you get in your police cruiser and drive east on River Road. You then turn right on Atlantic Avenue, left on Willow Street, right on Nathan Drive, right on Lumber Lane, and right onto Atlantic Avenue. At the first intersection, which of the following buildings will be on your left-hand side?

   A. the hospital
   B. the police station
   C. the diner
   D. the school

35. From the toy store, you travel south on Atlantic Avenue, west on Willow Street, and north on Push Lane. Then you get a call to respond to an emergency at point 3. In which direction must you travel next if your destination is point 3?

   A. north
   B. south
   C. east
   D. west

36. While speaking to the witness of a carjacking, you're told that the suspect was wearing jeans, white sneakers with red stripes, and a dark blue sweatshirt with a hood. The witness tells you that the suspect got in the car and sped away from the curb, nearly hitting a car traveling south in the opposite lane. The suspect drove for two blocks and then turned left.

According to the information you received, you would be most correct if you reported that the suspect was last seen traveling:

   A. north
   B. south
   C. east
   D. west

37. You're on a routine patrol when you walk past these buildings:

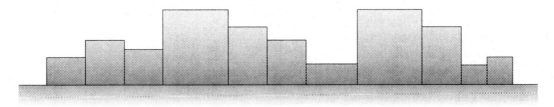

Your view of the buildings changes as you turn the corner. Which of the following most accurately represents your view from the back of the buildings?

A.

B.

C.

D.

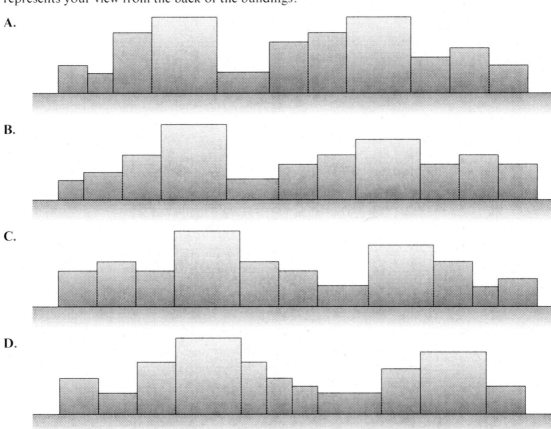

38. Detective Marsh sees a black male shove a woman to the ground outside the grocery store. They struggle, but the male is able to rip the purse from the woman and runs through the parking lot, nearly causing multiple car accidents. Detective Marsh runs after the suspect until he's out of breath. He knows that he followed the man north for a few blocks, then turned right down an alleyway and headed south once he emerged from between the buildings. He remembers making a right and then a left.

According to the information provided, Detective Marsh would be most accurate if he reported that the suspect was last seen traveling:

A. north
B. south
C. east
D. west

Questions 39 through 42 are based on the following photograph. Study the photograph for ten minutes; then cover the photograph and answer the questions based on your memory.

39. What does the sign in the foreground of this picture read?

    A. corn chips

    B. ncw

    C. soft drinks

    D. lemonade

40. Which of the following objects is the man in this picture *not* wearing?

    A. shirt

    B. shorts

    C. hat

    D. sandals

41. How many shelves are on the left side of the aisle?

    A. 4
    B. 5
    C. 6
    D. 7

42. Where is the stepstool positioned in proximity to the man in the aisle?

    A. in front of him and to his left
    B. in front of him and to his right
    C. behind him and to his left
    D. behind him and to his right

Questions 43 through 46 are based on the following photograph. Study the photograph for ten minutes; then cover the photograph and answer the questions based on your memory.

Photo credit: National Park Service

43. How many doors are visible in this photograph?

    A. 2
    B. 3
    C. 4
    D. 5

44. Which object is sitting next to the woman in the center of the photograph?

    A. a coat
    B. gloves
    C. a purse
    D. books

45. How many men are visible in this photograph?

    A. 1
    B. 2
    C. 3
    D. 4

46. What is the woman on the right side doing?

    A. walking
    B. jumping
    C. talking
    D. reading

47. You're on a routine patrol when you walk past these buildings:

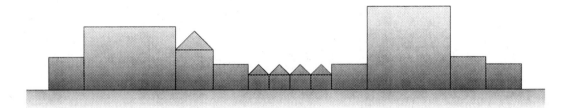

Your view of the buildings changes as you turn the corner. Which of the following most accurately represents your view from the back of the buildings?

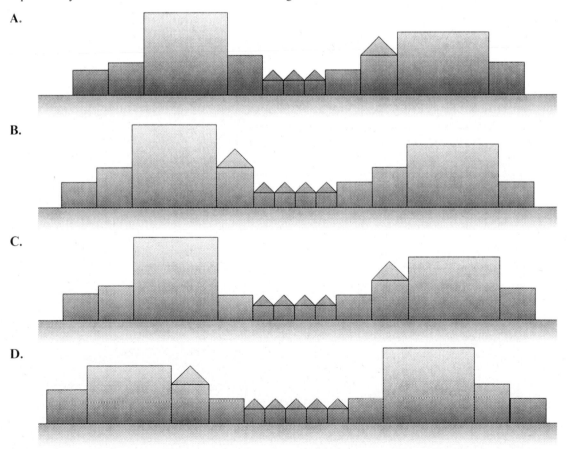

A.

B.

C.

D.

Questions 48 through 50 are based on the following map. The flow of traffic is indicated by the arrows. You must follow the flow of traffic.

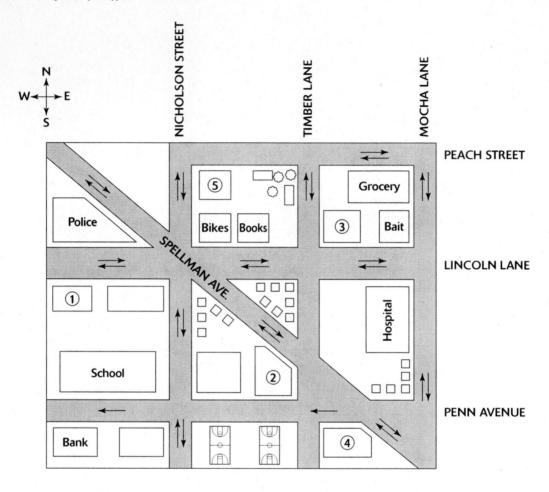

48. From the police station, which of the following is the quickest route to get to point 2?

A.   south on Nicholson Street, east on Penn Avenue

B.   southeast on Spellman Avenue, south on Timber Lane, west on Penn Avenue

C.   southwest on Spellman Avenue, south on Timber Lane, west on Penn Avenue

D.   north on Nicholson Street, east on Peach Street, south on Timber Lane, west on Penn Avenue

49. Starting at the westernmost soccer field, which of the following is the quickest route to the bait shop?

A.   north on Nicholson Street, east on Lincoln Lane

B.   north on Nicholson Street, west on Lincoln Lane

C.   east on Penn Avenue, southeast on Spellman Avenue, north on Mocha Lane

D.   east on Penn Avenue, north on Timber Lane, east on Lincoln Lane

50. After patrolling the park located on the corner of Peach Street and Timber Lane, Officer Lukes decides to patrol the surrounding area. He gets into his patrol car and travels south on Timber Lane. He then makes a right on Penn Avenue and another right on Nicholson Street. He turns east on Lincoln Lane and follows the road for a bit, traveling south on Timber Lane and then making a left. On which street is Officer Lukes now traveling?

A. Penn Avenue
B. Mocha Lane
C. Spellman Avenue
D. Peach Street

IF YOU FINISH BEFORE TIME IS CALLED, CHECK YOUR WORK ON THIS SECTION ONLY. DO NOT WORK ON ANY OTHER SECTION IN THE TEST.

Section 3: Mathematics

Time: 50 minutes

50 questions

Directions (1–50): Answer the questions solely on the basis of the information provided.

1. On Monday, Officer Costello walked 12 miles during his beat. If he patrolled the same route four more days that week, how many miles total did he travel?

   A. 24
   B. 60
   C. 72
   D. 120

2. Find the volume of the rectangle shown below using the formula $V = lwh$.

   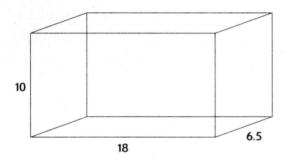

   A. 34.5
   B. 186.5
   C. 1,008
   D. 1,170

3. If one-fourth of the calls that Officer Moore responds to each week are nonemergency calls, and he typically responds to 32 calls per week, how many of those calls are emergencies?

   A. 8
   B. 10
   C. 16
   D. 24

4. During the past three weeks, Officer Hernandez worked on old incident reports. The first week, he finished 4 reports before lunch and 7 after lunch. The second week, he completed 9 reports before lunch and 2 reports after lunch. The third week, he finished 11 reports before lunch and 6 after lunch. How many reports did he write during the past three weeks?

   A. 26
   B. 32
   C. 39
   D. 41

Questions 5 through 6 refer to the following information.

In preparing a report on a home burglary, Sergeant Winslow listed the following stolen items and their values:

   MP3 player: $75
   Watch: $500
   Jewelry: $1,200
   Cash: $145
   TOTAL: $1,920

5. What is the total value of the stolen items except for the cash?

   A. $720
   B. $1,420
   C. $1,775
   D. $1,845

6. The homeowner finds the watch that she originally thought the burglars had taken, but then she realizes that her wedding band is also missing. The wedding band is worth $2,200. What is the new total value of the stolen items?

    A. $3,620
    B. $3,975
    C. $4,045
    D. $4,120

7. Find the area of the triangle shown below using the formula $A = \frac{1}{2}bh$.

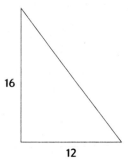

    A.   48
    B.   96
    C.   144
    D.   192

8. The number of arrests that Officer Chen made each week for the past three months was 5, 3, 9, 11, 7, 4, 5, 19, 3, 14, 1, and 4. What is the average number of arrests she made per week? Round to the nearest whole number.

    A.   4
    B.   7
    C.   11
    D.   14

9. During a drug bust, Officer Williamson netted 100 bags of marijuana. At the lab, it was determined that only 65% of the bags was filled with illegal drugs. How many bags were filled with illegal drugs?

    A.   45
    B.   50
    C.   65
    D.   90

10. If you can complete 12 training exercises in 6 days, how many training exercises can you complete in 18 days?

    A.   18
    B.   24
    C.   36
    D.   48

11. While responding to a burglary at a jewelry store, the store's owner tells Officer Muniz that the thieves stole 15 diamond rings, with a total worth of approximately $11,250. Each of the rings is worth the same amount. What is the approximate value of each diamond ring?

    A. $350
    B. $425
    C. $750
    D. $975

12. Solve $182.47 - 68.54 \times 0.17 + 12$, rounding to the nearest hundredth.

    A.   31.37
    B.   52.82
    C.   182.82
    D.   365.63

Questions 13 through 15 refer to the following information.

In the past three months, crime rates have increased and decreased. In January, 12 incidents of gang-related violence were reported. In March, 42 gang-related incidents were reported. At the beginning of the year, 9 robberies were reported. In March, 18 people reported that their businesses had been burglarized. In January, 6 arsons were reported, while March had only 2.

13. How many gang-related incidents and arsons were reported in March?

    A. 27
    B. 44
    C. 62
    D. 81

14. How much did the reports of gang-related violence increase from January to March?

    A. 50%
    B. 100%
    C. 150%
    D. 250%

15. Lieutenant Wong worked 13 security shifts over the past three weeks. They lasted 7 hours, 9 hours, 6 hours, 4 hours, 11 hours, 4 hours, 5 hours, 7 hours, 10 hours, 2 hours, 1 hour, 3 hours, and 6 hours. What is the average length of time he spent working security each shift? Round to the nearest whole number.

    A. 4 hours
    B. 5 hours
    C. 6 hours
    D. 7 hours

Questions 16 and 17 refer to the following information.

In preparing a report on a restaurant burglary, Officer Brogna listed the following stolen items and their values:

Cash: $7,500
Deep fryer: $12,000
Kitchen supplies: $600
Liquor: $1,700
Meat: $1,000
TOTAL: $22,800

16. What is the total value of the stolen items except for the deep fryer?

    A. $10,800
    B. $15,300
    C. $21,100
    D. $21,000

17. The restaurant owner finds some of the restaurant supplies that he originally thought were missing, but then he realizes that a case of wine is also missing. He calls Officer Brogna to update the report. The found restaurant supplies are worth $300 and the case of wine is worth $650. What is the new total value of the stolen items?

    A. $19,550
    B. $22,850
    C. $23,150
    D. $24,250

18. Find the volume of the rectangle shown below using the formula $V = lwh$.

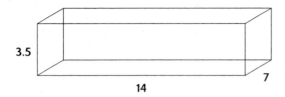

A. 24.5
B. 98
C. 294.5
D. 343

19. If you can complete 16 incident reports in 4 hours, how many incident reports can you complete in 12 hours?

A. 16
B. 24
C. 32
D. 48

20. Officer Petrilla usually drives to the county jail three days a week. The trip is 14 miles each way. If Officer Petrilla needs to drive to the county jail one more day this week, how many miles total will he have traveled this week?

A. 42
B. 56
C. 84
D. 112

21. Solve $447.50 - 63.75 \times 0.33 + 89$, rounding to the nearest hundredth.

A. 42.75
B. 250.50
C. 515.46
D. 895.44

22. If three-fourths of the calls Lieutenant Rogers responds to each week are for home invasions, and he typically responds to 96 calls per week, how many of those calls are *not* home invasions?

A. 12
B. 16
C. 24
D. 48

23. In the past four months, crime rates have increased in the town of Haydes. In May, 34 arsons were reported and that number increased to 46 in August. In May, local businesses reported 45 burglaries. In August, local businesses reported 64 burglaries. In May, 19 domestic abuse incidents were reported, while August had 21.

How much did the reports of local business burglaries increase from May to August?

A. 42%
B. 45.5%
C. 54%
D. 70%

24. Find the circumference of the circle shown below using the formula: $C = 2\pi r$. (**Note:** $\pi \approx$ 3.14.) Round to the nearest whole number.

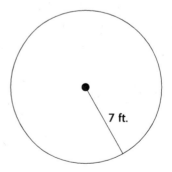

A. 27
B. 43.96
C. 44
D. 46.32

25. While responding to a burglary at an appliance store, Sergeant McMullen is told by the owner that the burglars stole 11 washing machines with a total worth of $6,325. If each washing machine is worth the same amount, what is the value of each washing machine?

    A. $450
    B. $575
    C. $650
    D. $775

26. On Wednesday, Officer Piko walked 7 miles during his beat. If he patrolled the same route four more days that week, how many total miles did he walk?

    A. 14 miles
    B. 28 miles
    C. 35 miles
    D. 39 miles

27. Find the area of the triangle below using the formula $A = \frac{1}{2}bh$.

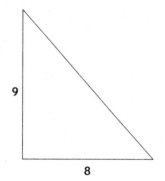

    A. 8
    B. 17
    C. 25
    D. 36

28. If three-fourths of the calls that Officer Michaels responds to each week are for noise complaints, and he typically responds to 60 calls per week, how many of those calls are *not* for noise complaints?

    A. 15
    B. 25
    C. 35
    D. 45

29. Over the past month, Officer Jeffries worked on old incident reports. The first week, he finished 3 reports before lunch and 6 more in the hours after lunch. The second week, he completed 10 reports before lunch, but only managed to finish 5 after lunch. The third week, he finished 9 reports before lunch and 5 more after lunch. The final week, he finished 4 reports before lunch and 5 after lunch. How many reports did he write over the past month?

    A. 27
    B. 38
    C. 47
    D. 56

Questions 30 and 31 refer to the following information.

In preparing a report on a home burglary, Sergeant Mulroney listed the following stolen items and their values:

HDTV: $650
Laptop: $500
Jewelry: $950
Cash: $275
TOTAL: $2,375

30. What is the total value of the stolen items except for the cash?

    A. $1,875
    B. $1,995
    C. $2,100
    D. $2,375

31. The homeowner finds the laptop that she originally thought the burglars took, but then she realizes that the gifts she bought for her husband's upcoming birthday are also missing. The gifts are worth $800. What is the new total value of the stolen items?

 A. $2,675
 B. $2,800
 C. $3,175
 D. $3,675

32. Find the circumference of the circle shown below using the formula $C = 2\pi r$.
 (*Note:* $\pi \approx 3.14$.)

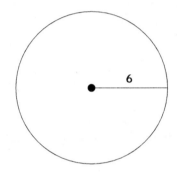

 A. 18.26
 B. 26.84
 C. 37.68
 D. 46.22

33. Officer Lombardi usually works the 10 p.m. to 6 a.m. shift five days a week. He's asked by his supervisor to report for duty at 9:30 p.m. four days this week. At the end of the week, how many hours of overtime will Officer Lombardi have worked?

 A. 1 hour, 30 minutes
 B. 2 hours
 C. 2 hours, 30 minutes
 D. 3 hours

34. During a search and seizure, Officer Arrowman netted 120 packages of ecstasy pills. At the lab, it was determined that only 55% of the packages contained illegal drugs. How many packages did *not* contain illegal drugs?

 A. 45
 B. 54
 C. 66
 D. 72

35. If you can complete 16 training exercises in 5 days, how many training exercises can you complete in 20 days?

 A. 30
 B. 44
 C. 50
 D. 64

36. While responding to a burglary at a pet store, Officer Pringle is told by the store owner that the thieves stole four purebred puppies worth approximately $6,480 in all. Each of the puppies is worth the same amount. What is the approximate value of each individual puppy?

 A. $1,240
 B. $1,430
 C. $1,620
 D. $1,810

37. Solve $217.88 - 4.02 \times 1.29 + 417.05$, rounding to the nearest hundredth.

 A. 600.40
 B. 629.74
 C. 632.20
 D. 692.93

Questions 38 and 39 refer to the following information.

In the past five months, crime rates have increased and decreased. In March, 8 incidents of domestic violence were reported. In August, 12 domestic-violence incidents were reported. Earlier in the year, 11 burglaries were reported. At the end of the summer, 21 people reported burglaries at their residences. In March, 8 arsons occurred, while August had only 3.

38. How many domestic-violence incidents and home invasions occurred in August?

A. 27
B. 33
C. 36
D. 40

39. How much did reports of arson decrease from March to August?

A. 37.5%
B. 41%
C. 50%
D. 62.5%

40. Lieutenant Kim worked 9 security shifts over the past 2 weeks. They lasted 5 hours, 6 hours, 4 hours, 3 hours, 8 hours, 6 hours, 5 hours, 8 hours, and 9 hours. What is the average length of time he spent working security each shift? Round to the nearest whole number.

A. 5 hours
B. 6 hours
C. 7 hours
D. 8 hours

Questions 41 and 42 refer to the following information.

In preparing a report regarding a car break-in, Officer Perbella listed the following stolen items and their values:

Cash: $45
CDs: $120
Stereo: $750
Textbooks: $320
Clothing: $50
TOTAL: $1,285

41. What is the total value of the stolen items except for the textbooks?

A. $965
B. $1,165
C. $1,285
D. $1,605

42. The car's owner finds some of the CDs he originally thought were stolen, but then he realizes that a portable GPS he kept locked in his glove compartment is also missing. He calls Officer Perbella to update the report. The recovered CDs are worth $40 and the GPS is worth $250. What is the new total value of the stolen items?

A. $1,245
B. $1,375
C. $1,495
D. $1,525

43. Find the width of the rectangle shown below using the formula $V = lwh$ if the volume is 288.

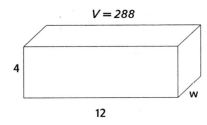

V = 288

4

12

w

- **A.** 2
- **B.** 4
- **C.** 6
- **D.** 8

44. If you can make 9 arrests in 4 days, how many arrests can you make in 12 days?

- **A.** 12
- **B.** 19
- **C.** 23
- **D.** 27

45. Officer Martin usually works a split shift from 9 a.m. to 1 p.m. and 4 to 8 p.m. five days a week. His supervisor asks him to stay until 2:30 p.m. three days this week. At the end of the week, how many hours of overtime will Officer Martin have worked?

- **A.** 3 hour, 30 minutes
- **B.** 4 hours
- **C.** 4 hours, 30 minutes
- **D.** 5 hours

46. Solve $414.05 - 6.09 \times 5.22 + 809$, rounding to the nearest hundredth.

- **A.** 924.32
- **B.** 1,191.26
- **C.** 1,462.18
- **D.** 2,000.14

47. If three-fifths of the calls that Lieutenant Franklin responds to each week are for trespassing, and he typically responds to 72 calls per week, about how many of those calls are not for trespassing?

- **A.** 29
- **B.** 34
- **C.** 40
- **D.** 43

48. Solve $12.58 + 74.59 \div 5.20 + 0.45 - 8.20$, rounding to the nearest hundredth.

- **A.** 17.45
- **B.** 18.53
- **C.** 19.17
- **D.** 20.12

49. Find the diameter of the circle shown below using the formula $D = 2r$. Round to the nearest tenth.

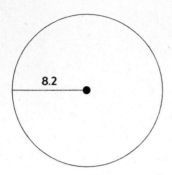

8.2

A. 8.2
B. 16
C. 16.4
D. 32

50. While responding to a burglary at an art gallery, the owner tells Sergeant O'Reilly that the burglars stole four paintings worth $8,460. If each painting is worth the same amount, what is the value of each individual painting?

A. $1,980
B. $2,000
C. $2,115
D. $2,200

IF YOU FINISH BEFORE TIME IS CALLED, CHECK YOUR WORK ON THIS SECTION ONLY. DO NOT WORK ON ANY OTHER SECTION IN THE TEST.

Section 4: Judgment and Problem Solving

Time: 50 minutes

50 questions

Directions (1–50): Answer the questions solely on the basis of the information provided.

Question 1 refers to the following information.

The collection and disposal ordinance in Akron, Ohio, is designed to set standards and rules for residents' trash removal. Stated in Section 52.11 of this ordinance titled "Containers—Collection" are requirements that all Akron, Ohio, residents must meet or they will be penalized. Requirements include the following:

- Residents must place garbage, household rubbish, and recyclables in city-supplied containers and deposit these containers on or near the curb directly in front of their residences no later than 4:30 a.m. on collection day and no earlier than 4:30 p.m. on the day prior to collection. After collection, residents should remove the containers from the curb and place them on their property by 6 p.m. on the day of collection. Garbage, household rubbish, and recyclables will not be collected unless they are placed in the designated containers and locations.
- Carpet and brush must be cut, bundled, and tied, and bundles must not exceed 4 feet in length.
- No automobile parts—except automobile tires, car seats, mufflers, and tail pipes—will be accepted.
- Concrete, construction or demolition material, dirt, sand, gravel, or bricks will not be accepted for curbside collection.
- Any violations, such as leaving garbage or rubbish on or near the curb for a period of four hours outside the designated pickup times, will not be tolerated and may warrant a citation.

1. According to the information provided, which of the following is the best example of an owner who is violating the collection and disposal ordinance?

   A. George will be out of town on collection day and asks a neighbor to place his refuse container on his property after collection.
   B. Marta, an auto mechanic, places a car's transmission on the curb in front of her residence for removal.
   C. Kevin is remodeling his house and bundles up an old carpet for removal. He ensures that the bundle is no more than 4 feet long.
   D. Phyllis is suffering from a bout of insomnia and decides to place her recyclables on the curb at 4 a.m. on pickup day.

2. You're on night patrol in the city park. As you enter a secluded section of the park, you see two individuals clearly engaged in a drug deal. Just as they complete their transaction, they notice you and run off in opposite directions. What would be the best way to handle this situation?

   A. Attempt to apprehend the suspect with the money.
   B. Attempt to apprehend the suspect with the drugs.
   C. Fire a warning shot and command the suspects to stop.
   D. Record a physical description of the suspects and issue arrest warrants.

3. Officer Leonard is working traffic control at a new construction site where the normal traffic patterns have recently been modified. He witnesses a driver commit an infraction. How should he proceed?

   A. Pull over the driver and give the driver a warning.
   B. Pull over the driver and give the driver a citation.
   C. Overlook the infraction because of the new traffic patterns.
   D. Record the license-plate number and issue a citation if the driver commits the infraction again.

Question 4 refers to the following information.

Police Captain Jim Edwards is addressing a class of new police recruits. He speaks to them about the procedures they should follow while dealing with domestic disputes. It is very important for recruits to understand the proper protocols for managing domestic dispute incidents, and with 35 years of experience, Captain Edwards is uniquely qualified to explain and teach the recruits. In the course of his presentation, Edwards highlights the following guidelines:

- Listen carefully to all information regarding the incident that you receive from the dispatcher. You'll need to learn as much as possible about the ongoing situation.

- Make a detailed assessment of the scene and approach cautiously. Be sure to note the behavior of the individuals involved, and look for any weapons or potentially dangerous objects.

- Speak calmly and respectfully to the involved parties—try not to further upset anyone. Listen carefully and develop a precise understanding of what has transpired.

- If any party attempts or threatens further violence, the individual should be subdued and restrained, if necessary.

- When you have a full understanding of the situation, take the appropriate actions. Remember to try to keep everyone calm and maintain order on the scene.

4. Based on the information provided, the recruits could correctly assume that the primary goal for an officer responding to a domestic dispute is to:

   A. arrest the suspect as quickly as possible.
   B. ensure and maintain your safety and the safety of others on the scene.
   C. get all the information you need for your report.
   D. keep the argumentative parties separated at all times.

5. You're en route to a crime in progress. While you're driving, your immediate supervisor issues you several commands over the radio, but you don't clearly hear them. How should you respond?

   A. Try to think like your supervisor and figure out what he or she would want you to do.
   B. Assume that the information wasn't important and proceed with your approach.
   C. Request that your supervisor repeat the instructions that he or she gave you.
   D. Determine how to handle the situation based on your police academy training.

Questions 6 and 7 refer to the following definitions.

Voluntary manslaughter: Someone charged with or convicted of voluntary manslaughter has unintentionally killed another person during a moment of intense rage or other emotion, or has killed someone while committing a less serious criminal offense such as a robbery. This charge implies that the person had no prior intent to kill and acted in the "heat of the moment." The provocation of the crime needs to be something that would cause a reasonable person to become distraught, lose control, and commit murder.

Involuntary manslaughter: Involuntary manslaughter is the unintentional killing of an individual through reckless, inattentive behavior, or any act that is considered unlawful, such as a misdemeanor or low-level felony.

Murder in the second degree: When a person intentionally kills another person without premeditation, or planning to kill that person, it's called murder in the second degree.

Murder in the third degree: When a person kills an individual as a result of negligence or disregard for the individual's life, it is called murder in the third degree. This includes a murder that occurs when a person intends to harm, not kill, an individual.

6. Which of the following is an example of voluntary manslaughter?

   A. Seth Burns finds his wife in bed with another man. A heated argument ensues and quickly evolves into a physical confrontation. As Seth and the stranger struggle, Seth accidentally pushes him over a third-floor balcony. The man plummets to the ground and dies.

   B. Three armed men are holding up a bank. One of the tellers attempts to activate an alarm but is caught by one of the men. The armed man shoots and kills the teller.

   C. Sandra Haverford discovers her wealthy husband is cheating on her. She wants to be rid of him but would like to hold on to his money, so she slowly poisons him.

   D. Two young brothers find their father's gun and are playing around with it when it suddenly goes off, killing one of them.

7. Which of the following is an example of murder in the second degree?

   A. After robbing a mini-mart, Frank Golden accidentally shoves a man into oncoming traffic while fleeing the scene and the man is killed.

   B. Sven Lewis is negotiating a transaction with a drug dealer. When he attempts to pay the man, he suddenly realizes that he doesn't have enough money. He's desperate, so he produces a gun and shoots the dealer, killing him.

   C. Two hunters are deep in the forest when one hunter mistakes the other for a deer and shoots him. The injured hunter dies.

   D. After George Goldstein's partner in a robbery attempt turned George in to the police, George was sentenced to 15 years in prison. When George is released from prison, he kills his former partner.

8. Increased police presence would be an effective deterrent for all the following crimes, *except:*

   A. grand theft auto
   B. larceny
   C. theft
   D. murder

Question 9 refers to the following information.

Officer Reynolds completed an incident report following an undercover drug arrest. The following five sentences were removed from the body of the report in no particular order:

1. The target asked the undercover dealer for cocaine.
2. Reginald Johnson was arrested and charged with purchasing drugs.
3. The target approached the undercover dealer's vehicle.
4. The undercover dealer told the target his price and the transaction proceeded.
5. The hidden arresting officers approached and apprehended the target.

9. Which of the following represents the correct chronological order of events?

   A. 2, 3, 1, 4, 5
   B. 3, 1, 4, 5, 2
   C. 3, 2, 4, 1, 5
   D. 5, 4, 3, 1, 2

Questions 10 and 11 refer to the following information.

Police officers are trained to spot suspicious behavior that may either lead to criminal mischief or indicate that a crime has already taken place.

10. Which of the following would police officers patrolling city streets early in the morning find *most* suspicious?

    A. a man waiting in a car outside of an apartment building with his hazard lights on
    B. a group of teenagers laughing and shouting at a corner bus stop
    C. a young man holding a pizza box, peering into the front window of a house
    D. a pair of women jogging in the road, pushing baby strollers

11. Which of the following would be the *least* suspicious to police officers who are patrolling city streets after school hours?

    A. a group of children on a playground without adult supervision
    B. a group of teenagers on the basketball courts, not playing basketball
    C. an older man standing outside of the school, talking to young female students
    D. a pair of teenagers walking quickly out of a nearby convenience store with an armful of soda and candy

Question 12 refers to the following information.

In class, recruit officers are told that when making an arrest, it's important that all police officers follow the proper procedures. An arrest can take place only if the crime was committed in the presence of police, if there is a warrant issued for an arrest, or if there is probable cause to believe a crime has taken place. If they stray from the following steps, their arrests and any evidence that may have been seized during the arrests may be deemed inadmissible and the suspects may be set free.

1. Read the suspect his or her Miranda rights.
2. Search the suspect and/or his or her vehicle for weapons or illegal substances.
3. Book the suspect and gather personal information, including fingerprints and photographs.
4. Create a written inventory of the suspect's personal property.

12. The class of recruits is presented with the following scenario: Officer Rodriguez is at a high school football game when he witnesses a fight between two men in the stands. As he attempts to separate the men, one of them takes a swing at him. Rodriguez's partner tells the man that he is under arrest for assaulting a police officer and then handcuffs him. What should the arresting officer do next?

   A. Search the suspect for concealed weapons and drugs.
   B. Ask Officer Rodriguez to log the man's personal property.
   C. Read the man his Miranda rights and escort him from the stands.
   D. Ask the man for his name, address, and work telephone number.

13. In which of the following situations is a police officer most likely to use force?

   A. A man is walking out of a grocery store with a shopping cart full of unpaid groceries.
   B. A woman is drunk in the downtown area and refuses to look both ways before she crosses the streets.
   C. A teenager is spray-painting on a local playground and runs away from the police when he is spotted.
   D. An elderly man is yelling at a convenience store clerk who printed the wrong lottery tickets for him.

Question 14 refers to the following information.

Officer Peters completed an incident report after a home robbery. The following five sentences were removed from the body of the report in no particular order:

1. Rodger Parsons is currently being held in the Wright County jail in lieu of $30,000 bail.
2. Value of property recovered: $275.
3. The suspect entered the home through an unlocked sliding door at the rear of the residence.
4. Rodger Parsons was arrested and charged with second-degree burglary.
5. Value of property stolen: $275.

14. Which of the following alternatives represents the correct chronological order of events?

   A. 4, 2, 3, 5, 1
   B. 3, 5, 2, 1, 4
   C. 3, 5, 2, 4, 1
   D. 5, 3, 2, 4, 1

15. An officer brings two prisoners in to the station after their arrests. As he returns to his squad car, he notices a gold ring on the floor of the back of the car. After retrieving the ring, what should the officer do?

   A. Take the ring to evidence control and file a written report on the matter.
   B. Keep it for himself.
   C. Discard it in the trash.
   D. Question the prisoners as to who owns the ring.

16. You are at a party and are talking with another guest. When you reveal to her that you're a police officer, she tells you about a traffic citation she received recently. She claims she shouldn't have been given the ticket and asks you to take care of it. How should you respond?

    A. Assure her that you'll take care of it.
    B. Say that you'll investigate her situation the next time you're at work.
    C. Tell her that you can't be sure of the ticket's legitimacy since you weren't there.
    D. Tell her that tickets are only issued when absolutely warranted.

17. At about 7:45 p.m. on Saturday, Officer Jacobs is on patrol in the vicinity of Charleston Avenue and Fifth Street when he hears two men arguing loudly in a nearby alley. As he approaches the alley, he sees the two men and notices that one of them (suspect #1) is holding a clear bag containing a white substance. Suddenly, the other man (suspect #2) pulls out a switchblade and stabs suspect #1 in the stomach. Suspect #1 clutches his stomach as he drops to the ground. He drops the bag and as suspect #2 bends down to pick it up, he sees Officer Jacobs and starts to run, leaving the bag on the ground. Officer Jacobs quickly enters the alley and proceeds to suspect #1. He sees that the man is bleeding very badly. He calls an ambulance for emergency medical support and tries to control the victim's bleeding until help arrives.

    What was the most likely reason that Officer Jacobs responded to the situation in the manner that he did?

    A. Officers should always immediately secure the suspect closest to them.
    B. When dealing with drugs, officers should always attempt to apprehend the suspect in possession of the drugs.
    C. Attending to a seriously injured suspect is an officer's primary objective in any case.
    D. Officers should not attempt to pursue a fleeing suspect when a second suspect can be apprehended easily.

18. Officer O'Brien is at the courthouse when a bystander approaches him and points out what appears to be a bomb under a stairwell. How should Officer O'Brien respond?

    A. Advise everyone to evacuate the courthouse.
    B. Contact the bomb squad and let them handle the situation.
    C. Inspect the bomb and attempt to defuse it.
    D. Inform courthouse security so that they may calmly evacuate the building.

Question 19 refers to the following information.

Recruit officers are learning about how the presence of streetlights along the sides of interstates and highways affects the number of accidents along these roadways each year. To demonstrate this information, the recruit officers review a handout containing the following information:

Interstate or Highway	Incidents (2009)	Streetlight
Highway 94	32	No
Interstate 80	15	Yes
Highway 222	19	No
Interstate 95	43	No
Interstate 476	28	Yes

19. After reviewing the table, what would it be most correct for a recruit officer to conclude?

    A. Streetlights do not affect the number of accidents on highways.
    B. Streetlights along highways and interstates result in more accidents.
    C. Streetlights do not affect the number of accidents on interstates.
    D. Streetlights along highways and interstates result in fewer accidents.

20. Around 3:30 a.m. on Saturday, Officer Gilardi is on patrol when he finds an unconscious man lying on a side street adjacent to a nightclub. Upon closer inspections, Gilardi finds an empty syringe next to the man. He is unable to revive the unidentified man. What should Officer Gilardi do next?

    A. Call an ambulance for transport to a hospital.
    B. Place the man under arrest for possession of drug paraphernalia.
    C. Leave the man where he is and continue on patrol.
    D. Take the man to a detoxification treatment center.

21. A recruit officer is admonished by his supervisor for always using the same route and timing schedule on his patrol. Which of the following is the most important reason why this practice is a bad policy?

    A. Staggering routes makes it seem as though police officers are always on patrol.
    B. Constant patrol patterns are recognized and taken advantage of by criminals.
    C. Staggering routes and times of patrols may confuse officers.
    D. Constant patrol patterns should be used only by senior officers.

Question 22 refers to the following definition.

> **Misappropriation of misdelivered or lost property:** Taking possession of lost or misdelivered property clearly identified as belonging to another individual and failing to make a reasonable effort to return the property

22. Which of the following is the most accurate example of misappropriation of misdelivered or lost property?

A. Earl Wilson receives a package that was addressed to his neighbor and opens it. He finds an MP3 player inside and decides to keep it.

B. Ronald Smith steals several CDs he finds in an unattended vehicle.

C. Rita Phillips threatens to reveal that her friend Mary has been having an affair with another woman's husband unless Mary pays her $1,000.

D. Frank Bruno takes a wallet from a man on the street. The wallet contains $279 in cash and traveler's checks.

Question 23 refers to the following information.

Officer Martinez is trying to reduce crime in his precinct. He is reviewing the following crime reports and last week's schedule.

Date	Day	Crime	Time	Location
8/2	Monday	Burglary	4:48 a.m.	400 block of 45th Street
8/2	Monday	Vandalism	11:09 p.m.	600 block of 14th Avenue
8/3	Tuesday	Arson	3:57 a.m.	900 block of 20th Avenue
8/3	Tuesday	Rape	8:43 p.m.	400 block of 14th Avenue
8/4	Wednesday	Arson	5:32 p.m.	300 block of 9th Street
8/5	Thursday	Burglary	6:21 p.m.	500 block of 19th Street
8/6	Friday	Vandalism	2:20 a.m.	4400 block of 8th Avenue
8/6	Friday	Burglary	4:25 p.m.	900 block of 6th Avenue
8/7	Saturday	Arson	6:30 a.m.	200 block of 13th Street
8/7	Saturday	Burglary	9:02 p.m.	100 block of 19th Street
8/8	Sunday	Burglary	8:45 p.m.	5000 block of 6th Avenue

Shift	Schedule
Tour I	7 a.m.–3 p.m.
Tour II	3–11 p.m.
Tour III	11 p.m.–7 a.m.

23. If Officer Martinez wants to assign extra police officers to reduce the number of burglaries, which of the following would most likely achieve that goal?

    A.   Assign a Tour III to patrol on Mondays at 45th Street and 8th Avenue.

    B.   Assign a Tour II and a Tour III to patrol Tuesdays and Wednesdays on 14th Avenue and 20th Avenue.

    C.   Assign a Tour I to patrol Fridays and Saturdays on 6th Avenue and 19th Street.

    D.   Assign a Tour II to patrol on Thursdays, Fridays, and Saturdays on 19th Street and 6th Avenue.

Question 24 refers to the following information.

Officer Torres completed an incident report following an undercover automobile theft. The following five sentences were removed from the body of the report in no particular order:

1. As Ms. Crane was entering her vehicle, an unknown assailant approached her and produced a knife.
2. Ms. Crane called for help, and I arrived on scene.
3. At approximately 9:45 p.m., the victim, Ms. Mary Crane, left a local bar and headed toward her vehicle.
4. The unknown assailant ordered Ms. Crane to exit the vehicle.
5. The unknown assailant drove away.

24. Which of the following represents the correct chronological order of events?

    A.   3, 1, 4, 5, 2
    B.   2, 3, 1, 4, 5
    C.   3, 1, 4, 2, 5
    D.   5, 4, 2, 1, 3

Question 25 refers to the following information.

The class of police recruits was excited to hear the evening's guest speaker, Sergeant Robert Remus. Sergeant Remus, a 20-year police veteran, was speaking to the class about driving under the influence (DUI) and driving while intoxicated (DWI) incidents. He spoke to the recruits about his experiences with DUI and DWI incidents, and he taught them about the proper procedures for handling such situations. During his lecture, Sergeant Remus outlined the following procedures for DUI and DWI incidents:

1. Always attempt to pull over vehicles exceeding the speed limit or swerving excessively.
2. When the suspect's vehicle stops, run the license-plate number and check the criminal database for outstanding warrants.
3. Cautiously approach the vehicle and question the suspect, paying careful attention to his or her speech and behavior patterns.
4. If you think the suspect may be intoxicated, ask him or her to exit the vehicle and monitor his or her ability to do so.
5. Once the suspect is out of the vehicle and away from the roadway, you may conduct a field sobriety test. Monitor the suspect and carefully note the state of his or her physical and mental conditions.
6. Ask the suspect to take a breathalyzer test.
7. Based on your observations and the suspect's test results, make a determination of the suspect's level of intoxication and take the appropriate actions.

25. What are the two main goals for an officer who pulls over a driver suspected of being intoxicated?

    A. maintaining public safety and getting the suspect into custody as quickly as possible
    B. maintaining public safety and determining the suspect's level of intoxication
    C. determining the suspect's level of intoxication and getting drunk drivers off the road
    D. determining the suspect's level of intoxication and accumulating as many traffic citations as possible

Question 26 refers to the following information.

The city of Fountainhead, Vermont, recently enacted a new ordinance regarding the use of mopeds within the city. The ordinance was designed to ensure the safety of moped drivers, other drivers, and the community at large. The ordinance contained the following regulations:

- Drivers must be at least 15 years of age and must obtain a moped license issued by the secretary of state. A valid driver's license is also acceptable.
- Any driver under 18 years of age must wear a safety helmet.
- Driving a moped on a sidewalk or bike path is prohibited.
- Mopeds driven on roadways must display valid permits, and drivers must obey all traffic laws. Moped drivers should stay as far to the right side of the road as possible.
- Moped drivers may not carry passengers at any time.
- All mopeds must be registered with the secretary of state, and a registration sticker must be in place on the rear of each vehicle.

26. Which of the following is the best example of an owner who is violating the city of Fountainhead's new moped ordinance?

    A. Sam, a 17-year-old high school student, puts on his helmet and drives his registered moped to school, being careful to always stay on the right-hand side of the road.
    B. Bill, 28, purchases a new moped, a helmet, and a leather jacket and then immediately drives off the sales lot on his new moped.
    C. Ann, 16, is excited to finally try out her new moped after waiting for her registration sticker to arrive in the mail. She applies the sticker, puts on a helmet, and drives away.
    D. Greg, 25, is showing off his moped for his friends. He decides to take a spin around the block and his friend Joe asks to ride with him. Greg declines, saying that he can't take any passengers.

Question 27 refers to the following information.

In bustling locations such as malls or amusement parks, children are sometimes separated from their parents. In class, recruit officers learn what to do when they're in a public area and a child approaches them without his or her parents. Officers should follow these steps in the order in which they are given:

1. Report the situation to the radio dispatcher and the desk officer.
2. Question people in the area who may have witnessed the child walk away from his or her parents.
3. If you can't locate the child's parents or caregiver, take them to the police station until you can make contact with the child's guardians.
4. Write an aid report with details about the incident.

27. A young boy named Marcus approaches Officer Landus's patrol car outside of a crowded grocery store on a Saturday morning. The 11-year-old boy seems upset but tries not to show it as he tells the officer that he can't find his father. What should Officer Landus do first?

   A. Ask shoppers if they've seen Marcus's father as they leave the store.
   B. Radio dispatch to let them know that he's helping a lost child.
   C. Tell Marcus to sit in the car while he looks for Marcus's father in the store.
   D. Request Marcus's full name and address to use later in his aid report.

28. Police officers rarely use force to maintain control over a situation, although the possibility is always present. Officers typically use force only to apprehend a suspect if the suspect is resisting arrest or if someone's life is in danger.

   In which of the following situations is a police officer least likely to use force?

   A. A prostitute is beating a man with her stiletto after he refused to pay her.
   B. A gang member is approaching a member of a rival gang with a gun in his hand.
   C. A drug dealer is cursing at an undercover police officer who is arresting him for selling drugs.
   D. A thief is running through a crowded mall after robbing a store at gunpoint.

Question 29 refers to the following information.

A class of new police recruits reports to the seminar hall for a presentation by guest speaker Sergeant Paul Lester. Sergeant Lester, an experienced police officer and police helicopter pilot, is speaking to the students about the proper procedures in the event of a high-speed police pursuit. Sergeant Lester highlights the following guidelines:

1. If a suspect refuses to pull over or attempts to flee the scene of a crime in a motor vehicle, immediately inform your superiors that a motor-vehicle pursuit is in progress and follow the suspect.
2. Try to maintain visual contact with the suspect's vehicle at all times, while being sure to drive as safely as possible.
3. When other officers have joined the pursuit, maintain open communication and coordinate your actions.
4. Carefully employ specialized tactics designed to stop the fleeing suspect. Remember to consider the safety of other drivers on the road while attempting to stop the suspect.
5. When the suspect's vehicle has stopped, approach cautiously, assess the scene, assess the suspect for injuries, and proceed accordingly with arrest or medical assistance.

29. Based on the passage, the recruits would be correct to assume that the primary goal for an officer engaged in a high-speed pursuit is to:

   A. Ensure the safety of everyone in and around the scene and quickly stop the suspect.
   B. Drive as fast as possible to keep up with the suspect.
   C. Stop and arrest the suspect as quickly as possible.
   D. Alert as many fellow officers to the situation as possible, so that everyone may join the chase.

30. You've been dispatched to a domestic dispute. As you arrive on the scene, your supervisor issues you special instructions over the radio, but there is significant interference and you can't understand her. You decide that you already know what to do and proceed with the investigation. This decision is:

   A. right, because you have been extensively trained for this situation and should be able to handle it on your own

   B. right, because you can deduce what the special instructions were by what you find on the scene

   C. wrong, because the special instructions may be vital to the investigation or your safety and should be fully understood before you proceed

   D. wrong, because you'll need to include this information in your incident report

Questions 31 through 33 refer to the following definitions.

Assault/battery: Assault/battery occurs when one individual attempts to strike or actually strikes another person. Using threatening behavior to scare someone into thinking that you're about to harm him or her is also considered assault/battery.

Aggravated assault/battery: When a person attempts to cause severe injury, actually causes severe injury, or causes severe injury with a deadly weapon, the offending person is charged with aggravated assault/battery.

Sexual assault: Sexual assault is any form of assault that involves nonconsensual and/or offensive sexual contact.

Rape: The act of forcing another into nonconsensual sexual intercourse through the use of physical force, threatening behavior, or any other means is referred to as rape.

31. Which of the following is an example of aggravated assault/battery?

   A. While drinking at a local bar, Stan Kelly gets into an argument with another patron and punches him in the face, knocking him unconscious.

   B. As store clerk Latisha Johnson returns to her register from the restroom, she finds a burglar stealing cash from the drawer. He says he has a knife in his pocket and threatens to stab her if she screams.

   C. Jim Phillips is hired to make sure that a baseball pitcher is unable to play in an important upcoming game. He finds the man and breaks his pitching arm with a club.

   D. Samantha Peters is walking through the park late at night when an unknown assailant jumps out of the brush and attempts to pull her into a ditch. He hits and fondles her during the struggle.

32. Which of the following is an example of assault/battery?

   A. Sarah Jones is repeatedly groped by an intoxicated man while at a bar.

   B. Jennifer Gonzales is attacked by an unidentified man in the stairwell of a parking garage. He forces her into sexual intercourse.

   C. George Franklin gets into a bar fight with another man and stabs him with a pocketknife.

   D. Michael Salvo realizes that he has just been ripped off by a street vendor. After a heated argument, Salvo punches the man.

33. Which of the following is an example of sexual assault?

   A. Julie Chen is being verbally harassed by a man at a bar, so she kicks him in the groin.
   B. Peter Martin is at a house party. As the last guests start to leave, he puts something in the host's drink. Within a few minutes, she has passed out and he has sexual intercourse with her while she is unconscious.
   C. Maria Brown is in the mosh pit at a concert when a man behind her tries to lift up her shirt.
   D. Manuel Sanchez sneaks up on a woman walking through an alley and proceeds to hit and choke her.

Question 34 refers to the following information.

Officer Walsh completed an incident report following a shoplifting incident. The following five sentences were removed from the body of the report in no particular order:

1. Store security apprehended the suspect and contacted police.
2. A clerk witnessed a woman placing a pair of earrings into her purse.
3. I arrested Mary Parker and charged her with shoplifting.
4. The woman headed toward the exit and attempted to leave the store.
5. The clerk notified store security.

34. Which of the following represents the correct chronological order of events?

   A. 4, 2, 1, 3, 5
   B. 3, 1, 2, 4, 5
   C. 2, 5, 4, 3, 1
   D. 2, 4, 5, 1, 3

35. Officer Lopez is patrolling the city park when he sees a mugging in progress. The suspect has a knife to the victim's throat and orders him to hand over his wallet. When the victim refuses, the suspect slashes the victim's throat and takes the wallet. Just then, he sees Officer Lopez and runs off and out of the park. Instead of chasing the suspect, Lopez attends to the victim. Why is this course of action appropriate?

   A. He would not have been able to catch the suspect anyway.
   B. The victim was seriously injured and in need of immediate medical attention.
   C. A mugging does not constitute the need for a pursuit.
   D. He was assigned to patrol the park and could not follow the suspect outside that area.

36. Officer Lawrence is on patrol at 2:45 a.m. when he's dispatched to a shipping warehouse where a silent burglar alarm has been activated. Lawrence's lights and sirens are off as he approaches the scene. Why is he correct to approach in this way?

   A. It's very late and he doesn't want to wake up any sleeping neighbors.
   B. He isn't sure if a crime is actually in progress, so lights and sirens aren't necessary.
   C. He doesn't want the burglars to be aware of his presence.
   D. Lights and sirens shouldn't be turned on until backup arrives.

Question 37 refers to the following information.

The city of Mandeville, Oregon, recently enacted a new ordinance concerning the construction of additions being built onto existing physical structures. The ordinance contains the following provisions:

- Required building permits for such construction projects must be acquired from city hall.
- Proof of building permits must be kept on visible display throughout the course of construction.
- Construction zone must be properly enclosed with temporary fencing.
- Structural additions shouldn't exceed the size of the existing property.
- All construction equipment must be properly secured when not in use.
- Construction may take place only between the hours of 7 a.m. and 9 p.m.

37. Which of the following addition construction projects would be in violation of the city's new ordinance?

   A. a project with a building permit displayed in a window of the existing structure

   B. a project measuring 245 square feet added to an existing structure measuring 530 square feet

   C. a project enclosed with wooden barricades

   D. a project that is closed at 5 p.m. every day

38. Officer Freeland is on patrol when he passes a restaurant that has just closed for the night. As he walks around the rear of the building, he smells smoke and sees a fire in the kitchen through a window. Someone left the stove on and a nearby greasy rag ignited. The fire is spreading quickly. What should the officer do first?

   A. Break the window and attempt to put out the fire.

   B. Inform the restaurant owner.

   C. Request instructions from his supervisor.

   D. Call for support from the fire department.

Question 39 refers to the following information.

Officer Gutierrez completed an incident report following an armed robbery. The following five sentences were removed from the body of the report in no particular order:

   1. Shawn Jackson was arrested and charged with armed robbery.

   2. The clerk complied and the suspect fled after receiving the money.

   3. The suspect entered the convenience store, produced a gun, and ordered the clerk to give him the money in the register.

   4. Shawn Jackson is currently being held in the Sutter County jail in lieu of $25,000 bail.

   5. Police were called and the suspect was apprehended a few blocks away from the store.

39. Which of the following represents the correct chronological order of events?

   A. 4, 3, 2, 5, 1

   B. 3, 2, 5, 1, 4

   C. 3, 5, 2, 1, 4

   D. 5, 3, 2, 4, 1

40. Officer Williams brings a suspect who has just been arrested for public intoxication to the precinct for booking. As he returns to his squad car, he sees a small bag of white powder that he believes is cocaine on the back seat. What should the officer do with the bag?

    A. Discard it in the trash.
    B. Question the suspect about it.
    C. File a report and submit the bag to evidence control.
    D. Ignore the bag and let someone else find it.

41. You're at a family gathering and a cousin approaches you. He knows that you're a police officer. He tells you about a speeding ticket he received recently and asks you to do something about it. How should you respond?

    A. Tell him that he wouldn't have gotten a ticket if it weren't warranted.
    B. Tell him that there's nothing you can do because you didn't issue the ticket.
    C. Tell him that you'll check it out during your next shift.
    D. Tell him that you'll take care of it.

Questions 42 and 43 refer to the following passage.

Officer Larry Jones is on patrol at 9:15 p.m. Friday when he's dispatched to a private residence for a domestic dispute. When he arrives at the home, Officer Jones quickly assesses the scene outside the residence and sees no immediate danger. As he approaches the front door, a woman comes out yelling frantically about the situation. Officer Jones speaks calmly and respectfully to the woman and asks her to relax and tell him what's going on. The woman composes herself and tells him that her sister and brother-in-law have been arguing about which of them will get custody of their son after their upcoming divorce. She says that she called the police after her brother-in-law began to threaten them with violence. Jones thanks the woman and enters the home, assessing the interior scene as he does so. When he finds the arguing couple, he speaks to them separately, calmly asking each of them for his or her own side of the story and recording all pertinent information. When he's satisfied that no crime has been committed, he encourages the husband to leave the residence, which he agrees to do.

42. What is Officer Jones's primary goal throughout this situation?

    A. to assess and secure the scene and maintain order
    B. to defuse the situation as quickly as possible
    C. to determine if a crime had been committed and make any necessary arrests
    D. to remove the suspect from the scene by any means necessary

43. Why doesn't Officer Jones immediately approach the arguing couple upon entering the home?

    A. He wants to listen to them before they become aware of his presence.
    B. He needs to check the scene for any potential dangers.
    C. He needs to determine whether he should call for backup.
    D. He doesn't think the situation is serious enough to merit immediate intervention.

Questions 44 and 45 refer to the following information.

Police Chief Johnson is reviewing his town's vehicular-accident records. He must determine whether the city should invest in installing more traffic lights at various intersections in town and make his recommendations to the city council. He examines the following chart to gather some information.

Intersection	Accidents (2009)	Traffic-Control Device
Broad and Patterson	13	Traffic light
Park and Sutherland	11	Traffic light
Market and Chestnut	27	Stop signs
South Walnut and Frederick	9	Traffic light
Cedar and Main	22	Stop signs
Fleet and Thrasher	19	Stop signs

44. It would be most correct for Chief Johnson to conclude that:

    A. Traffic lights do not have a significant impact on the number of accidents at an intersection.

    B. Traffic lights lead to more accidents than stop signs.

    C. Stop signs lead to more accidents than traffic lights.

    D. Neither traffic lights nor stop signs are effective at preventing accidents.

45. Which of the following recommendations would be most appropriate?

    A. installing traffic lights at Fleet and Thrasher

    B. installing traffic lights at Cedar and Main

    C. installing stop signs at Park and Sutherland

    D. installing traffic lights at Market and Chestnut

46. A rookie police officer regularly uses the same route and timing while on his patrol. This would be considered:

    A. good policy, because officers may become confused by staggered routes and times

    B. good policy, because this method will help the officer become better acquainted with his area of patrol

    C. bad policy, because only experienced officers should patrol in this fashion

    D. bad policy, because criminals can become aware of constant patterns of patrol and use them to their advantage

Question 47 is based on the following definition.

Wire fraud: Using interstate wires (for example, television, radio, telephone, Internet) to acquire money or other property through fraudulent means

47. Which of the following is the most accurate example of wire fraud?

   A. Gene Sanderson receives a call from a friend who works in the stock market. His friend offers him an insider-trading tip, which Sanderson then uses to make a considerable amount of money.

   B. Roy Harlow is scamming elderly victims by calling them and pretending to be a bill collector.

   C. Simon Matthews is running a telemarketing scam in which he convinces victims to send him a fee for entry into a $500,000 sweepstakes that will never actually occur.

   D. Jim Jenkins steals a wallet out of another man's bag at the gym and later uses his credit card at a department store.

Questions 48 and 49 refer to the following information.

Police Chief Bill Patrick wants to reduce the crime rate in his precinct. While devising a new crime-prevention strategy, he reviews the following crime report.

Date	Day	Crime	Time	Location
11/1	Sunday	Assault	10:49 p.m.	6th Street and Granger Avenue
11/2	Monday	Burglary	4:10 a.m.	15th Street and Park Avenue
11/2	Monday	Vandalism	11:45 p.m.	9th Street and Granger Avenue
11/3	Tuesday	Assault	3:23 p.m.	3rd Street and Wallace Avenue
11/4	Wednesday	Burglary	12:56 a.m.	17th Street and Spruce Avenue
11/4	Wednesday	Burglary	1:57 a.m.	19th Street and Granger Avenue
11/5	Thursday	Rape	2:55 a.m.	30th Street and Park Avenue
11/6	Friday	Arson	3:02 a.m.	12th Street and Granger Avenue
11/6	Friday	Vandalism	3:30 a.m.	26th Street and Washington Avenue
11/6	Friday	Assault	4:28 p.m.	5th Street and Spruce Avenue
11/7	Saturday	Burglary	11:50 p.m.	18th Street and Wallace Avenue

48. What action should Chief Patrick take to achieve the greatest overall reduction in crime?

A. Assign more officers to patrol Granger Avenue at night.

B. Assign more officers to patrol Park Avenue at night.

C. Assign more officers to patrol Granger Avenue during the day.

D. Assign more officers to patrol Wallace Avenue at night.

49. What action should Chief Patrick take specifically to reduce the number of burglaries in his precinct?

A. Assign more officers to patrol Granger Avenue at night.

B. Assign more officers to patrol between 15th and 20th streets.

C. Assign more officers to patrol between 20th and 30th streets.

D. Assign more officers to patrol Park Avenue at night.

Question 50 refers to the following information.

Officer Li completed an incident report following an assault. The following five sentences were removed from the body of the report in no particular order:

1. Mr. Smith attacked Mr. Sanford, punching him several times before being subdued by the bartender.

2. Leroy Smith and Bob Sanford were drinking at a local pub when they became engaged in a heated argument.

3. The bartender called police.

4. Leroy Smith was arrested and charged with assault.

5. Leroy Smith is being held at the Clark County jail in lieu of $5,000 bail.

50. Which of the following represents the correct chronological order of events?

A. 2, 3, 1, 4, 5

B. 5, 2, 1, 3, 4

C. 4, 2, 1, 3, 5

D. 2, 1, 3, 4, 5

IF YOU FINISH BEFORE TIME IS CALLED, CHECK YOUR WORK ON THIS SECTION ONLY. DO NOT WORK ON ANY OTHER SECTION IN THE TEST.

Answer Key

Section 1: Verbal

1. B	14. B	27. D	40. B
2. A	15. B	28. A	41. Amelia Martinez
3. C	16. A	29. B	42. 235
4. B	17. B	30. D	43. 75 Maddox St.
5. A	18. B	31. C	44. November 18
6. C	19. A	32. D	45. Brown
7. C	20. B	33. A	46. $85
8. C	21. B	34. A	47. 35
9. B	22. C	35. A	48. 3265 Lake St.
10. B	23. D	36. C	49. White pants
11. C	24. C	37. C	50. MP3 player
12. A	25. A	38. A	
13. D	26. D	39. B	

Section 2: Memory and Visualization

1. D	14. D	27. C	40. C
2. C	15. B	28. D	41. C
3. D	16. D	29. B	42. A
4. A	17. A	30. A	43. B
5. B	18. B	31. D	44. C
6. C	19. B	32. C	45. A
7. D	20. A	33. C	46. D
8. C	21. B	34. B	47. C
9. B	22. B	35. C	48. B
10. C	23. C	36. D	49. A
11. A	24. C	37. A	50. C
12. B	25. B	38. B	
13. C	26. A	39. C	

Section 3: Mathematics

1. B	14. D	27. D	40. B
2. D	15. C	28. A	41. A
3. D	16. A	29. C	42. C
4. C	17. C	30. C	43. C
5. C	18. D	31. A	44. D
6. A	19. D	32. C	45. C
7. B	20. D	33. B	46. B
8. B	21. C	34. B	47. A
9. C	22. C	35. D	48. C
10. C	23. A	36. C	49. C
11. C	24. B	37. B	50. C
12. C	25. B	38. B	
13. B	26. C	39. D	

Section 4: Judgment and Problem Solving

1. B	14. C	27. B	40. C
2. B	15. A	28. C	41. B
3. A	16. C	29. A	42. A
4. B	17. C	30. C	43. B
5. C	18. D	31. C	44. C
6. A	19. D	32. D	45. D
7. B	20. A	33. C	46. D
8. D	21. B	34. D	47. B
9. B	22. A	35. B	48. A
10. C	23. D	36. C	49. B
11. A	24. A	37. C	50. D
12. C	25. B	38. D	
13. C	26. B	39. B	

Answer Explanations

Section 1: Verbal

1. **B** The correct answer is *their*. The possessive adjective *their* modifies the noun *arms*. *There* is an adverb used to show placement, while *they're* is a contraction for *they are*. Both are homophones of the correct answer, *their*. *(See Chapter V, Section B.)*

2. **A** The correct answer is *incidents*, which is a plural noun. Choices B *(incidents')* and C *(incident's)* are incorrect because they're possessives nouns. *(See Chapter V, Section B.)*

3. **C** The correct answer is the singular possessive noun *teenager's*. The sentence is talking about one teenager. Choice A *(teenagers')* is incorrect because it's a plural possessive noun, and choice B *(teenagers)* is incorrect because it's a plural noun. *(See Chapter V, Section B.)*

4. **B** The correct answer is the singular possessive noun *suspect's*. Choice C *(suspects')* is incorrect because it's a plural possessive noun, and choice A *(suspects)* is incorrect because it's a plural noun. *(See Chapter V, Section B.)*

5. **A** The correct answer is the plural noun *posters*. Choices B *(poster's)* and C *(posters')* are incorrect because they're possessives nouns. *(See Chapter V, Section B.)*

6. **C** The correct answer is *victims'*. The world *lives* indicates that the plural possessive is necessary. Choice B *(victim's)* is incorrect because it's a singular possessive noun, and choice A *(victims)* is incorrect because it's a plural noun. *(See Chapter V, Section B.)*

7. **C** The correct answer is the possessive adjective *your*. The possessive adjective *your* modifies the noun *hands*. *You're* is the contraction for *you are* and is a homophone for the correct answer, *your*. *(See Chapter V, Section B.)*

8. **C** The correct answer is *two*, which is an adjective used to describe how many warrants the judge must approve. *Too* means "also," while *to* is a preposition or an infinitive. When used as an infinitive, it precedes a verb. Both are homophones of the correct answer, *two*. *(See Chapter V, Section B.)*

9. **B** The correct answer is *where*. The word *where* is an adverb that means "at" or "what place." *Wear* is a verb that means "to have on," and *ware* is a noun that means "good" or "item." *Wear* and *ware* are homophones of the correct answer, *where*. *(See Chapter V, Section B.)*

10. **B** The correct answer is *towed*. *Towed* is the past tense of the verb *tow*, which means "to drag or pull along behind." The verb *toed*, which is a homophone of *towed*, means "having toes." The noun *toad* is the name of a type of amphibian. *(See Chapter V, Section B.)*

11. **C** The correct answer is *street*. This word should be capitalized because it's part of a proper noun. *(See Chapter V, Section B.)*

12. **A** The phrase *Police Presence* should not be capitalized because it isn't a proper noun. *(See Chapter V, Section B.)*

13. **D** The phrase *who lives at 64 Dover Avenue* is a nonrestrictive, or nonessential, phrase and should be set off by commas. *(See Chapter V, Section B.)*

14. **B** The example sentence contains two independent clauses that should be separated by a semicolon (;). *(See Chapter V, Section B.)*

15. **B** Section 11 on the blank incident report requires the name of the suspect. Based on the information in the paragraph, this section can't be completed because there is no information about the suspect. *(See Chapter V, Section A.)*

16. **A** The paragraph states that the house located at 313 Blackwell Dr. was burglarized. *(See Chapter V, Section A.)*

17. **B** The incident report cannot be completely filled out. *(See Chapter V, Section A.)*

18. **B** Ms. Moore's purse contained three, not four, credit cards. *(See Chapter V, Section A.)*

19. **A** The statement is true because sections 4 and 5 of the incident report can be completely filled out. *(See Chapter V, Section A.)*

20. **B** The statement is false because the victim's name is José Roberts, not José Sanchez. *(See Chapter V, Section A.)*

21. **B** The word *informent* is spelled incorrectly. The correct spelling is *informant. (See Chapter V, Section B)*

22. **C** The word *apparant* is spelled incorrectly. The correct spelling is *apparent. (See Chapter V, Section B.)*

23. **D** The word *avidence* is spelled incorrectly. The correct spelling is *evidence. (See Chapter V, Section B.)*

24. **C** The word *disaibled* is spelled incorrectly. The correct spelling is *disabled. (See Chapter V, Section B.)*

25. **A** The word *voluntear* is spelled incorrectly. The correct spelling is *volunteer. (See Chapter V, Section B.)*

26. **D** The word *coroperation* is spelled incorrectly. The correct spelling is *cooperation. (See Chapter V, Section B.)*

27. **D** The word *effecient* is spelled incorrectly. The correct spelling is *efficient. (See Chapter V, Section B.)*

28. **A** Sentence I is correct, but sentence II uses the incorrect verb tense. The present tense *(see)* should be replaced with the past tense *(saw). (See Chapter V, Section B.)*

29. **B** Sentence II is correct, but sentence I is a run-on sentence. A period should be placed after the word *juvenile,* and the word *he* should be capitalized to create a separate sentence. *(See Chapter V, Section B.)*

30. **D** Both sentence I and sentence II are correct. Each sentence uses the correct subject-verb agreement, pronoun agreement, and correct verb tenses. *(See Chapter V, Section B.)*

31. **C** Neither sentence I nor sentence II is correct. In sentence I, the incorrect pronoun is used. The possessive adjective *our* should be replaced with the possessive adjective *her,* because it modifies the subject, *daughter.* Sentence II contains the incorrect verb tense. The present tense of the verb *call* should be replaced with the past tense *called. (See Chapter V, Sections B.)*

32. **D** Both sentence I and sentence II are grammatically correct. *(See Chapter V, Section B.)*

33. **A** Sentence I is grammatically correct, but sentence II contains a grammar error. Sentence II is a sentence fragment and should contain an independent clause. *(See Chapter V, Section B.)*

34. **A** Mrs. Janoski's initials are sewn on the handkerchief. *(See Chapter V, Section A.)*

35. **A** *Littered,* which means "made a mess," is closest in meaning to the word *strewn,* which means "scattered." *(See Chapter V, Section A.)*

36. **C** Mrs. Janoski told the officers that her husband was out of town visiting their son. *(See Chapter V, Section A.)*

37. **C** Mrs. Janoski told the officers that the thief stole a purse, a wallet, and a watch; she did not report that a necklace had been stolen. *(See Chapter V, Section A.)*

38. **A** The female whom Mrs. White saw in the hallway was wearing khaki pants and a pink polo shirt. *(See Chapter V, Section A.)*

39. **B** The safe in Mr. and Mrs. Loucks's apartment was located in a closet of the master bedroom, where Mrs. Loucks's jewelry also was stolen. *(See Chapter V, Section A.)*

40. **B** The Loucks live in apartment 2B. *(See Chapter V, Section A.)*

41. The victim's name is Amelia Martinez. *(See Chapter V, Section A.)*

42. The responding police officer's badge number is 235. *(See Chapter V, Section A.)*

43. The suspect's address is 75 Maddox St. *(See Chapter V, Section A.)*

44. The victim's date of birth is November 18. *(See Chapter V, Section A.)*

45. The suspect's hair color is brown. *(See Chapter V, Section A.)*

46. The stolen item's value is $85. *(See Chapter V, Section A.)*

47. The suspect is 35 years old. *(See Chapter V, Section A.)*

48. The incident took place at 3265 Lake St. *(See Chapter V, Section A.)*

49. The suspect is wearing white pants. *(See Chapter V, Section A.)*

50. The suspect stole an MP3 player from the victim. *(See Chapter V, Section A.)*

Section 2: Memory and Visualization

1. **D** If you followed the suspect traveling north and then took two right turns, a left turn, and two more right turns, you would be traveling west. *(See Chapter VI, Section B.)*

2. **C** This diagram correctly shows the directions in which the vehicles were traveling. Although choice D may *look* correct, vehicle 1 is traveling east in this diagram, not west as indicated in the passage. *(See Chapter VI, Section C.)*

3. **D** Choice D is correct. This diagram correctly shows the directions in which the vehicles were traveling. Choice C may look correct, but vehicle 1 is traveling north in this diagram, not south as indicated in the passage. *(See Chapter VI, Section C.)*

4. **A** Starting on 98th Street, if you travel north on Minor Street, east on 96th Street, and north on Maffet Street, you'll be closest to the police station. Mo's Diner is also in that area, but it isn't one of the answer choices. *(See Chapter VI, Section C.)*

5. **B** Because you need to obey all traffic regulations, including one-way streets, you have to travel south on River Road, west on 98th Street, north on Minor Street, east on 96th Street, north on Maffet Street, and west on 94th Street to reach the neighborhood described. *(See Chapter VI, Section C.)*

6. **C** If you're located at point 2, Mo's Diner, and travel north, then west, then south, you'll be closest to point 3, the pizza shop. Although you're also close to the tattoo parlor and the mall, those are not answer choices. *(See Chapter VI, Section C.)*

7. **D** Traveling from the police station to the south entrance of the mall parking lot, your most direct route would be to travel west on 94th Street, south on Locust Street, east on 96th Street, south on River Road, and west on 98th Street. *(See Chapter VI, Section C.)*

8. **C** If the owner of the convenience store watched the suspect travel south and then saw him make a left turn, it would be most accurate to report that the suspect was last seen traveling east. *(See Chapter VI, Section B.)*

9. **B** If the suspect was last seen traveling south and took a left-hand turn and then a right-hand turn, it would be most accurate to report that the suspect was last seen traveling south. *(See Chapter VI, Section B.)*

10. **C** Your view from the back should be the opposite of your view from the front. All the buildings should be in the same order; none of the roofs should be switched on any of the buildings and none of the buildings should move from their original locations. *(See Chapter VI, Section B.)*

11. **A** If the owner of the bakery is correct, then it would be most accurate to report that the suspect was last seen traveling north. *(See Chapter VI, Section B.)*

12. **B** The man standing to the left of the ticket booth is carrying two bags. One is a shopping bag, while the other is a shoulder bag used to carry office supplies, books, or even a laptop computer. *(See Chapter VI, Section A.)*

13. **C** The sign hanging on the fence outside the carousel reads WET PAINT. There are two signs signaling that the fence may be wet. One is located in the far left of the photograph, and the other is slightly to the left of the man in the hat. *(See Chapter VI, Section A.)*

14. **D** The design of the carousel doesn't feature any birds. There are birds on the ticket booth, but the photograph doesn't show any birds on the carousel itself. There are, however, faces of angels, paintings of clouds, and large butterflies on the top of the carousel. *(See Chapter VI, Section A.)*

15. **B** The lines on the bottom of the ticket stand are grouped in threes and run vertically. A screen covers the window where a worker would sell the tickets and speak to the guests, with lines running horizontally and vertically. *(See Chapter VI, Section A.)*

16. **D** There are eight people standing outside the cabin. There are three people on the left side, two people near the door, and three people walking away from the cabin on the right side. *(See Chapter VI, Section A.)*

17. **A** There is a pair of antlers hanging above the doorway of the cabin. *(See Chapter VI, Section A.)*

18. **B** The sign on the left reads THEODORE ROOSEVELT'S MALTESE CROSS CABIN. *(See Chapter VI, Section A.)*

19. **B** Your view from the back should be the opposite of your view from the front. All the buildings should be in the same order; none of the roofs should be switched on any of the buildings and none of the buildings should move from their original locations. *(See Chapter VI, Section B.)*

20. **A** There is one animal in this photograph. You can see a sheep standing in front of the truck beyond the clothesline. *(See Chapter VI, Section A.)*

21. **B** There are several sheets hanging on the clothesline in the foreground of the photograph. There are several pairs of socks hanging from the clothesline in the background. *(See Chapter VI, Section A.)*

22. **B** Three windows are visible on the first house on the right. Although the house may have more windows, they are not visible in this photograph. *(See Chapter VI, Section A.)*

23. **C** Barrels are propped up against the side of each house. The barrels are sitting on wood platforms. *(See Chapter VI, Section A.)*

24. **C** There are three vehicles in this photograph. Two trucks are parked next to each other and another car is in the background. *(See Chapter VI, Section A.)*

25. **B** The quickest route to get to the library from the police station, obeying all traffic and safety regulations, is to travel west on Oak Street, north on Second Street, and east on Willow Street. Because Willow Street is a one-way street traveling east, you wouldn't be able to travel north on Third Street and west on Willow Street to get to the library. *(See Chapter VI, Section C.)*

26. **A** Starting at point 5, the art studio, the quickest route you could travel to get to point 6, the deli, is north on First Street, east on Willow Street, and south on Third Street. Since Oak Street is a one-way street traveling west, you can't travel east on Maple Street, north on Second Street, and east on Oak Street. *(See Chapter VI, Section C.)*

27. **C** Officer Bean should find himself at the intersection of Second Street and Oak Street, facing the side of the bookstore. *(See Chapter VI, Section C.)*

28. **D** If you're located on Oceanside Drive and you travel north on New Street and then turn east on Mountain View Road and south on Fickle Lane, you'll be closest to the pet store. The grocery store, baseball field, and points 4 and 5 also are located on Fickle Lane. *(See Chapter VI, Section C.)*

29. **B** The most direct route from the bank to the neighborhood on Mountain View Road and Fickle Lane is to travel south on Marcus Road, east on Oceanside Drive, and north on Fickle Lane. *(See Chapter VI, Section C.)*

30. **A** If you're located at point 5 and travel north, then turn west onto Mountain View Road and south on Marcus Road, you'll be closest to point 1. Point 2 is close, as well, but traveling Marcus Road will bring you to the school, which is next to point 1. *(See Chapter VI, Section C.)*

31. **D** Your most direct route to the east entrance of the baseball field is south on Marcus Road, east on Oceanside Drive, and south on Fickle Lane. If you wanted to enter the baseball field from the west, you would travel south on New Street. *(See Chapter VI, Section C.)*

32. **C** From point 5, the first direction in which you'll travel to eventually reach point 4 is east on Lumber Lane. Although point 4 is located north of point 5, you can't cut through the block of buildings, homes, and trees with your police cruiser. Instead, you'll have to travel east, north, west, and then north again. *(See Chapter VI, Section C.)*

33. **C** The quickest route from the bank to the pizza shop is to travel east on River Road, south on Atlantic Avenue, and west on Willow Street. Choices A and B are incorrect because you can't travel south on Push Lane, a one-way street traveling north. Choice D is incorrect because you want to travel west on Willow Street, not east. *(See Chapter VI, Section C.)*

34. **B** After traveling east on River Road, you turn right (south) on Atlantic Avenue, left (east) on Willow Street, right (south) on Nathan Drive, right (west) on Lumber Lane, and finally right (north) onto Atlantic Avenue. Because you're now traveling north, at the first intersection the police station will be on your left. *(See Chapter VI, Section C.)*

35. **C** After traveling south on Atlantic Avenue, west on Willow Street, and north on Push Lane, you're facing north. From that position, point 3 is southeast of your patrol car. To eventually reach point 3, you must first travel east on River Road. From there, you would travel south on Nathan Drive, and point 3 would be on your right. *(See Chapter VI, Section C.)*

36. **D** You would be most correct if you reported that the suspect was last seen traveling west. When the suspect drove away, the witness said he almost hit a car traveling south in the opposite lane. You can assume that the suspect was then traveling north, which means that a left turn would take him west. *(See Chapter VI, Section C.)*

37. **A** Your view from the back should be the opposite of your view from the front. All the buildings should be in the same order; none of the roofs should be switched on any of the buildings, and none of the buildings should move from their original locations. *(See Chapter VI, Section B.)*

38. **B** Detective Marsh would be most correct if he reported that the suspect was last seen traveling south. After traveling north, east, and south, and then making a right (west) and a left (south), Detective Marsh last saw the suspect traveling south. *(See Chapter VI, Section B.)*

39. **C** The sign in the foreground of this photograph reads soft drinks. Signs for corn chips, lemonade, potato chips, and batteries also appear in this photograph, but the sign for soft drinks is closest to the camera. *(See Chapter VI, Section A.)*

40. **C** The man in this photograph is wearing a shirt, shorts, and sandals, but he is not wearing a hat. *(See Chapter VI, Section A.)*

41. **C** The left side of the aisle is lined with six shelves, while the right side of the aisle is lined with seven. The bottom shelves on the left side of the aisle are taller to allow for boxes of canned soft drinks, while the shelves on the bottom of the right side of the aisle only need to be tall enough to hold bags of chips. *(See Chapter VI, Section A.)*

42. **A** In proximity to the man in this photograph, the stepstool in the aisle is positioned in front of him and to his left. *(See Chapter VI, Section A.)*

43. **B** Three doors are visible in this photograph. There is a door at the top of the stairs, a door underneath the stairs, and a door in the center of the picture. *(See Chapter VI, Section A.)*

44. **C** There is a purse sitting next to the woman in the center of the picture. The woman is sitting on a short wall and her purse sits off to the left. *(See Chapter VI, Section A.)*

45. **A** There is one man visible in this photograph. He is talking with a woman who has her back to the camera. *(See Chapter VI, Section A.)*

46. **D** The woman on the right side of the photograph is reading a book. *(See Chapter VI, Section A.)*

47. **C** Your view from the back should be the opposite of your view from the front. All the buildings should be in the same order; none of the roofs should be switched on any of the buildings and none of the buildings should move from their original locations. *(See Chapter VI, Section B.)*

48. **B** From the police station, the quickest route to point 2 would be to travel southeast on Spellman Avenue, south on Timber Lane, and west on Penn Avenue. You can't travel south on Nicholson Street and east on Penn Avenue because Penn Avenue is a one-way street traveling west. *(See Chapter VI, Section C.)*

49. **A** From the westernmost soccer field, the quickest route to the bait shop is to travel north on Nicholson Street and east on Lincoln Lane. You can't travel east on Penn Avenue because it's a one-way street traveling west. *(See Chapter VI, Section C.)*

50. **C** After traveling south on Timber Lane, right (east) on Penn Avenue, right (north) on Nicholson Street, east on Lincoln Lane, south on Timber Lane, and then making a left (east), Officer Lukes would be traveling southeast on Spellman Avenue. *(See Chapter VI, Section C.)*

Section 3: Mathematics

1. **B** He traveled 60 miles. You can either add the number of miles a day each of the five days (12 + 12 + 12 + 12 + 12 = 60) or multiply the number of miles walked each day by the number of days (12 × 5 = 60). *(See Chapter VII, Sections A and B.)*

2. **D** The volume of the rectangle shown is 1,170. $V = 18 \times 6.5 \times 10 = 1,170$. *(See Chapter VII, Section B.)*

3. **D** Each week, 24 calls are emergencies. Either multiply the total number of calls by the percentage of nonemergency calls and subtract that number from the total number of calls (32 × 0.25 = 8 and 32 – 8 = 24) or multiply the total number of calls by the percentage of emergency calls (32 × 0.75 = 24). *(See Chapter VII, Sections A and B.)*

4. **C** He wrote 39 reports. Add the numbers of reports done each week before and after lunch: 4 + 7 + 9 + 2 + 11 + 6 = 39. *(See Chapter VII, Section A.)*

5. **C** The total value of stolen items except for the cash is $1,775. To find the correct answer, subtract the cash from the total amount: $1,920 – $145 = $1,775. *(See Chapter VII, Section A.)*

6. **A** The new value is $3,620. Subtract the watch from the total amount and then add the value of the wedding band: $1,920 – $500 = $1,420 and $1,420 + $2,200 = $3,620. *(See Chapter VII, Section A.)*

7. **B** The area of the triangle shown is 96. $A = \frac{1}{2} \times 12 \times 16 = 96$. *(See Chapter VII, Section B.)*

8. **B** The average number of arrests per week is 7. Add the number of arrests each week and then divide by the number of weeks: 5 + 3 + 9 + 11 + 7 + 4 + 5 + 19 + 3 + 14 + 1 + 4 = 85 and 85 ÷ 12 = 7.083. Then round to the nearest whole number: 7. *(See Chapter VII, Section A.)*

9. **C** Only 65 bags contained illegal drugs. Multiply the number of bags by the percentage of illegal drugs: 65% = 0.65, so 100 × 0.65 = 65. *(See Chapter VII, Section B.)*

10. **C** You can complete 36 training exercises in 18 days. Begin with the ratio you're given: 12:6. You know that 18 is three times 6, so multiple 12 times 3 and you get 36. *(See Chapter VII, Section B.)*

11. **C** The approximate value of each ring is $750. Divide the total amount that the rings are worth by the number of rings: $11,250 ÷ 15 = $750. *(See Chapter VII, Section B.)*

12. **C** To solve this problem, follow the order of operations. First, multiply 68.54 × 0.17; then subtract the product from 182.47; and finally, add 12. So, 182.47 – 11.6518 + 12 = 182.8182. Round to the nearest hundredth and the answer is 182.82. *(See Chapter VII, Section C.)*

13. **B** There were 44 gang-related incidents and arsons reported. Add the number of gang-related incidents and arsons for the month of March: 42 + 2 = 44. *(See Chapter VII, Section A.)*

14. **D** Gang-related violence increased by 250%. The percent increase is the difference between the end and the beginning amounts divided by the beginning amount. So, 42 – 12 = 30, and 30 divided by 12 is 2.5, or 250%. *(See Chapter VII, Section C.)*

15. **C** The average security shift lasted 6 hours. Add the number of hours worked over the past three weeks and divide by the number of shifts: 7 + 9 + 6 + 4 + 11 + 4 + 5 + 7 + 10 + 2 + 1 + 3 + 6 = 75 and 75 ÷ 13 = 5.77 hours. Round to the nearest whole number, and you get 6 hours. *(See Chapter VII, Section A.)*

16. **A** The total value except for the deep fryer is $10,800. To find the correct answer, subtract the deep fryer total from the total amount: $22,800 – $12,000 = $10,800. *(See Chapter VII, Section A.)*

17. **C** The new total value is $23,150. Subtract $300 from the total for the found restaurant supplies and add the case of wine to that total: $22,800 – $300 = $22,500 and $22,500 + $650 = $23,150. *(See Chapter VII, Section A.)*

18. **D** The volume of the rectangle shown is 343. $V = 14 \times 7 \times 3.5 = 343$. *(See Chapter VII, Section C.)*

19. **D** You can complete 48 incident reports in 12 hours. Begin with the ratio you're given: 16:4. You know that 12 is 3 multiplied by 4; therefore, you should multiply 16 by 3 to get 48. *(See Chapter VII, Section B.)*

20. **D** He drove 112 miles. You can either add the number of miles driven each for four days (28 + 28 + 28 + 28 = 60) or multiply the number of miles driven each day by the number of days (28 × 4 = 112). *(See Chapter VII, Sections A and B.)*

21. **C** To solve this problem, follow the order of operations. First, multiply 63.75×0.33, then subtract the product from 447.50, and then add 89. So, 447.50 – 21.0375 + 89 = 515.4625. Round to the nearest hundredth, and the answer is 515.46. *(See Chapter VII, Section C.)*

22. **C** Of these calls, 24 are not for home invasions. To find the answer, you can multiply the total number of calls by the percentage of home invasion calls and subtract that number from the total number of calls: 96 × 0.75 = 72 and 96 – 72 = 24. You also can multiply the total number of calls by the percentage of emergency calls: 96 × 0.25 = 24. *(See Chapter VII, Section B.)*

23. **A** Reports of local business burglaries increased by 42%. The percent increase is 64 – 45 = 19, and then 19 divided by 45 is about 42.2%. *(See Chapter VII, Section C.)*

24. **B** The circumference of the circle shown is $C = 2 \times 3.14 \times 7 = 43.96$, which rounds to 44. *(See Chapter VII, Section C.)*

25. **B** Divide the total amount the washing machines are worth by the number of washing machines: $6,325 ÷ 11 = $575. *(See Chapter VII, Section B.)*

26. **C** He walked 35 miles. To determine the correct answer, you can either add the number of miles he walked per day each of the five days (7 + 7 + 7 + 7 + 7 = 35) or multiply the number of miles walked each day by the number of days (7 × 5 = 35). *(See Chapter VII, Section A.)*

27. **D** The area of the triangle shown is 36. $A = \frac{1}{2} \times 8 \times 9 = 36$. *(See Chapter VI, Section C.)*

28. **A** To solve, multiply the total number of calls by the percentage of noise complaints and subtract the product from the total number of calls. So, 60 × 0.75 = 45 and 60 – 45 = 15. You also can multiply the total number of calls by the percentage of calls that are not noise complaints: 60 × 0.25 = 15. *(See Chapter VII, Section C.)*

29. **C** He wrote 47 reports. Add the numbers of reports done each week before and after lunch to get the total: 3 + 6 + 10 + 5 + 9 + 5 + 4 + 5 = 47. *(See Chapter VII, Section A.)*

30. **C** The total value of stolen items except for the cash is $2,100. Subtract the cash from the total value: $2,375 – $275 = $2,100. *(See Chapter VII, Section A.)*

31. **A** The new value is $2,675. Subtract the laptop from the total amount and then add the value of the gifts: $2,375 – $500 = $1,875 and $1,875 + $800 = $2,675. *(See Chapter VII, Section A.)*

32. **C** The circumference of the circle shown is 37.68. $C = 2 \times 3.14 \times 6 = 37.68$. *(See Chapter VII, Section C.)*

33. **B** Officer Lombardi's supervisor asked him to come in a half-hour early four days: $4 \times \frac{1}{2} = 2$. *(See Chapter VII, Section C.)*

34. **B** Out of all the packets, 54 did not contain illegal drugs. Multiply the total number of packets by the percentage of legal substances. $100\% - 55\% = 45\%$, and $120 \times 0.45 = 54$. *(See Chapter VII, Section C.)*

35. **D** You can complete 64 training exercises in 20 days. Begin with the ratio you're given, 16:5. Then make another ratio using x to represent the unknown number. So, x exercises:20 days :: 16 exercises:5 days. Then, cross-multiply both sides of the equation, and divide each side by 5. In the end, you learn that you can complete 64 training exercises. *(See Chapter VII, Section C.)*

36. **C** The approximate value of each puppy is $1,620. Divide the total amount the puppies are worth by the number of puppies: $\$6,480 \div 4 = \$1,620$. *(See Chapter VII, Section B.)*

37. **B** To solve this problem, follow the order of operations. First, multiply 4.02×1.29, then subtract the product from 217.88 and add 417.05. So, $217.88 - 5.1858 + 417.05 = 629.7442$. Rounding to the nearest hundredth, you get 629.74. *(See Chapter VII, Section B.)*

38. **B** There were 33 domestic-violence incidents and home invasions reported in August. Add the number of domestic-violence incidents and home invasions for the month of August: $12 + 21 = 33$. *(See Chapter VII, Section A.)*

39. **D** Arsons decreased by 62.5% from March to August. The percent decrease is the difference between the beginning and end divided by the beginning amount. So, 5 divided by 8 is 62.5%. *(See Chapter VII, Section C.)*

40. **B** The average security shift lasted six hours. Add the number of hours worked over the past two weeks and divide by the number of shifts: $5 + 6 + 4 + 3 + 8 + 6 + 5 + 8 + 9 = 54$ and $54 \div 9 = 6$. *(See Chapter VII, Section A.)*

41. **A** The total value except for the textbooks is $965. Subtract the value of the textbooks from the total amount: $\$1,285 - \$320 = \$965$. *(See Chapter VII, Section A.)*

42. **C** The new total value is $1,495. Subtract $40 from the total for the recovered CDs and add the value of the GPS to that total: $\$1,285 - \$40 = \$1,245$ and $\$1,245 + \$250 = \$1,495$. *(See Chapter VII, Section A.)*

43. **C** The width of the rectangle shown is 6. Start with $288 = 4 \times w \times 12$. Multiply 4×12 to get 48. Then divide both sides by 48 to get $6 = w$. *(See Chapter VII, Section B.)*

44. **D** You can make 27 arrests in 12 days. Begin with the ratio you're given, 9:4. Use the ratio to create an equation (where x represents the unknown number), cross-multiply, and divide each side by 4. *(See Chapter VII, Section C.)*

45. **C** Officer Martin's supervisor asks him to stay $1\frac{1}{2}$ hours later for three days. So, $1\frac{1}{2} \times 3 = 4\frac{1}{2}$. *(See Chapter VII, Section C.)*

46. **B** To solve this problem, follow the order of operations. First, multiply 6.09×5.22, and then subtract the product from 414.05 and add 809. So, $414.05 - 31.7898 + 809 = 1,191.2602$. Round to the nearest hundredth, and you get 1,191.26. *(See Chapter VII, Section B.)*

47. **A** You can multiply the total number of calls by the total number of trespassing calls and subtract the product from the total number of calls: $72 \times \frac{3}{5} = \frac{216}{5} = 43\frac{1}{5}$ and $72 - 43.2 = 28.8$. Or you can multiply the total number of calls by the total number of emergency calls: $72 \times \frac{2}{5} = \frac{144}{5} = 28\frac{4}{5}$. Rounded to the nearest whole number, that's 29. *(See Chapter VII, Section C.)*

48. **C** To solve this problem, follow the order of operations. First, divide $74.59 \div 5.20$, and then perform the addition and subtraction necessary for the rest of the problem: $12.58 + 14.84423 + 0.45 - 8.20 = 19.17$. *(See Chapter VII, Section C.)*

49. **C** The diameter of the circle shown is 16.4. $D = 2 \times 8.2 = 16.4$. *(See Chapter VII, Section C.)*

50. **C** Each painting is worth $2,115. Divide the total amount the paintings are worth by the number of paintings: $8,460 \div 4 = $2,115. *(See Chapter VII, Section B.)*

Section 4: Judgment and Problem Solving

1. **B** Marta is violating the ordinance by placing a car's transmission on the curb for removal. The third bullet states that only automobile tires, car seats, mufflers, and tail pipes will be accepted for curbside collection. *(See Chapter VIII, Section D.)*

2. **B** You should attempt to apprehend the suspect with the drugs. The suspect holding the drugs is actively committing a crime, so he should be your prime target. The other suspect may be implicated as the investigation progresses. Although issuing arrest warrants would be acceptable, you would have a significantly better chance of apprehending the suspects if you gave chase. Firing warning shots could present a public safety hazard and would not be an acceptable action. *(See Chapter VIII, Section D.)*

3. **A** Officer Leonard should pull over the driver and give him a warning. Since the new traffic patterns have only recently taken effect, some leniency should be shown, as drivers who frequently travel the same routes may become complacent. A warning would be more suitable than a citation in this scenario because this would alert the driver to the new traffic patterns without unnecessary penalization. No traffic infraction should be ignored, as this could lead to accidents or injuries. *(See Chapter VIII, Section D.)*

4. **B** Based on the passage, the primary goal for an officer responding to domestic dispute is to ensure and maintain your safety and the safety of others on the scene. The guidelines that Captain Edwards mentioned are all designed to help ensure that the scene is safe for both officers and the parties involved and that safety is maintained at all times. *(See Chapter VIII, Section D.)*

5. **C** Good communication is a vital element of properly coordinating police activities. If you don't clearly hear or understand any instructions you're given, you should always request that your supervisor repeat the instructions, instead of making critical decisions on your own. All police operations require effective teamwork for efficient execution. None of the other choices would support this concept. *(See Chapter VIII, Section D.)*

6. **A** Seth Burns did not intend to kill the man he found in bed with his wife. He killed the man accidentally while he was in a rage. *(See Chapter VIII, Section D.)*

7. **B** Sven Lewis's murder of the drug dealer is an example of murder in the second degree because he didn't plan to kill the drug dealer until the opportunity arose. *(See Chapter VIII, Section D.)*

8. **D** In the majority of cases, murder is a spontaneous crime that is not premeditated. Grand theft auto, larceny, and theft are all crimes of a more predictable nature that can often be deterred effectively with increased police presence. *(See Chapter VIII, Section B.)*

9. **B** The officer's report would begin with the target of the drug sting approaching the undercover dealer's vehicle. The officer would then record the target's request, followed by the transaction. The apprehension of the suspect would come next. Finally, the officer would identify the target and report his arrest and charges. *(See Chapter VIII, Section B.)*

10. **C** Since the police officers are patrolling in the early morning, they should be most suspicious of a young man holding a pizza box, peering into the front window of a house. Most people don't order pizza at this time of day. In fact, many pizza places are closed early in the morning. *(See Chapter VIII, Section A.)*

11. **A** You would expect to see a group of children on a playground without adult supervision after school hours. Many parents don't have the opportunity to pick up their children after school; therefore, many kids walk home with friends and neighbors. They may spend time on a nearby playground instead of going directly home. *(See Chapter VIII, Section A.)*

12. **C** Since the officers witnessed a crime take place—assaulting a police officer—they're free to arrest the man without a warrant. They must be sure to read the man his Miranda rights and escort him from the stands before they attempt to search him or gather his personal information, however. *(See Chapter VIII, Section B.)*

13. **C** Police officers would most likely use force to apprehend a teenager who is spray-painting on a local playground and runs away from the police when he is spotted. Since the suspect is showing resistance and refusal to cooperate with police, officers would most likely chase him down and use the least amount of force necessary to handcuff him. *(See Chapter VIII, Section A.)*

14. **C** The officer's report would begin with the suspect's entry and, then, the amount of property stolen. Next, the report would indicate the amount of property recovered. The report would then move on to the arrest of the suspect and, finally, his present status. *(See Chapter VIII, Section B.)*

15. **A** The officer should take the ring to evidence control and file a written report on the matter. This action will prevent the officer from being implicated in any claim of theft. Keeping the ring or simply throwing it away would be illegal and unethical. Such behavior would not be acceptable from a police officer. Choice D is incorrect because prisoners may be questioned only by investigators assigned to their cases. *(See Chapter VIII, Section A.)*

16. **C** If you tell her that you can't be sure of the ticket's legitimacy since you weren't there, you can offer the woman an honest answer that will neither further aggravate her, nor indicate that you'll take any action to fix it. The other choices would only irritate the woman or give her false hope. *(See Chapter VIII, Section C.)*

17. **C** Officer Jacobs's decision to attend to the injured suspect, rather than to pursue the fleeing suspect, was based primarily on the fact that attending to a seriously injured suspect is an officer's primary objective in any case. This protocol supersedes all others in this situation. *(See Chapter VIII, Section D.)*

18. **D** The best thing Officer O'Brien could do is inform courthouse security so that they may calmly evacuate the building. Defusing the bomb presents tremendous risk to O'Brien and the public and would be ill advised without the proper training. Informing everyone about the bomb could incite a panic, which would only exacerbate the situation. Finally, although it would be a good idea to notify the bomb squad, he shouldn't simply wait for them to arrive, as this valuable time could be used for an evacuation. *(See Chapter VIII, Section C.)*

19. **D** According to the handout, a higher number of accidents occurred on highways and interstates that did not have streetlights, so choice D is the correct answer. *(See Chapter VIII, Section D.)*

20. **A** The need for emergency medical care is the key element in this scenario. Because Officer Gilardi is unable to revive the man and the empty syringe indicates a likelihood of illicit drug use, Officer Gilardi should call an ambulance for transport to a hospital. Although a detoxification treatment center could offer support for the unconscious man, they would not be equipped to supply emergency medical care. The other choices don't provide for any medical care. *(See Chapter VIII, Section A.)*

21. **B** The most important reason that no officer should always use the same route and timing schedule when on patrol is because constant patrol patterns are recognized and utilized by criminals. *(See Chapter VIII, Section A.)*

22. **A** When Earl Wilson keeps the contents of the package that was clearly meant for his neighbor, he commits misappropriation of misdelivered or lost property. *(See Chapter VIII, Section D.)*

23. **D** To reduce the number of burglaries, Officer Martinez should assign a Tour II to patrol on Thursdays, Fridays, and Saturdays on 19th Street and 6th Avenue. *(See Chapter VIII, Section D.)*

24. **A** The officer's report would begin with the victim exiting the bar and approaching her vehicle. The officer would then record the approach of the unknown assailant. This would be followed by the assailant telling the victim to get out of the car and driving away. Finally, the officer would report the victim's call for help and his arrival on scene. *(See Chapter VIII, Section B.)*

25. **B** Based on the passage, the two main goals for an officer who pulls over a driver suspected of being intoxicated are maintaining public safety and determining the suspect's level of intoxication. By pulling over any driver suspected of being intoxicated, the officer is helping to ensure the public's safety by getting a potentially dangerous driver off the road. In many cases, this also will ensure the safety of the suspect. Once the suspect is safely pulled over, an officer's next goal is to determine the driver's level of intoxication. This determination will indicate the most appropriate actions for the officer to take. *(See Chapter VIII, Section D.)*

26. **B** Bill is in violation of the new moped ordinance because he is operating his moped before he has obtained the proper registration. *(See Chapter VIII, Section D.)*

27. **B** The first thing Officer Landus should do is radio dispatch to let them know that he's helping a lost child. After he has contacted both dispatch and his desk officer, he should take Marcus into the store and attempt to find his father by asking shoppers and grocery store clerks if they've seen him. He also may choose to make an announcement via the store's PA system. Common sense should tell you that the officer shouldn't leave Marcus alone in the parking lot while he goes inside, nor should he worry about his aid report at that moment. *(See Chapter VIII, Section B.)*

28. **C** Police officers are not likely to use force to apprehend a drug dealer who is cursing at an undercover police officer who is arresting him for selling drugs. This statement does not indicate that the dealer is putting up a fight or resisting arrest. He may be verbally abusive, but he is assumedly obedient and no one is in danger. *(See Chapter VIII, Section A.)*

29. **A** Based on the passage, the primary goal for an officer engaged in a high-speed pursuit is to ensure the safety of everyone in and around the scene and quickly stop the suspect. Maintaining public safety and stopping the suspect quickly are the top priorities for an officer in this situation. High-speed pursuits are very dangerous for everyone involved, including the suspects, police, and other drivers and pedestrians on the road, so officers should try to execute the pursuit as safely as possible and get the suspect off the road as quickly as possible. *(See Chapter VIII, Section B.)*

30. **C** Your decision to enter the scene without first clarifying your supervisor's instructions is wrong, because the special instructions may be vital to the investigation or your safety and should be fully understood before you proceed. Officers must always clarify any special instructions that they don't fully understand, as these instructions are very important and may affect the integrity of the investigation or may impact your safety or the safety of others on the scene. *(See Chapter VIII, Section A.)*

31. **C** Choice C would be an example of aggravated assault because Jim Phillips has intentionally inflicted a serious injury upon his victim. *(See Chapter VIII, Section D.)*

32. **D** When Michael Salvo punches the street vendor, he commits assault/battery. This wouldn't be considered aggravated assault because he didn't use a weapon. *(See Chapter VIII, Section D.)*

33. **C** Maria Brown is sexually assaulted when the unidentified man at the concert attempts to lift up her shirt. The host in choice B can rightfully press charges of rape on Peter Martin. *(See Chapter VIII, Section D.)*

34. **D** The officer's report would begin with the clerk witnessing the suspect placing a pair of earrings in her purse. After the suspect attempted to leave the store, the clerk informed store security. Security then apprehended the woman and called police. Finally, Officer Walsh placed the woman under arrest and charged her with shoplifting. *(See Chapter VIII, Section B.)*

35. **B** Officer Lopez's decision not to pursue the suspect in favor of attending to the victim was appropriate because the victim was seriously injured and in need of immediate medical attention. *(See Chapter VIII, Section C.)*

36. **C** Lawrence made the correct choice because he doesn't want the burglars to be aware of his presence. The officer's advantage in this situation is the element of surprise. Arriving on the scene with lights and sirens on would negate this advantage. *(See Chapter VIII, Section A.)*

37. **C** The project in choice C would be in violation of the new city ordinance because, although it has been enclosed, the property owner used wooden barricades rather than temporary fencing, as indicated in the ordinance. *(See Chapter VIII, Section D.)*

38. **D** The officer's first response should be to call for support from the fire department. He should not attempt to put out the fire himself, because this could be dangerous and should be done by professional firefighters. *(See Chapter VIII, Section A.)*

39. **B** The officer's report would begin with the suspect entering the store and holding up the clerk. This would be followed by the clerk complying with the suspect's demands and the suspect fleeing the scene. After the police were called, the report would continue with the suspect's capture and arrest. The report would end with the statement of the suspect's present status. *(See Chapter VIII, Section B.)*

40. **C** Officer Williams should file a report and submit the bag to evidence control. Questioning of suspects should be done only by investigators; discarding or ignoring the bag would be unacceptable. *(See Chapter VIII, Section C.)*

41. **B** You should tell him there's nothing you can do because you didn't issue the ticket. This answer is the best choice because it explains the situation to your cousin without making him frustrated or making him think you'll attempt to nullify the ticket. *(See Chapter VIII, Section C.)*

42. **A** Officer Jones's primary goal during the situation described in the passage was to assess and secure the scene and maintain order. The officer's main concern throughout the situation was making sure that the scene was safe for everyone involved, including himself, and that everyone remained calm and under control. Taking these precautions can help to reduce the risk of further violence or injury. *(See Chapter VIII, Section D.)*

43. **B** Officer Jones doesn't immediately approach the arguing couple upon entering the home because he needs to check the scene for any potential dangers. For this reason, Jones carefully performs a scene assessment when he enters the home, looking for any weapons or other potential dangers that might present a risk for anyone on the scene. *(See Chapter VIII, Section D.)*

44. **C** Based on the information in the chart, Chief Johnson could conclude that stop signs lead to more accidents than traffic lights. In 2009, more accidents occurred at stop signs than at traffic lights. *(See Chapter VIII, Section D.)*

45. **D** The best recommendation that Chief Johnson could make would be to install traffic lights at Market and Chestnut. This intersection, which has only stop signs, has seen the highest number of accidents and is most in need of stricter traffic control. *(See Chapter VIII, Section D.)*

46. **D** Always using the same route and timing while on patrol would be considered bad policy, because criminals can become aware of constant patterns of patrol and use them to their advantage. *(See Chapter VIII, Section A.)*

47. **B** Roy Harlow's phone scam is a clear example of wire fraud. Choice A would be an example of securities fraud, as the suspect has used an insider-trading tip to illegally make money off the stock market. Simon Matthews's telemarketing scam is a telemarketing fraud, rather than wire fraud. Because it involves the use of a credit card, choice D is an example of credit card fraud. *(See Chapter VIII, Section D.)*

48. **A** Chief Patrick should assign more officers to patrol Granger Avenue at night. Granger Avenue has the highest crime rate of any location on the chart, and all the crimes there occurred at night. *(See Chapter VIII, Section D.)*

49. **B** If he wants to reduce the number of burglaries in his precinct, Chief Patrick should assign more officers to patrol between 15th and 20th streets. All the burglaries on the crime report occurred within that area. *(See Chapter VIII, Section D.)*

50. **D** Officer Li's report would begin with the two men drinking at the bar and getting into an argument. This would lead to Mr. Smith's attack on Mr. Sanford and the bartender's call to police. The report would then continue with the arrest of Mr. Smith and end with the statement of his current status. *(See Chapter VIII, Section B.)*

II. Two-Month Cram Plan

	Verbal	Memorization and Visualization	Mathematics	Judgment and Problem Solving
8 weeks before the test	**Study Time:** 4½ hours ❑ Take the **Diagnostic Test** and review the answer explanations. ❑ Based on your errors on the Diagnostic Test, identify difficult topics and their corresponding chapters. These are your targeted chapters.			

7 weeks before the test	**Study Time:** 1 hour
	❑ Chapter V
	   ❑ Read sections A and C.
	   ❑ Do practice questions 1–3 in each section.
	   ❑ For targeted areas, do practice questions 1–7 in each section.
		Study Time: 1 hour
		❑ Chapter VI
		   ❑ Read sections A–B.
		   ❑ Do practice questions 1–3 in each section.
		   ❑ If Section A is a targeted area, do practice questions 1–7.
		   ❑ Review the answer explanations for any questions you answer incorrectly.
			Study Time: 1 hour
			❑ Chapter VII
			   ❑ Read sections A–B.
			   ❑ Do practice questions 1–2 in each section.
			   ❑ For targeted areas, do practice questions 1–5 in each section.
				Study Time: 1 hour
				❑ Chapter VIII
				   ❑ Read sections A–B.
				   ❑ Do practice questions 1–4 in each section.
				   ❑ For targeted areas, do practice questions 1–6 in each section.

6 weeks before the test	**Study Time:** 1 hour
	❑ Chapter V
	   ❑ Review sections A and C.
	   ❑ Do practice questions 4–10 in each section.
		Study Time: 1 hour
		❑ Chapter VI
		   ❑ Review sections A–B.
		   ❑ Complete the remaining practice questions in Section A.
		   ❑ Redo any practice questions you answered incorrectly in Section B last week.
			Study Time: 1 hour
			❑ Chapter VII
			   ❑ Review sections A–B.
			   ❑ Do practice questions 3–10 in each section.
			   ❑ Make a list of the questions that you answered incorrectly in each section.
				Study Time: 1 hour
				❑ Chapter VIII
				   ❑ Review sections A–B.
				   ❑ Do practice questions 5–10 in each section.

continued

	Verbal	Memorization and Visualization	Mathematics	Judgment and Problem Solving

5 weeks before the test	**Study Time:** 1 hour
	❏ Chapter V
	  ❏ Read parts 1–4 of Section B.
	  ❏ Do practice questions 1–4.
	  ❏ If Section B is a targeted area, do practice questions 1–8.
		Study Time: 1 hour
		❏ Chapter VI
		  ❏ Read sections C–D.
		  ❏ Do practice questions 1–4 in each section.
		  ❏ For targeted areas, do practice questions 1–6 in each section.
			Study Time: 1 hour
			❏ Chapter VII
			  ❏ Read Section C.
			  ❏ Do practice questions 1–2.
			  ❏ If Section C is a targeted area, do practice questions 1–5.
				Study Time: 1 hour
				❏ Chapter VIII
				  ❏ Read sections C–D.
				  ❏ Do practice questions 1–5 in each section.
				  ❏ For targeted areas, do practice questions 1–8 in each section.

4 weeks before the test	**Study Time:** 1 hour
	❏ Chapter V
	  ❏ Read parts 5–9 of Section B.
	  ❏ Do practice questions 9–16.
		Study Time: 1 hour
		❏ Chapter VI
		  ❏ Review sections C–D.
		  ❏ Do practice questions 5–8 in each section.
		  ❏ For targeted areas, do practice questions 5–10.
			Study Time: 1 hour
			❏ Chapter VII
			  ❏ Review Section C.
			  ❏ Do practice questions 3–10.
			  ❏ Add the questions that you answer incorrectly to the list you created 6 weeks before the test.
				Study Time: 1 hour
				❏ Chapter VIII
				  ❏ Review sections C–D.
				  ❏ Do practice questions 6–10.

3 weeks before the test	**Study Time:** 1 hour
	❏ Chapter V
	  ❏ Review part 7 of Section B.
	  ❏ Highlight any words that are unfamiliar or difficult to spell.
	  ❏ Review the highlighted words during the next five study sessions.
		Study Time: 1 hour
		❏ Chapter VI
		  ❏ Continue reviewing sections C–D.
		  ❏ Do practice questions 11–12 in Section C.
		  ❏ Redo any questions in Section D that you answered incorrectly last week.
			Study Time: 1 hour
			❏ Chapter VII
			  ❏ Review sections A–C.
			  ❏ Review the list of questions that you answered incorrectly in previous study sessions.
			  ❏ Redo all the questions you answered incorrectly in each section.
				Study Time: 1 hour
				❏ Chapter VIII
				  ❏ Redo the practice questions in sections A–D.
				  ❏ Make a list of any questions you answered incorrectly in these sections.

	Verbal	Memorization and Visualization	Mathematics	Judgment and Problem Solving
2 weeks before the test	**Study Time:** 2½ hours ❏ Take the **Practice Test** and review the answer explanations. ❏ Based on your errors on the Practice Test, identify difficult topics and their corresponding chapters. These chapters are now your targeted areas.			
	Study Time: 1 hour ❏ Based on the Practice Test, review any sections in Chapter V that still present a problem. ❏ Redo any Verbal questions that you answered incorrectly on the Practice Test.	**Study Time:** 1 hour ❏ Review any sections in Chapter VI that remain problematic. ❏ Redo two practice problems in each section of Chapter VI.	**Study Time:** 1 hour ❏ Redo any Mathematics problems you answered incorrectly on the Practice Test. ❏ Highlight any sections of Chapter VII that need further attention.	**Study Time:** 1 hour ❏ Review any Judgment and Problem Solving questions that you answered incorrectly on the Practice Test. ❏ Determine which sections require the most attention in the Judgment and Problem Solving chapter.

7 days before the test	**Study Time:** 30 minutes
	❏ Chapter V
	   ❏ Review Section A.
	   ❏ Redo practice questions 4–7.
	   ❏ Continue reviewing the highlighted words from part 7 of Section B during the next six study sessions.
		Study Time: 30 minutes
		❏ Chapter VI
		   ❏ Review Section A.
		   ❏ Redo practice questions 6–10.
			Study Time: 30 minutes
			❏ Preparing for Mathematics
			❏ Chapter VII
			   ❏ Review Section A.
			   ❏ Redo practice questions 1–5.
				Study Time: 30 minutes
				❏ Chapter VIII
				❏ Review sections A–B.
				❏ Redo questions 5–6 in each section.
				❏ Review the list of questions you created three weeks before the test. Redo any questions you answered incorrectly in sections A–B.

continued

	Verbal	Memorization and Visualization	Mathematics	Judgment and Problem Solving

6 days before the test	**Study Time:** 30 minutes
	❏ Chapter V
	    ❏ Review parts 1–4 of Section B.
	    ❏ Redo practice questions 1–4 and 7–8.
	    ❏ Remember to review the highlighted words from part 7 of Section B.
		Study Time: 30 minutes
		❏ Chapter VI
		    ❏ Review Section B.
		    ❏ Redo practice questions 1–3.
			Study Time: 30 minutes
			❏ Preparing for Mathematics
			❏ Chapter VII
			    ❏ Continue reviewing Section A.
			    ❏ Redo practice questions 6–10.
			    ❏ Make a list of any questions you answered incorrectly in Section A.
			    ❏ Review these questions during your next four study sessions.
				Study Time: 30 minutes
				❏ Chapter VIII
				    ❏ Continue reviewing sections A–B.
				    ❏ Redo questions 7–10 in Section A.
				    ❏ Redo questions 9–10 in Section B.

5 days before the test	**Study Time:** 30 minutes
	❏ Chapter V
	    ❏ Review parts 5–9 of Section B.
	    ❏ Redo practice questions 5–6 and 9–16.
	    ❏ Read through the highlighted words from Section 7.
		Study Time: 30 minutes
		❏ Chapter VI
		    ❏ Continue reviewing Section A.
		    ❏ Redo practice questions 1–5.
			Study Time: 30 minutes
			❏ Chapter VII
			❏ Review Section B.
			❏ Redo practice questions 6–10.
			❏ Review the questions you answered incorrectly in Section A.
				Study Time: 30 minutes
				❏ Chapter VIII
				    ❏ Review sections C–D.
				    ❏ Redo questions 1–3 in each section.
				    ❏ Review the list of questions you created three weeks before the test. Redo any questions you answered incorrectly in sections C–D.

	Verbal	Memorization and Visualization	Mathematics	Judgment and Problem Solving
4 days before the test	**Study Time:** 30 minutes ❏ Chapter V 　❏ Review Section C. 　❏ Redo practice questions 1–5. 　❏ Ask a friend or study partner to read aloud the highlighted words from part 7 of Section B. Write the words on a separate piece of paper and review your answers. Based on your errors, continue reviewing words that still present difficulties.	**Study Time:** 30 minutes ❏ Chapter VI 　❏ Review sections C–D. 　❏ Redo practice questions 7–12 in Section C. 　❏ Redo practice questions 1–7 in Section D.	**Study Time:** 30 minutes ❏ Chapter VII 　❏ Continue reviewing Section B. 　❏ Redo practice questions 1–5. 　❏ Add any questions you answered incorrectly in Section B to the list of questions you answered incorrectly in Section A. Continue to review these questions during your next two study sessions.	**Study Time:** 30 minutes ❏ Chapter VIII 　❏ Continue reviewing sections C–D. 　❏ Redo questions 4–8 in each section.
3 days before the test	**Study Time:** 30 minutes ❏ Chapter V 　❏ Review Section C. 　❏ Redo practice questions 6–10. 　❏ Continue reviewing the highlighted words from part 7 of Section B that still present problems.	**Study Time:** 30 minutes ❏ Chapter VI 　❏ Continue reviewing sections C–D. 　❏ Redo practice questions 1–6 in Section C. 　❏ Redo practice questions 8–10 in Section D.	**Study Time:** 30 minutes ❏ Chapter VII 　❏ Review Section C. 　❏ Redo all the practice questions. 　❏ Add any questions you answered incorrectly in Section C to the list of questions you answered incorrectly in sections A–B.	**Study Time:** 30 minutes ❏ Chapter VIII 　❏ Briefly read through sections A–D. 　❏ Continue to review troublesome questions from the list you created three weeks before the test.

continued

	Verbal	Memorization and Visualization	Mathematics	Judgment and Problem Solving

2 days before the test	**Study Time:** 30 minutes
	❏ Chapter V
	   ❏ Reread sections A–C.
	   ❏ Do two practice questions in each section.
		Study Time: 30 minutes
		❏ Chapter VI
		   ❏ Briefly read through sections A–D.
		   ❏ Carefully review any practice problems that you answered incorrectly during your previous study sessions.
			Study Time: 30 minutes
			❏ Chapter VII
			   ❏ Briefly read through sections A–C.
			   ❏ Redo the questions that you answered incorrectly in these sections.
			   ❏ Carefully review the answer explanations for any questions that still present problems.
				Study Time: 30 minutes
				❏ Chapter VIII
				   ❏ Continue reviewing sections A–D.
				   ❏ Redo any Judgment and Problem Solving questions you answered incorrectly on the Practice Test.

1 day before the test	❏ Take a break! You're well prepared for the test. ❏ Get a good night's rest.			

Morning of the test	**Reminders:**
	❏ Eat a healthy breakfast.
	❏ Take with you to the testing facility:
	   ❏ Two forms of identification, including photo ID
	   ❏ Several no. 2 pencils
	   ❏ Any documentation that is required by the testing facility
	❏ Try to arrive at the testing facility early to give yourself time to prepare for the test.
	❏ Stay calm during the test and take deep breaths if you feel nervous.
	❏ Have confidence in your ability to do well on the test.			

III. One-Month Cram Plan

	Verbal	Memorization and Visualization	Mathematics	Judgment and Problem Solving
4 weeks before the test	**Study Time:** 4½ hours ❏ Take the **Diagnostic Test** and review the answer explanations. ❏ Based on your errors on the Diagnostic Test, identify difficult topics and their corresponding chapters. These are your targeted chapters.			
	Study Time: 2 hours ❏ Chapter V ❏ Read sections A–C. ❏ Do practice questions 1–7 in Section A. ❏ If Section A is a targeted area, do practice questions 1–7 and 9–10. ❏ Do practice questions 1–6 in Section B. ❏ If Section B is a targeted area, do practice questions 1–8. ❏ Do practice questions 1–5 in Section C. ❏ If Section C is a targeted area, do practice questions 1–7.	**Study Time:** 2 hours ❏ Chapter VI ❏ Read sections A–D. ❏ Do practice questions 1–3 in Section B. ❏ Do practice questions 1–5 in sections A, C, and D. ❏ Do two additional practice questions in any targeted areas.	**Study Time:** 2 hours ❏ Chapter VII ❏ Read sections A–C. ❏ Do practice questions 1–4 in each section. ❏ For targeted areas, do two additional practice questions in each section. ❏ Make a list of any questions that you answered incorrectly in each section.	**Study Time:** 2 hours ❏ Chapter VIII ❏ Read sections A–D. ❏ Do practice questions 1–4 in each section. ❏ For targeted areas, do practice questions 1–6. ❏ Keep track of the questions you answered incorrectly.
3 weeks before the test	**Study Time:** 1½ hours ❏ Chapter V ❏ Review sections A–C. ❏ Do practice questions 8–9 in Section A. ❏ Do practice questions 7–16 in Section B. ❏ Do practice questions 6–10 in Section C.	**Study Time:** 1 hour ❏ Chapter VI ❏ Review sections A–D. ❏ Do practice questions 6–10 in sections A, C, and D. ❏ Make note of any practice questions that you answer incorrectly.	**Study Time:** 1 hour ❏ Chapter VII ❏ Review sections A–C. ❏ Do practice questions 5–10 in each section. ❏ Continue noting any questions that you answered incorrectly.	**Study Time:** 1 hour ❏ Chapter VIII ❏ Review sections A–D. ❏ Do practice questions 5–10 in each section. ❏ Continue to note questions that you miss.

continued

	Verbal	Memorization and Visualization	Mathematics	Judgment and Problem Solving

2 weeks before the test	**Study Time:** 1 hour
	❑ Chapter V
	   ❑ Continue reviewing sections A–C.
	   ❑ Highlight any words that are unfamiliar or difficult to spell in part 7 of Section B.
	   ❑ Review these words over the next six study sessions.
		Study Time: 1 hour
		❑ Chapter VI
		   ❑ Continue reviewing sections A–D.
		   ❑ Redo any practice questions you answered incorrectly in your previous study sessions.
			Study Time: 1 hour
			❑ Chapter VII
			   ❑ Continue reviewing sections A–C.
			   ❑ Redo any practice questions that you answered incorrectly.
				Study Time: 1 hour
				❑ Chapter VIII
				   ❑ Continue reviewing sections A–D.
				   ❑ Review the list of questions you answered incorrectly in your previous study sessions.

7 days before the test	**Study Time:** 2½ hours ❑ Take the **Practice Test** and review the answer explanations. ❑ Based on your errors on the Practice Test, identify difficult topics and their corresponding chapters. These chapters are now your targeted areas.			
6 days before the test	**Study Time:** 1 hour ❑ Based on your errors on the Practice Test, review the sections that still present problems. ❑ Ask a friend or study partner to read aloud the highlighted words from part 7 of Section B. Write them on a separate piece of paper and review your answers. Based on your errors, continue reviewing words that still present difficulties.	**Study Time:** 1 hour ❑ Redo any Memorization and Visualization questions that you answered incorrectly on the Practice Test. ❑ Review any sections of Chapter VI that still require your attention.	**Study Time:** 1 hour ❑ Review any sections in Chapter VII that still present problems. ❑ Redo the practice problems in these sections.	**Study Time:** 1 hour ❑ Redo any Judgment and Problem Solving questions you answered incorrectly on the Practice Test. ❑ Review any sections of Chapter VIII that still present problems.

5 days before the test	**Study Time:** 1 hour
	❑ Chapter V
	   ❑ Review Section A.
	   ❑ Redo practice questions 8–10.
	   ❑ Continue reviewing any difficult words from part 7 of Section B.
		Study Time: 1 hour
		❑ Chapter VI
		   ❑ Review sections A–B.
		   ❑ Redo practice questions 1–3 in Section B.
		   ❑ Redo practice questions 6–10 in Section A.
			Study Time: 1 hour
			❑ Chapter VII
			   ❑ Review sections A–B.
			   ❑ Redo practice questions 6–10 in Section A.
			   ❑ Redo practice questions 1–6 in Section B.
				Study Time: 1 hour
				❑ Chapter VIII
				   ❑ Review sections A–B.
				   ❑ Redo practice questions 1–6 in each section.

	Verbal	**Memorization and Visualization**	**Mathematics**	**Judgment and Problem Solving**

4 days before the test	**Study Time:** 30 minutes
	❑ Chapter V
	  ❑ Review Section B.
	  ❑ Redo practice questions 9–14.
		Study Time: 30 minutes
		❑ Chapter VI
		  ❑ Continue reviewing sections A–B.
		  ❑ Redo practice questions 1–5 in Section A.
			Study Time: 30 minutes
			❑ Chapter VII
			  ❑ Continue reviewing sections A–B.
			  ❑ Redo practice questions 1–5 in Section A.
			  ❑ Redo practice questions 7–10 in Section B.
				Study Time: 30 minutes
				❑ Chapter VIII
				  ❑ Continue reviewing sections A–B.
				  ❑ Redo practice questions 7–10 in each section.

3 days before the test	**Study Time:** 30 minutes
	❑ Chapter V
	  ❑ Review Section C.
	  ❑ Redo practice questions 6–10.
		Study Time: 1 hour
		❑ Chapter VI
		  ❑ Review sections C–D.
		  ❑ Redo practice questions 1–6 in Section C.
		  ❑ Redo practice questions 8–10 in Section D.
			Study Time: 30 minutes
			❑ Chapter VII
			  ❑ Review Section C.
			  ❑ Redo practice questions 1–4.
				Study Time: 1 hour
				❑ Chapter VIII
				  ❑ Review sections C–D.
				  ❑ Redo practice questions 6–10 in each section.

2 days before the test	**Study Time:** 30 minutes
	❑ Chapter V
	  ❑ Briefly review sections A–C.
	  ❑ Quiz yourself on any highlighted words from part 7 of Section B that still present problems.
		Study Time: 30 minutes
		❑ Chapter VI
		  ❑ Continue reviewing sections C–D.
		  ❑ Redo practice questions 7–12 in Section C.
		  ❑ Redo practice questions 1–7 in Section D.
			Study Time: 30 minutes
			❑ Chapter VII
			  ❑ Continue reviewing Section C.
			  ❑ Redo practice questions 1–4.
				Study Time: 30 minutes
				❑ Chapter VIII
				  ❑ Continue reviewing sections C–D.
				  ❑ Redo practice questions 1–5 in each section.

1 day before the test	❑ Take a break! You're well prepared for the test. ❑ Get a good night's rest.			

Morning of the test	**Reminders:**
	❑ Eat a healthy breakfast.
	❑ Take with you to the testing facility:
	  ❑ Two forms of identification, including photo ID
	  ❑ Several no. 2 pencils
	  ❑ Any documentation that is required by the testing facility
	❑ Try to arrive early so you can take a few minutes to go outside and relax before the test.
	❑ Stay calm during the test and take deep breaths if you feel nervous.			

IV. One-Week Cram Plan

	Verbal	Memorization and Visualization	Mathematics	Judgment and Problem Solving
7 days before the test	**Study Time:** 4½ hours ❑ Take the **Diagnostic Test** and review the answer explanations. ❑ Based on your errors on the Diagnostic Test, identify difficult topics and their corresponding chapters. These are your targeted chapters.			

6 days before the test	**Study Time:** 1 hour
	❑ Chapter V
	  ❑ Read Section B.
	  ❑ Do practice questions 7–14.
	  ❑ If Section B is a targeted area, do practice questions 7–16.
	  ❑ Review part 7 of Section B and highlight any words that are unfamiliar or difficult to spell.
	  ❑ Review the highlighted words during the next five study sessions.
		Study Time: 1 hour
		❑ Chapter VI
		  ❑ Read sections A–B.
		  ❑ Do practice questions 1–5 in Section A.
		  ❑ If Section A is a targeted area, do practice questions 1–7.
		  ❑ Do practice questions 1–3 in Section B.
			Study Time: 1 hour
			❑ Chapter VII
			  ❑ Read sections A–B.
			  ❑ Do practice questions 1–5 in each section.
			  ❑ For targeted areas, do practice questions 1–7.
				Study Time: 1 hour
				❑ Chapter VIII
				  ❑ Read sections A–B.
				  ❑ Do practice questions 1–5 in each section.
				  ❑ For targeted areas, do practice questions 1–7.

5 days before the test	**Study Time:** 1 hour
	❑ Chapter V
	  ❑ Review Section B.
	  ❑ Do practice questions 1–6 and 15–16.
	  ❑ Review the highlighted words from part 7 of Section B.
	  ❑ Note any practice questions you answered incorrectly.
		Study Time: 1 hour
		❑ Chapter VI
		  ❑ Review sections A–B.
		  ❑ Do practice questions 6–10 in Section A.
		  ❑ Note any practice questions you answered incorrectly.
			Study Time: 1 hour
			❑ Chapter VII
			  ❑ Review sections A–B.
			  ❑ Do practice questions 6–10 in each section.
			  ❑ Note any practice questions you answered incorrectly.
				Study Time: 1 hour
				❑ Chapter VIII
				  ❑ Review sections A–B.
				  ❑ Do practice questions 6–7 in each section.
				  ❑ Note any practice questions you answered incorrectly.

continued

	Verbal	Memorization and Visualization	Mathematics	Judgment and Problem Solving

4 days before the test	**Study Time:** 1½ hours
	❑ Chapter V
	   ❑ Read sections A and C.
	   ❑ Do practice questions 1–7 in Section A.
	   ❑ If Section A is a targeted area, do practice questions 1–8.
	   ❑ Do practice questions 1–5 in Section C.
	   ❑ If Section C is a targeted area, do practice questions 1–7.
	   ❑ Continue reviewing the words from part 7 of Section B.
		Study Time: 1 hour
		❑ Chapter VI
		   ❑ Read sections C–D.
		   ❑ Do practice questions 1–6 in Section C.
		   ❑ If Section C is a targeted area, do practice questions 1–8.
		   ❑ Do practice questions 1–5 in Section D.
		   ❑ If Section D is a targeted area, do practice questions 1–7.
			Study Time: 1 hour
			❑ Chapter VII
			   ❑ Read sections C–D.
			   ❑ Do practice questions 1–5 in each section.
			   ❑ For targeted areas, do practice questions 1–7.
				Study Time: 1 hour
				❑ Chapter VIII
				   ❑ Read sections C–D.
				   ❑ Do practice questions 1–5 in each section.
				   ❑ For targeted areas, do practice questions 1–7.

3 days before the test	**Study Time:** 2½ hours ❑ Take the **Practice Test** and review the answer explanations. ❑ Based on your errors on the Practice Test, identify difficult topics and their corresponding chapters. These chapters are now your targeted areas.			

2 days before the test	**Study Time:** 1½ hours
	❑ Chapter V
	   ❑ Review sections A and C.
	   ❑ Do practice questions 8–10 in Section A.
	   ❑ Do practice questions 6–10 in Section C.
	   ❑ Note any practice questions you answered incorrectly in sections A and C.
	   ❑ Ask a friend or study partner to read aloud the highlighted words from part 7 of Section B. Write the words on a separate piece of paper and review your answers.
		Study Time: 1 hour
		❑ Chapter VI
		   ❑ Review sections C–D.
		   ❑ Do practice questions 7–10 in Section C.
		   ❑ Do practice questions 6–10 in Section D.
		   ❑ Redo any practice questions that you answered incorrectly in sections A–D.
			Study Time: 1 hour
			❑ Chapter VII
			   ❑ Review sections C–D.
			   ❑ Do practice questions 6–10 in each section.
			   ❑ Note any practice questions you answered incorrectly.
				Study Time: 1 hour
				❑ Chapter VIII
				   ❑ Review sections C–D.
				   ❑ Do practice questions 6–10 in each section.
				   ❑ Note any practice questions you answered incorrectly.

	Verbal	Memorization and Visualization	Mathematics	Judgment and Problem Solving
1 day before the test	**Study Time:** 1 hour ❏ Chapter V ❏ Briefly review sections A–C. ❏ Redo any practice questions you answered incorrectly in sections A–C.	**Study Time:** 1 hour ❏ Chapter VI ❏ Briefly review sections A–D. ❏ Redo any Memorization and Visualization questions that you answered incorrectly on the Practice Test.	**Study Time:** 1 hour ❏ Chapter VII ❏ Briefly review sections A–D. ❏ Redo any practice questions you answered incorrectly in sections A–D. ❏ Redo any questions you answered incorrectly on the Practice Test.	**Study Time:** 1 hour ❏ Chapter VIII ❏ Briefly review sections A–D. ❏ Redo any practice problems you answered incorrectly in sections A–D. ❏ Redo questions 1–14 on the Practice Test.
Morning of the test	**Reminders:** ❏ Eat a healthy breakfast. ❏ Take with you to the testing facility: ❏ Two forms of identification, including photo ID ❏ Several no. 2 pencils ❏ Any documentation that is required by the testing facility ❏ Try to arrive at the testing facility early to give yourself time to prepare for the test. Walk around outside before the test. ❏ Stay calm during the test and take deep breaths if you feel nervous. ❏ Most important: Have confidence in your ability to do well on the test.			

V. Verbal

Believe it or not, writing is an important part of every police officer's job. Reports, notifications, and inter-office memos must be completed on a daily basis. That's why every police officer must have excellent communication skills.

Imagine that you're reading an incident report completed by a co-worker:

> The mail suspect described as having brown hare, bleu eyes, wearing blac pants, orange sneacers, and a red banada covering her face.

This sentence isn't easy to understand. Think about what's wrong with it. First, it isn't really a complete sentence—it's a fragment. In addition, it contains numerous errors in agreement and spelling.

Now, consider the following revision:

> The male suspect has brown hair and blue eyes and is wearing black pants, orange sneakers, and a red bandana, which is covering his face.

This sentence is much easier to understand. It communicates all the necessary information in a logical manner. *Remember:* Your co-workers and supervisors are going to read your reports and memos—make sure that they can understand what you write.

You have to take several written exams before you become a police officer. Fortunately, you can prepare yourself for these exams by reviewing the rules of grammar, punctuation, and spelling. You probably learned these rules in English classes, but in case you've forgotten, in this chapter we review what you can expect to see on the police officer exam. Each police department is different, but the questions on the exams are very similar. On the verbal section of the police officer exam, expect to see reading comprehension questions, grammar and spelling questions, and writing questions.

Don't worry if English isn't your strong suit. We provide the basic skills you need to succeed on the exam.

A. Reading Comprehension

On the reading comprehension section of the police officer exam, you'll be asked to read a passage and answer questions based on that passage. Some passages may contain only a few sentences; others are much longer. Most of the passages relate to law enforcement.

Don't worry—you don't need to know specific police procedures to understand these passages or answer the questions. Everything you need to answer the questions is found in the passages themselves. In addition, you can refer back to the passages while answering the questions.

Tip: Read the reading comprehension questions before you read the passage. This helps you pinpoint the exact information you need as you read.

The questions you encounter on the police officer exam are based on four types of reading passages: short reading passages, long reading passages, definitions, and incident reports. The questions that follow short and long reading passages usually require you to recall certain facts or details about what you've read. Some passages provide a list of definitions that you must interpret to answer the questions. The final type of passage you may encounter on the test is an incident report; an incident report is completed by a police officer after he or she responds to a call. Multiple-choice or true/false questions usually follow these types of passages.

1. Short Passages

Some of the reading passages on the police officer exam contain only a few sentences. These passages are often about law enforcement, but you don't need to understand police procedures to answer questions based on them. Short passages often contain information about town ordinances or steps that police officers should follow in a given situation. The following is an example of a short reading comprehension passage and several questions based on that passage.

EXAMPLES:

It's that time of year again! The Lenore Police Department would like to remind residents about the upcoming Eggplant Festival, which starts Wednesday, July 20, and ends Sunday, July 24. The department would also like to remind residents of a few rules, regulations, and restrictions that will take effect when the festival begins. These restrictions, which are meant to protect our residents, will be lifted on Monday, July 25.

- Residents attending the festival should not park in private parking lots during regular business hours. This includes the parking lots of banks, grocery stores, and other businesses. Violators will be fined and/or towed.
- The left lane of Main Boulevard will be closed. Parking will also be restricted in this area. Violators will be fined and/or towed.
- The sidewalk in front of the Times Bank Building on Washington Street will be closed due to construction. Residents attending the festival should avoid using this area.
- On Saturday, July 23, Washington Street will be closed in both directions from noon until 2 p.m. for the parade. Motorists should find an alternate route during this time.
- Juveniles under the age of 14 must have adult supervision while on festival grounds. Curfew for juveniles under the age of 18 is 10:30 p.m. and will be strictly enforced during the festival.
- Pets will not be allowed on festival grounds.
- No outside food or beverages may be brought on festival grounds.
- Authorities have the right to search all purses, backpacks, and other bags.

---

1. According to the passage, parking during the Eggplant Festival is restricted:
   A. in public parking lots
   B. in the right lane of Main Boulevard
   C. in front of the municipal building after 10:30 p.m.
   D. in private parking lots during regular business hours

The correct answer is **D.** Parking during the Eggplant Festival is restricted in private parking lots during regular business hours and in the left lane of Main Boulevard.

> **2.** According to the passage, a 12-year-old is allowed entry to the festival without adult supervision.
>
> **A.** True
> **B.** False

The correct answer is **B.** Juveniles under the age of 14 are not allowed entry to the festival without adult supervision, so the correct answer is False.

> **3.** According to the passage, which of the following statements would be accurate?
>
> **A.** The regulations are in effect for the entire month of July.
> **B.** The goal of the regulations is to ensure the safety of Lenore's residents.
> **C.** The regulations allow the police department to issue more citations.
> **D.** The Eggplant Festival helps raise money for the city of Lenore.

The correct answer is **B.** The goal of the regulations is to ensure the safety of Lenore's residents.

2. Long Passages

Longer passages on the police officer exam often describe what officers discovered when they responded to a call. These passages often contain very specific information, such as the time officers arrived at the scene and witnesses' accounts of what has taken place. Because long passages may contain many details and numbers, you should go back to the passage and find the information you need to answer questions about these passages.

The following is an example of a long reading comprehension passage and several questions based on that passage.

EXAMPLES:

Officers James Maleski and Rebecca Light responded to a report of a burglary by Mr. Eli Goldstein at the Cigar Room located at 47 Major St. at 8:57 a.m. on Friday, April 2, 2010. They arrived at the business at 9:06 a.m. and were greeted by Mr. Goldstein, the owner of the business. He explained that he locked up the shop the previous night around 9:02 p.m. before heading home. Mr. Goldstein returned to the shop around 8:40 a.m. on Friday morning. At this time, he noticed that the front window of the store was smashed. He opened the front door, which was still locked and appeared untouched. He said that the business was completely ransacked, so he immediately called 911. Mr. Goldstein said he looked around the shop and noticed that the glass counters were smashed and emptied out. The cash register was pulled off the counter and thrown onto the floor, spilling coins everywhere. His humidor room was completely destroyed. Chairs in the smoking area were overturned and slashed open. A safe in his office was opened and emptied.

In addition to the damage, Mr. Goldstein reported that $2,500 was taken from the safe, $150 was taken from the register, and more than 10,000 cigars were removed from the business.

While Officer Light interviewed Mr. Goldstein, Officer Maleski searched the property and spoke with other business owners in the strip mall.

Mr. Haines, the owner of the hair salon at 45 Major St., told Officer Maleski that he had just arrived and was surprised to hear what happened. He told Officer Maleski that he closed his business around 7 p.m. the previous evening and that he hadn't notice anything out of the ordinary.

Mrs. Riviera, the owner of the Coffee Beanery Cafe, said she left the cafe around 12:30 a.m. Friday after a long night of baking pastries for the following morning. She stated that she had the radio playing loudly and didn't hear anything unusual. As she prepared to leave, however, she noticed a brand-new black Subaru Legacy sedan in the parking lot near the Cigar Room. The driver had turned off the car's lights, but he never got out of the vehicle.

Although patrons of the bar across the street sometimes park in the lot late at night, Mrs. Riviera was still frightened by the driver's suspicious behavior. She kept an eye on the car while she closed up, but no one ever got out of the car. She immediately called her husband and told him about the vehicle. He stayed on the phone with her as she walked to her car. Mrs. Riviera was able to see the car's license plate. She gave the numbers to her husband and told him to write them down. After a quick phone call to her husband, Mrs. Riviera provided Officer Maleski with the car's license plate number: 433-NRT.

Officer Maleski returned to the Cigar Room, and he and Officer Light returned to the police station to file a report.

---

1. According to the passage, Mrs. Riviera was still at the Coffee Beanery Cafe at 12:30 a.m. Friday because:

   A. She was cleaning the windows of the business.
   B. She was dancing to loud music.
   C. She was waiting for her husband to give her a ride home.
   D. She was baking pastries for the following morning.

The correct answer is **D**. Mrs. Riviera was at the Coffee Beanery Cafe until 12:30 a.m. because she was baking pastries for the following morning.

---

2. Which word could best replace the word *ransacked* in the following sentence?

   He said the business was completely ransacked, so he immediately called 911.

   A. plundered
   B. cleaned
   C. attacked
   D. procured

The correct answer is **A**. The word *ransacked,* which means "to search thoroughly to commit robbery," can best be replaced with the word *plundered,* which means "to rob or steal using violence or force."

---

3. According to the passage, the vehicle's license plate number is 433-NRT.

   A. True
   B. False

The correct answer is **A**. The vehicle's license plate number is 433-NRT.

> 4. According to the passage, what was the total amount of money stolen from the Cigar Room?
>
> A. $150
> B. $2,350
> C. $2,500
> D. $2,650

The correct answer is **D.** Mr. Goldstein reported that $2,500 was taken from the safe and $150 was taken from the register, so $2,650 total cash was stolen from the Cigar Room.

3. Definition Passages

Definition passages provide a few definitions that you must interpret to answer the scenario-based questions that follow. For example, you might be asked to choose the action that best fits a definition.

> **Tip: You may see questions similar to these in Chapter VIII, which discusses judgment and problem-solving abilities.**

The following is an example of a definition passage.

EXAMPLE:

> **Accomplice:** An individual who aids another person in an act of wrongdoing.
> **Juvenile:** Another name for a youth or young person not yet of adult age.
> **Suspect:** An individual who is suspected of an act of wrongdoing with or without proof.
> **Victim:** An individual who is acted on and usually adversely affected by another individual.

> Which of the following best describes an accomplice?
>
> A. Marie's purse was stolen from her shopping cart when she turned her back.
> B. Bailey, a 16-year-old, was arrested for vandalizing a park.
> C. Angie agreed to hide a sweater that her friend stole from the mall.
> D. Edward reported to police that his house was broken into while he was away.

The correct answer is **C.** Angie is an accomplice because she agreed to hide the sweater that her friend stole.

4. Incident Reports

A police officer fills out an incident report like the one shown here after he or she investigates a crime. The incident report contains spaces for information pertaining to the incident, such as the address of the incident, name of the victim, name of the suspect, charges, and so on.

INCIDENT REPORT –– POLICE DEPARTMENT			
1. ADDRESS OF INCIDENT	2. OFFENSE	3. CODE	4. DATE
5. NAME OF VICTIM: INDIVIDUAL OR BUSINESS	6. ADDRESS	PHONE	
7. ASSIGNED OFFICERS/BADGE NUMBERS	8. AGE OF VICTIM	9. RACE OF VICTIM	10. VICTIM'S DATE OF BIRTH
11. NAME OF SUSPECT	12. ADDRESS		
13. AGE 14. RACE 15. SEX	16. DATE OF BIRTH	17. HEIGHT	18. WEIGHT
19. HAIR 20. EYES	21. PHYSICAL DESCRIPTION		
22. CHARGES			
23. ITEM 24. BRAND	25. SERIAL NUMBERS	26. VALUE	
27. ITEM 28. BRAND	29. SERIAL NUMBERS	30. VALUE	
31. ITEM 32. BRAND	33. SERIAL NUMBERS	34. VALUE	
35. _____ SIGNATURE OF OFFICER/BADGE NUMBER			

The written police officer exam contains two types of questions about incident reports:

- **True/false:** The first type of question is a true/false question based on an image of a blank incident report form and a paragraph of information about an accident or crime. These true/false questions may ask if the paragraph contains enough information to complete the blank incident report. They may also ask about details in the paragraph. These questions are just like other reading-comprehension questions, and you should base your answer only on what you've read. *Remember:* You can refer back to this information as needed.

- **Fill in the blank:** The second type of question asks you to fill in parts of the incident report. You learn more about this type of question in Section C of this chapter.

EXAMPLES:

INCIDENT REPORT –– POLICE DEPARTMENT			
1. ADDRESS OF INCIDENT	2. OFFENSE	3. CODE	4. DATE
5. NAME OF VICTIM: INDIVIDUAL OR BUSINESS	6. ADDRESS		PHONE
7. ASSIGNED OFFICERS/BADGE NUMBERS	8. AGE OF VICTIM	9. RACE OF VICTIM	10. VICTIM'S DATE OF BIRTH
11. NAME OF SUSPECT		12. ADDRESS	
13. AGE / 14. RACE / 15. SEX	16. DATE OF BIRTH	17. HEIGHT	18. WEIGHT
19. HAIR / 20. EYES	21. PHYSICAL DESCRIPTION		
22. CHARGES			
23. ITEM / 24. BRAND	25. SERIAL NUMBERS		26. VALUE
27. ITEM / 28. BRAND	29. SERIAL NUMBERS		30. VALUE
31. ITEM / 32. BRAND	33. SERIAL NUMBERS		34. VALUE
35. _____ SIGNATURE OF OFFICER/BADGE NUMBER			

Martino Vulz, owner of Music World at 2222 World Dr., called police headquarters at 9:55 a.m. on Thursday, August 19, to report that his business had been burglarized sometime between 10 p.m. on Wednesday, August 18, and 9:50 a.m. on Thursday, August 19. Officers Marvin Amesbury and Jillian Peoples arrived at the store at 10:15 a.m. to investigate the incident. Mr. Vulz reported that the suspect took $675 from the cash register and two electric guitars. Mr. Vulz has a security camera in his store that recorded footage of the incident. He was able to identify the suspect as Roger Stream, a homeless man whom Mr. Vulz passes on his way to work every day.

---

1. The incident report can be fully completed based on the information in the paragraph.

A. True
B. False

The correct answer is **B.** Although the description of the incident contains a lot of information, it doesn't contain enough to fully complete the incident report form, so the correct answer is False.

---

2. The incident was reported on August 18.

A. True
B. False

The correct answer is **B.** The incident description states that the incident was reported on August 19, but the burglary could've happened on the night of August 18.

Practice

Directions (1–10): Answer the questions solely on the basis of the information provided.

Questions 1 through 3 refer to the following passage.

At 12:42 a.m. on April 2, 2010, Officer Janudo pulled over a white Honda Accord that failed to stop at a stop sign at the intersection of Rock Street and Cemetery Street. He activated his lights and sirens and attempted to pull over the driver. The driver of the car traveled for a few blocks before pulling into an empty church parking lot on Mayberry Lane.

Officer Janudo approached the driver's side of the parked vehicle, shined a flashlight on the driver, and asked why he didn't stop at the stop sign. The driver shrugged his shoulders and handed the officer his license and registration. Officer Janudo repeated his question, but the man remained silent. Officer Janudo took the paperwork to his police cruiser to run the plates and pulled up the man's driving record information. The driver's record came back clean, and the car's registration showed no problems.

Officer Janudo returned to the car and handed the driver his paperwork. He considered letting the driver go with a warning, but the driver started acting strangely. He asked the driver if he had been drinking, and the man shook his head and remained silent. Officer Janudo asked the driver to step out of the vehicle and conducted a field sobriety test. The driver passed the test, and Officer Janudo determined that the man was not intoxicated and asked him to get back in his car. He informed the driver that he would let him go with a warning, but the driver only continued to stare. Again, Officer Janudo waited for a response, but the driver just nodded. Frustrated, Officer Janudo asked the driver if he understood. The driver nodded and explained that he speaks only some English.

1. According to the passage, where did the driver fail to stop at the stop sign?

A. Rock Street and Cemetery Street
B. Cemetery Street and Mayberry Lane
C. Mayberry Lane and Rock Street
D. Mayberry Lane and Main Street

2. During the field sobriety test, Officer Janudo asked the driver to count from 1 to 100.

    A. True

    B. False

3. According to the passage, the driver of the vehicle did not say anything to Officer Janudo because:

    A. He believed the officer pulled him over in error.

    B. He was under the influence of alcohol.

    C. He could speak only some English.

    D. He was deaf.

Questions 4 through 7 refer to the following passage.

Officers William Hansen and Dena Pagnarti responded to a call of a possible kidnapping at 99 Lemon Lane at 1:32 p.m. on Sunday, March 21, 2010. They arrived at the house at 1:35 p.m. and were greeted by a hysterical Mr. and Mrs. Wilson. Mr. Wilson told the officers that his daughter was missing. The couple returned home from church around 1:25 p.m. to find the front door wide open. Mr. Wilson told the officers that he suspected something was wrong because his 14-year-old daughter, Madison, would never leave the door open.

The couple rushed inside, calling for their daughter. Both parents checked their cellphones, and there were no messages. They called their daughter's cellphone repeatedly, but Madison didn't answer. While Mr. Wilson called 911, Mrs. Wilson discovered a letter on their dining room table. The letter was a ransom note stating that Madison had been kidnapped. The note also stated that the kidnappers wanted $100,000 for Madison's safe return. There was no further information listed in the note.

Officer Hansen called for backup and asked the Wilsons for a few recent photographs of their daughter as well as a physical description. Mr. Wilson described Madison Amy Wilson as a 14-year-old girl with long blond hair and blue eyes. She is 4'11" tall, weighs 100 pounds, and has a red birthmark on her left shoulder. She was last seen wearing jean shorts, a green polo shirt adorned with flowers, and white sneakers.

Officer Hansen searched the house for clues as he waited for backup to arrive. Officer Pagnarti decided to speak with a few of the Wilsons' neighbors.

She knocked on the door of the house at 100 Lemon Lane, and the owner, Mrs. Ginari, answered. Mrs. Ginari seemed upset after Officer Pagnarti explained what happened. She told Officer Pagnarti that she saw a red convertible pull up to the house around 11:30 a.m., shortly after the Wilsons left for church. She said she could hear the music blaring from the car's speakers in her kitchen, which is on the other side of the house. She said that the driver was a white male juvenile with a shaved head and the passenger was a white male juvenile with dark hair. Both wore red T-shirts. The driver beeped the horn, and Madison ran out of the house and hopped into the back of the convertible.

Officer Pagnarti thanked Mrs. Ginari and returned to the Wilsons' house to share what she had learned. When she arrived at the house, she noticed two more police cruisers. She went inside and asked the Wilsons if any of Madison's friends drives a red convertible. Mrs. Wilson told her that one of Madison's friends drives a convertible. Mr. and Mrs. Wilson do not approve of this friend, and Madison is not allowed to ride in the car with him. Officer Pagnarti told the Wilsons and the other officers what Mrs. Ginari saw that morning. Mrs. Wilson called the friend's house, but there was no answer. Mrs. Wilson gave the officers the address of the house where Madison's friend lives.

The officers arrived at the house and noticed a red convertible parked outside. When the officers knocked on the door, a male juvenile wearing a red T-shirt answered. The officers questioned him, and he nervously told them that the kidnapping was just a joke and that Madison was inside the house. The officers arrested the juvenile and took Madison back to the police station to answer a few questions.

4. According to the passage, which of the following statements would be accurate?

   A. Madison was kidnapped by her neighbor.
   B. Madison has a friend who drives a red convertible.
   C. Madison's parents do not like their neighbor.
   D. Madison's parents do not know any of her friends.

5. Which word could best replace the word *adorned* in the following sentence?

   She was last seen wearing jean shorts, a green polo shirt adorned with flowers, and white sneakers.

   A. littered
   B. defaced
   C. embellished
   D. savored

6. According to the passage, Mrs. Ginari lives at 100 Lemon Lane.

   A. True
   B. False

7. According to the passage, Madison:

   A. Has long dark hair
   B. Drives a red convertible
   C. Always leaves the front door open
   D. Has a red birthmark on her left shoulder

Question 8 refers to the following definitions.

Robbery: The act of removing or attempting to remove a piece of property from its owner's possession by use of force, intimidation, or threat of violence

Larceny: The unlawful taking of personal property with intent to deprive the rightful owner of it permanently

Confiscation: The legal taking or seizure of something

Fraud: When something is not as it seems or as it is represented

8. Which of the following best describes fraud?

   A. Josef broke the restaurant's window, climbed into the unoccupied establishment, and took $350 from the cash register.
   B. While Joanne was at the grocery store, she slipped a steak into her purse and quickly left the store unnoticed.
   C. Melanie took her older sister's driver's license from her purse and used it to buy beer for the party.
   D. Jaime found a wallet on the ground near his school. He opened it, took out the cash, and placed the wallet back on the ground where he found it.

Questions 9 and 10 refer to the following information.

INCIDENT REPORT —— POLICE DEPARTMENT			
1. ADDRESS OF INCIDENT	**2. OFFENSE**	**3. CODE**	**4. DATE**
5. NAME OF VICTIM: INDIVIDUAL OR BUSINESS	**6. ADDRESS**		**PHONE**
7. ASSIGNED OFFICERS/BADGE NUMBERS	**8. AGE OF VICTIM**	**9. RACE OF VICTIM**	**10. VICTIM'S DATE OF BIRTH**
11. NAME OF SUSPECT		**12. ADDRESS**	
13. AGE **14. RACE** **15. SEX**	**16. DATE OF BIRTH**	**17. HEIGHT**	**18. WEIGHT**
19. HAIR **20. EYES**	**21. PHYSICAL DESCRIPTION**		
22. CHARGES			
23. ITEM **24. BRAND**	**25. SERIAL NUMBERS**		**26. VALUE**
27. ITEM **28. BRAND**	**29. SERIAL NUMBERS**		**30. VALUE**
31. ITEM **32. BRAND**	**33. SERIAL NUMBERS**		**34. VALUE**
35. _____ SIGNATURE OF OFFICER/BADGE NUMBER			

    Margaret Alecto, owner of a house located at 1 Friendship Drive, called police headquarters at 5:35 p.m., Wednesday, May 13, to report that her house had been broken into sometime between 8:30 a.m. and 5:25 p.m. on Wednesday. Officer Antonio Rubino arrived at the house at 5:42 p.m. to investigate the incident. Mrs. Alecto reported that the suspect took $900 from a safe and a jewelry box from her dresser, both of which were located in her first-floor bedroom. Nothing else in the house appeared to be missing. Mrs. Alecto has a security camera on her front porch, but there was nothing unusual on the tape when she played it for Officer Rubino. There was no other evidence other than an open window in Mrs. Alecto's bedroom.

9. The incident was reported on May 13 at 5:25 p.m.

   A. True
   B. False

10. The incident report can be fully completed based on the information in the paragraph.

    A. True
    B. False

Answers

1. **A** The driver failed to stop at the stop sign at Rock Street and Cemetery Street.

2. **B** The passage does not say that Officer Janudo asked the driver to count from 1 to 100, so the correct answer is False.

3. **C** The driver of the vehicle did not say anything to Officer Janudo because he could speak only some English.

4. **B** According to the passage, Mrs. Wilson told the officer that Madison has a friend who drives a red convertible.

5. **C** The word *embellished,* which means "beautified," would best replace *adorned,* which means "decorated."

6. **A** The passage states that Mrs. Ginari lives at 100 Lemon Lane, so the correct answer is True.

7. **D** According to the passage, Madison has a red birthmark on her left shoulder.

8. **C** Melanie committed fraud when she took her older sister's license to buy beer.

9. **B** The incident description states that the incident was reported on Wednesday, May 13, at 5:35 p.m., so the correct answer is False.

10. **B** Although the description of the incident contains many details, it doesn't contain enough to fully complete the incident report form, so the correct answer is False.

B. Grammar and Spelling

Almost everyone makes grammatical mistakes when speaking, but such mistakes are more noticeable in writing. That's why it's important to check your writing for proper grammar, spelling, and usage.

Some written police officer exams may focus more on grammar and spelling than others do, so it's important to brush up on these skills before taking the exam.

This section reviews the skills you need to successfully answer questions regarding grammar and spelling.

1. Pronouns

The verbal section of the police officer written exam will likely contain questions that ask you to choose the correct pronoun to use in a sentence. A **pronoun** is a word used in place of a noun. There are a variety of types of pronouns; it's important that you're able to recognize when to use each type so that you can answer questions correctly on your exam. Here is a list of different types of pronouns:

- **Subject pronouns** take the place of the subject in the sentence. The subject typically appears in a sentence before the verb or after *than* or *as*. You can use a subject pronoun when a compound subject contains a noun and a pronoun. You also can use a subject pronoun to rename a subject. Subject pronouns include *I, you, he, she, it, we, you, they,* and *who*.
- **Object pronouns** take the place of the object in the sentence. The object typically appears after the verb. You can use an object pronoun when a compound object contains a noun and a pronoun. You can also use an object pronoun as the object of a prepositional phrase. Object pronouns include *me, you, him, her, it, us, them,* and *whom*.
- **Possessive pronouns** show ownership, or possession. Possessive pronouns include *its, yours, his, hers, ours, theirs,* and *mine*. **Possessive adjectives** resemble possessive pronouns and also show ownership, but they really modify nouns in sentences. Possessive adjectives include *its, your, his, her, our, their,* and *my*. You should use possessive adjectives before nouns ending in *–ing*. Neither possessive pronouns nor possessive adjectives need apostrophes to show possession.
- **Reflexive pronouns** refer back to another word in the sentence. Reflexive pronouns include *myself, yourself, yourselves,* and *ourselves*.
- **Indefinite pronouns** don't refer to a specific person or thing. They may be singular or plural. If you use a singular indefinite pronoun in a sentence with another pronoun, the other pronoun should also be singular. Singular indefinite pronouns include *another, anybody, anyone, anything, each, either, everybody, everything, everyone, nobody, no one, nothing, somebody, someone,* and *something*. Plural indefinite pronouns include *few, many, others,* and *several*.
- **Demonstrative pronouns** refer to the nouns that come after them. Demonstrative pronouns include *that, this, those,* and *these*.

Examples:

---

1. When we were younger, it was obvious that my brother, Nick, wasn't as strong as _____.

   A. I
   B. me
   C. us
   D. them

The correct answer is **A**. Subject pronouns, such as *I*, are used after *than* and *as*. To check your answer, complete the sentence: When we were younger, it was obvious that my brother, Nick, wasn't as strong as *I was*.

---

2. Officer Andrews often envisions _____ in the near future; she hopes to receive her detective shield within the coming year.

   A. her
   B. herself
   C. she
   D. hers

The correct answer is **B.** Reflexive pronouns refer back to another word in the sentence. In this case, *herself* refers to Officer Andrews.

---

3. Everyone knows when my squad car pulls up; the noise from _____ muffler is loud enough to disrupt any and all conversations.

    A. his
    B. its
    C. it's
    D. their

The correct answer is **B.** Possessive adjectives show ownership and modify nouns. In this sentence, the muffler belongs to the car, and the possessive adjective *its* modifies *muffler*. Remember that *it's* is a contraction for *it is*.

2. Adjectives

You also may have to identify the correct use of adjectives on the written police officer test. **Adjectives** are words used to describe nouns; words that describe colors, placement, and personality traits are all considered adjectives. There are three main types of adjectives:

- **Positive adjectives** stand alone, meaning they are the only adjectives used to describe the noun. Positive adjectives don't offer a comparison. For example:

  The suspect's <u>yellow</u> shirt made him stand out in the crowd.

- **Comparative adjectives** compare two people, places, things, or ideas. Add an *–er* to the end of an adjective if you want to use it to compare two items. Add *more* or *less* before the adjective if it has three or more syllables. For example:

  Officer Nickels is <u>faster</u> than I am.

  I am <u>more intelligent</u> than my neighbor.

- **Superlative adjectives** compare three or more people, places, ideas, or items. Add an *–est* ending to these adjectives if they have one or two syllables. If they contain three or more syllables, use *most* or *least* before the adjective. For example:

  I am the <u>oldest</u> of my parents' three children.

  Detective Sheridan is the <u>most respected</u> member of the force.

Examples:

---

1. Officer Rodriguez chose _____ shirts for his team to wear during the annual softball tournament.

    A. orange
    B. orangest
    C. more orange
    D. most orange

The correct answer is **A.** Because the sentence is describing one noun, *shirts,* the adjective must be a positive adjective.

2. Everyone agrees that Officer Chin is the _____ player on the department's softball team.

    A.   talented
    B.   talentest
    C.   more talented
    D.   most talented

The correct answer is **D.** Since the sentence is comparing Chin to all the other players on the team, you need to use a superlative adjective. *Talented* has three syllables, so you have to add the word *most* before *talented*.

3. After graduating from the police academy, my aim was _____ than it was before I enrolled.

    A.   accurate
    B.   accurater
    C.   more accurate
    D.   most accurate

The correct answer is **C.** This sentence is comparing the person's aim after completing training to his or her aim before training. Because the sentence is comparing two things, a comparative adjective is required. *Accurate* has three syllables, so you need to use *more* before the word.

3. Fragments and Complete Sentences

A **fragment** is an incomplete sentence that is typically missing a subject, a verb, or punctuation. Fragments may be dependent clauses, meaning they contain a subject and a verb but don't necessarily express a complete thought.

When you correct a fragment, you incorporate it into, or make a new, **complete sentence.** A complete sentence contains a subject and a verb. In addition, the complete sentence expresses a complete thought. To fix a fragment, add the missing components to express a complete thought. You also could remove the period that ends the fragment and combine it with an independent clause.

On the exam, you may be asked to fix sentence fragments and eliminate redundancy, as in the following examples.

Examples:

1. Although the cashier was terrified. The cashier gave the money to a man who entered Mo's Convenient Shack with a gun on Monday, January 19.

    A.   Although the cashier was terrified, the cashier gave the money to a man who entered Mo's Convenient Shack with a gun on Monday, January 19.
    B.   Although the cashier was terrified, and the cashier gave the money to a man who entered Mo's Convenient Shack with a gun on Monday, January 19.
    C.   Although the cashier was terrified, she gave the money to the man who entered Mo's Convenient Shack with a gun on Monday, January 19.
    D.   Although the cashier was terrified; however, she gave the money to the man who entered Mo's Convenient Shack with a gun on Monday, January 19.

The correct answer is **C.** *Although the cashier was terrified* is a fragment because it doesn't express a complete thought. The word *although* signifies that an exception or a contradiction is coming, but the period at the end of the fragment doesn't allow for the completion of the thought. Adding a comma and changing *the cashier* to a pronoun, such as *she,* creates a complete sentence and eliminates redundancy.

---

2. Officers Jenkins and Rodge arrested two suspects last night. One involved in a burglary. One accused of assault.

    A.   Officers Jenkins and Rodge arrested two suspects last night; however, one involved in a burglary, but one accused of assault.

    B.   Officers Jenkins and Rodge arrested two suspects last night; therefore, one involved in a burglary, or one accused of assault.

    C.   Officers Jenkins and Rodge arrested two suspects last night, and one involved in a burglary, however, one accused of assault.

    D.   Officers Jenkins and Rodge arrested two suspects last night: one involved in a burglary and one accused of assault.

The correct answer is **D.** *One involved in a burglary* and *One accused of assault* are fragments because they are incomplete thoughts. To create a complete sentence, use a colon to connect the independent clause stating that the officers made two arrests and separate the two fragments using *and.*

4. Verbs

Verbs are action words—they tell the reader what's happening. **Tense** is an indicator of time; it tells the reader when an action takes place.

A verb's form may change as the tense of a sentence is altered. For example, when describing your exercise routine to a co-worker, you might say, "I walk 5 miles every day." Because this sentence describes an ongoing action that takes place in the present, the verb must also be in the present tense.

Now, think about how the sentence would change if you described something that took place yesterday:

    I walked 5 miles yesterday.

Notice how the verb tense changes when you describe an action that took place in the past.

Verbs also can describe actions that will take place in the future. Imagine telling your co-worker what you'll do tomorrow:

    I will walk 5 miles tomorrow.

Remember: Good communication skills are an important part of every police officer's job. Using the correct verb tenses will make your written reports easier to understand.

On the police officer exam, you'll encounter several types of questions that ask you to identify or use the correct verb tense. Here's a list of the verb tenses, including examples of each.

- **Present tense:** A verb in the present tense expresses an action that is happening right now. It also describes an action that happens continually or regularly. For example:
  - The ocean <u>is</u> beautiful.
  - I <u>wake</u> at 5:30 a.m. every morning.
- **Past tense:** A verb in this tense describes an action that was completed at a particular point in the past. For example:
  - I <u>went</u> to the movie theater last night.
  - They <u>completed</u> their training last week.
- **Future tense:** A verb in the future tense describes an action that will take place at a certain point in the future. For example:
  - I <u>will run</u> tomorrow morning.
  - She <u>will finish</u> the report by Friday.
- **Present perfect tense:** A verb in the present perfect tense describes an action that began in the past and either continues in the present or is completed in the present. For example:
  - His mother <u>has taught</u> kindergarten for many years.
  - I <u>have located</u> the suspect.
- **Past perfect tense:** A verb in the past perfect tense describes an action that began in the past and was completed in the past. For example:
  - They <u>had expected</u> more customers on Monday morning.
  - She <u>had finished</u> the movie by 11 p.m.
- **Future perfect tense:** A verb in the future perfect tense describes an action that will begin in the future and will be completed at a specific time in the future. For example:
  - By this time tomorrow, I <u>will have graduated</u> from college.
  - In a few years, she <u>will have saved</u> enough money to buy a new car.

Another important consideration when working with verbs is whether the verb is regular or irregular. Most **regular verbs** can be transformed into the past tense by adding –d or –ed. For example, the word *accept* is changed to the past tense by adding –ed to make the word *accepted*. In this case, the past participle of the word *accept* is also *accepted*. The past participle is the –ed form of most verbs and indicates an action that has been completed. The **past participle** often uses an auxiliary verb to describe an action that took place in the past. For example:

I <u>have accepted</u> the position of deputy inspector.

Irregular verbs don't always use –d or –ed to form the past tense or the past participle. Think about the word *steal*. The past tense of *steal* is *stole*, not *stealed*, and the past participle is *stolen*. For example:

Past tense: The criminals <u>stole</u> $500 from a local bakery.

Past participle: The criminals <u>have stolen</u> money from many local businesses.

Although there are fewer than 200 irregular verbs in the English language, it's important that you recognize the irregular verbs so you know how to *conjugate* them (change them from one verb form to another). Unfortunately, there's really no rhyme or reason as to how irregular verbs are conjugated. The only way to learn the different forms is to memorize them.

Infinitives consist of *to* plus the plain form of the verb. An infinitive can function as a noun, an adjective, or an adverb. For example:

> To know her is to love her.

Take a few moments to review the table of common irregular verbs before moving on to the example questions.

Common Irregular Verbs					
Present Tense	**Past Tense**	**Past Participle**	**Present Tense**	**Past Tense**	**Past Participle**
am, be	was, were	been	ring	rang	rung
begin	began	begun	rise	rose	risen
break	broke	broken	run	ran	run
bring	brought	brought	see	saw	seen
catch	caught	caught	set	set	set
choose	chose	chosen	shake	shook	shaken
come	came	come	show	showed	shown
do	did	done	sing	sang	sung
drive	drove	driven	sink	sank	sunk
eat	ate	eaten	speak	spoke	spoken
fall	fell	fallen	spring	sprang	sprung
fight	fought	fought	steal	stole	stolen
fly	flew	flown	swear	swore	sworn
freeze	froze	frozen	swim	swam	swum
give	gave	given	swing	swung	swung
go	went	gone	take	took	taken
grow	grew	grown	tear	tore	torn
hide	hid	hidden	throw	threw	thrown
know	knew	known	wake	woke, waked	waked
lead	led	led	wear	wore	worn
ride	rode	ridden	write	wrote	written

Examples:

1. When I work sobriety checkpoints at night, I use a flashlight to _____ the vehicle for evidence of open alcohol containers.

    A. inspect
    B. inspecting
    C. inspected
    D. had inspected

The correct answer is **A.** This sentence is not describing an activity that is acting in the past, present, or future; therefore, it's best to use the regular form of the verb to accompany the infinitive *to*.

2. During my previous vehicle pursuit, I _____ my squad car into a sidewalk fruit stand to avoid hitting a bicyclist.

   A. crash
   B. crashed
   C. will crash
   D. crashing

The correct answer is **B.** This sentence refers to something that happened in the past. You know this because of the word *previous*.

3. By the end of today, I _____ 10 incident reports, 11 aid reports, and 3 found-property reports.

   A. complete
   B. completing
   C. will be completing
   D. will have completed

The correct answer is **D.** This sentence uses the future perfect tense because it describes an action that will both begin and end in the future. The verb phrase *will have completed* is correct.

5. Subject-Verb Agreement

Every complete sentence needs a subject and a verb, and they need to agree with each other. If you have a singular subject, you should have a singular verb. If you're using a plural subject, your verb should also be in the plural form. Apply the following rules when answering questions on the verbal section of the police officer written exam:

- Use a singular verb with a singular subject. For example:
  - Keisha plays the guitar. (*Keisha* is a singular subject; *plays* is a singular verb.)
  - The puppy knows its name. (*Puppy* is a singular subject; *knows* is a singular verb.)
- Use a plural verb with a plural subject. For example:
  - Teachers appreciate students who participate in class. (*Teachers* is a plural subject; *appreciate* is a plural verb.)
  - The *puppies enjoy* playing in the backyard. (*Puppies* is a plural subject; *enjoy* is a plural verb.)
- Use a plural verb when at least two subjects are connected by *and*. For example:
  - *Keisha and Jamie play* the guitar. (This sentence has a plural subject—*Keisha and Jamie*—and a plural verb—*play*.)
  - Ms. Martinez, Mr. Drake, and Mrs. Shiffer are in charge of the school play. (The subject of this sentence is plural: *Ms. Martinez, Mr. Drake, and Mrs. Shiffer*. The verb *are* is also plural.)
- Use a singular verb with *neither/nor* or *either/or* when they connect singular subjects, and use a plural verb when they connect plural subjects. For example:
  - Neither Sarah nor John drives a car. (*Sarah/John* are singular subjects; *drives* is a singular verb.)
  - Either Casey and James or Eric and Wanda play on the basketball team. (This sentence has two plural subjects joined by either/or: *Casey and James/Eric and Wanda*, so the plural verb *play* is used.)

- Use a singular verb when two singular subjects are connected by *or* or *nor.* For example:
  - The dog or the cat sleeps on that sofa. (This sentence has two singular subjects joined by *or: dog/cat.* Therefore, the singular verb *sleeps* is used.)
  - Neither Rita nor Ray eats red meat. (This sentence has two singular subjects joined by *nor: Rita/Ray,* so the singular verb *eats* is used.)
- Use a singular verb in sentences with *each, everyone, every one, someone, somebody, anyone,* and *anybody.* For example:
  - Each senior girl has a class ring. (This sentence contains the word *each,* so the singular verb *has* is used.)
  - Everyone in the group uses his or her free movie pass on the weekend. (*Everyone* is singular so it requires a singular verb: *uses.*)
- Use a singular verb when dealing with time or money. For example:
  - Two years is a long time to be away from home. (The subject of this sentence—*two years*—deals with time, so the singular verb *is* is used.)
  - Six dollars is the price of admission. (The subject of this sentence—*six dollars*—deals with money, so a singular verb is used.)
- Use a singular verb with collective nouns such as *team* and *group.* For example:
  - The team is in the locker room. (*Team* is singular; the verb *is* is also singular.)
  - The group practices each day after school. (*Group* is singular; the verb *practices* is also singular.)
- If a phrase appears between the subject and the verb, make sure the verb agrees with the subject, not the phrase. For example:
  - The teacher, as well as her students, hopes to win the contest. (*Teacher* is singular, so the singular verb *hopes* is used.)
  - The man on our street who lives in the red house likes to run each morning. (*Man* is singular, so the singular verb *likes* is used.)
- If a compound subject has both a singular and a plural subject joined by *or* or *nor,* the verb should agree with the part of the subject that appears closest to the verb. For example:
  - The keys or the automatic door opener is in the drawer. (Since *automatic door opener* is closest to the verb, the verb is singular.)
  - Neither Ms. Murphy nor the students are pleased with the new textbook. (Since *students* is closest to the verb, the verb is plural.)
- If *there* or *here* begins a sentence, the subject of the sentence should follow the verb. The verb should agree with the subject. For example:
  - There is Melissa. (The subject of the sentence—*Melissa*—is singular, so the singular verb *is* is used.)
  - Here are your keys. (The subject of the sentence—*keys*—is plural, so the plural verb *are* is used.)

Examples:

---

1. Larry and Qadry _____ video games after police training every night.

   A. play
   B. plays
   C. playing
   D. will plays

The correct answer is **A.** The word *and* connects *Larry* and *Qadry*, so you should use the plural verb *play.*

---

2. Everyone in the department _____ the Mayoral Ball at the end of September.

    A. attend
    B. attends
    C. attending
    D. will attends

The correct answer is **B.** Sentences in which *everyone* is the subject use the singular verb. *Attends* is correct.

---

3. There _____ multiple reasons as to why we can arrest you this very second.

    A. is
    B. are
    C. was
    D. were

The correct answer is **B.** The subject of the sentence is *reasons.* Because *reasons* is plural, you have to use the plural verb *are.*

6. Pluralizing

Although you were probably taught the rules for pluralizing in school, you may have forgotten them by now. Admittedly, these rules can be confusing. How are you supposed to know when the *–y* ending changes to *–i?* And when is it okay to add *–es* instead of *–s?* Brush up on the following rules while you study for the verbal section of the police officer exam.

- The most common way to pluralize a noun is to add *–s,* such as *dog/dogs.*
- For words that end in *–ch, –x, –s,* or *s*-like sounds, add *–es,* such as *stitch/stitches.*
- Be aware of irregular nouns such as *child/children* and *person/people.*
- Some irregular words keep their original Latin or Greek form when plural, such as *syllabus/syllabi.*
- When a word ends in a consonant before *–y,* change *–y* to *–i* and add *–es,* such as *penny/pennies.*
- Most words that end in *–f* or *–fe* are pluralized by adding *–ves,* such as *scarf/scarves.*
- For words that end in *–is,* change the *–is* to *–es,* such as *analysis/analyses.*
- When a word ends in *–um* or *–on,* add *–a* to the root to pluralize, such as *criterion/criteria.*
- Words that end in *–a* are pluralized by adding *–ae,* such as *alumna/alumnae.*
- Words that end in *–ex* or *–ix* are pluralized by adding *–in* or *–ices* to the root, such as *appendix/appendices.*
- When a word ends in *–us,* make it plural by adding *–i* or *–a,* such as *octopus/octopi.*
- For words that end in *–eau,* change it to *–eaux,* such as *tableau/tableaux.*
- Nouns that usually come in pairs are plural, such as *glasses.*
- Some nouns don't change form whether they're singular or plural, like *deer* and *sheep.*

Note that you don't have to memorize every spelling rule in this chapter. Most spelling questions on the police officer test are fairly easy. When you come across a word you can't spell on the job, consult a dictionary for the correct spelling.

Examples:

---

1. A recent string of carjackings has left six of Mr. Wright's best _____ without vehicles this week.

   A. customer
   B. customers
   C. customer's
   D. customers'

The correct answer is **B.** Six cars have been stolen, so you know that multiple people are without vehicles. The plural of *customer* is *customers*.

Tip: Using an apostrophe and adding an –s doesn't make a noun plural. Instead, this makes the noun possessive. If you want to write about more than one student, the word will not be students' or student's. Instead, just add the –s and make it students, the plural form of student.

---

2. Conducting investigations outside during autumn is difficult because _____ fall from the trees and mask crucial evidence.

   A. leaf
   B. leafs
   C. leave
   D. leaves

The correct answer is **D.** Obviously, one leaf isn't enough to cover evidence at a crime scene, so you know you're dealing with more than one. To make plural most words that end in –f, drop the –f and add –ves. *Leaves* is correct.

---

3. The witness reported that the suspect wore a black sweatshirt with a hood, a pair of black _____ with a white stripe down the side, and red running shoes.

   A. pant
   B. pants
   C. pant's
   D. pants'

The correct answer is **B.** The word *pants* is plural.

7. Spelling

When you're a police officer, it's important that your reports are grammatically correct and free of spelling errors. However, you shouldn't rely on a spell-checker to correct your work. Always double-check your reports for spelling errors. If something seems incorrect, look it up in the dictionary.

The following list will help you brush up on spelling rules before taking the police officer exam:

- In most words, *i* comes before *e,* unless the *i* and the *e* appear after a *c* or if they make the *ay* sound. For example, it's *beige* and *neighbor*, but *thief* and *believe.*

- When the letter *c* follows a short vowel, it's usually doubled. For example, it's *raccoon* and *hiccups.*

- The letters *ck* are used instead of *cc* if the letter following the *c* sound is *e, i,* or *y.* Examples include *lucky, picking,* and *finicky.*

- If the *j* sound follows a short vowel, the word is usually spelled with *dge.* Examples include *badge* and *gadget.*

- In most cases, the *ch* sound is spelled *tch* after a short vowel. Examples include *witch* and *kitchen.*

- In words with a short vowel sound, you'll find two consonants between the vowel and an *–le* ending. Consider the words *little* and *handle.*

- When a word has a silent *e,* you need to drop the *e* before adding a vowel suffix (that is, a suffix that begins with a vowel), such as *–ing.* Examples include *convince/convincing* and *shake/shaking.*

- When the *ee* sound comes before a vowel suffix, the sound is usually spelled using the letter *i.* Consider the words *obvious* and *material.*

- The ending *–ist* is typically used to refer to a person, while the ending *–est* is used to create superlative adjectives. For example, a *pianist* is a person, and *fastest* is a superlative adjective.

- The ending *–cian* always refers to a person, but the endings *–tion* and *–sion* refer to ideas or things.

The commonly misspelled words in the following table don't abide by any rules; you just have to memorize them.

Commonly Misspelled Words		
acceptable	discipline	indispensable
accommodate	embarrass	inoculate
amateur	equipment	intelligence
apparent	exceed	jewelry
argument	existence	judgment
calendar	gauge	kernel
category	grateful	leisure
cemetery	guarantee	license
changeable	harass	lightning
collectible	height	maintenance
committed	ignorance	millennium
conscience	independent	miniature

(continued)

Commonly Misspelled Words *(continued)*		
misspell	playwright	separate
noticeable	questionnaire	sergeant
occasionally	recommend	supersede
occurrence	referred	vacuum
pastime	relevant	
personnel	rhythm	

In addition to commonly misspelled words, it's important to recognize commonly confused words, including **homophones** (words that sound the same, but have different meanings). It's quite easy to make a mistake involving some of these words. Consider the following sentence:

Dad doesn't want to drive threw the center of town; traffic is always horrible at this hour.

The word *threw* is the past tense of the verb *throw,* which often means "to propel through the air." In this case, the writer most likely wanted to use the word *through,* which means "to indicate movement into one side or point and out another."

See how easy it can be to confuse one word for another? *Remember:* It's important to use the correct word so you don't confuse your readers or obscure the meaning of your writing.

Review the following list of commonly confused words before looking at the example questions.

Commonly Confused Words		
accept: to receive (e.g., He accepted the raise.) **except:** to take or leave out (e.g., Please bring all the bags except the black one.)	**cite:** to quote by way of example (e.g., Please cite all sources in your report.) **sight:** something that is seen (e.g., The sunset was such a beautiful sight.) **site:** the location of a structure (e.g., We visited the site of the first Woodstock festival.)	**precede:** to come before (e.g., A guitar solo preceded the singer's finale.) **proceed:** to go forward (e.g., The president proceeded according to plan.)
affect: n., expressed or observed emotional response (e.g., The suspect showed no affect when confronted with his victim.); v., to influence (e.g., His decision affected the entire team.) **effect:** n., result (The storm had a devastating effect on the town.); v., to accomplish (e.g., The senator hoped to effect sweeping reform in the tax structure.)	**complement:** n., something that completes (e.g., The usual complement of education and experience is required.); v., to complete (e.g., That color of the dress complements your eyes.) **compliment:** n., praise (e.g., He flattered her with compliments all evening.); v., to praise (e.g., He complimented her on her victory.)	**principal:** adj., most important (e.g., Eggs are the principal ingredient in this dish.); n., a person in authority (e.g., The high school welcomed a new principal.) **principle:** a general or fundamental law (e.g., The students studied the basic principles of physics.)

ascent: the act of rising or moving upward (e.g., The ascent up the hill was very steep.) assent: to agree to something (e.g., He assented to the terms of the contract.)	its: of or belonging to it (e.g., The car lost its muffler on the highway.) it's: contraction of it is (e.g., It's time to go to bed.)	right: adj., being in accordance with what is just or proper (e.g., He provided the professor with the right answer.); n., something to which one has a just claim (e.g., She has the right to say whatever she likes.) rite: a ceremonial act or action (e.g., Obtaining a driver's license is a rite of passage for most teenagers.) write: to express in literary form (e.g., Henry writes a column about sports.)
buy: to purchase (e.g., He will buy some flowers for the dinner party.) by: in proximity to; near (e.g., The book is by the computer.) bye: the automatically advanced position of a participant in a tournament (e.g., The team has a bye during the second week of the season.)	lead: n., a type of metal (e.g. The pencil contains lead.) led: v., past tense of lead (e.g., She led the dog down the road.)	their: of or relating to them or themselves (e.g., Their hands were frozen.) there: in or at that place (e.g., We have lived there for many years.) they're: contraction of they are (e.g., They're headed to the concert after dinner.)
capital: a city serving as the seat of government (e.g., Harrisburg is the capital of Pennsylvania.) capitol: a building in which a legislative body meets (e.g., The senators met at the capitol building.)	lose: v., to fail (e.g., The team didn't want to lose the game.) loose: not fastened securely (e.g., The dress was too loose.)	threw: past tense of throw (e.g., He threw the ball to first base.) through: indicates movement into one side or point and out another (e.g., We passed through Maryland on our way to Virginia.)
cent: monetary unit equal to 1/100th of a basic unit of value (e.g., The bracelet costs 99 cents.) scent: an odor (e.g., The scent of pancakes filled the house.) sent: past tense of send (e.g., I sent the package to him last week.)	passed: past tense of pass (e.g., He passed the store on his way home.) past: having existed or taken place in a period before the present (e.g., The photograph was taken in the past.)	to: indicates movement or action toward a place (e.g., We are headed to the city tonight.) too: to an excessive degree (e.g., She poured too much milk in her cereal.); also (e.g., He is going to the movies, too.) two: the number (e.g., Her son turns two on Friday.)

In the following examples, look for the misspelled word in each sentence.

Examples:

1. On February 22, Officer Jackson was called to investigate vandelism at the cemetery on municipal property.

   A. February
   B. investigate
   C. vandelism
   D. cemetery

The correct answer is **C.** The correct spelling is *vandalism*.

> **2.** When the officer searched the vehicle, he found an open container of alcohol, marijuana, and drug paraphanalia.
>
> A. vehicle
> B. alcohol
> C. marijuana
> D. paraphanalia

The correct answer is **D.** The correct spelling is *paraphernalia.*

> **3.** Officer Richards responded to a domestec dispute at 115 Randall St.
>
> A. Officer
> B. responded
> C. domestec
> D. dispute

The correct answer is **C.** The correct spelling is *domestic.*

> **4.** The business owner was the principle suspect in the case.
>
> A. business
> B. owner
> C. principle
> D. suspect

The correct answer is **C.** *Principle* means "a general or fundamental law." In this case, the writer most likely wanted to use the word *principal,* which means "most important."

8. Capitalization

Every sentence starts with a capital letter. **Proper nouns** (names of particular people, places, things, or ideas) are also capitalized.

But there are many additional rules of capitalization that you should review before taking the police officer exam. The following table explains some general rules of capitalization.

General Rules of Capitalization	
Always Capitalize	**Examples**
Days of the week	Friday, Saturday, Sunday
Months	January, February, March
Holidays, religious holy days	New Year's Eve, Passover
Periods, events in history	Enlightenment, Cold War
Political parties	Democratic Party, Republican Party
Official documents	Constitution of the United States, Declaration of Independence

Always Capitalize	Examples
Acts, treaties, and government programs	Thirteenth Amendment, Stamp Act
Awards, prizes	Academy Award, Nobel Peace Prize
Trade names	Toyota, Apple, Microsoft
Formal epithets	Catherine the Great, Ivan the Terrible
Planets, celestial bodies	Mars, Big Dipper
Continents	Asia, Africa, North America
Countries	France, Peru, South Africa
States, provinces	Rhode Island, New Jersey, Ontario
Official state nicknames	Empire State, Sunshine State
Counties	Lackawanna County, Orange County
Cities, towns, villages	New York City, Middletown, Monticello
Streets, roads, highways	Wall Street, River Road, Interstate 84
Landforms	Appalachian Mountains, Mojave Desert
Bodies of water	Atlantic Ocean, Mississippi River, Red Sea
Public areas	Yosemite National Park
Abbreviations of titles and organizations	CEO, FBI, TSA

There are, however, some challenging capitalization rules that you should memorize. Review these special capitalization rules before taking the police officer written exam:

- **Official titles:** Religious, political, military, and professional titles are capitalized when they immediately precede a personal name. These titles also are capitalized when they stand in the place of a personal name in direct address, as in, *Thank you, Mr. President.* For example:
  - Pope John Paul II *but* the pope
  - President Barack Obama *but* the president of the United States
  - General George S. Patton *but* the general
  - Professor Jones *but* the professor
- **Titles of works:** Capitalize the first word, the last word, and every word in between (except articles like *a, an,* and *the* and short prepositions) of titles of books, newspapers, magazines, poems, plays, songs, films, works of art, and stories. For example:
  - *The Once and Future King* (book)
  - *The New York Times* (newspaper)
  - *Newsweek* (magazine)
  - "Stopping by Woods on a Snowy Evening" (poem)
  - *Romeo and Juliet* (play)
  - "What a Wonderful World" (song)
  - *The Godfather* (film)
  - *Starry Night* (work of art)
  - "The Woman in the Room" (short story)

- **Regions of a country:** Words that indicate specific sections or regions of a country are proper nouns and, therefore, must be capitalized. Words that simply imply direction should be lowercased. For example:
  - East Coast (refers to the eastern United States)
  - the South (specific region of the country) *but* the couple was moving south
  - Central America (proper noun) *but* central Illinois (implies direction)
- **Earth:** When referring to the planet, *Earth* is capitalized. However, when referring to dirt or ground, *earth* is lowercased. For example:
  - The asteroid may hit Earth.
  - The earth is fertile in this region of the country.

In the following example, look for the word or phrase that reflects an error in capitalization.

Examples:

---

1. Law enforcement officials will be on hand Monday morning, when senator John McCain will give a speech at the Lincoln Memorial.

   A. Monday
   B. senator
   C. John McCain
   D. Lincoln Memorial

The correct answer is **B.** The word *senator* precedes the personal name *John McCain;* therefore, *senator* must be capitalized.

---

2. Police were called to the east coast headquarters of *USA Today* yesterday.

   A. *USA Today*
   B. headquarters
   C. east coast
   D. yesterday

The correct answer is **C.** The title *east coast* refers to a specific region of the country and should be capitalized.

---

3. The White House, which is located at 1600 Pennsylvania avenue in Washington, D.C., is always surrounded by law enforcement officials.

   A. White House
   B. Pennsylvania
   C. avenue
   D. Washington, D.C.

The correct answer is **C.** The word *avenue* is part of a specific street name and needs to be capitalized.

9. Punctuation

Knowing when and where to place a comma or how to properly use a semicolon can be difficult. This section briefly reviews some of the most common punctuation rules you may encounter when taking the police officer written exam.

End Punctuation

Periods mark the end of most sentences. Periods are also commonly used after initials, such as in the name J. Edgar Hoover. Periods are also used in common abbreviations, such as a.m., p.m., and U.S.A.

An **exclamation point** is used to express a strong emotion. It can be used after a complete sentence, a phrase, or a single word. For example:

> I can't believe I got accepted to the academy!
>
> Get out!
>
> Help!

Remember: Exclamation points should be used sparingly.

A **question mark** is used at the end of a direct question. An indirect question does not require a question mark. For example:

> Question mark required: Are you attending the meeting on Friday?
>
> No question mark required: I was wondering if you could help me with this incident report.

Commas

A **comma** indicates a break, or pause, in sentence structure. Commas are commonly used between two independent clauses joined by a coordinating conjunction such as *and, but, or, for, nor, so,* and *yet.* For example:

> Amy will attend the meeting, but her partner will be on vacation that day.

The comma is used before a conjunction only to connect two independent clauses. Commas are not always necessary when the words *and, but, or, for, nor, so,* and *yet* appear. For example:

> Benjamin completed the incident report and filed it before leaving for the evening.

Commas also are used to separate words or phrases in a series. For example:

> The suspect is charged with trespassing, burglary, and assault.

Commas are used to separate **coordinate adjectives,** adjectives that equally modify the same noun. For example:

> The suspect was wearing a lightweight, gray, hooded sweater.

Commas are used with introductory adverbial phrases. For example:

> After receiving the call, the officers raced to the scene of the crime.

Commas are used to enclose **nonrestrictive** (or nonessential) phrases and clauses. These phrases are not essential to the basic meaning of the sentence. For example:

> The suspect, who is a local business owner, will be arraigned on Tuesday.

The phrase *who is a local business owner* is not essential to this sentence. It is merely giving the reader additional information.

Restrictive phrases, which are necessary to the meaning of the sentence, are not set off with commas. For example:

> The suspect who is wearing a red shirt is a local business owner.

The phrase *who is wearing a red shirt* implies that there is more than one suspect in this case. Therefore, the phrase becomes crucial to the reader's understanding.

Example:

Officers Harris Lopez and Frank were headed to the meeting but traffic delayed their arrival.

- **A.**   Officers Harris; Lopez; and Frank were headed to the meeting: but traffic delayed their arrival!
- **B.**   Officers Harris, Lopez, and Frank were headed to the meeting; but traffic delayed their arrival.
- **C.**   Officers Harris, Lopez, and Frank were headed to the meeting but traffic delayed their arrival.
- **D.**   Officers Harris, Lopez, and Frank were headed to the meeting, but traffic delayed their arrival.

The correct answer is **D**. This choice correctly uses commas to separate a series and to separate two independent clauses joined by a coordinating conjunction.

Semicolons

A **semicolon** is used to join two or more independent clauses that are not connected with a coordinating conjunction. In these situations, both clauses can stand alone as separate sentences. For example:

> Officer James was extremely tired; he just completed a 14-hour shift.

Semicolons also are used to separate groups of words or phrases that already contain commas. For example:

> The list of suspects includes Karen Weaver of Flint, Michigan; Percy Jones of Dayton, Ohio; and Jayden Smith of Pittsburgh, Pennsylvania.

Colons

A **colon** is used to introduce an element or series of elements that adds emphasis or further explains what has preceded the colon. For example:

> Paperwork is an important part of every police officer's job: It's tedious, but it has to be done.

A colon can also be used to introduce a list. For example:

> Officer Kendrick's emergency kit includes the following items: bandages, aspirin, extra batteries, a pocket knife, and tape.

Example:

The officers inspected the vehicle for the following items open containers of alcohol illegal drugs and unregistered firearms.

- **A.** The officers inspected the vehicle for the following items: open containers of alcohol, illegal drugs, and unregistered firearms.
- **B.** The officers inspected the vehicle for the following items, open containers of alcohol; illegal drugs; and unregistered firearms.
- **C.** The officers inspected the vehicle for the following items; open containers of alcohol, illegal drugs, and unregistered firearms.
- **D.** The officers inspected the vehicle for the following items open containers of alcohol, illegal drugs, and unregistered firearms?

The correct answer is **A.** This choice correctly uses commas to separate a series and uses a colon to introduce a list.

Practice

Directions (1–4): Choose the word or words that best complete the sentence.

1. Our police _____ fiftieth birthday is next week, so we've decided to throw him a surprise party.

   - **A.** chief
   - **B.** chiefs
   - **C.** chief's
   - **D.** chiefs'

2. Although high-speed police chases don't occur often, you _____ receive training on the EVOC course when you enter the police academy next month.

   - **A.** will
   - **B.** would
   - **C.** will have
   - **D.** would have

3. Officers Muncy and Pauley don't usually patrol together, but both of _____ partners took vacation days this week, and the lieutenant asked them to share a squad car.

   A. there
   B. they're
   C. their
   D. they are

4. According to your _____ statement, the suspect was last seen heading north on Belle Boulevard.

   A. witness
   B. witnesses
   C. witness'
   D. witness's

Directions (5–6): Answer the following questions solely on the basis of the information provided.

A recruit officer is preparing a report for a homework assignment. As she reads the report, she examines the following two sentences:

   I. A police officer needs to be aware of a family's cultural background when they enter the family's home.

   II. Sometimes a uniformed officer may suspect that a crime has occurred when the activities reported to police are actually part of a religious or cultural ritual or tradition.

5. Which of the following best describes the above sentences?

   A. Only sentence I is grammatically correct.
   B. Only sentence II is grammatically correct.
   C. Neither sentence I nor sentence II is grammatically correct.
   D. Both sentence I and sentence II are grammatically correct.

An academy instructor is reading a stack of papers his class turned in earlier in the day. As he reads one essay in particular, he encounters the following sentences:

   I. While searching for evidence, police officers, need to keep the Fourth Amendment in mind.

   II. The Fourth Amendment guarantees protection against unreasonable searches and seizures.

6. Which of the following best describes the above sentences?

   A. Only sentence I is grammatically correct.
   B. Only sentence II is grammatically correct.
   C. Neither sentence I nor sentence II is grammatically correct.
   D. Both sentence I and sentence II are grammatically correct.

Directions (7–8): Choose the answer that best fixes the sentence fragments.

7. The officers were grateful that the search took place without incident. Except for a small argument between the mother and her teenage son.

   A. The officers were grateful that the search took place without incident, except for a small argument between the mother and her teenage son.
   B. The officers were grateful that the search took place without incident; except for a small argument between the mother and her teenage son.
   C. The officers were grateful that the search took place without incident, but except for a small argument between the mother and her teenage son.
   D. The officers were grateful that the search took place without incident; however, except for a small argument between the mother and her teenage son.

8. While on a stakeout. Officer Schmidt watches a man matching her suspect's description attempt to enter the building through the side entrance.

   A. While on a stakeout and Officer Schmidt watches a man matching her suspect's description attempt to enter the building through the side entrance.
   B. While on a stakeout but Officer Schmidt watches a man matching her suspect's description attempt to enter the building through the side entrance.
   C. While on a stakeout; Officer Schmidt watches a man matching her suspect's description attempt to enter the building through the side entrance.
   D. While on a stakeout, Officer Schmidt watches a man matching her suspect's description attempt to enter the building through the side entrance.

Directions (9–12): Select the misspelled word in each sentence.

9. Officers Suarez and Verret receive a call conserning an altercation between two passengers on a bus traveling downtown.

   A. receive
   B. conserning
   C. altercation
   D. passengers

10. While patrolling a quiet neighborhood in the middle of the day, an officer sees a ladder propped against the side of a house and suspects that a burglery may be in progress.

    A. patrolling
    B. neighborhood
    C. suspects
    D. burglery

11. Officer Henry lead the suspect through the crowd of reporters.

    A. Officer
    B. lead
    C. suspect
    D. through

12. Officers Banks and Rogan past the station on the way to the traffic accident.

    A. past
    B. station
    C. way
    D. traffic

Directions (13–14): Choose the word or words that reflect an error in capitalization.

13. Police officers will set up sobriety checkpoints early on saturday morning in preparation for the Fourth of July.

    A. officers
    B. sobriety
    C. saturday
    D. Fourth of July

14. Officer Henderson responded to a call at 244 W. Franklin St. in glen cove.

    A. Henderson
    B. responded
    C. Franklin St.
    D. glen cove

Directions (15–16): Choose the sentence that corrects the error(s) in punctuation.

15. The police officers must take the suspect in for questioning but they need to stop for gas on the way to the station.

    A. The police officers must take the suspect in for questioning: but they need to stop for gas on the way to the station.
    B. The police officers must take the suspect in for questioning; but they need to stop for gas on the way to the station.
    C. The police officers must take the suspect in for questioning, but they need to stop for gas on the way to the station.
    D. The police officers, must take the suspect in for questioning but they need to stop for gas on the way to the station.

16. Officer James attended a meeting finished incident reports and interrogated a suspect before noon.

    A.   Officer James attended a meeting, finished incident reports: and interrogated a suspect, before noon.

    B.   Officer James attended a meeting: finished incident reports, and interrogated a suspect before noon.

    C.   Officer James attended a meeting, finished incident reports, and interrogated a suspect before noon.

    D.   Officer James attended a meeting finished; incident reports; and interrogated a suspect before noon?

Answers

1. **C** Since you have only one police chief with a birthday approaching, the singular possessive *chief's* is correct. Choice B is plural and choice D is a plural possessive; therefore, both are incorrect.

2. **A** The sentence implies that you'll be entering the police academy in the future, so you *will* receive training on the EVOC course. Choice C is incorrect because you aren't using the future perfect tense.

3. **C** Because the sentence refers to two officers, Muncy and Pauley, you need to use the plural possessive adjective *their*. The *partners,* in a sense, belong to the officers and the possessive adjective *their* modifies *partners.*

4. **D** As it appears, you have spoken to only one witness; therefore, the correct answer is *witness's,* the singular possessive. The statement belongs to the witness. This ownership eliminates choices A and B. Choice C is incorrect because it's missing the possessive *–s.*

5. **B** The recruit officer's first sentence is not grammatically correct. The subject doesn't agree with the pronoun used later in the sentence. The recruit officer mentions a single police officer but then uses the plural pronoun *they* later on. The sentence would be correct if the officer swapped *they* for the singular *his or her.*

6. **B** The first sentence in the essay the instructor is reading is not grammatically correct. After *police officers,* the student has placed an unnecessary comma. This causes the reader to pause and may lead to confusion. Removing the comma would make the sentence grammatically correct.

7. **A** The second sentence is a fragment that can easily be tacked on to the end of the first sentence, an independent clause, through the use of a comma. You don't need to add any words or phrases to these sentences to correct them. Choice A is correct.

8. **D** The first sentence is a fragment because it is not a complete thought or idea. You can add the fragment to the independent clause, the second sentence, by dropping the period and replacing it with a comma. Choice D is correct.

9. **B** The misspelled word is *conserning.* The correct spelling is *concerning.*

10. **D** The misspelled word is *burglery.* The correct spelling is *burglary.*

11. **B** The misspelled word is *lead.* The correct word is *led.*

12. **A** The misspelled word is *past.* The correct word is *passed.*

13. **C** The word *saturday* is a day of the week. These words are always capitalized.

14. **D** In this sentence, *glen cove* refers to a town, which should be capitalized.

15. **C** This sentence correctly uses a comma between two independent clauses joined by a coordinating conjunction.

16. **C** This sentence correctly uses commas in a series.

C. Writing

The police officer written exam tests your writing skills. Police officers need to have excellent writing skills to communicate important information to co-workers, superiors, lawyers, judges, and members of the media. Although paperwork may seem tedious, it's an important part of every police officer's job. Fortunately, the proper writing skills can help you complete reports in an efficient and timely manner.

For some questions, you have to read a completed incident report and answer the questions that follow in the space provided.

Because this section tests your writing skills, it's important that you answer all questions in complete, grammatically correct sentences. Even if you write down the correct answer on the police officer exam, you won't receive full credit unless that answer uses proper grammar, spelling, and punctuation.

In the following examples, answer the questions using complete, grammatically correct sentences.

Examples:

INCIDENT REPORT —— POLICE DEPARTMENT			
1. ADDRESS OF INCIDENT 252 Rio Rd.	2. OFFENSE Trespassing	3. CODE H1-9890	4. DATE 04/18
5. NAME OF VICTIM: INDIVIDUAL OR BUSINESS Janet Mandel		6. ADDRESS 252 Rio Rd.	PHONE 555-0607
7. ASSIGNED OFFICERS/BADGE NUMBERS Stephanie Salvatore	8. AGE OF VICTIM 43	9. RACE OF VICTIM White	10. VICTIM'S DATE OF BIRTH 05/31/1967
11. NAME OF SUSPECT Damon Gilbert		12. ADDRESS 814 Edward St.	

13. AGE 27	14. RACE White	15. SEX Male	16. DATE OF BIRTH 9/17	17. HEIGHT 5'10"	18. WEIGHT 165

19. HAIR Brown	20. EYES Brown	21. PHYSICAL DESCRIPTION Wearing jeans and a black sweatshirt

22. CHARGES Criminal trespass			
23. ITEM	24. BRAND	25. SERIAL NUMBERS	26. VALUE
27. ITEM	28. BRAND	29. SERIAL NUMBERS	30. VALUE
31. ITEM	32. BRAND	33. SERIAL NUMBERS	34. VALUE

35. *Stephanie Salvatore #1422*
SIGNATURE OF OFFICER/BADGE NUMBER

1. How much does the suspect weigh?

_____

The following is an example of a correct response:

The suspect weighs 165 pounds.

Note that this response not only offers the correct information but also uses proper grammar, spelling, and punctuation. The following are examples of incorrect responses:

- **165 pounds.** Although 165 pounds is correct, it would be marked as incorrect because it was not written as a complete sentence, and the directions explicitly say to use "complete, grammatically correct sentences." **_Remember:_** A complete sentence expresses a complete thought. It includes a subject and a verb, as well as proper punctuation and capitalization.
- **Suspect weighs 165 pounds.** This response would be considered incorrect because the word _the_ is missing.
- **The suspect weights 165 pounds.** This response is incorrect because the word _weights_ should be _weighs_.

2. Where did the incident take place?

_____

The following is an example of a correct response:

The incident took place at 252 Rio Rd.

The answer is given in the form of a complete sentence.

The following are examples of incorrect responses:

- **the incident took place at 252 Rio Rd.** This response would be marked as incorrect because it is missing proper capitalization. All complete sentences begin with a capital letter.
- **The icindent took place at 252 rio rd.** Spelling counts on this section of the exam. Responses must include proper spelling and capitalization of proper nouns.

Other questions on the police officer written exam test your ability to express information in a clear, concise manner. These questions often appear as multiple-choice questions that ask you to summarize notes from an incident so that others can understand what happened.

Examples:

Question 1 refers to the following information.

While on patrol, Officer Ramirez responded to a traffic accident. The following details were recorded at the scene:

Place of accident: Intersection of Eighth Street and Drinker Street
Time of accident: 4:15 p.m.
Vehicle involved: 2007 Toyota Prius

Driver: Jason Schwartz

Damage: Vehicle struck a fire hydrant after driver swerved to miss a dog, causing a large dent in the passenger-side door.

---

1. Officer Ramirez must complete a report of the incident. Which of the following expresses the above information most clearly, accurately, and completely?

   A. Driving a 2007 Toyota Prius, Jason Schwartz, at the intersection of Eighth Street and Drinker Street, struck a fire hydrant, causing a dent in the passenger-side door at 4:15 p.m.

   B. Jason Schwartz was the driver of a 2007 Toyota Prius. At 4:15 p.m., Schwartz hit a fire hydrant at the intersection of Eighth Street and Drinker Street. There is a dent in the passenger-side door.

   C. At 4:15 p.m., Jason Schwartz was driving a 2007 Toyota Prius at the intersection of Eighth Street and Drinker Street. He struck a fire hydrant, causing a dent in the passenger-side door.

   D. A 2007 Toyota Prius driven by Jason Schwartz struck a fire hydrant at the intersection of Eighth Street and Drinker Street at 4:15 p.m., causing a dent in the passenger side door.

The correct answer is **D**. This answer provides a clear and accurate summary of the incident. It uses simple wording to help the reader understand exactly what happened. The other answers provide accurate information but are written in such a way that they could confuse the reader. For example, the many commas in choice A make the sentence difficult to read; it sounds as if the dent occurred at 4:15 p.m. rather than the accident. In choice B, it is not clear that the Toyota Prius was involved in the accident; the details just say that Jason Schwartz drives this kind of car. In choice C, it isn't clear when Jason Schwartz struck the fire hydrant.

Question 2 refers to the following information.

While on patrol, Officer Johnson responds to a domestic abuse call. The following details were recorded at the scene:

Place of crime: 57 Sanford Ave.

Time of crime: 3:33 a.m.

Victim: Jessica Delaney

Crime: Assault

Suspect: Stefan Delaney

---

2. Officer Johnson must complete a report of the crime. Which of the following expresses the above information most clearly, accurately, and completely?

   A. Jessica Delaney was assaulted by Stefan Delaney at 57 Sanford Ave. at 3:33 a.m.

   B. At 57 Sanford Ave., at 3:33 a.m., Jessica Delaney was assaulted by Stefan Delaney.

   C. At 3:33 a.m., Stefan Delaney, at 57 Sanford Ave., assaulted Jessica Delaney.

   D. Jessica Delaney, at 57 Sanford Ave. at 3:33 a.m., was assaulted by her husband.

The correct answer is **A**. This answer provides all the necessary information in a clear and concise statement. The other answers are either confusing or do not provide all the necessary information. Choice B is not as clear as choice A because the details come before the subject of the sentence, Jessica Delaney. In choice C, it's unclear if the assault happened at 57 Sanford Ave. or if this is where Stefan Delaney lives.

Practice

Directions (1–5): Read the incident report and answer the questions using complete, grammatically correct sentences.

INCIDENT REPORT —— POLICE DEPARTMENT			
1. ADDRESS OF INCIDENT **1013 Adams Ave.**	2. OFFENSE **Burglary**	3. CODE **G9-0974**	4. DATE **07/06**
5. NAME OF VICTIM: INDIVIDUAL OR BUSINESS **Paul Jenkins**		6. ADDRESS **1013 Adams Ave.**	PHONE **555-0624**
7. ASSIGNED OFFICERS/BADGE NUMBERS **Rashad Wilson #1121**	8. AGE OF VICTIM **29**	9. RACE OF VICTIM **Black**	10. VICTIM'S DATE OF BIRTH **05/22/81**
11. NAME OF SUSPECT **Wendy Harris**		12. ADDRESS **271 Wyoming Ave.**	

13. AGE **27**	14. RACE **White**	15. SEX **Female**	16. DATE OF BIRTH **1/2**	17. HEIGHT **5'5"**	18. WEIGHT **135**

19. HAIR **Blonde**	20. EYES **Brown**	21. PHYSICAL DESCRIPTION **Wearing jeans and a blue sweater**

22. CHARGES
Burglary

23. ITEM **Cash**	24. BRAND	25. SERIAL NUMBERS	26. VALUE **$400**
27. ITEM **Watch**	28. BRAND **Rolex**	29. SERIAL NUMBERS	30. VALUE **$750**
31. ITEM **Guitar**	32. BRAND **Fender -Stratocaster**	33. SERIAL NUMBERS **XNF6677017**	34. VALUE **$500**

35. ___*Rashad Wilson #1121*___
SIGNATURE OF OFFICER/BADGE NUMBER

1. What is the value of the stolen guitar?

_____

2. What was the suspect wearing?

_____

3. What is the victim's address?

_____

4. What is the suspect's address?

_____

5. What is the name of the suspect?

_____

Directions (6–10): Read each set of notes and choose the answer that best summarizes the information.

Question 6 refers to the following information.

While on patrol, Officer Johnson responds to a burglary. The following details were recorded at the scene:

Place of crime: 72 W. Locust St.
Time of crime: 11:19 p.m.
Victim: Angelique Monroe
Crime: Burglary, purse stolen
Suspect: Unidentified

6. Officer Johnson must complete a report of the crime. Which of the following expresses the above information most clearly, accurately, and completely?

   A. A purse belonging to Angelique Monroe at 72 W. Locust St. at 11:19 p.m. was stolen by an unidentified suspect.
   B. An unidentified suspect at 72 W. Locust St. at 11:19 p.m. stole Angelique Monroe's purse.
   C. Angelique Monroe's purse was stolen by an unidentified suspect at 72 W. Locust St. at 11:19 p.m.
   D. At 72 W. Locust St. at 11:19 p.m., an unidentified suspect stole a purse.

Question 7 refers to the following information.

While on patrol, Officer Jamison responds to the scene of a traffic accident. The following details were recorded at the scene:

Place of accident: 22nd Street
Time of accident: 7:55 p.m.
Vehicle involved: 1989 Honda Civic
Driver: Dianna Chin
Damage: Vehicle crossed into the left lane, striking another vehicle. Both vehicles received extensive damage, but both drivers suffered only minor injuries.

7. Officer Jamison must complete a report of the incident. Which of the following expresses the above information most clearly, accurately, and completely?

   A. At 7:55 p.m., Dianna Chin was driving a 1989 Honda Civic on 22nd Street when she crossed into the left lane, striking another vehicle. Although both vehicles received extensive damage, both drivers suffered only minor injuries.

   B. Driving a 1989 Honda Civic at 7:55 p.m., Dianna Chin, crossed into the left lane on 22nd Street, striking another vehicle. Both vehicles received extensive damage. Both drivers suffered only minor injuries.

   C. On 22nd Street at 7:55 p.m., Dianna Chin, who was driving a 1989 Honda Civic, crossed into the left lane. Chin struck another vehicle. Both drivers suffered minor injuries, but the vehicles received extensive damage.

   D. Dianna Chin, who was driving a 1989 Honda Civic, crossed into the left lane on 22nd Street at 7:55 p.m.

Question 8 refers to the following information.

While on patrol, Officer Patterson responds to an assault. The following details were recorded at the scene:

Place of crime: 1251 Davis St.

Time of crime: 1:15 a.m.

Victim: James Sheppard

Crime: Assault

Suspect: Jack Ford

8. Officer Patterson must complete a report of the crime. Which of the following expresses the above information most clearly, accurately, and completely?

   A. At 1251 Davis St., at 1:15 a.m., Jack Ford assaulted someone.
   B. Jack Ford and James Sheppard were involved in an assault at 1:15 a.m.
   C. James Sheppard was assaulted at 1251 Davis St. at 1:15 a.m.
   D. At 1:15 a.m., James Sheppard was assaulted by Jack Ford at 1251 Davis St.

Question 9 refers to the following information.

While on patrol, Officer Fernandez responds to the scene of a traffic accident. The following details were recorded at the scene:

Place of accident: Intersection of Third Street and Rutter Avenue

Time of accident: 7:23 a.m.

Vehicle involved: 2004 Chevrolet Aveo

Driver: Patrick Hendricks

Damage: Vehicle struck a telephone pole, denting the front fender

9. Officer Fernandez must complete a report of the incident. Which of the following expresses the above information most clearly, accurately, and completely?

    A. A 2004 Chevrolet Aveo struck Patrick Hendricks causing a dent in the front fender at the intersection of Third Street and Rutter Avenue at 7:23 a.m.

    B. At 7:23 a.m., a 2004 Chevrolet Aveo driven by Patrick Hendricks struck a telephone pole at the intersection of Third Street and Rutter Avenue, denting the front fender.

    C. Patrick Hendricks, driving a 2004 Chevrolet Aveo at the intersection of Third Street and Rutter Avenue, struck a telephone pole and dented the front fender at 7:23 a.m.

    D. At the intersection of Third Street and Rutter Avenue at 7:23 a.m., driving a 2004 Chevrolet Aveo, Patrick Hendricks struck a telephone pole and dented his front fender.

Question 10 refers to the following information.

While on patrol, Officer Gilmore responds to a robbery. The following details were recorded at the scene:

    Place of crime: 37 River St.

    Time of crime: 8:19 a.m.

    Victim: Lea Finely, owner of River Street Bakery

    Crime: Robbery

    Suspect: An unidentified male wearing a baseball cap and a black sweater

10. Officer Gilmore must complete a report of the crime. Which of the following expresses the above information most clearly, accurately, and completely?

    A. An unidentified male wearing a baseball cap and a black sweater robbed Lea Finely, owner of the River Street Bakery, at 37 River St. at 8:19 a.m.

    B. At 37 River St. at 8:19 a.m., Lea Finely, wearing a baseball cap and a black sweater, was robbed by the owner of the River Street Bakery.

    C. At 8:19 a.m., the owner of the River Street Bakery was robbed by an unidentified male.

    D. At 37 River St., Lean Finely was robbed at 8:19 a.m.

Answers

1. **The value of the stolen guitar is $500.** This response correctly answers the question using a complete sentence.

2. **The suspect was wearing jeans and a blue sweater.** This response uses a complete sentence and provides the correct information.

3. **The victim's address is 1013 Adams Ave.** This response gives the victim's address using a complete, grammatically correct sentence.

4. **The suspect's address is 271 Wyoming Ave.** This response provides the necessary information in a complete and grammatically correct sentence.

5. **The name of the suspect is Wendy Harris.** This response uses a complete sentence to identify the suspect.

6. **C** This answer provides all the necessary information in a concise statement. Choices A and B are confusing. Choice D does not identify the victim.

7. **A** This answer summarizes all the necessary information in a way that is easy for the reader to understand. Choices B and C could confuse the reader. Choice D does not provide any information about the damage to the vehicles.

8. **D** This answer provides all the necessary information in a short, easy-to-read statement. Choices A, B, and C do not provide all the necessary information.

9. **B** This answer provides all the necessary information in a concise statement. Choices A, B, and C could confuse the reader.

10. **A** This answer provides all the necessary information. The other statements are either incomplete or confusing.

VI. Memorization and Visualization

Imagine that you're chasing a suspect. Suddenly, he jumps a fence and you lose sight of him. Do you remember what he looks like? Does he have any identifiable characteristics, such as tattoos or scars? What was he wearing? What is his body type?

Police officers must observe and recall details like these all the time. Aside from recalling facts about suspects, police officers must also be able to remember the names of streets, unique landmarks, phone numbers, and directions.

Some of the questions on the police officer exam test your memorization skills by asking you to answer questions based on details from a photograph. You'll have a certain amount of time to review the photo before answering the questions. It's important to note that you won't be able to refer to the photo again once your review time is up. On some tests, you're asked to seal a booklet of photographs with a sticker or hand in the photographs before answering the questions.

Other questions test your visualization skills by asking you to examine a row of buildings and then determine what they look like from behind.

Some questions ask you to interpret maps. You'll often be asked to find the shortest or quickest routes between two points in these types of questions.

Finally, spatial-orientation questions ask about directions. You may be asked to figure out which direction a suspect was last seen traveling, or you may have to select a diagram that illustrates the events that led to a motor-vehicle accident.

In this chapter, we show you how to hone your memorization and visualization skills so you're prepared to answer memorization and visualization questions on the police officer exam.

A. Memorization

Memorization questions on the police officer exam ask you to look at a photograph and memorize as many details as you can in a certain amount of time. You must then answer questions based on the photograph. You aren't allowed to take notes while examining the photograph and you can't look at the photograph when answering the questions.

The questions ask you about specific details in the photo. For example, you may be asked about a person's attire or the numbers on a particular building.

Tip: When memorizing details in a photograph, focus on the most important details and try to connect them to things in your life. For example, you may be wearing a color that is featured in the photograph. Making connections will help you remember the information.

Look closely at the photograph and try to take in as much as you can about it. What is in the photograph? What is happening in the photograph? What are the people in the photograph doing?

Think about the following questions when you examine the photograph:

- Are there people in the photograph?
- How many people are in the photograph?
- What are they wearing?
- Are they carrying any items?
- What are they doing?
- Are there buildings in the photograph?
- What is the order of the buildings?
- What are the shapes and colors of the buildings?
- How many floors does each building have?
- Are there any names or phone numbers in the photograph?
- Is there any additional writing in the photograph?
- Are there any vehicles in the photograph?
- What types of vehicles are in the photograph?
- What are the colors of the vehicles?
- Are there animals in the photograph?
- What types of animals are in the photograph?
- Where are the animals located?
- What are the animals doing?

In the following examples, study each photograph for ten minutes. Then cover the photograph and answer the questions that follow.

EXAMPLES:

Photo credit: CDC / Dawn Arlotta

---

1. How many people are in the photograph?

   A. 2
   B. 3
   C. 5
   D. 7

The correct answer is **B.** One middle-aged man and two young girls are in the photograph.

---

2. What is the girl on the right side of the photograph doing?

   A. Playing with a ball
   B. Painting the wall
   C. Jumping rope
   D. Riding a scooter

The correct answer is **D.** The girl on the right side of the photograph is riding a scooter, and the other girl is playing with a ball.

---

3. How many shelves are in the photograph?

   A. 1
   B. 2
   C. 3
   D. 5

The correct answer is **D.** The total number of shelves in the photograph is five. The man is placing an item on the fourth shelf from the bottom.

---

4. What is on the top shelf?

   A. A birdhouse
   B. A gas can
   C. A basketball
   D. A basket

The correct answer is **B.** There is a gas can on the top shelf. A birdhouse is on the third shelf from the bottom, a basketball is on the second shelf from the bottom, and a basket is on the bottom shelf.

---

5. What is hanging on the right side of the wall in the back of the garage?

   A. A lawn chair
   B. Children's toys
   C. A ladder
   D. Gardening tools

The correct answer is **A.** A lawn chair is hanging on the right side of the wall in the back of the garage.

How were your memorization skills? Did you answer all the questions correctly? If not, try another photograph. Remember to follow the tips mentioned earlier when studying the photograph.

EXAMPLES:

---

6. What is printed on the sign in the photograph?

    A.   VISITOR PARKING

    B.   CAR LOT

    C.   VISITORS CAR PARK

    D.   CAR PARK

The correct answer is **C.** The words VISITORS CAR PARK are printed on the sign on the right side of the photograph.

---

7. Which direction is the arrow on the sign pointing?

    A.   Left

    B.   Right

    C.   Up

    D.   Down

The correct answer is **B.** The arrow on the sign is pointing to the right.

---

8. What type of gate is at the entrance of the building?

    A.   Wooden

    B.   Barbed wire

    C.   Electric

    D.   Wrought iron

The correct answer is **D.** A wrought-iron gate is at the entrance of the building.

---

9. How many chimneys are visible on the main building?

    A.   2

    B.   4

    C.   5

    D.   6

The correct answer is **C.** Although the main building may have other chimneys, only five are visible in this photograph.

---

10. How many trees are in the photograph?

    A.   1

    B.   2

    C.   3

    D.   4

The correct answer is **A.** Several bushes are on the left side of the photograph, but only one tree is on the ride side of the photograph.

Practice

Directions (1–10): Answer the questions solely on the basis of the corresponding photograph. Study the photograph for ten minutes; then cover the photograph and answer the questions based on your memory.

Questions 1 through 5 refer to the following photograph.

1. How many floors does the building have?

    A. 1
    B. 2
    C. 3
    D. 4

2. What does the business on the left side of the photograph sell?

    A. Meat
    B. Video games
    C. Coffee
    D. Cellphones

3. Which way is the arrow on the sign pointing?

   A. Up
   B. Down
   C. Left
   D. Right

4. What is the approximate number of shops in the building?

   A. 25
   B. 50
   C. 75
   D. 100

5. All the following are located on the bottom floor, except:

   A. Restrooms
   B. An elevator
   C. Shops
   D. A restaurant

Questions 6 through 10 refer to the following photograph.

Photo credit: National Park Service

6. How many people are wearing baseball caps in the photograph?

   A. 1
   B. 3
   C. 5
   D. 6

7. What is hanging on the right side of the wall?

   A. Topographical maps
   B. Pictures of animals
   C. Portraits of U.S. presidents
   D. Meeting notes

8. How many people are in the photograph?

   A. 2
   B. 7
   C. 8
   D. 12

9. What type of shoes is the man on the right side of the photograph wearing?

   A. Sneakers
   B. Loafers
   C. Boots
   D. Sandals

10. What is on the chair in the foreground of the photograph?

   A. An umbrella
   B. A jacket
   C. A notebook
   D. A backpack

Answers

1. **C** The sign above the business says 3 FLOORS, so you can assume the building has three floors.

2. **A** The sign above the business on the left side of the photograph says MEAT. You can assume that the business sells meat.

3. **B** The arrow on the sign is pointing down.

4. **B** The writing on the sign indicates that there are over 50 shops to serve you, so you can assume there are about 50 shops in the building.

5. **D** The sign indicates that restrooms, an elevator, and shops are on the bottom floor. It does not indicate that there is a restaurant on the bottom floor.

6. **B** There are 12 people total in the photograph, and 3 of them are wearing baseball caps.

7. **A** Topographical maps are hanging on the right side of the wall. Pictures of animals, portraits of U.S. presidents, and meeting notes are incorrect.

8. **D** There are 12 people in the photograph. One person is standing and the rest are sitting around a table.

9. **D** The man on the right side of the photograph is wearing glasses, shorts, a T-shirt, and sandals. He is not wearing sneakers, loafers, or boots.

10. **B** There is a jacket on the chair in the foreground of the photograph.

B. Visualization

Imagine that you've been called to the scene of a domestic dispute. As you near the house, which is one unit in a row of town houses, you can hear screaming and glass breaking. Your partner knocks on the door and announces that he's a police officer. The noise in the house stops briefly and then picks up again. When no one comes to the door, your partner signals that he's going to kick it in. You head around back in case anyone flees from a window or rear exit.

When you get to the back of the row of town houses, you pause. You can no longer hear any noises from inside the home. How do you know which house you're supposed to be watching?

You have to envision the house from the front and picture what the houses on the street look like from the rear. Try to remember the color, the shape, and the location of the building from the end of the street. These details will help you recognize the building from the rear.

To answer some questions on the police officer exam, you have to envision what a diagram would look like from a different perspective. One of the ways to do this is to pay attention to the shape of the buildings from the front. Pick out the tallest or shortest building and memorize its position in the row. Noting the positions of wide or narrow buildings will also help.

Look at the following diagram. Pay attention to the size of the buildings and answer the accompanying example question.

Example:

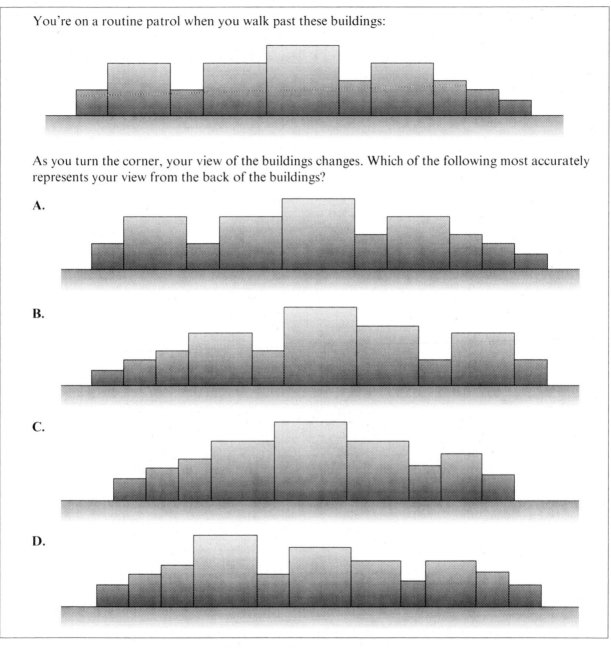

You're on a routine patrol when you walk past these buildings:

As you turn the corner, your view of the buildings changes. Which of the following most accurately represents your view from the back of the buildings?

A.

B.

C.

D.

The correct answer is **B.** Your view from the back should be the exact opposite of your view from the front. The buildings should be in the same order, but reversed. None of the bigger buildings should suddenly appear between the smaller ones, and none of the buildings should go missing. Choice B is correct because it shows the buildings in the correct order but reversed. Choice A is incorrect because it represents the view from the front of the building. Choice C is incorrect because it's missing a smaller building, and choice D is incorrect because it includes an extra building.

Tip: The fourth building from the left when you're facing the buildings from the front is the fourth building from the right when you're facing the buildings from behind.

Another way to answer these questions is to examine the rooftops of the buildings in the diagram. If the third house from the left has a pointed roof when you look at it from the front, then the third house from the right should also have a pointed roof when you view it from the rear. Pay attention to the shapes of the roofs, as well. Some may be half-roofs, while others may be full. Some roofs may be slanted to the right when looking at them from the front, so they should appear slanted to the left from the back.

Now, try an example question that includes buildings with roofs.

Example:

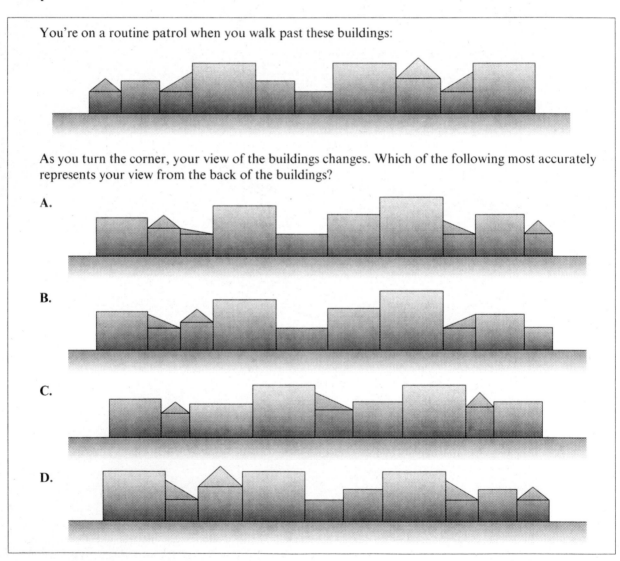

The correct answer is **D.** Your view from the back should be the exact opposite of your view from the front, so choice D is correct. In choice D, none of the roofs has been misplaced and the buildings are all in their original positions but reversed. The house that is the second from the left when you look at the buildings from the back is the second house from the right when you look at the building from the front. Choice A is incorrect because two of the buildings are in the wrong positions. Choice B is incorrect because the last building in the row is missing a roof. Choice C is incorrect because the last building in the row is missing.

As you work on the practice problems, remember to count the total number of buildings, pay attention to the size of each building, and look for defining features like roofs.

Practice

Directions (1–10): Answer the questions solely on the basis of the diagrams provided.

1. You're on a routine patrol when you walk past these buildings:

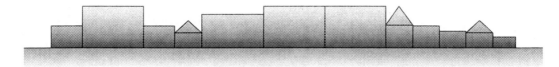

As you turn the corner, your view of the buildings changes. Which of the following most accurately represents your view from the back of the buildings?

A.

B.

C.

D.

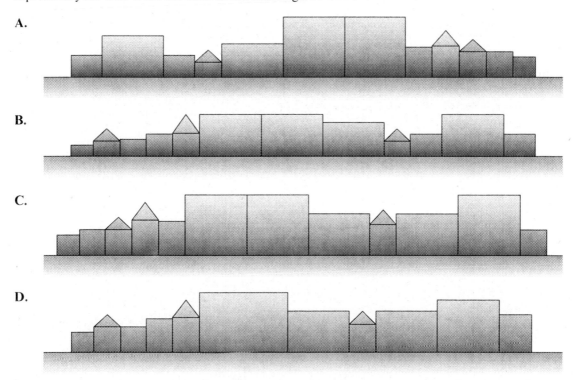

2. You're on a routine patrol when you walk past these buildings:

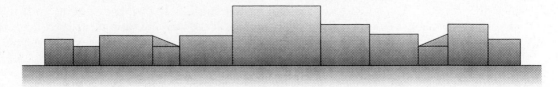

As you turn the corner, your view of the buildings changes. Which of the following most accurately represents your view from the back of the buildings?

A.

B.

C.

D.

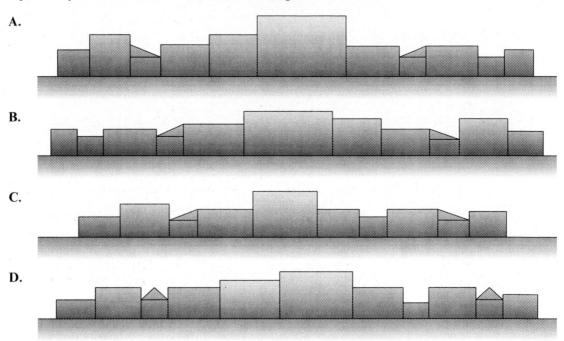

3. You're on a routine patrol when you walk past these buildings:

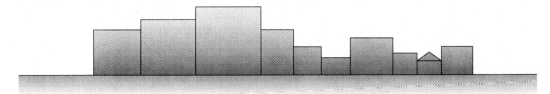

As you turn the corner, your view of the buildings changes. Which of the following most accurately represents your view from the back of the buildings?

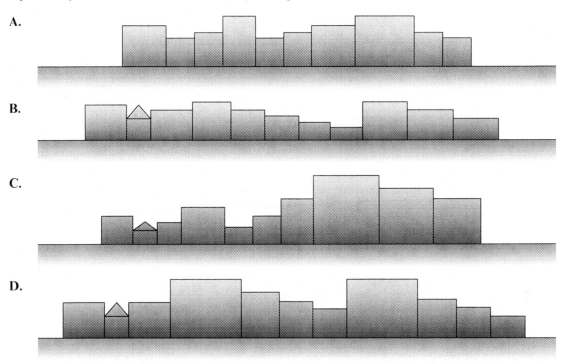

A.

B.

C.

D.

Answers

1. **B** Choice B presents an image that features the correct number of buildings, the correct placement of the buildings, and the correct number and placement of roofs. Choice A is incorrect because it is the view from the front of the street. The roofs in choice C are incorrect, and the image in choice D is missing a building.

2. **A** Choice A presents an image that features the correct number of buildings, the correct placement of the buildings, and the correct number and placement of roofs. Choice B is incorrect because it represents the view from the front of the street, but with the roofs flipped. Choice C is incorrect because it's missing a building, and choice D is incorrect because the image contains full roofs instead of half-roofs.

3. **C** Choice C presents an image that features the correct number of buildings, the correct placement of the buildings, and the correct number and placement of the roofs. Choice A is incorrect because the second building from the left is missing a roof. Choice B is incorrect because the buildings are in the wrong positions, and choice D is incorrect because an extra building is included in the image.

C. Map Reading

Every police officer exam includes a section on interpreting maps. Although many police officers know the streets they patrol on a daily basis, they still rely on maps and directions to help them find their way in unfamiliar neighborhoods.

You're probably wondering why anyone needs to be able to read a map when GPS is readily available in most modern vehicles and even on some cellphones. Although convenient for family vacations or out-of-town trips, GPS isn't always reliable or available. This is why map-reading skills are so important to police officers.

1. Directions

To read a map, the first thing you should do is locate the compass rose. The *compass rose* is a figure on a map that indicates the four main directions: north, south, east, and west. The areas between these directions represent northeast, southeast, southwest, and northwest. Almost all the map questions you'll encounter on the exam will include some type of direction you must follow. When you're given directions, you should visualize yourself moving through the area the map depicts.

Remember: When you're facing north, east will always be to your right. If you're moving south, however, east will be to your left. Beware of questions that ask you to turn south and make a right. You would think that the right turn would lead you east, but you'll really be traveling west. These types of questions can be especially challenging, so take your time.

2. Symbols

When you're interpreting a map, you need to pay attention to everything the map depicts, including symbols. Map symbols provide valuable pieces of information. Here are two types of symbols that you should always look for when reading a map:

- **Keys or legends:** If you see a symbol on a map and you're unsure what it means, look for a box in the corner of the map. This box is called the *key* or *legend.* Legends and keys for maps may include symbols that help you distinguish houses from apartment buildings, streetlights from stop signs, and even one-way streets from two-way streets. They also may include symbols for historical monuments or dead ends.
- **Directional cues:** Many maps include arrows indicating direction. As previously mentioned, a compass rose will help you distinguish which way is north, south, east, or west. Be sure to pay attention to how many arrows appear and in which direction they're pointing—you don't want to confuse a one-way street running west with a two-way street running east.

Sometimes numbers, rather than names, will represent points on a map. These maps are easy to read because there are fewer words to confuse and distract you. When you're looking for point 2, you know you're looking for a building with the numeral 2 on it, rather than a bank, a daycare, or Gerald's Perfect Pizza.

Now, try answering a few questions based on a map without words or phrases. Be sure to pay attention to the numbers on the buildings and the directions in which you must travel.

Examples:

Questions 1 through 5 refer to the following map.

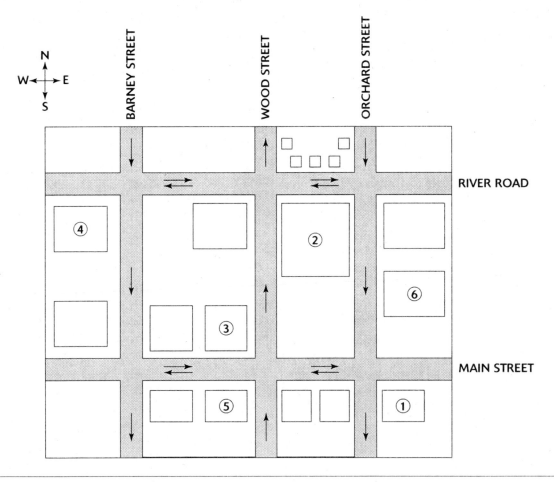

1. If you're at point 2, in which direction must you travel to reach point 4?

   A. North
   B. South
   C. East
   D. West

The correct answer is **D.** If you're at point 2 and you need to travel to point 4, you'll most likely travel west on River Road. There are plenty of different routes you may use to get there, but point 4 is generally located west of point 2.

2. You're traveling on Orchard Street and you need to respond to a burglary that occurred at point 4. Which of the following is the most direct route for you to take in your patrol car, making sure to obey all traffic regulations?

A. North on Orchard Street, west on River Road, south on Barney Street
B. South on Orchard Street, west on Main Street, north on Barney Street
C. South on Orchard Street, west on Main Street, north on Wood Street, west on River Road, south on Barney Street
D. North on Orchard Street, west on River Road, south on Wood Street, west on Main Street, north on Barney Street

The correct answer is **C**. Orchard, Wood, and Barney streets all run one way in varying directions, so you need to obey traffic patterns and regulations when traveling on them. The most direct route for you to take in your patrol car, making sure to obey all traffic regulations, is south on Orchard Street, west on Main Street, north on Wood Street, west on River Road, and south on Barney Street.

3. Starting at point 5, if you travel north on Wood Street, west on River Road, south on Barney Street, and east on Main Street, stopping at the intersection of Main and Wood streets, you'll find yourself between points:

A. 1 and 2
B. 1 and 6
C. 3 and 4
D. 3 and 5

The correct answer is **D**. Starting at point 5, if you travel north on Wood Street, west on River Road, south on Barney Street, and east on Main Street, stopping at the intersection of Main and Wood streets, you'll find yourself between points 3 and 5.

4. Starting at point 4, if you travel south on Barney Street, make a left and continue on that street for two blocks, which point are you closest to?

A. 1
B. 2
C. 3
D. 5

The correct answer is **A**. Starting at point 4, if you travel south on Barney Street and make a left, you'll be traveling east on Main Street. If you stay on this street for two blocks, you'll find yourself closest to point 1, which will be on your right side.

5. After responding to a domestic disturbance at one of the houses across from point 2, you receive instructions to respond to a mugging that took place behind point 1. Which of the following is the quickest route from point 2 to point 1?

A. East on River Road, south on Orchard Street
B. West on River Road, south on Orchard Street
C. West on River Road, south on Wood Street, east on Main Street
D. East on River Road, south on Barney Street, west on Main Street

The correct answer is **A.** Starting at point 2, if you travel east on River Road and south on Orchard Street, you'll reach point 1 in a shorter amount of time than you would traveling any other route on the map. Traveling south on Wood Street is illegal because it's a one-way street running north. Choices B and D are incorrect because you can't reach Orchard Street by traveling west from point 2, nor can you reach Barney Street traveling east from point 2.

3. Words

Symbols are extremely important when you're reading a map, but you need to be careful never to overlook words. As you saw in the last example, words on maps often provide specific information about the area that you can't get from studying symbols alone. The words that you'll see on the maps on the police officer exam will most likely include the names of streets and buildings. Here are some of the types of words you'll encounter on the test:

- **Captions:** A caption is a word, phrase, or sentence explaining the purpose of the map that includes additional information about streets, signs, or buildings depicted in the diagram. Captions may tell you the exact location of the map you're studying or may include a historical fact about the area.

- **Labels:** Labels are words or phrases that identify an item on a map, such as the name of a street or building. The label may be placed on top of or inside the image it represents. A line or arrow may extend from the label to a word that describes the item. Labels make it easy to find community facilities and businesses, such as Moe's Bike Shop, located at the intersection of Barney Street and Woodlawn Avenue.

Tip: Remember to pay close attention to both the name of a street and the direction in which traffic flows. Sometimes maps featuring labels instead of, or combined with, numbers may look crowded and confusing. Use your compass rose and visualize yourself moving through the area in your patrol car.

Try answering a few questions based on a map with words. The buildings will be labeled, as will the streets, so take your time and be sure to read the question and all your answer options completely before selecting an answer. Traffic flow is indicated by arrows, and you must follow the flow of traffic.

Examples:

Questions 1 through 5 refer to the following map.

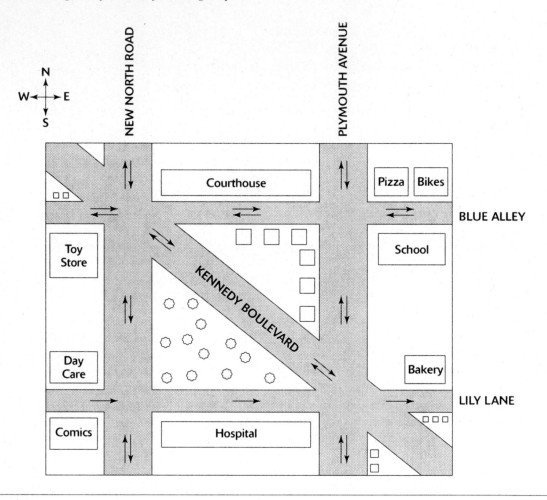

---

1. Starting at the bike shop, in which direction must you travel to reach the courthouse?

A. North

B. South

C. East

D. West

The correct answer is **D.** From the bike shop, you must travel west to reach the courthouse. Rely on your compass rose, located in the upper-left corner of this map, if you're not sure what direction you must travel.

2. You're traveling southeast on Kennedy Boulevard. If you were to bear left onto Lily Lane, what would you find yourself closest to?

   A. The bakery
   B. The hospital
   C. The day care
   D. The comic-book store

The correct answer is **A.** If you were to bear left onto Lily Lane while traveling southeast on Kennedy Boulevard, you would find yourself closest to the bakery. The hospital, day care, and comic-book store are all located on Lily Lane, but they aren't accessible at this point because Lily Lane is a one-way street running east. *Remember:* When traveling south, a right turn means you'll be traveling west, so a left turn will take you east.

3. You're instructed to escort a county judge from the hospital to the courthouse. He is in a hurry and asks you to take the most direct route. You should travel:

   A. West on Lily Lane, north on New North Road, west on Blue Alley
   B. East on Lily Lane, north on Plymouth Avenue, west on Blue Alley
   C. East on Lily Lane, north on Plymouth Avenue, east on Blue Alley
   D. West on Lily Lane, north on New North Road, east on Blue Alley

The correct answer is **B.** The most direct route from the hospital to the courthouse is to travel east on Lily Lane, north on Plymouth Avenue, and west on Blue Alley. You should know from the start that you can eliminate choices A and D because Lily Lane is a one-way street running east; therefore, you can't travel west using that street. Choice C is incorrect because turning east on Blue Alley instead of west would cause you to miss the courthouse entirely.

4. After responding to a theft at the toy store, you're instructed to patrol the surrounding area. Starting at the toy store, if you travel south on New North Road, east on Lily Lane, northwest on Kennedy Boulevard, east on Blue Alley, and south on Plymouth Avenue, which building will be on your right?

   A. The bakery
   B. The school
   C. The hospital
   D. The courthouse

The correct answer is **C.** If you travel south on New North Road, east on Lily Lane, northwest on Kennedy Boulevard, east on Blue Alley, and south on Plymouth Avenue, the building on your right side will be the hospital. As you travel south, the bakery and school will be on your left. The only way you'd reach the courthouse would be to travel north on Plymouth Avenue, not south.

5. Starting at the comic-book store, you travel east on Lily Lane and then make a left onto Plymouth Avenue. You make three more left turns and continue straight. What is on your left?

    A. The comic-book store
    B. The courthouse
    C. The day care
    D. The bakery

The correct answer is **D.** If you travel east on Lily Lane and then make a left onto Plymouth Avenue, you're now traveling north. The first left turn will take you west on Blue Alley. If you turn left again, you'll find yourself traveling south on New North Road. One final left turn will bring you back to traveling east on Lily Lane. If you continue straight on this street, you'll see the bakery on your left.

4. Finding the Shortest Route

As you've already seen in the previous example questions, the questions on the police officer exam often ask you to find the shortest or quickest route to a particular point. Many times, the question will begin with a scenario that tells you where your cruiser is located on the map. The scenario will also tell you where you must go. Read the entire scenario thoroughly, but pay special attention to the instructions or directions you're given rather than the reason you're traveling to that location. In a real emergency, details about the crime in progress will be critical, but on the police officer exam they're irrelevant. Regardless of whether you're responding to a burglary at Pistol Pete's or an aggravated assault at the corner of Carey Avenue and Market Street, you need to reach the location quickly and legally.

The first thing you have to do is find your starting point. When the question tells you that you're currently at point 1, find point 1 on the map. Next, figure out where you need to travel. If you have to respond to an emergency at point 4, find point 4 on the map. Now you know where you are and where you need to go. The next step is to find the shortest or quickest way to get there.

There are two ways to find the answers to these questions. The first way is to use the answer options given to you. Read each option carefully and test them out on the map. If you have difficulty envisioning yourself moving throughout the streets on the map, try using a prop such as a coin or an eraser. If you're not allowed to have props on your desk at the testing site, draw on the map. Use your pen or pencil to trace out the route. Eliminate any answer options that include illegal moves, such as traveling east on a one-way street that runs west or cutting through a parking lot. Of the remaining options, which route appears to be the shortest? That's your answer.

You also can answer these questions by tracing out a route without using the answer options. Once again, locate your starting point and your final destination. Now, obeying all traffic laws, trace the quickest route. When you think you've found it, compare your route with the answer options. If your solution is not among the choices, try again or work with the options available to you.

> **Tip: If choice A lists only two streets and choice B lists three, this doesn't automatically mean the route in choice A will be quicker than the route in choice B.**

These strategies also work with questions that ask you to determine which direction you're facing after making a series of turns. If you're told that you're driving east on George Avenue and you make a U-turn, followed by a right turn, you may be a bit confused at first. That's okay—just refer to your map and work your way through the question. Find your starting point, do a bit of drawing (lines, cars, people—whatever works for you), and you'll soon see that if you make a U-turn while traveling east, you'll be traveling west. If you make a right turn while traveling west, you'll be traveling north. This makes the process a little less confusing.

Use these strategies to answer the practice questions. Remember to take your time, read the questions and answer options thoroughly, and refer to the compass rose whenever necessary.

Practice

Directions (1–12): Answer the questions solely on the basis of the map provided. The flow of traffic is indicated by the arrows. You must follow the flow of traffic.

Questions 1 through 6 refer to the following map.

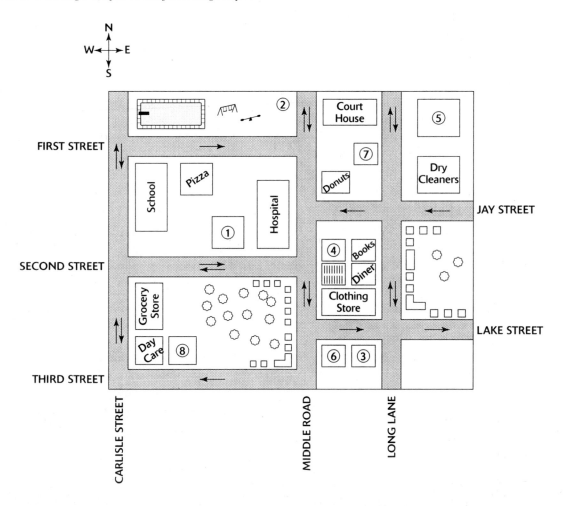

1. You're at the donut shop. In which direction must you first travel to reach the dry cleaners?

   A. North
   B. South
   C. East
   D. West

2. The quickest route from the day care to the pool and playground is:

   A. East on Third Street, north on Middle Road
   B. West on Third Street, north on Carlisle Street
   C. West on Third Street, north on Carlisle Street, east on Second Street, north on Middle Road
   D. East on Third Street, north on Middle Road, west on Second Street, north on Carlisle Street

3. While at the courthouse, you receive a report of a carjacking that took place in the parking lot between point 4 and the clothing store. Your cruiser is parked outside the easternmost entrance of the courthouse. Which of the following is the quickest route to the parking lot?

   A. South on Middle Road, east on Lake Street, north on Long Lane
   B. South on Long Lane, west on Lake Street, north on Middle Road
   C. South on Long Lane, west on Jay Street, south on Middle Road
   D. South on Middle Road, east on Jay Street, south on Middle Road

4. After patrolling the forested area behind the homes located on Second Street and Middle Road, you get in your police cruiser and travel west. You turn north on Carlisle Street and east on First Street before you turn south on to Middle Road. You stop at the second intersection and look to your left. You see:

   A. The donut shop
   B. The hospital
   C. The clothing store
   D. The diner

5. While at the bookstore, you receive a report of a fight outside the school. Obeying all traffic laws, which of the following routes will take you to the school in the least amount of time?

   A. North on Long Lane, west on Jay Street, north on Middle Road, west on First Street
   B. South on Long Lane, west on Lake Street, north on Middle Road, west on Second Street, north on Carlisle Street
   C. South on Long Lane, west on Lake Street, south on Middle Road, west on Third Street, north on Carlisle Street
   D. North on Long Lane, west on Jay Street, south on Middle Road, west on Second Street, north on Carlisle Street

6. Starting at point 5, you travel south and then make the first right. At the next intersection, you make a left, a right, and another right. After making two more right turns, you continue straight and then turn left. You stop at the next intersection. Which point is on your right?

    A. 1
    B. 3
    C. 5
    D. 7

Questions 7 through 12 refer to the following map.

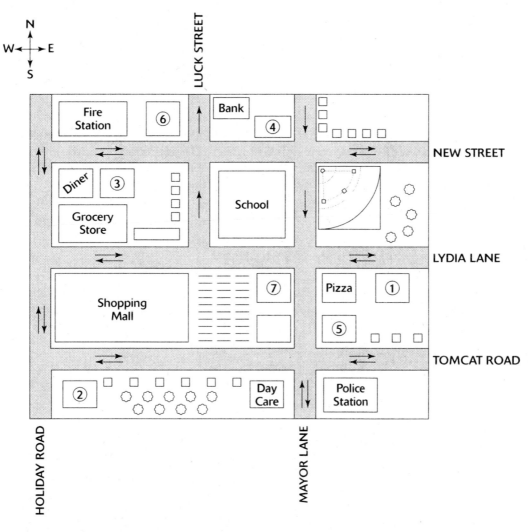

7. You would be most accurate if you stated that the fire station is located:

    A. East of the baseball field
    B. North of the pizza shop
    C. West of the shopping mall
    D. Northwest of the police station

8. Starting at point 2, if you travel north on Holiday Road for two blocks, make a right, and stop at the first intersection, which point is to your left?

    A. 4
    B. 5
    C. 6
    D. 7

9. The quickest route from the easternmost entrance of the day care to the westernmost entrance of the school is:

    A. North on Mayor Lane, west on New Street, south on Luck Street
    B. North on Mayor Lane, west on Lydia Lane, north on Luck Street
    C. North on Mayor Lane, west on Tomcat Road, north on Holiday Road, east on Lydia Lane, north on Luck Street
    D. North on Mayor Lane, west on Tomcat Road, north on Holiday Road, west on New Street, south on Luck Street

10. After patrolling the wooded area behind the houses on Tomcat Road, you decide to patrol the surrounding area in your cruiser. You start by traveling west on Tomcat Road and then make a right turn. You continue straight for two blocks before turning right and continuing through an intersection before making another right. You then make a left. What is nearest to you?

    A. The shopping mall
    B. The pizza shop
    C. The grocery store
    D. The day care

11. While parked in the lot between the shopping mall and point 7, you receive instructions to respond to a robbery at the bank. If you leave the parking lot from the southernmost exit, which of the following is the quickest route to the bank?

    A. West on Lydia Lane, north on Luck Street
    B. East on Lydia Lane, north on Mayor Lane
    C. West on Tomcat Road, north on Holiday Road, east on New Street, north on Luck Street
    D. East on Tomcat Road, north on Mayor Lane, west on New Street, north on Luck Street

12. Starting at the baseball field, you make a left onto Mayor Lane. You then make four consecutive rights and continue straight for one block. You then make a left. In which direction are you traveling?

    A. North
    B. South
    C. East
    D. West

Answers

1. **B** You must first travel south on Middle Road if you want to reach the dry cleaners. Although your ending point is located just down the street from the starting point, you can't travel east on Jay Street because it's a one-way street running west. To reach the dry cleaners, you must travel south on Middle Road, east on Lake Street, and north on Long Lane.

2. **B** The quickest route from the day care to the pool and playground is west on Third Street and north on Carlisle Street. You can immediately eliminate choices A and D since Third Street is a one-way street running west, which means you can't legally travel east using this street. Choice C will get you to your destination but will take longer than choice B.

3. **C** The quickest route from the easternmost entrance of the courthouse to the parking lot between point 4 and the clothing store is to travel south on Long Lane, west on Jay Street, and south on Middle Road. Choice A is incorrect because this would take you back to the courthouse. Since Jay Street is a one-way street running west, you can't travel east using it, so choice D is also incorrect. The route in choice B will take you to the parking lot, but it will take longer than the route in choice C.

4. **C** After patrolling the forested area behind the homes located on Second Street and Middle Road, you get in your police cruiser and travel west on Second Street. You turn north on Carlisle Street and east on First Street before you turn south onto Middle Road. If you stopped at the second intersection on Middle Road and looked to your left, you would see the clothing store. Since you're facing south, anything on your left would be on the easternmost part of the map.

5. **D** The shortest route from the bookstore to the school will require you to travel north on Long Lane, west on Jay Street, south on Middle Road, west on Second Street, and north on Carlisle Street. Choices A, B, and C are incorrect because Lake Street and First Street are both one-way streets running east; you can't legally travel west on these streets.

6. **B** Starting at point 5, you travel south (on Long Lane) and then make the first right (west on Jay Street). At the next intersection, you make a left (south on Middle Road), a right (west on Second Street), and another right (north on Carlisle Street). After making two more right turns (east on First Street and south on Middle Road), you continue straight for a while and then turn left (east on Lake Street). You stop at the intersection of Lake Street and Long Lane and see point 3 on your right.

7. **D** You would be most accurate if you stated that the fire station is located northwest of the police station. Although it would be somewhat accurate to state that the fire station is located north of the pizza shop, it would be more accurate to state that it's located northwest of the pizza shop, the day care, and the police station. It's also located north of the shopping mall and west of the baseball field.

8. **C** Starting at point 2, if you traveled north on Holiday Road for two blocks, made a right (onto New Street), and stopped at the first intersection (of New Street and Luck Street), point 6 would be on your left. If you stopped at the intersection of New Street and Mayor Lane, point 4 would be on your left.

9. **C** The quickest route from the easternmost entrance of the day care to the westernmost entrance of the school requires traveling north on Mayor Lane, west on Tomcat Road, north on Holiday Road, east on Lydia Lane, and north on Luck Street. You can't travel north on Mayor Lane beyond the intersection of Mayor Lane and Tomcat Road; the only portion of Mayor Lane that runs two ways is the part located between the day care and the police station. Instead, you must make a left onto Tomcat Road and travel from there. Choice D is incorrect because you can't travel south on Luck Street.

10. **B** You start by traveling west on Tomcat Road and then make a right turn (onto Holiday Road). You continue straight for two blocks before turning right (on New Street), continuing through an intersection, and making another right (onto Mayor Lane). You then make a left (onto Lydia Lane). The building closest to you is the pizza shop. Had you made a right onto Lydia Lane, the shopping mall would have been on your left and the grocery store would have been on your right.

11. **C** The quickest route from the southernmost exit of the parking lot behind the shopping mall to the bank is west on Tomcat Road, north on Holiday Road, east on New Street, and north on Luck Street. Had you left the parking lot from the northernmost exit, you would have been able to briefly travel west on Lydia Lane and turn north onto Luck Street.

12. **C** Starting at the baseball field, if you made a left (south) onto Mayor Lane and then made four consecutive rights (west, north, east, and south), you would have ended up on Mayor Lane once again. If you had continued straight for one block and then made a left, you would have been traveling east.

D. Spatial Orientation

Imagine that you're pursuing a suspect on foot. You're traveling north when the suspect makes a left turn. The suspect then makes a right turn and another left turn. Based on this information, in which direction are you traveling now?

The first thing to remember is that you start out traveling north. If you make a left turn, you're traveling west. If you turn right, you're traveling north again. If you make another left, you're traveling west, so west is the correct answer to the question. Knowing the direction that you started out traveling in will help you figure out the answers to questions like this one with little difficulty.

As a police officer, you must have a good sense of direction and excellent spatial-orientation skills. Spatial-orientation questions on the police officer exam test your ability to determine a location based on either a directional passage like the one above or a directional passage that gives you four diagrams to choose from as your answer choices.

The following sections review what you need to know to succeed on this portion of the police officer exam.

1. Directional Passages

Directional passages are just like the reading-comprehension passages in Chapter V. To solve spatial-orientation questions based on directional passages, read the passage and use the information in the passage to answer the question that follows.

Tip: Use a compass rose and sketch out a map on scrap paper using the information from the passage.

Examples:

---

1. While questioning a crime victim, you're told that suspect 1 grabbed the victim from behind and covered her mouth as suspect 2 took her purse. Both suspects then headed north. The victim chased the pair for two blocks. Suspect 1 stopped and got into a vehicle that turned left. Suspect 2 stayed on foot and turned right.

   According to the information in the passage, you would be most correct if you reported that suspect 1 was last seen traveling:

   A.   North
   B.   South
   C.   East
   D.   West

The correct answer is **D.** If suspect 1 had originally been running north and was last seen in a car that turned left, then it would be most correct to report that he was last seen traveling west. If you look at a compass rose, you would see that west is on the left side of the compass.

---

2. While questioning a witness to a robbery, you're told that the suspect shoved the victim against a car and then ran down the street, heading south. He slipped through a busy intersection, ran two more blocks, and then turned right, disappearing around the corner of a brick building.

   According to the information you received, you would be most correct if you reported that the suspect was last seen traveling:

   A.   North
   B.   South
   C.   East
   D.   West

The correct answer is **D.** If the suspect was last seen turning right after originally running south, then it would be most correct to report that the suspect was last seen traveling west. If you're heading south, east is always on your left and west is always on your right.

---

3. You're traveling north while pursuing a suspect on foot. You follow as the suspect makes two right turns and then a left turn.

   According to the information in the passage, in which direction are you traveling now?

   A.   North
   B.   South
   C.   East
   D.   West

The correct answer is **C.** If you're facing north and you stick out your right hand, it'll point east. If you're facing south and you stick out your right hand, it'll point west. In this case, if you followed the suspect traveling north and then took two right turns, you would be traveling south.

4. While speaking with a witness at the scene of a crime, you're told that the suspect left a computer store carrying two laptops. The suspect, a black male, headed east and got into a cab. The cab turned left and then right before the witness lost track of it.

   According to the information you received, you would be most correct if you reported that the suspect was last seen traveling:

   A. North
   B. South
   C. East
   D. West

The correct answer is **C**. The cab was originally traveling east. If the cab turned left and then right, it would be most correct to report that the cab was last seen traveling east.

5. You're investigating a robbery. The crime victim tells you that the suspect held a knife to her throat as she was walking to her car. The suspect, a white female, then demanded cash from the victim. After the victim handed over her purse, the suspect headed west. A witness chased the suspect, who made two left turns and then a right turn. The witness then lost sight of the suspect.

   According to the information you received, you would be most correct if you reported that the suspect was last seen traveling:

   A. North
   B. South
   C. East
   D. West

The correct answer is **B**. If the suspect was originally running west and then took two left turns and then a right turn, it would be most correct to report that the suspect was last seen traveling south.

2. Directional Passages with Diagrams

Directional passages with diagrams are just like the directional passages in the preceding section, except that the answer choices are diagrams instead of directions. To solve spatial-orientation questions based on directional passages with diagrams, read the passage and use the information in the passage to choose the diagram that correctly answers the question that follows.

Tip: Use the compass rose provided along with the information from the passage to answer these types of questions.

Examples

1. Officer Hernandez responds to the scene of a motor-vehicle accident on May Street and River Road. The man driving vehicle 1 tells the officer that he was traveling east on May Street when vehicle 2, traveling south on River Road, failed to stop at a stop sign and continued straight through the intersection. Vehicle 2 hit vehicle 1 in the intersection. Vehicle 1 was then struck from behind by vehicle 3.

   Which diagram is most consistent with the driver's statement?

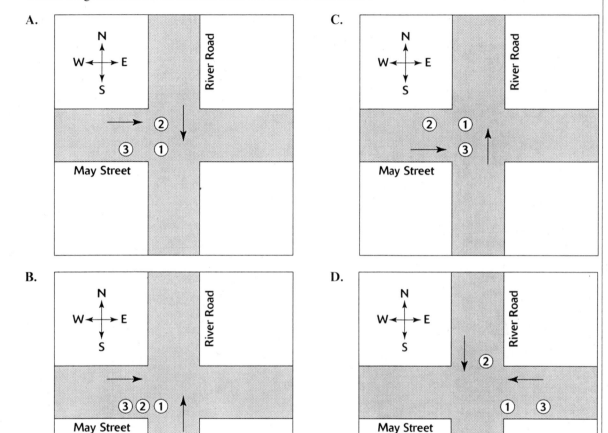

The correct answer is **A.** This diagram correctly shows the directions in which the vehicles were traveling. Although choice D may look correct, vehicle 1 is traveling west in this diagram, not east as indicated in the passage.

2. Officer Chin responds to the scene of a motor-vehicle accident on Pringle Street and Curtis Lane. The woman driving vehicle 1 tells the officer that she was traveling north on Pringle Street when vehicle 2, traveling west on Curtis Lane, failed to stop at a stop sign and continued straight through the intersection. Vehicle 2 hit vehicle 1 and caused vehicle 1 to hit vehicle 3, which was traveling east on Curtis Lane.

Which diagram is most consistent with the driver's statement?

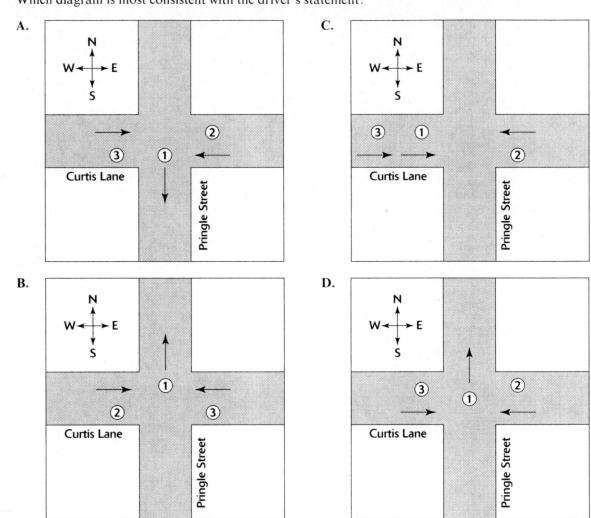

The correct answer is **D.** This diagram correctly shows the directions in which the vehicles were traveling. Although choice A may look correct, vehicle 1 is traveling south in this diagram, not north as indicated in the passage.

Practice

Directions (1–10): Answer the questions solely on the basis of the corresponding passages.

1. While questioning a crime victim, you're told that the suspect grabbed the victim's purse and then headed south. The crime victim chased the suspect for three blocks. The suspect made a left turn and then a right turn. The victim then lost sight of the suspect.

   According to the information in the passage, you would be most correct if you reported that the suspect was last seen traveling:

   A. North
   B. South
   C. East
   D. West

2. While speaking with a witness at the scene of a crime, you're told that the suspect left a jewelry store clutching a diamond necklace. The suspect, an Asian female, headed west and then turned left before getting on the subway.

   According to the information you received, you would be most correct if you reported that the suspect was last seen traveling:

   A. North
   B. South
   C. East
   D. West

3. You're traveling east while pursuing a suspect on foot. You follow as the suspect makes a right turn and two left turns.

   According to the information in the passage, in which direction are you traveling now?

   A. North
   B. South
   C. East
   D. West

169

4. While questioning a crime victim, you're told that suspect 1 held a gun to the victim as suspect 2 took the victim's wallet and watch. Both suspects then headed west after robbing the victim. A witness chased the suspects for one block and watched as suspect 1 made a right turn. Suspect 2 got into a cab, which then turned right.

According to the information in the passage, you would be most correct if you reported that suspect 1 was last seen traveling:

A. North
B. South
C. East
D. West

5. You're traveling north in pursuit of a suspect. You follow as the suspect makes three left turns. You lose him at the subway station.

According to the information in the passage, in which direction are you traveling now?

A. North
B. South
C. East
D. West

6. While questioning a crime victim, you're told that the suspect held a knife to the victim's neck and demanded her purse. After grabbing the purse, the suspect headed east. The crime victim chased the suspect for six blocks. The suspect then made two right turns before hopping in a cab that turned left.

According to the information in the passage, you would be most correct if you reported that the suspect was last seen traveling:

A. North
B. South
C. East
D. West

7. While speaking with a witness, you're told that the suspect was last seen running north from the scene of the crime. The suspect turned left and then right before getting on the subway.

According to the information you received, you would be most correct if you reported that the suspect was last seen traveling:

A. North
B. South
C. East
D. West

8. Officer Cullen responds to the scene of a motor-vehicle accident on James Street and Laurel Lane. The man driving vehicle 2 tells the officer that he was traveling east on James Street when vehicle 1, which was traveling north on Laurel Lane, cut across the intersection. This caused vehicle 2 to hit vehicle 1. Vehicle 2 was then was struck from behind by vehicle 3.

Which diagram is most consistent with the driver's statement?

A.

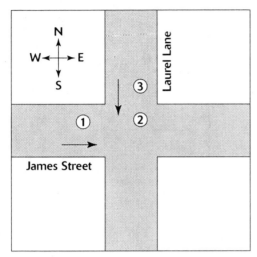

C.

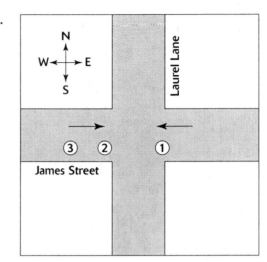

B.

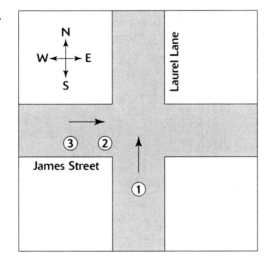

D.

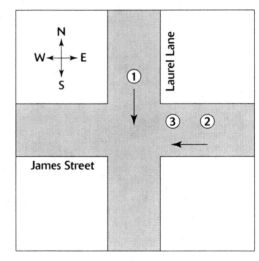

9. Officer Kellogg responds to the scene of a motor-vehicle accident on State Boulevard and Swing Way. The woman driving vehicle 2 tells the officer that she was traveling east on Swing Way when vehicle 1, which was traveling south on State Boulevard, failed to stop at a stop sign and continued straight through the intersection. Vehicle 2 hit vehicle 1. This caused vehicle 1 to hit vehicle 3, which was traveling west on Swing Way.

Which diagram is most consistent with the driver's statement?

A.

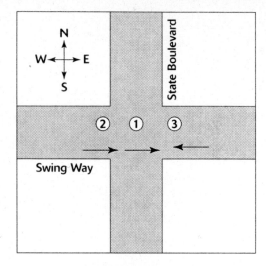

B.

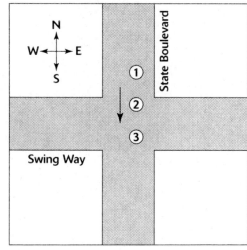

C.

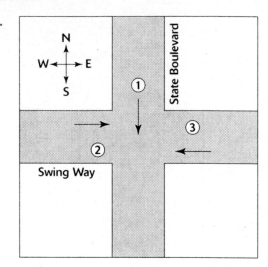

D.

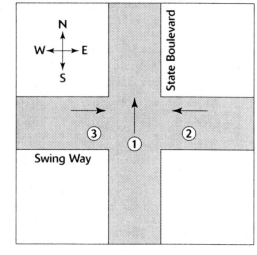

10. Officer Sully responds to the scene of a motor-vehicle accident on Benedict Street and Wyoming Avenue. The man driving vehicle 2 tells the officer that he was traveling south on Benedict Street when vehicle 1, traveling east on Wyoming Avenue, cut across the intersection. This caused vehicle 2 to hit vehicle 1. Vehicle 2 was then struck from behind by vehicle 3.

Which diagram is most consistent with the driver's statement?

A.

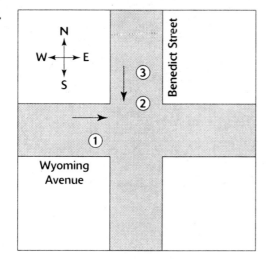

C.

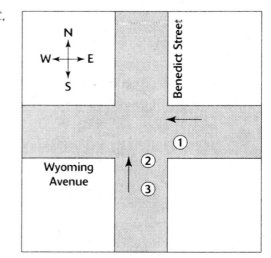

B.

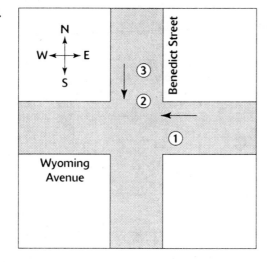

D.

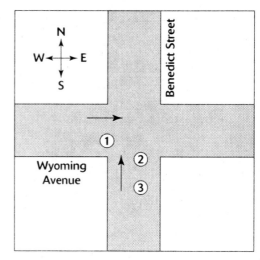

Answers

1. **B** If the suspect was last seen turning right and had originally been running south, then it would be most correct to report that the suspect was last seen traveling south. The suspect started out traveling south, then turned left and was traveling east, then turned right and was last seen traveling south again.

2. **B** If the suspect was last seen turning left after originally traveling west, it would be most correct to report that the suspect was last seen traveling south.

3. **A** If you're traveling east and you make a right, you're now traveling south. If you then make a left, you're traveling east again. If you turn left again, you're traveling north.

4. **A** If suspect 1 had originally been running west and was last seen turning right, then it would be most correct to report that the suspect was last seen traveling north.

5. **C** If you're traveling north and then make three left turns, you would be traveling east.

6. **B** The suspect was originally running east and then made two right turns. If the suspect was last seen getting into a cab that turned left, then it would be most correct to report that the suspect was last seen traveling south.

7. **A** If the suspect was last seen turning left and then right after originally traveling north, it would be most correct to report that the suspect was last seen traveling north.

8. **B** The diagram in choice B correctly shows the directions in which the vehicles were traveling. Choice D may look correct, but vehicle 1 is traveling south in this diagram, not north as indicated in the passage.

9. **C** The diagram in choice C correctly shows the directions in which the vehicles were traveling. Choice D may look correct, but vehicle 2 is traveling west in this diagram, not east as indicated in the passage.

10. **A** The diagram in choice A correctly shows the directions in which the vehicles were traveling. Choice B may look correct, but vehicle 1 is traveling west in this diagram, not east as indicated in the passage.

VII. Mathematics

You respond to the scene of a home burglary. The homeowner tells you that his watch, valued at $500, and his wedding band, valued at $1,000, are missing. He also tells you that $2,500 in cash and his wife's diamond earrings, valued at $1,500, were taken from a safe in the bedroom. You record the missing items in your notes and return to the police station to fill out an incident report. While you're filling out your report, the homeowner calls to inform you that he found his wife's earrings, but noticed that two of his wife's necklaces are missing. They're valued at $500 each. You include the value of the missing necklaces in your report and subtract the value of the earrings.

Police officers use basic math skills every day in a variety of situations. Even if you're using a calculator, you need to know when to add, subtract, multiply, and divide. You also need to know how to solve problems involving averages, decimals, percentages, fractions, time, circumference, area, and ratios. The math section of the police officer exam features multiple-choice questions based on real-life situations that you could face on the job. These questions focus on basic equations that can be solved without the aid of a calculator. Don't worry if math isn't one of your strong suits. In this chapter, we review basic math skills and explain how to solve the math problems you may encounter on the police officer exam.

A. Addition and Subtraction

Addition and subtraction questions on the math section of the police officer exam may ask you to determine the total value of stolen items or calculate the total distance traveled during the course of a day. Most of these questions involve the use of basic addition and subtraction skills. In this section, we review the skills you need to succeed on this portion of the exam.

1. Addition

Addition questions on the police officer exam often ask you to solve problems involving a total number of miles, minutes, values, or feet. These types of problems usually appear as a word problem or a passage that contains critical information, such as numbers or key words, to help you solve the problem. Some key words used in addition problems include *all together, greater, more, sum,* and *total.* These key words should indicate that you must use addition to solve the problem.

Unless you're working with negative numbers, note that the *sum* (total) of the numbers in an addition problem should always be greater than the *addends* (numbers added together). For example, suppose you're asked to determine how many bottles of soda were stolen from two food stands at the fair. You're told that four bottles of soda were taken from one stand and three bottles were stolen from another stand. Before you even begin to solve the problem, you can eliminate any answer choices that contain the numbers 4, 3, 2, or 1 because the sum must be greater than the addends (4 and 3). To solve this question, you would use addition: 4 + 3 = 7.

Try a few addition questions on your own. ***Remember:*** You can eliminate any answer choices that are less than or equal to the addends.

Examples:

Questions 1 and 2 refer to the following information.

While preparing a report on a burglary at a coffee shop, Officer Patrice lists the following stolen items and their values:

> Coffee: $300
>
> Espresso machine: $1,200
>
> Cash: $500

---

1. What is the total value of the stolen items?

   A. $500
   B. $750
   C. $1,000
   D. $2,000

The correct answer is **D.** The total value of the stolen items is $2,000. To find the total value of the stolen items, add the values of the coffee, espresso machine, and cash: $300 + $1,200 + $500 = $2,000. You also can solve this problem without adding by automatically eliminating choices A, B, and C because these choices are less than the highest addend ($1,200).

---

2. What is the total value of the stolen items except for the cash?

   A. $500
   B. $1,200
   C. $1,500
   D. $2,000

The correct answer is **C.** The total value of the stolen items except the cash is $1,500. To find the total value of the stolen items except for the cash, add the values of the coffee and espresso machine: $300 + $1,200 = $1,500. You can automatically eliminate choices A and B because these choices are less than or equal to the highest addend ($1,200).

Tip: Remember to look out for words such as *except* when answering these types of questions. If you missed this word when answering question 2, you might have added all the values and answered the question incorrectly.

3. During the past three days, Officer McCarthy worked on old incident reports. The first day, he finished two reports before lunch and nine after lunch. The second day, he completed five reports before lunch and seven reports after lunch. The third day, he finished ten reports before lunch and six after lunch. How many reports did he write during the past three days?

A. 10
B. 22
C. 34
D. 39

The correct answer is **D.** Officer McCarthy completed 39 incident reports during the past three days. To find the total number of reports Officer McCarthy worked on during the past three days, add the number of reports completed each day before and after lunch: 2 + 9 + 5 + 7 + 10 + 6 = 39.

2. Subtraction

Subtraction questions on the police officer exam are similar to addition questions. Instead of being asked to combine values to determine a total, you're asked to remove numbers from a total. These types of questions also appear as word problems that contain numbers or key words that help you determine the answer to the question. Some of the key words used in subtraction problems are *difference, fewer, left over, less,* and *remain.* These words tell you that you must use subtraction to solve the problem.

Use common sense when solving subtraction problems. If you're asked to subtract, your *difference* (the answer to a subtraction problem) should not be greater than your *minuend* (largest number). Go back to the stolen soda example in the addition section. If seven sodas were stolen, and four were from one stand, then the number of missing sodas should not be greater than seven. You can eliminate any answer choices that are larger than the minuend.

Now, try a few subtraction questions. ***Remember:*** You can eliminate any answer choices that are greater than the minuend.

Examples:

1. During a typical work week, Officer Munez drives his police cruiser approximately 1,500 miles, which is about 300 miles a day. Officer Munez called in sick on Tuesday and only worked four days this week. About how many miles did Officer Munez drive this week?

A. 1,000 miles
B. 1,200 miles
C. 1,500 miles
D. 1,800 miles

The correct answer is **B.** Officer Munez drove 1,200 miles this week. Since Officer Munez didn't work on Tuesday, he only drove his police cruiser for four days this week. To solve this problem, you have to subtract the miles he would have driven on Tuesday from the number of miles he typically drives in one week: 1,500 miles – 300 miles = 1,200 miles. You can automatically eliminate Choice D because this choice is larger than the minuend (1,500).

Did you notice that this example used the word *total?* Addition questions aren't the only types of questions that ask you to find totals. This is why it's important to read each passage carefully when answering mathematics questions. Don't rely solely on key words when determining which operation you should use to solve a problem. Make sure you understand what you're being asked to find before attempting to answer the question.

---

2. Officer Johnson patrols a particular neighborhood known for high crime rates 50 times each work week, which is about 10 times per day. Officer Johnson was asked to complete some paperwork on Thursday, so he didn't patrol the neighborhood that day. How many times did he patrol the neighborhood this week?

 A. 30
 B. 40
 C. 50
 D. 60

The correct answer is **B.** Officer Johnson patrolled the neighborhood 40 times this week. Since Officer Johnson didn't patrol the neighborhood on Thursday, and he normally patrols it 10 times a day, subtract 10 patrols from his total number of weekly patrols: 50 – 10 = 40.

After responding to a home burglary, Officer Lenore lists the following stolen items and their values:

   Wedding band: $150
   Watch: $350
   Stamp collection: $1,000
   Laptop computer: $450
   TOTAL: $1,950

---

3. What is the total value of the stolen items except for the laptop computer?

 A. $1,500
 B. $1,600
 C. $1,700
 D. $1,800

The correct answer is **A.** The total value of the stolen items except for the laptop computer is $1,500. To solve this problem using simple subtraction, subtract the value of the laptop computer from the total value of all the stolen items: $1,950 – $450 = $1,500.

3. Time

Police officers need to know how to tell time. Now, you might wonder why the police officer exam would include questions on telling time when you can just look at a clock, watch, or cellphone and read the time. Being able to read the time on a clock is simple, but calculating increments of time is slightly more complex.

Police officers must perform these types of operations to determine how many hours they work during a shift or how long it takes to travel from point A to point B.

Questions involving time on the police officer exam aren't that different from addition or subtraction problems. These types of questions usually ask you to determine how many extra or fewer hours or minutes a police officer has worked in a particular day or week. These types of questions usually ask about 15-minute increments of time.

Remember: There are four 15-minute intervals in 60 minutes and 60 minutes in 1 hour. A typical work week usually consists of 40 hours worked over 5 days, which averages out to about 8 hours a day.

Now, try a few example questions regarding time.

Examples:

---

1. Officer Muldoon usually works from 11 p.m. to 7 a.m., five days a week. His supervisor asks him to report for duty at 9 p.m. every day this week. At the end of the week, how many hours of overtime will Officer Muldoon have worked?

   A. 4 hours
   B. 6 hours, 30 minutes
   C. 10 hours
   D. 12 hours, 30 minutes

The correct answer is **C.** At the end of the week, Officer Muldoon will have worked 10 hours of overtime. To solve this problem, you must use both subtraction and addition. Officer Muldoon is asked to come in at 9 p.m. instead of 11 p.m. every day this week. Use subtraction to determine how many extra hours he works each day: $11 - 9 = 2$ hours. Then, use addition to determine how many additional hours he will work over the course of five days: $2 + 2 + 2 + 2 + 2 = 10$ hours.

Tip: Time questions also can be solved using multiplication skills. In the preceding problem, you can multiply the number of hours Officer Muldoon is asked to come in early each day (2 hours) by the number of days worked in a week (5 days): $2 \times 5 = 10$. You'll read more about multiplication skills later in this chapter.

---

2. Officer Jackson usually works from 9 a.m. to 5 p.m., five days a week. His supervisor asks him to report to work at 8:30 a.m. on Monday, Wednesday, and Friday of this week to relieve an officer who needs to leave early. At the end of the week, how many hours of overtime will Officer Jackson have worked?

   A. 1 hour, 30 minutes
   B. 2 hours
   C. 2 hours, 30 minutes
   D. 3 hours

The correct answer is **A.** If Officer Jackson comes in 30 minutes early on Monday, Wednesday, and Friday, he will have worked 1 hour, 30 minutes of overtime at the end of the week: $30 + 30 + 30 = 90$ minutes and because there are 60 minutes in an hour, the answer is 1 hour, 30 minutes.

3. Officer Mortimer usually works from 4 p.m. to 12 a.m., five days a week. Her supervisor asks her to report to work at 2:15 p.m. on Tuesday and Thursday for two training sessions before the start of her shift. At the end of the week, how many hours of overtime will Officer Mortimer have worked?

    A.   1 hour, 30 minutes

    B.   2 hours

    C.   3 hours, 30 minutes

    D.   3 hours

The correct answer is **C.** If Officer Mortimer comes in at 2:15 p.m. two days this week, she will have worked 3 hours, 30 minutes of overtime at the end of the week: 1 hour, 45 minutes + 1 hour, 45 minutes = 3 hours, 30 minutes.

4. Perimeter

The perimeter of an object is the total distance around the outside of the object. Determining the perimeter of an object requires addition and subtraction skills. These types of problems on the police officer exam will present you with either a passage or a diagram containing all the information you need to solve the problem, including a formula.

Here are a few of the perimeter formulas you may see on the police officer exam:

Shape	Formula
Square	Perimeter = length + length + length + length ($P = l + l + l + l = 4l$)
Rectangle	Perimeter = length + length + width + width ($P = l + l + w + w = 2l + 2w$)
Triangle	Perimeter = the lengths of the three sides ($P = a + b + c$)

> **Tip: The perimeter of a circle is called the circumference. Circumference is covered later in this chapter.**

For example, to find the perimeter of a square that has sides with a length of 2, you use the formula $P = l + l + l + l$. Plug in the values: $P = 2 + 2 + 2 + 2$, so $P = 8$. You can also find this number easily using multiplication: $P = 4l = 4 \times 2 = 8$.

Occasionally, you'll be given the perimeter of an object and asked to find the length or width. For example, a rectangle's perimeter is 60 feet and its width is 18 feet. Using the equation $P = l + l + w + w$, plug in the values: $60 = l + l + 18 + 18$ or $60 = l + l + 36$. To solve for l, subtract 36 from both sides: $60 - 36 = l + l + 36 - 36$, so $24 = 2l$. Next, divide each side by 2: $24 \div 2 = 12$.

Now, try a few questions that require you to find the perimeter of an object.

Examples:

---

1. Find the perimeter of the triangle shown below using the formula $P = a + b + c$.

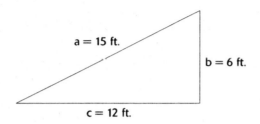

a = **15 ft.**

b = **6 ft.**

c = **12 ft.**

    A.   18 feet
    B.   27 feet
    C.   33 feet
    D.   48 feet

The correct answer is **C**. The perimeter of the triangle is 33 feet. To find the perimeter of the triangle using the formula $P = a + b + c$, plug the values into the equation: $P = 15 + 6 + 12 = 33$.

---

2. Find the perimeter of the square shown below using the formula $P = 2l + 2w$.

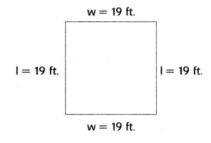

w = **19 ft.**

l = **19 ft.**

l = **19 ft.**

w = **19 ft.**

    A.   19 feet
    B.   38 feet
    C.   64 feet
    D.   76 feet

The correct answer is **D**. The perimeter of the square is 76 feet. To find the perimeter of the square using the formula $P = l + l + l + l$, plug the values into the equation: $P = 19 + 19 + 19 + 19 = 76$.

3. Sergeant Phillips strings police tape around a crime scene. The tape encompasses a 24-x-16-foot rectangle. Using the formula $P = l + l + w + w$, what is the perimeter of the crime scene?

   A.   40 feet
   B.   64 feet
   C.   72 feet
   D.   80 feet

The correct answer is **D**. The perimeter of the crime scene is 80 feet. To find the perimeter of a rectangle, use the formula $P = l + l + w + w$: $P = 24 + 24 + 16 + 16 = 80$.

Practice

Directions (1–10): Answer these questions solely on the basis of the information provided.

Questions 1 and 2 refer to the following information.

After responding to a report of a burglary at a local jewelry store, Officer Bishop lists the following stolen items and their values:

   Necklace: $200
   Ring: $1,000
   Earrings: $400
   Cash: $900

1. What is the total value of the stolen items?

   A. $1,000
   B. $1,500
   C. $2,000
   D. $2,500

2. What is the total value of the stolen items except for the cash?

   A. $1,600
   B. $1,800
   C. $2,500
   D. $2,600

3. During the past two days, Officer Franklin worked on incident reports. The first day, he finished 6 reports before lunch and 5 after lunch. The second day, he completed 4 reports before lunch and 12 reports after lunch. How many reports did he complete during the past two days?

   A.   19
   B.   27
   C.   33
   D.   37

4. Each week, Officer Maynard drives his police cruiser approximately 800 miles, which is about 160 miles a day. Officer Maynard is on vacation for two days this week. What is the approximate number of miles that Officer Maynard will drive this week?

   A.   320 miles
   B.   480 miles
   C.   600 miles
   D.   980 miles

5. Sergeant Bilbow patrols a particular parking lot known for gang activity 25 times during a workweek, which is about 5 times a day. Sergeant Bilbow calls in sick on Wednesday, so he doesn't patrol the parking lot that day. How many times did he patrol the neighborhood this week?

   A.   20
   B.   35
   C.   45
   D.   50

Question 6 refers to the following information.

While responding to a burglary at a local eatery, Officer Malone lists the following stolen items and their values:

   Deep fryer: $900
   10 pounds of steaks: $50
   1 case of wine: $3,000
   Cash: $1,725
   TOTAL: $5,675

6. What is the total value of the stolen items except for the steaks?

   A. $5,720
   B. $5,625
   C. $6,050
   D. $6,295

7. Officer Chang usually works from 9 a.m. to 7 p.m., four days a week. His supervisor asks him to report for duty at 7 a.m. and work until 7 p.m. for four days this week. At the end of the week, how many hours of overtime will Officer Chang have worked?

   A.   2 hours
   B.   4 hours, 30 minutes
   C.   8 hours
   D.   10 hours, 30 minutes

8. Officer LaMarka usually works from 9 a.m. to 5 p.m., five days a week. His supervisor asks him to report to work at 7:45 a.m. on Monday and Tuesday this week to train a new officer. At the end of the week, how many hours of overtime will Officer LaMarka have worked?

    A.   45 minutes
    B.   1 hour, 15 minutes
    C.   2 hours
    D.   2 hours, 30 minutes

9. Find the perimeter of the rectangle shown below using the formula $P = l + l + w + w$.

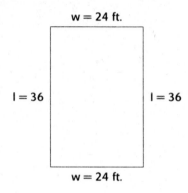

w = 24 ft.
l = 36   l = 36
w = 24 ft.

    A.   60 feet
    B.   120 feet
    C.   180 feet
    D.   220 feet

10. Find the perimeter of the triangle shown below using the formula $P = a + b + c$.

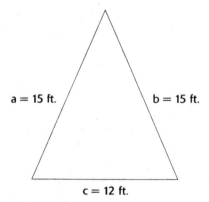

a = 15 ft.   b = 15 ft.
c = 12 ft.

    A.   27 feet
    B.   42 feet
    C.   55 feet
    D.   61 feet

Answers

1. **D** The total value of the stolen items is $2,500. To find the total value of the stolen items, add the values of the necklace, ring, earrings, and cash: $200 + $1,000 + $400 + $900 = $2,500. You can automatically eliminate choice A because this choice is less than or equal to the highest addend ($1,000).

2. **A** The total value of the stolen items except the cash is $1,600. To find the total value of the stolen items except the cash, add the values of the necklace, ring, and earrings: $200 + $1,000 + $400 = $1,600.

3. **B** He wrote 27 reports. Add the number of reports completed each day before and after lunch: 6 + 5 + 4 + 12 = 27.

4. **B** Officer Maynard drove 480 miles this week. Since Officer Maynard is on vacation for two days, he drove only three days this week. To solve this problem, you have to subtract the miles he would've driven in two days from the number of miles he typically drives in one week: 800 miles – 160 miles – 160 miles = 480 miles. You can automatically eliminate choice D because this choice is larger than the minuend (800).

5. **A** Sergeant Bilbow patrolled the parking lot 20 times this week. Since Sergeant Bilbow did not patrol the parking lot on Wednesday and he normally patrols it five times a day, subtract five patrols from his total number of weekly patrols: 25 – 5 = 20.

6. **B** The total value of stolen items except the steaks is $5,625. To solve this problem, subtract the value of the steaks from the total value of all the stolen items: $5,675 – $50 = $5,625.

7. **C** Officer Chang will work 8 hours of overtime this week. To solve this problem, use subtraction and addition. Officer Chang is asked to come in at 7 a.m. instead of 9 a.m. every day this week, meaning that he'll come in two hours early each day. He works four days a week, so 2 + 2 + 2 + 2 = 8 hours.

8. **D** If Officer LaMarka comes in 1 hour, 15 minutes early two days this week, he will have worked 2 hours, 30 minutes of overtime at the end of the week: 1 hour, 15 minutes + 1 hour, 15 minutes = 2 hours, 30 minutes.

9. **B** The perimeter of the rectangle is 120 feet. To find the perimeter of the rectangle using the formula $P = l + l + w + w$, plug the values into the equation: $P = 36 + 36 + 24 + 24 = 120$.

10. **B** The perimeter of the triangle is 42 feet. To find the perimeter of the triangle using the formula $P = a + b + c$, plug the values into the equation: $P = 15 + 15 + 12 = 42$.

B. Multiplication and Division

You'll often use multiplication and division to solve similar types of questions on the police officer exam. These questions will ask you to determine percentages, find the area of a shape, or solve for *A* or *B* using both multiplication, division, and possibly even addition and subtraction. Take the time to review the basics of multiplication and division so that you're prepared for these types of questions when you take the exam.

Tip: Always follow the order of operations when solving math problems. Work with anything in parentheses first, then exponents, and then multiplication, division, addition, and subtraction. Use the mnemonic device Please Excuse My Dear Aunt Sally to remember the order.

1. Multiplication

As you may recall from your elementary mathematics lessons, multiplication is really an advanced way to add. Because of this, multiplication questions that appear on the police officer exam may look like addition questions at first. As you read the passages and accompanying questions, you'll probably realize it would be easier to use multiplication to find the correct answer.

When using multiplication, remember these two rules:

- Any number multiplied by 0 will always equal 0 (for example, $5 \times 0 = 0$).
- Any number multiplied by 1 will equal itself (for example, $12 \times 1 = 12$).

Remember to look for key words in questions. Recall that the answer to a multiplication equation is called the *product,* while the numbers you're multiplying are called *factors.* Look for the words *of, product,* and *times* as you read. These words indicate that you should use multiplication to find the correct answer.

Examples:

Questions 1 and 2 refer to the following information.

While preparing a report on a home burglary, Sergeant Watkins listed the following stolen items and their values:

> 2 MP3 players: $90 each
> 1 watch: $500
> 3 HDTVs: $1,200 each
> 2 DVD players: $60 each
> Cash: $145
> TOTAL: $4,545

---

1. What is the total value of the stolen HDTVs?

   A. $1,200
   B. $2,400
   C. $3,600
   D. $4,800

The correct answer is **C.** To find the total value of the stolen HDTVs, you have to multiply the number of stolen TVs by the value of each individual TV: $3 \times \$1,200 = \$3,600$. Choice A is incorrect because this is the value of one HDTV. Choice B is incorrect because this would be the value of two TVs, and choice D is incorrect because $4,800 is the value of four TVs.

2. Later that day, the homeowner calls Sergeant Watkins to report that another MP3 player is missing. This MP3 player has the same value as the other MP3 players. What is the total value of the stolen MP3 players?

   A. $90
   B. $180
   C. $270
   D. $360

The correct answer is **C.** To find the total value of the stolen MP3 players, you have to multiply the number of players stolen by the value of each individual player: 3 × $90 = $270. Choice A is incorrect because this is the value of one MP3 player. Choice B is incorrect because this would be the value of two players, and choice D is incorrect because $360 is the value of four players.

3. 24 + 8 × 2 + 15 = ?

   A.   55
   B.   79
   C.   160
   D.   624

The correct answer is **A.** To solve this problem, you have to follow the order of operations. First multiply, and then add: 8 × 2 = 16, and 24 + 16 + 15 = 55. Choices B, C, and D are incorrect because these are answers you would get if you didn't follow the order of operations. Always multiply (or divide) before you add (or subtract).

2. Division

Expect to see several division questions on the written police officer exam. Division is used in fractions, percentages, and many geometry problems. Division questions regularly provide you with a large number (values, miles, arrests, and so on) and ask you to break it down into smaller parts.

Like multiplication, there are a few easy rules to remember when dividing:

- Zero divided by any other number is always 0 (for example, 0 ÷ 8 = 0).
- Any number divided by one always equals itself (for example, 6 ÷ 1 = 6).
- Numbers are *not* divisible by 0.

Although the answer to a division problem is called a *quotient,* and the parts you use to divide are *divisors* and *dividends,* you won't see these words used in many problems on the written exam. Instead, look for the words *each* and *per.* The word *per* may be substituted for *each* and typically appears in phrases such as *per hour, per day,* or *per mile.*

Examples:

---

1. $5 \times 8 + 12 \div 4 - 1 = ?$

    A.   12
    B.   20
    C.   24
    D.   42

The correct answer is **D.** Following the order of operations, you have to divide and multiply before you can add and subtract. After completing the first two operations, your equation would look like this: $40 + 3 - 1$. The answer is 42. Choices A, B, and C are incorrect because these are the answers you would get if you didn't follow the order of operations.

---

2. After pulling a driver over for speeding, Officer Rodriguez discovers eight bags of cocaine in the passenger seat of the car. At the station, another officer estimates the total value of all the cocaine to be $1,200. What is the value of each bag of cocaine if each bag is worth the same amount?

    A. $150
    B. $300
    C. $500
    D. $750

The correct answer is **A.** You know this is a division problem because the question asks you to find the value of each bag. To solve this problem, you have to divide the total value of the drugs by the number of bags discovered in the car: $1,200 \div 8 = $150.

Question 3 refers to the following information.

While preparing a report on a mugging, Officer Michaels listed the following stolen items and their values:

    1 cellphone: $150
    1 watch: $220
    2 MP3 players: $480
    2 bracelets: $110
    Cash: $85
    TOTAL: $1,045

3. When the victim of the mugging gets back to her house, she calls Officer Michaels and tells him that she found one of the bracelets that she originally reported stolen. Assuming that both bracelets are worth the same amount, what is the new total value of the stolen items?

   A. $935
   B. $990
   C. $1,135
   D. $1,155

The correct answer is **B**. This problem requires the use of two operations: division and subtraction. First, you must divide to find the value of each individual bracelet. To do so, divide the total value of the bracelets by the number of bracelets the victim had previously reported stolen: $110 ÷ 2 = $55. Next, subtract the value of one bracelet from the original total value of items stolen: $1,045 − $55 = $990.

3. Area and Volume

On the written police officer exam, you may be asked to find the area or volume of specific geometric figures, such as squares or rectangles.

Determining the area or volume of an object requires multiplication. The problems you'll find on the police officer exam will present you with a diagram of an object. The diagram will contain all the information you need to solve for the area, volume, height, width, or length. The problem will most likely present you with the formula you'll need to use to find the answer. You may see the following formulas on the test:

Area of a rectangle	Area = length × width $(A = lw)$
Area of a square	Area = length × width $(A = s^2)$
Area of a circle	Area = π × radius × radius $(A = \pi r^2)$
Diameter of a circle	Diameter = 2 × radius $(D = 2r)$
Volume of a rectangular prism (box)	Volume = length × width × height $(V = lwh)$

Tip: Pi (π) is equal to 3.14159265, but for the purposes of the police officer exam you can round this number to 3.14.

Occasionally, you'll be given the area or volume of an object and asked to find its height or width. For example, you may be told that a rectangle's area is 24 and its length is 6. Your equation will look like this: $A = lw$ and $24 = 6w$. In this case, you're solving for w. To find w, divide both sides of the equation by 6 and you get $w = 4$.

You'll also see problems that ask you to find the area of a triangle. You'll learn more about this in the next section.

Now, try a few math questions involving area and volume.

Examples:

1. Find the area of the object below using the formula $A = lw$.

5

12

- A. 12
- B. 17
- C. 30
- D. 60

The correct answer is **D.** To find the area of the object, substitute the numbers provided for the l and the w and multiply: $A = lw = 12 \times 5 = 60$. If you needed to solve for length or width, you would have used division. Since you only need to find the area, the only operation you need to perform is multiplication.

2. Find the area of the object below using the formula $A = \pi r^2$.

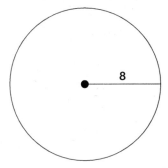

8

- A. 25.12
- B. 50.24
- C. 100.48
- D. 200.96

The correct answer is **D.** To find the area of the object presented, simply plug in 8 for r and multiply: $A = \pi r^2 = 3.14 \times 8^2 = 3.14 \times 64 = 200.96$.

3. Find the volume of the object below using the formula $V = lwh$.

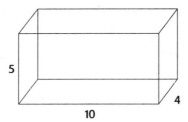

5

10

4

A. 40
B. 50
C. 100
D. 200

The correct answer is **D.** To find the volume of the object presented, substitute the numbers provided in the appropriate positions in the formula and multiply: $V = lwh = 10 \times 4 \times 5 = 200$.

4. Averages

Averages are commonplace in police work. You'll often be asked to calculate the average number of incident or aid reports you finish in a week, the average number of miles you put on your police cruiser each month, or even the average number of arrests you've made each year since receiving your shield.

An *average* is sometimes referred to as a *mean*. Averages may be whole numbers or may have a remainder in a decimal or fraction form. To eliminate tricky remainders, some questions on the police officer exam ask you to estimate or round to the nearest value.

Calculating an average is easy: Just use addition and division. To find an average, add together all values and then divide by the number of values you added. For example, if you wanted to find the average of 2, 4, and 6, you would add the numbers and then divide by 3: $(2 + 4 + 6) \div 3 = 12 \div 3 = 4$. The average of 2, 4, and 6 is 4.

You'll know when you need to find an average because the questions will use the words *average* or *mean*. It's as easy as that!

Try the following examples.

Examples:

---

1. The number of incident reports Officer Dickenson wrote each week for the past two months was 9, 8, 6, 7, 10, 4, 8, and 5. What is the average number of incident reports he wrote each week? Round to the nearest whole number.

   A. 5
   B. 6
   C. 7
   D. 8

The correct answer is **C.** To find the average number of incident reports Officer Dickenson wrote each week, you have to add up the incident reports he completed during a two-month span and divide by the number of weeks. Since each month is four weeks, you'd have to divide by 8: $9 + 8 + 6 + 7 + 10 + 4 + 8 + 5 = 57$ and $57 \div 8 = 7.125$. Round to the nearest whole number, and you get 7 reports per week.

---

2. Officers King and Barre made a total of 40 arrests over the last 3 months. If Officer King made 13 of those arrests, what is the average number of arrests Office Barre made each month?

   A. 6
   B. 7
   C. 8
   D. 9

The correct answer is **D.** To find the average number of arrests Office Barre made each month, you must subtract and divide. First, subtract the number of arrests King made from the total: $40 - 13 = 27$. Then, divide the number of arrests Barre made by the number of months: $27 \div 3 = 9$ arrests per month.

---

3. Officer Medina patrols the local park four times over the course of four days. At the end of each day, he records the number of hours spent patrolling that day. If Officer Medina recorded two hours, three hours, five hours, and one hour, what is the average amount of time he spent patrolling the park per day? Round to the nearest whole number.

   A. 1
   B. 2
   C. 3
   D. 4

The correct answer is **C.** To find the average amount of time Officer Medina spent patrolling the park per day, you have to add and then divide by the number of days: $2 + 3 + 5 + 1 = 11$ and $11 \div 4 = 2.75$. Rounded to the nearest whole number, you get 3 hours per day.

Practice

Directions (1–10): Answer the questions solely on the basis of the information provided.

Questions 1 and 2 are based on the following information.

While preparing a report on a burglary at a sporting-goods store, Officer Mantione listed the following stolen items and their total values:

  1 golf club: $130
  2 pairs of sneakers: $220
  4 thermal jackets: $350
  1 tent: $70
  2 backpacks: $160

1. What is the value of each thermal jacket if each jacket has the same value?

    A. $87.50
    B. $175
    C. $262.50
    D. $350

2. After Officer Mantione finishes his report, the owner of the sporting-goods store calls to say he located one pair of sneakers that was originally reported as stolen. What is the new total value of all the stolen items if each pair of sneakers has the same value?

    A. $710
    B. $820
    C. $930
    D. $1,040

3. Solve: $4 + 8 \times 10 - 14 \div 2$.

    A. 18
    B. 28
    C. 53
    D. 77

4. Solve: $7 \times 5 + 4 - 2 + 10 \div 2$.

    A. 17.5
    B. 23.5
    C. 27
    D. 42

5. Find the volume of the object below using the formula $V = lwh$.

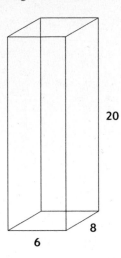

20

8

6

   A.   280
   B.   540
   C.   960
   D.   1,120

6. Find the area of the object below using the formula $A = \pi r^2$. Round to the nearest whole number.

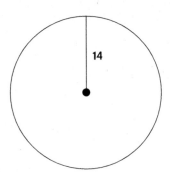

14

   A.   44
   B.   264
   C.   528
   D.   615

7. Detective Sheridan often takes security shifts in addition to her regular shifts at the police department. Over the past two weeks, she's worked six security shifts that lasted five hours, three hours, two hours, eight hours, two hours, and four hours. What is the average amount of time she spent working security on each shift?

   A.   2 hours
   B.   4 hours
   C.   6 hours
   D.   8 hours

8. In the past week, Officer White patrolled his assigned area on foot five times. The distance he covered during each shift was 5 miles, 6 miles, 4 miles, 3 miles, and 7 miles, respectively. What is the average distance he walked during each shift?

   A.   5 miles
   B.   10 miles
   C.   20 miles
   D.   25 miles

Questions 9 and 10 refer to the following information.

While preparing a report on a burglary at a pet store, Officer Webber listed the following stolen items and their total values:

   1 puppy: $300
   2 kittens: $450
   3 frogs: $75
   5 turtles: $80
   1 snake: $115
   10 goldfish: $50

9. What is the value of one kitten and three goldfish if each kitten and each goldfish has the same value?

   A. $240
   B. $275
   C. $465
   D. $500

10. Once Officer Webber finishes his report, the owner of the pet store calls to report that two of the turtles are accounted for, but another frog is missing. What is the new total value of the stolen items?

   A. $1,038
   B. $1,063
   C. $1,070
   D. $1,079

Answers

1. **A** The value of each thermal jacket is $87.50. To answer this question, you have to divide the total value of the thermal jackets by 4: $350 ÷ 4 = $87.50.

2. **B** The new total value of the stolen items is $820. To solve, you must first divide to find the value of one pair of sneakers: $220 ÷ 2 = $110. Then you must add the values listed, with the substitution of the price of one pair of sneakers instead of two, to find the new total: $130 + $110 + $350 + $70 + $160 = $820.

3. **D** The correct answer is 77. To solve this problem, you must follow the order of operations. First, multiply and divide. Your new equation will look like this: 4 + 80 − 7. Now, add and subtract: 84 − 7 = 77. Choices A, B, and C represent the answers you would get if you didn't follow the order of operations when solving this problem.

4. **D** The correct answer is 42. To solve this problem, you must follow the order of operations. First, multiply and divide. Your new equation will look like this: 35 + 4 − 2 + 5. Now, add and subtract: 35 + 4 − 2 + 5 = 42. Choices A, B, and C represent the answers you would get if you did not follow the order of operations when solving this problem.

5. **C** The volume of the rectangle presented is 960. To find the answer, plug the numbers from the figure into the formula: $V = lwh = 6 \times 8 \times 20 = 960$.

6. **D** The area of the object presented is approximately 615. To find the answer, plug the numbers from the figure into the formula: $A = \pi r^2 = 3.14 \times 14^2 = 615$.

7. **B** The average amount of time Detective Sheridan spent on security shifts over the past two weeks is 4 hours. To find the average, you must add the hours that she worked and then divide by the number of shifts: 5 + 3 + 2 + 8 + 2 + 4 = 24 and 24 ÷ 6 = 4 hours.

8. **A** The average distance Officer White patrolled during each shift is 5 hours. To find the average, you must add the number of miles he patrolled and then divide by the number of shifts: 5 + 6+ 4 + 3 + 7 = 25 miles and 25 ÷ 5 = 5 miles.

9. **A** The value of one stolen kitten and three goldfish is $240. To find this answer, you must divide, multiply, and add. First, divide the total value of the stolen kittens by the number of kittens stolen to find the value of one kitten: $450 ÷ 2 = $225. Now, do the same for the goldfish: $50 ÷ 10 = $5. The question asks you to find the value of one kitten and three goldfish: 3 goldfish × $5 per goldfish = $15. Finally, add the price of one kitten to the price of three goldfish. $225 + $15 = $240.

10. **B** The new total value is $1,063. To solve this problem, you must divide, multiply, and add. First, find the value of one turtle. To do this, divide the total value of the stolen turtles by the number of turtles stolen: $80 ÷ 5 = $16. Next, multiply the price of one turtle by how many turtles were actually stolen: $16 × 3 = $48. Now, do the same with the frogs: $75 ÷ 3 = $25 and $25 × 4 = $100. Now, add the values of the pets stolen using this new information: $300 + $450 + $100 + $48 + $115 + $50 = $1,063.

C. Fractions and Decimals

1. Fractions

As a police officer, you'll need to know how to work with fractions so you can solve questions on the police officer exam that involve ratios and proportions, formulas, decimals, and percentages.

Don't let fractions intimidate you. Think of a fraction as "part over a whole," or $\frac{part}{whole}$. Any whole number can be turned into a fraction by putting it over 1; for example, the whole number 10 would become a fraction by putting it over 1: $\frac{10}{1}$. This is an example of an improper fraction, which is one of the three different types of fractions you'll encounter on the exam:

- **Proper fraction:** A fraction with a smaller number in the *numerator* (the top number) and a larger number in the *denominator* (the bottom number). Example: $\frac{3}{4}$.

- **Improper fraction:** A fraction with a larger number in the numerator and a smaller number in the denominator. Example: $\frac{25}{12}$.

- **Mixed number:** A fraction that includes a whole number and a proper fraction. Example: $4\frac{1}{2}$.

A fraction is a rational number that can be added, subtracted, multiplied, and divided. To solve questions involving fractions on the police officer exam, you only need to know how to multiply fractions. To do this, you multiply the two numerators and the two denominators.

To multiply fractions, multiply across the numerators, and then multiply across the denominators. Reduce to lowest terms, if necessary. If you need to multiply a mixed number and a fraction, convert the mixed number to an improper fraction before you multiply.

Take a look at the following multiplication example:

$$\frac{3}{4} \times \frac{3}{9}$$

First, multiply:

$$\frac{3}{4} \times \frac{3}{9} = \frac{9}{36}$$

Because 36 is divisible by 9, you can reduce this fraction by dividing the numerator and denominator by 9:

$$\frac{9}{36} = \frac{1}{4}$$

Here's another example involving a mixed number:

$$2\frac{1}{2} \times \frac{4}{5}$$

First, convert the mixed number to a fraction. Multiply the denominator by the whole number and then add this product to the numerator. Place the answer over the original denominator:

$$2 \times 2 + 1 = 5$$

$$2\frac{1}{2} = \frac{5}{2}$$

Multiply the fractions:

$$\frac{5}{2} \times \frac{4}{5} = \frac{20}{10}$$

Now, reduce:

$$\frac{20}{10} = \frac{2}{1} = 2$$

You'll use this method to solve questions on the police officer exam involving the area of a triangle. In Section B, we reviewed how to find the area and volume of objects, such as squares, circles, and rectangles. We left out triangles because you need to know how to multiply fractions to solve for the area of a triangle. These types of problems will present you with either a passage or a diagram containing all the information you'll need to solve the problem, including the formula.

To find the area of a triangle, use the formula $A = \frac{1}{2}bh$, where b is the base and h is the height.

Try the following area question.

EXAMPLE:

Find the area of the triangle shown below using the formula $A = \frac{1}{2}bh$.

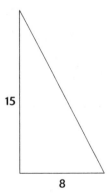

15

8

A. 45
B. 60
C. 90
D. 120

The correct answer is **B**. The area of the triangle shown is 60. Plug the given values into the equation: $A = \frac{1}{2} \times 8 \times 15$. Next, put the whole number 8 over 1 to make it a fraction. This allows you to multiply the fractions: $\frac{1}{2} \times \frac{8}{1} = \frac{8}{2} = 4$. Now, multiply the whole numbers: $A = 4 \times 15 = 60$.

198

Occasionally, you'll be given the area of a triangle and asked to find the height or base. For example, you may be told that a triangle's area is 25 and its base is 10. Your equation will look like this:

$$25 = \frac{1}{2} \times 10 \times h$$

First, turn 10 into a fraction and multiply by $\frac{1}{2}$:

$$\frac{10}{1} \times \frac{1}{2} = \frac{10}{2} = 5$$

So, 25 = 5h. To find h, divide both sides of the equation by 5:

$$\frac{25}{5} = \frac{\cancel{5}h}{\cancel{5}}$$
$$\frac{25}{5} = h$$
$$5 = h$$

The height of the triangle is 5.

To solve equations, you have to use reverse operations. For example, if one side of the equation uses multiplication, you have to use division to cancel out that information and solve for the variable. Anything you do to one side of the equation must be done to the other side of the equation. For example, if you multiply one side by 4, you must multiply the other side by 4.

Take a look at the following example:

$$\frac{2}{3} = \frac{x}{5}$$

Cross-multiply to get:

$$3x = 10$$

To solve the equation, divide each side by 3:

$$\frac{\cancel{3}x}{\cancel{3}} = \frac{10}{3}$$
$$x = \frac{10}{3} = 3\frac{1}{3}$$

Now, try this example.

EXAMPLE:

If two-thirds of the calls Officer Nemetz responds to each week are for violent crimes, and he typically responds to 42 calls per week, how many of those calls are for violent crimes?

A.   14
B.   19
C.   28
D.   36

The correct answer is **C**. Officer Nemetz responds to 28 violent crime calls each week. Let x be the number of calls for violent crimes. Cross-multiply to solve this problem: $\frac{2}{3} = \frac{x}{42}$ and $3x = 84$. Divide each side by 3: $\frac{3x}{3} = \frac{84}{3}$ and $x = \frac{84}{3} = 28$.

Now that you know how to multiply fractions and solve equations, try a few example questions.

Examples:

1. Find the area of the triangle shown below using the formula $A = \frac{1}{2}bh$.

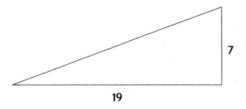

19

7

A. $44\frac{1}{2}$
B.   60
C. $66\frac{1}{2}$
D.   133

The correct answer is **C**. The area of the triangle shown is $66\frac{1}{2}$. Plug the given values into the equation: $A = \frac{1}{2} \times 19 \times 7$. Next, put the whole number 19 over 1 to make it a fraction and then multiply by $\frac{1}{2}$: $\frac{1}{2} \times \frac{19}{1} = \frac{19}{2}$. Now, put 7 over 1 to make it a fraction, so you can solve the problem: $\frac{19}{2} \times \frac{7}{1} = \frac{133}{2} = 66\frac{1}{2}$.

2. If one-fourth of the calls Lieutenant Marsh responds to each week are nonemergency calls, and she typically responds to 84 calls per week, how many of those calls are emergency calls?

A. 21
B. 42
C. 55
D. 63

The correct answer is **D.** Lieutenant Marsh responds to 63 emergency calls each week. Let x be the number of nonemergency calls. Cross-multiply to solve this problem: $\frac{1}{4} = \frac{x}{84}$ and $4x = 84$. Divide each side by 4: $\frac{4x}{4} = \frac{84}{4}$ and $x = \frac{84}{4} = 21$ nonemergency calls. To find the number of emergency calls, subtract 21 from the total number of calls (84) to get 63.

3. Find the height of a triangle with an area of 108 and a base of 12 using the formula $A = \frac{1}{2}bh$.

A. 9
B. 12
C. 15
D. 18

The correct answer is **D.** The height of the triangle is 18. Plug the given values into the equation: $108 = \frac{1}{2} \times 12 \times h$. First, turn 12 into a fraction and multiply: $\frac{1}{2} \times \frac{12}{1} = \frac{12}{2} = 6$, so $108 = 6h$. Next, divide both sides of the equation by 6: $\frac{108}{6} = \frac{6h}{6}$ and $\frac{108}{6} = h$ and $h = 18$.

a. Ratios/Proportions

Police officers use ratios and proportions to compare things, such as the number of police officers to the number of suspects, the number of arrests made in one day to the number of arrests made in one month, the number of incident reports completed in one day to the number of incident reports completed in three days, and so on. A ratio is a comparison of two numbers. A ratio can be written as a ratio notation (3:5) or as a fraction ($\frac{3}{5}$).

For example, the Erie Police Department has 22 police officers, and the Summerville Police Department has 16 police officers. The ratio of Erie police officers to Summerville police officers is 22:16. The ratio can also be expressed as the fraction $\frac{22}{16}$.

A proportion is an equation with a ratio on each side:

$$3:5 :: 22:16 \text{ or } \frac{3}{5} = \frac{22}{16}$$

Ratio questions on the police officer exam test your ability to solve proportions. You'll use information given in the problem to solve for an unknown variable. Consider the following problem:

If you can complete 30 incident reports in 6 hours, how many incident reports can you complete in 9 hours?

Let x represent the number of incident reports completed in 9 hours:

$$x \text{ incident reports} : 30 \text{ incident reports} :: 9 \text{ hours} : 6 \text{ hours} \text{ or } \frac{x \text{ incident reports}}{30 \text{ incident reports}} = \frac{9 \text{ hours}}{6 \text{ hours}}$$

Now, cross multiply:

$$\frac{x}{30} = \frac{9}{6}$$
$$6x = 270$$

Next, divide each side by 6:

$$\frac{6x}{6} = \frac{270}{6}$$
$$x = \frac{270}{6} = 45$$

You can complete 45 incident reports in 9 hours.

Now, try a few example problems.

Examples:

---

1. If you can complete 25 training exercises in 5 days, how many training exercises can you complete in 15 days?

   A. 30
   B. 55
   C. 60
   D. 75

The correct answer is **D.** You can complete 75 training exercises in 15 days. Begin with the ratio you're given:

$$x \text{ exercises} : 25 \text{ exercises} :: 15 \text{ days} : 5 \text{ days} \text{ or } \frac{x \text{ exercises}}{25 \text{ exercises}} = \frac{15 \text{ days}}{5 \text{ days}}$$

Then, cross-multiply both sides of the equation: $\frac{x}{25} = \frac{15}{5}$ and $5x = 375$. Next, divide each side by 5:

$$\frac{5x}{5} = \frac{375}{5}$$
$$x = \frac{375}{5} = 75$$

2. If you can make 24 arrests in 6 days, how many arrests can you make in 18 days?

    A.   65
    B.   72
    C.   81
    D.   99

The correct answer is **B.** You can make 72 arrests in 18 days. Begin with the ratio you're given:

$$x \text{ arrests} : 24 \text{ arrests} :: 18 \text{ days} : 6 \text{ days}$$

Next, cross-multiply: $\frac{x}{24} = \frac{18}{6}$ and $6x = 432$. Divide each side by 6:

$$\frac{6x}{6} = \frac{432}{6}$$

$$x = \frac{432}{6} = 72$$

3. If you can complete 49 incident reports in 7 days, how many incident reports can you complete in 21 days?

    A.   147
    B.   149
    C.   156
    D.   167

The correct answer is **A.** You can complete 147 incident reports in 21 days. Begin with the ratio you're given:

$$x \text{ incident reports} : 49 \text{ incident reports} :: 21 \text{ days} : 7 \text{ days or } \frac{x}{49} = \frac{21}{7}$$

Next, cross-multiply: $7x = 1{,}029$. Then, divide each side by 7 to get 147.

2. Decimals

Decimals are similar to fractions because both types of numbers represent parts of a whole. Like fractions, decimals are rational numbers you can add, subtract, multiply, and divide. The decimal point (.) in a decimal is what gives this type of number its name. It may fall before, after, or between a set of numbers. The position of the decimal point determines not only the name of the decimal, but also the value of the number.

Each time a decimal point moves one place to the left, the name of the decimal changes and the value of the number decreases:

$0.1 = \text{one-tenth} = \frac{1}{10}$

$0.01 = \text{one-hundredth} = \frac{1}{100}$

$0.001 = \text{one-thousandth} = \frac{1}{1{,}000}$

Each time a decimal point moves one place to the right, the value of the number increases:

0.01 = one-hundredth = $\frac{1}{100}$

0.1 = one-tenth = $\frac{1}{10}$

1.0 = one = 1

You can add or subtract two decimals without finding a common link between them—all you have to do is line up the points before you add or subtract. Sometimes, you may want to add a zero to the end of the number to make the decimal points line up. Adding a zero to the end of the number won't affect its value. For example, if you have to add 8.25 and 9.1, you'll want to align the decimals first. When you do so, you'll see that there's a blank spot beneath the 5 in 8.25. To fix this, just make 9.1 into 9.10. This doesn't alter the value and it makes adding easier. Now that every number is aligned, just add the numbers:

$$\begin{array}{r} 8.25 \\ +9.10 \\ \hline 17.35 \end{array}$$

Multiplying decimals is slightly more difficult than adding decimals. The easiest way to multiply decimals is to take the decimal points out of the numbers and then add them back in later.

For example, instead of multiplying 4.2 by 0.35, multiply 42 by 35: $42 \times 35 = 1,470$. To add the decimals back in, count the total number of numerals behind the decimal point in both of the numbers you multiplied. In 4.2, the 2 was the only numeral to the right of the decimal point. In 0.35, two numbers fell behind the decimal. Therefore, three numbers fell behind the decimal points, so the answer should have three numbers behind the decimal point. The correct answer is 1.470.

Tip: You'll be given scrap paper to work out problems like this when you take your written exam.

The movement of the decimal point also complicates the division of numbers with decimals. When decimal points are present in division problems, first move the decimal point in the *divisor* (the number by which you're dividing) to the right until it becomes a whole number. Then move the decimal point in the *dividend* (the number you're dividing) the same number of places to the right. Now, put a decimal point in the *quotient* (the answer) directly above the decimal point in the dividend. Finally, divide—but don't touch those decimal points!

Confused yet? Here's an example: To divide 6.420 by 0.02, you would first move the decimal point in the divisor two places to the right to get a whole number. Therefore, 0.02 becomes 2. Now that you've moved the decimal point two places to the right in the divisor, you have to move it two places to the right in the dividend. Therefore, 6.420 becomes 642.0. Your work for this equation may look like this (the *x*'s act as placeholders):

$$0.02\overline{)6.420}^{\,x} \rightarrow 2\overline{)642.0}^{\,x.x} \rightarrow 2\overline{)642.0}^{\,321.0}$$

Now, try a few example problems.

Examples:

> **1.** Solve: $5.2 + 1.7 \times 0.3 - 0.05$.
>
>   A.   2.02
>   B.   5.23
>   C.   5.63
>   D.   5.66

The correct answer is **D**. To solve this problem, you have to align your decimals, but you also have to follow the order of operations. The presence of decimal points doesn't mean you shouldn't follow all the basic rules you've learned thus far. First, you have to multiply: $1.7 \times 0.3 = 0.51$. Then, you have to add and subtract: $5.2 + 0.51 - 0.05 = 5.66$. Choices A, B, and C represent the answers that you may have gotten if you didn't follow the order of operations.

> **2.** Solve: $8.25 \div 0.5 + 1.4 - 0.045$.
>
>   A.   3.8921
>   B.   4.4474
>   C.   17.855
>   D.   19.210

The correct answer is **C**. To solve this problem, you must follow the order of operations and work with your decimal points. You can divide after shifting the decimals one place to the right: $8.25 \div 0.5$ becomes $82.5 \div 5 = 16.5$. Now, just add and subtract: $16.5 + 1.4 - 0.045 = 17.855$. Choices A, B, and C represent the answers that you may have gotten if you didn't follow the order of operations.

> **3.** At the end of each shift, Officer Montana and Officer Wright search the back seats of their patrol cars, looking for anything that may have fallen out of suspects' pockets. Occasionally, they find a few personal possessions or some illegal substances. When they find spare change, they add the coins to a collection for missing persons. In the past week, Montana found $0.75, $0.45, and $2.12 in change. Wright found $1.13, $0.33, and $0.02. What is the combined value of the change that Montana and Wright found this week?
>
>   A. $1.48
>   B. $3.32
>   C. $4.80
>   D. $5.58

The correct answer is **C**. The word *combined* should draw your attention to the fact that you should add the numbers in this word problem together: $0.75 + $0.45 + $2.12 + $1.13 + $0.33 + $0.02 = $4.80. Choice A is incorrect because this is merely the total that Officer Montana collected. Choice B is the total that Officer Wright collected. Choice D is a result of incorrect addition.

3. Percentages

The word *percent* is defined as "per 100 parts," so it makes sense that a percent is a fraction that always has a denominator of 100. Even if you didn't know what the word *percent* meant before, a quick glance at the word should allow you to see that it has something to do with the number 100.

Percentages may appear on the police officer exam in three ways:

> As a percentage: 20%
>
> As a fraction: $\frac{20}{100}$
>
> As a decimal: 0.20

Determining a percentage isn't too hard as long as you're comfortable working with fractions. ***Remember:*** These types of fractions always have a denominator of 100. Don't let percentages (or fractions, for that matter) intimidate you.

Suppose you're asked to find 10% of 80. One way to find the answer to this question is to convert the numbers to fractions and multiply. One fraction will always be your percentage (a number over 100). Use x to represent the number you don't know.

You already know that 10% is $\frac{10}{100}$. This is your first fraction. The other will be $\frac{x}{80}$. You then need to solve for x.

When you're dealing with fractions, think of the fraction as "part over a whole," or $\frac{part}{whole}$. The x in this example goes in the numerator because you've been asked to find *part* of 80. Had the question told you that 80 was 10% of a bigger number, then the x would go in the denominator because you'd have to find the bigger number, or the "whole."

Start with your equation:

$$\frac{10}{100} = \frac{x}{80}$$

Next, multiply diagonally:

$$10 \times 80 = 100 \times x$$
$$800 = 100x$$

Then, divide by 100 to find x:

$$\frac{800}{100} = \frac{\cancel{100}x}{\cancel{100}}$$
$$8 = x$$

So, 10% of 80 is 8.

Another way to find 10% of 80 is to use decimals. You already know that 10% is 0.10. So, all you have to do is multiply 80 by 0.10 to find your answer: $80 \times 0.10 = 8.0$.

Use the method you feel most comfortable with. If you can't seem to find the right answer using decimals, try cross-multiplying fractions and vice versa.

Examples:

---

1. What is 40% of 32?

   A.   10.6
   B.   12.8
   C.   15.4
   D.   19.2

The correct answer is **B**. To answer this question, you can either cross-multiply fractions or multiply decimals. If you choose to cross-multiply fractions, your work should look like this:

$$\frac{40}{100} = \frac{x}{32}$$
$$100x = 1,280$$
$$\frac{100x}{100} = \frac{1,280}{100}$$
$$x = 12.8$$

If you chose to multiply decimals, you know that 40% = 0.40. You'd then multiply: $0.40 \times 32 = 12.8$. Choice D is incorrect because 19.2 is 60% of 32, while choices A and C are the results of incorrect multiplication.

---

2. What percent of 224 is 56?

   A.   25%
   B.   35%
   C.   45%
   D.   55%

The correct answer is **A**. To solve this problem, you can either cross-multiply fractions or simply divide to get a decimal. If you choose to cross-multiply fractions, your work should look similar to the following:

$$\frac{56}{224} = \frac{x}{100}$$
$$5,600 = 224x$$
$$\frac{5,600}{224} = \frac{224x}{224}$$
$$25 = x$$

Since x is part of your percent, the answer would need a percent sign: 56 is 25% of 224.

Another way to solve this problem is to divide to get a decimal: $56 \div 224 = 0.25$ and $0.25 = 25\%$. Choices B, C, and D are incorrect because they're the results of incorrect division or multiplication.

3. During a routine drug bust, you find 84 bags of marijuana in a chest in a suspect's living room. In the closet, you find 36 bags of pills. What percentage of drugs did you discover in the closet?

   A.   30%
   B.   40%
   C.   42%
   D.   70%

The correct answer is **A.** To solve this problem, regardless of which method you choose, you must first add to find the total number of bags seized during the drug bust: 84 + 36 = 120 bags. Now, you can either cross-multiply or divide to find this answer. If you choose to cross-multiply, your work should look like this:

$$\frac{36}{120} = \frac{x}{100}$$
$$120x = 3,600$$
$$\frac{120x}{120} = \frac{3,600}{120}$$
$$x = 30$$

Since you're looking for part of a fraction, you'd add the percent sign to get 30%.

If you choose to divide to get a decimal, you'd simply divide the number of bags found in the closet by the total number of bags: 36 ÷ 120 = 0.30 and 0.30 = 30%. Choices B, C, and D are the results of incorrect addition or multiplication.

Practice

Directions (1–10): Answer these questions solely on the basis of the information provided.

1. In July, the number of parking tickets issued in a town increased dramatically. In June, only 35 parking tickets were issued. In July, 315 parking tickets were issued. By what percent did the number of parking tickets issued increase between June and July?

   A.   35%
   B.   89%
   C.   110%
   D.   800%

2. Find the area of the circle shown below using the formula $A = \pi r^2$. Round to the nearest tenth. ($\pi \approx 3.14$.)

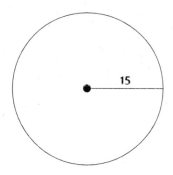

15

   A.   47.10
   B.   225.0
   C.   706.5
   D.   1,413

3. Solve: $98.15 + 75.20 \div 1.60 - 12.40 \times 0.62$. Round to the nearest hundredth.

   A.   59.49
   B.   65.17
   C.   98.15
   D.   137.46

4. Find the area of the triangle shown below using the formula $A = \frac{1}{2}bh$.

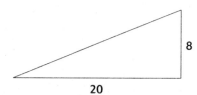

8

20

   A.   40
   B.   60
   C.   80
   D.   160

5. If you can make 21 arrests in 3 days, how many arrests can you make in 7 days?

   A.   28
   B.   32
   C.   42
   D.   49

6. What is 25% of 625? Round to the nearest hundredth.

   A. 156.25
   B. 312.50
   C. 425.00
   D. 468.75

7. While preparing an incident report for a burglary at a ski shop, Officer O'Malley must include the total value of the stolen items. He was told that 4 sets of skis were stolen, with a total value of $1,525.20. The owner reported that 3 helmets were also taken, valued at $62.75 each. Later, the owner tells him that 5 sets of skis, not 4, were stolen and each set of skis has the same value. What is the total value of all the stolen items?

   A. $1,332.15
   B. $1,587.95
   C. $1,713.45
   D. $2,094.75

8. Find the height of a triangle with an area of 54 and a base of 6 using the formula $A = \frac{1}{2}bh$.

   A. 6
   B. 9
   C. 12
   D. 18

9. Find the circumference of the circle shown below using the formula $C = 2\pi r$. Round to the nearest hundredth.

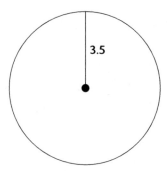

   A. 6.28
   B. 10.14
   C. 10.99
   D. 21.98

10. If four-fifths of the calls Officer Barber responds to each week are emergency calls, and he typically responds to 96 calls per week, how many of those calls are nonemergency calls? Round to the nearest whole number.

    A. 19
    B. 42
    C. 76
    D. 77

Answers

1. **D** The number of parking tickets increased by 800% from June to July. Begin by subtracting 35 from 315: 315 − 35 = 280. Then divide 280 by 35, which equals 8. Now multiply 8 by 100: 8 × 100 = 800%.

2. **C** The area of the circle shown is 706.5. Using the formula $A = \pi r^2$, you would plug in the correct numbers and simply multiply: $A = 3.14 \times 15^2 = 706.5$.

3. **D** The answer is 137.46. To solve this problem, you must follow the order of operations. First, divide: 75.20 ÷ 1.60 = 47. Then, multiply: 12.40 × 0.62 = 7.688. Now, just add and subtract: 98.15 + 47 − 7.688 = 137.462. Rounded to the nearest hundredth, 137.462 = 137.46. Choices A, B, and C represents the answer you may have gotten if you didn't follow the order of operations.

4. **C** The area of the triangle shown is 80. Plug the given values into the equation: $A = \frac{1}{2} \times 20 \times 8 = 10 \times 8 = 80$.

5. **D** You can make 49 arrests in 7 days. Begin with the ratio you're given: $\frac{x}{21} = \frac{7}{3}$. Next, cross-multiply and then divide each side by 3 to get 49.

6. **A** To solve this problem, replace the equation with $\frac{x}{625} = \frac{25}{100}$ or $\frac{x}{625} = \frac{1}{4}$. Isolate x: $x = \frac{625}{4} = 156.25$. You also can multiply using decimals. If you choose to multiply using decimals, first convert 25% to 0.25. Then, multiply: 625 × 0.25 = 156.25.

7. **D** The total value of the stolen items is $2,094.75. To solve this problem, you have to divide, multiply, and add decimals. First, you have to divide the initial value of stolen skis by the reported number of stolen ski sets to find the price of one set of skis: $1,525.20 ÷ 4 = $381.30. Since each set of skis costs $381.30 and the owner reported that 5 sets were stolen, not 4, you must multiply the price of one set of skis by 5 to find the total value of the stolen skis: $381.30 × 5 = $1,906.50. Next, you have to multiply the cost of one helmet by 3 to find the total value of the stolen helmets: $62.75 × 3 = $188.25. Now, add the totals together to find the total value of all stolen items: $1,906.50 + $188.25 = $2,094.75.

8. **D** Plug the given values into the equation and multiply the fractions: $54 = \frac{1}{2}(6)(x)$, or 54 = 3x. Solve the equation: $x = \frac{54}{3}$ or $x = 18$.

9. **D** To find the circumference, you have to use the formula $C = 2\pi r$ and multiply decimals. You know that $r = 3.5$ and $\pi = 3.14$. Plug these numbers into the formula and multiple: $C = 2 \times 3.14 \times 3.5 = 21.98$.

10. **A** Officer Barber responds to 19 nonemergency calls each week. If four-fifths of the calls are emergency, then one-fifth of the calls are nonemergency:

$$\frac{1}{5} = \frac{x}{96}$$
$$5x = 96$$
$$\frac{\cancel{5}x}{\cancel{5}} = \frac{96}{5}$$
$$x = 19.2$$

Round down to the nearest whole number, and the answer is 19.

VIII. Judgment and Problem Solving

You're responding to a call on Maple Lane. While en route, you remember that there is construction a few blocks from your destination that could potentially hold you up for a few minutes. Every minute is crucial when responding to a call, so you must quickly think of another route to your destination.

As a police officer, you'll need to use sound reasoning, good judgment, and common sense to make critical decisions. Most times, you'll have mere seconds to make a decision under dangerous or stressful conditions. A good police officer is able to think on his or her feet and make rational decisions.

Reasoning and judgment questions on the police officer exam may seem difficult at first, but as long as you remember the following tips, you should do well on this section of the test:

- Read each scenario and question carefully. Make sure you're able to identify the problem before you answer the question.
- If you're stuck deciding between two possible answers, choose the one that you can apply to any situation.
- Reread the question and apply the answer choice you think is correct. Make sure your answer satisfies every part of the question.

The types of questions you may see in the judgment and problem-solving section of the police officer exam may be based on your knowledge of following procedures and reacting to complicated situations. Your ability to follow directions and perform steps in a logical order will also be assessed. You'll also be tested on your ability to interact with people, such as other police officers, victims, suspects, emergency personnel, and members of the public. You'll need to use inductive and deductive reasoning to draw conclusions about specific incidents or information.

A. Following Procedures

Knowing how to handle certain situations is a huge part of being a police officer. You have to know the rules and apply these rules when handling situations requiring police intervention. These types of questions test your common sense and ability to follow proper protocol. The first type of question presents a situation and then asks, "What would you do?" The second type of question asks you to observe a situation and determine whether something is likely to go wrong in a particular situation.

1. Situational Judgment

You won't need to know specific laws or policies to answer these questions, but you will need to determine the *best* course of action. The easiest way to answer these types of questions is to put yourself in a police officer's shoes. Read the questions and ask yourself what you would do in that particular situation. Remember to follow proper protocol at all times.

EXAMPLES:

1. Officer Burke is on patrol on a college campus when he discovers a gas leak at the rear of one of the dormitories. What should he do next?

   A. Enter the dormitory and order all occupants to evacuate.
   B. Attempt to stop the leak.
   C. Inform campus maintenance about the problem.
   D. Secure the scene and notify the gas utility company.

The correct answer is **D.** Although choices A and C are conceivably good answers, an evacuation may not be necessary and campus maintenance would probably just call the gas utility company, so the *best* answer is to secure the scene and notify the gas utility company. Common sense should tell you that no one other than the gas utility company should attempt to do anything to fix the leak, so you can eliminate choice B.

Tip: "What would you do?" Keep this question in mind when answering situational judgment questions.

2. While working the overnight shift, Officer Howard is dispatched to a bank where a silent alarm has been tripped. When handling this situation, Officer Howard should *not:*

   A. Carefully approach the front of the bank in an indirect manner.
   B. Enter the scene with lights and sirens activated.
   C. Prevent civilians from entering the premises before conducting a search.
   D. Try to secure the building until backup arrives.

The correct answer is **B.** The most important factor in a situation involving a silent alarm is the element of surprise. If the officer attempts to enter the scene with lights and sirens activated, he'll nullify his advantage over the suspects. The other choices are acceptable procedures, so they're incorrect.

3. You're on a late-night patrol in the downtown shopping district. As you're walking, you hear two men talking around the corner. You hear what they're saying and it becomes clear that they're in the midst of the sale of an illegal firearm. When you approach them, you see two men: one holding the weapon, and the other holding a wad of cash. When they see you, one man runs east and the other runs west. How should you proceed in this situation?

   A. Chase the suspect with the weapon.
   B. Chase the suspect with the money.
   C. Write down the suspects' physical descriptions.
   D. Order the suspects to stop, and fire a warning shot.

The correct answer is **A.** Your first action should be to chase the suspect with the weapon. The suspect with the illegal firearm is currently violating the law and could be a danger to others. You can't be sure that the other suspect has committed a crime, so you should chase the suspect you know has broken the law. Recording a physical description of the suspects may be helpful later in the investigation, but arresting the suspect with the firearm should be your first priority. Firing warning shots may present a danger to public safety and normally should not be attempted.

2. Problem Sensitivity

Problem sensitivity questions present you with a situation and ask you to recognize a problem. These questions can be difficult to answer if you don't understand the question. Make sure you read these questions carefully to identify the problem. After you've determined the problem, you must identify a possible solution.

For example, you may be asked in what situation a police officer should patrol an area more closely for traffic violations. One possible answer to the question may be that a police officer should patrol an area more closely for traffic violations when the area becomes a construction zone.

Tip: Don't be afraid of this type of question. Read each question carefully and choose the answer you think best fits the situation. If you get stuck, choose the answer that best ensures the safety of the police officer, the suspect, the victim, and any witnesses or bystanders.

Examples:

Occasionally, police officers are instructed to warn drivers of road conditions by changing the operation of traffic lights from an alternating red-amber-green to a steady flashing amber or red.

---

1. In which of the following conditions would police officers most likely alter the operation of traffic lights in a residential area?

    A. The county is trying to save money by conserving water and electricity.
    B. Strong winds have knocked down large trees on a nearby roadway.
    C. A traffic accident on the highway has created a traffic jam.
    D. A dangerous snowstorm is approaching the region.

The correct answer is **B.** Although a traffic accident would justify altering the operation of traffic lights, the accident in choice C has occurred on a highway, so the lights in a residential neighborhood would not be affected. Instead, police officers would most likely alter the operation of traffic lights if strong winds have knocked down large trees on a nearby roadway.

In the event of a serious medical emergency, officers may need to delay placing a suspect under arrest until appropriate medical treatment is administered.

---

2. Which of the following scenarios would *not* warrant a delay in arrest?

    A. A suspect breaks his leg while fleeing from officers.
    B. A suspect in a bar fight suffers an injury to the eye.
    C. A suspect suffers an abrasion during an altercation.
    D. A suspect suffers a third-degree burn on his arm.

The correct answer is **C.** If a suspect suffers an abrasion during an altercation, the officer should not delay arresting the suspect. The abrasion is a mild injury that does not warrant emergency medical attention. In the other choices, the suspect has suffered more serious injuries that require emergency medical attention.

Practice

Directions (1–10): Answer these questions solely on the basis of the information provided.

1. On some occasions, police officers must determine whether a person is actually missing before they file a report and begin a search. In which of the following situations would police officers most likely consider a person missing?

    A. At 4:30 p.m., a woman calls police and frantically states that her child was supposed to arrive home a few minutes after school, which dismissed at 3:15 p.m.

    B. A young man with a mental disorder goes to the store down the street from his house at 6:15 p.m., and a neighbor notices that he doesn't return home that night.

    C. The parents of 16-year-old twin girls call to report that their children aren't home nearly two hours after their curfew on a Friday night.

    D. A woman comes home after a three-day business trip to find that all of her husband's clothes are missing from their closets, the safe is empty, and his wedding ring is on the nightstand.

2. Officer Stewart is on patrol when he witnesses two men in a heated confrontation. As Officer Stewart approaches the scene, one of the men pulls out a gun and shoots the other man in the abdomen. The shooter flees, and the victim falls to the ground. When Officer Stewart reaches the victim, the officer can clearly see that he is losing a great deal of blood. What should Officer Stewart do first?

    A. Question witnesses and drive the victim to the hospital.

    B. Try to control the bleeding and call for an ambulance.

    C. Pursue and attempt to arrest the shooter.

    D. Submit an incident report about the situation.

3. Officer Kingston has been assigned to traffic control in the downtown area during the city's annual summer festival. For the duration of the festival, the city enacts special traffic and parking regulations due to the closure of several streets used for the festival. Officer Kingston finds a vehicle that is illegally parked according to the temporary regulations. What should she do in this situation?

    A. Ignore the infraction because the regulation the driver broke is only temporary.

    B. Write the driver a citation for breaking the regulation.

    C. Record the vehicle's information and write a citation if the driver breaks another regulation.

    D. Give the driver a warning for breaking the regulation.

4. Officer Morgan is patrolling a residential neighborhood after a severe storm and discovers a downed power line in the roadway. There is no obvious arcing or burning. How should Officer Morgan proceed?

    A. File the proper report and continue patrolling.

    B. Drag the wire to the side of the road so it does not pose a hazard.

    C. Use some sort of object to move the wire without making direct contact.

    D. Make sure the scene is secured and notify the electric utility company.

Questions 5 and 6 refer to the following information.

Police officers are trained to spot suspicious behavior that may either lead to criminal mischief or indicate that a crime has already taken place.

5. Which of the following should police officers patrolling city streets late at night be most suspicious of?

    A. screaming and yelling coming from a house
    B. a man and a woman walking down the street with a stroller
    C. a pizza delivery man on the porch of a brightly lit house
    D. loud noises coming from the back door of a local restaurant

6. Which of the following should police officers patrolling city streets late at night be least suspicious of?

    A. a man and a woman walking a dog down the street
    B. a woman walking up and down the block numerous times
    C. a child crying on the porch of an unlit house
    D. a teenager running from an all-night store

Questions 7 and 8 refer to the following information.

Police officers who patrol busy streets at night often have special training to help them spot drivers who may be operating their vehicles while under the influence of alcohol or other drugs.

7. Which of the following would be most likely to indicate an intoxicated driver?

    A. use of excessive speed
    B. inability to stay within marked lanes
    C. improper use of turn signals
    D. tailgating

8. Which of the following would be least likely to indicate an intoxicated driver?

    A. excessive swerving
    B. delayed reaction times
    C. cutting off another driver
    D. veering off the road

9. Officer Braden is dispatched to a local park to investigate calls from various people about a dog terrorizing people in the park. When Officer Braden arrives on the scene, he sees a loose dog fitting the description of the dog from the complaints. What should he do next?

    A. Euthanize the dog immediately.
    B. Try to capture the dog.
    C. Call the local pound for assistance.
    D. Question people on the scene.

10. Officer Hall is responding to a domestic abuse call. On her way, she notices smoke coming from a closed pizzeria. What should she do next?

    A.   Stop at the scene and try to put out the fire.
    B.   Ignore the fire and respond to the original call.
    C.   Call the fire department and continue on to the original call.
    D.   Secure the scene and call the fire department.

Answers

1. **B** The scenario of the person with a mental disorder not returning home is the most likely to be a missing person. Although parents are understandably concerned when their kids are late getting home, being late by an hour or two doesn't yet qualify someone as a missing person. Choice D points to a man leaving his wife, not to a missing person.

2. **B** As soon as Officer Stewart recognizes that the victim is bleeding profusely, his first priority should be to try to control the bleeding and call for an ambulance. The officer should not drive the victim to the hospital because an emergency medical crew could care for the victim on the way to the hospital.

3. **D** Officer Kingston should give the driver a warning for breaking the regulation. Since the regulation is temporary, she should issue a warning instead of a citation. A warning informs the driver of the violation and encourages the driver not to break the regulation again. Simply ignoring the violation because of the situation would not be acceptable; the temporary regulations are in place for specific reasons and should be enforced.

4. **D** Regardless of any arcing or burning, any downed power line should be treated as if it is active and should not be touched directly or indirectly. The most appropriate action would be for the officer to make sure the scene is secured and notify the electric utility company.

5. **A** The police officers should be most suspicious of screaming and yelling coming from a house. The screaming could be people arguing, but the arguing could lead to violence or a domestic abuse situation. The man and woman walking with the stroller are most likely trying to get their child to fall asleep. More people tend to order pizza at night and turn on their lights for the pizza delivery man. The back door of a restaurant would most likely lead to the kitchen, where loud noises are common.

6. **A** The police officers should be least suspicious of a man and a woman walking a dog down the street. Dogs need to be walked at all times of the day and night, so this situation should not cause concern to a police officer.

7. **B** The inability to stay within marked lanes would be the most likely indicator of an intoxicated driver. This problem is a likely sign that the driver is impaired as a result of using drugs or alcohol. The other choices are common traffic infractions and would not necessarily indicate an intoxicated driver.

8. **C** Cutting off another driver is the least likely indicator of an intoxicated driver. This is a common traffic infraction and would not necessarily indicate an intoxicated driver. The other choices are common signs that a driver is impaired by drugs or alcohol.

9. **C** Because the dog is a threat, Officer Braden should not try to capture the dog on his own and should call the local pound for assistance. He should not euthanize the dog unless it attacks him or someone else. He should question people on the scene while waiting for assistance.

10. **D** Officer Hall should secure the scene and call the fire department. After assistance arrives, the officer should continue on to the original call. She should not try to put out the fire herself or ignore the fire. The officer should not leave the scene until the fire department arrives.

B. Logical Ordering

Some of the judgment and problem solving questions you'll see on the written police officer exam will test your ability to following directions and perform steps in a logical order. You may be asked to identify the correct order in which a set of tasks should be completed, or you may be presented with a scenario and asked how a police officer should respond. The questions on the police officer exam don't require you to have any previous knowledge of policing, so many of these questions can simply be answered by using common sense. Two types of logical ordering questions you'll encounter on the exam are information-ordering passages and sentence-order logistics.

1. Information-Ordering Passages

The information-ordering passages you'll answer on the police officer exam will contain instructions about completing specific tasks related to police work, from pulling over drivers who have violated a traffic law to helping a lost child find his or her parent in a busy store. The instructions are listed as steps and appear in the order in which police should complete them.

A brief scenario about a police officer who must perform a particular task accompanies each information-ordering passage. The scenario will contain information about which steps the officer has previously completed. The question will ask you to identify which step the police officer must complete first, next, or last. You may also be asked which step the officer skipped while performing his or her duties.

The purpose of information-ordering questions is to test your ability to follow rules in the correct order. As a recruit at the academy, you'll quickly learn the importance of protocol and following procedures. These questions ask you to show that you're capable of following instructions before you actually start training.

To answer this type of question, thoroughly read the passage and the accompanying scenario and be sure that you understand what you're asked to find (the first step, the last step, a missing step, and so on). Then refer back to the passage to determine the correct answer.

> **Tip:** If you're a visual learner, it may help to cross out the steps the police officer in the scenario has already completed. Once you're finished marking up the passage, it should be clear which steps the officer skipped or which steps he has left to complete. Before you make stray marks in your test booklet, however, you should read the directions and make sure you're allowed to write in the booklet.

Carefully examine the following information-ordering examples and rely on your reading-comprehension skills to help you answer the accompanying questions. If you're uncomfortable with reading passages, refer to Chapter V for tips on understanding what you read.

Examples:

At the police academy, recruit officers learn how to handcuff a suspect properly. They're told never to handcuff male and female prisoners together, never to apply handcuffs over jewelry or clothing, and never to leave a handcuffed suspect alone. In general, applying handcuffs includes the following steps:

1. Place the suspect's hands behind his or her back. If the suspect is injured or pregnant, you can handcuff him or her in the front.

2. Put the handcuffs between the hands and wrist bones and be sure that the suspect's palms are facing upward.

3. If the suspect is on his or her knees, have the suspect sit on the ground with his or her legs outstretched.

4. If you must cuff two suspects together, cuff them with both of their right or left wrists together.

5. Remove the suspect from the view of the public by placing them in the police cruiser or inside a building.

---

1. The class is then given the following scenario: Officer Darnel is handcuffing a man suspected of robbing a jewelry store. The man is kneeling on the ground in an alleyway, facing a chain-link fence. He places the man's hands behind his back and places the handcuffs between the man's wrist and hands. The man is wearing a watch, so he positions the handcuffs so that they don't press the watch into the man's arm. What should the officer do next?

   A. Remove the man from the view of the public.
   B. Handcuff the man to the door of the jewelry store.
   C. Ask the suspect to sit on the ground with his legs stretched out.
   D. Check the suspect for injuries that the handcuffs may aggravate.

The correct answer is **C.** After Officer Darnel has handcuffed the suspect, he should ask the suspect to sit on the ground with his legs stretched out in front of him. Before he handcuffed the suspect, the officer should've checked the suspect for injuries. The officer should move the suspect to the police cruiser after the suspect sits on the ground.

In class, recruit officers are learning about specific procedures that they must perform when responding to emergencies involving fire. They receive a handout detailing the responsibilities of first responding police officers at the scene of a fire:

1. Make notes of the time you arrive on scene, the color of the flames, and the color and odor of the smoke.

2. Evacuate the homes and areas surrounding the fire, paying special attention to the location and behavior of the people you evacuate.

3. Make note of any materials you notice that may have been placed against windows or doors to delay the discovery of the fire. Such items may include blankets, shades, or pieces of paper.

4. Make note of any materials you notice that may have been placed in front of doors or windows to delay access to the building that is on fire. Such items may include piles of books or bricks, large appliances, and tables.

5. Never enter a burning building, but pay attention to how firefighters access the building. Note if any doors were unlocked or opened before firefighters entered them.

2. Recruits then receive the following scenario: Officer Mendez is one of several officers who respond to the scene of a house fire. Firefighters assume that the fire started in the basement and has since spread to the first and second floors. Officer Mendez tells his partner to record that the flames are an orange color and the smoke is a dark black as they pull up to the scene at 3:45 p.m. What should Officer Mendez do next?

   A.   Look for open doors or windows.
   B.   Make note of obstructions to entrances.
   C.   Evacuate the homes next to the fire.
   D.   Enter the building to search for victims.

The correct answer is **C**. After noting the appearance of the fire and the smoke and recording the time he arrived on scene, Officer Mendez should evacuate the homes next to the fire. Once all neighbors are out of harm's way, he can look for signs of an arsonist. Common sense (and rule 5) should tell you that choice D is incorrect—officers should never enter a burning building.

2. Sentence-Order Logistics

The second type of logical ordering questions you'll encounter on the police officer exam is sentence-order logistics. These questions look similar to information-ordering questions because both include a short passage and are accompanied by a list, but they're quite different. Although information-ordering questions present a list of rules or steps that need to be completed in a specific order, sentence-order logistic questions give you a list of events in random order that you must rearrange chronologically.

These questions typically appear with a passage that states that a police officer is writing an incident report about an emergency to which he or she responded. You're told that five random details have been pulled from the report and it's your job to determine the correct order in which the five sentences should appear in the report.

To answer these questions correctly, you need to rely on common sense and logic to make reasonably informed judgments or draw educated conclusions about the most likely order of the events. You need to thoroughly read the passage and the list and then analyze the answer choices before selecting what you believe to be the correct answer.

The first thing you should do when presented with a sentence-order logistics question is determine which step or event happened first. Then identify the event that occurred last. Once you're certain of the first and last incidents, look for answer options that begin and end with those specific details. Eliminate any answer option that doesn't fit. Read the remaining options and determine which one makes the most sense. The correct answer will flow smoothly and won't make the reader of the incident report struggle to make connections or draw conclusions.

Now, try the following example problems. Be sure to read each sentence thoroughly and compare it to the others before you decide where to it belongs in the report.

Examples:

Officer Paulson completed an incident report following a fatal shooting. The following five sentences were removed from the body of the report in no particular order:

1. Mrs. Hunter entered the parking garage after the department store closed at 9 p.m.

2. The handgun Mrs. Hunter used to shoot Mr. Montauk was licensed to her husband, Mr. Hunter.

3. Mr. Montauk grabbed Mrs. Hunter from behind and shoved her against her car, a green 2005 Ford.

4. Mrs. Hunter called 911 at 9:09 p.m. and reported that she had shot a man.

5. Mr. Montauk and Mrs. Hunter struggled, exchanged punches, and then Mrs. Hunter shoved Mr. Montauk to the ground.

---

1. Which of the following represents the correct order in which these events would appear in Officer Paulson's police report?

   A. 1, 3, 5, 4, 2
   B. 4, 1, 5, 3, 2
   C. 2, 1, 4, 3, 5
   D. 1, 3, 5, 2, 4

The correct answer is **A**. Officer Paulson's report begins with statement 1, where the incident began. The attack would not have taken place if Mrs. Hunter had not entered the garage alone at night after the department store had closed. Next in the report is statement 3, which states that Mr. Montauk initiated the attack by shoving Mrs. Hunter against her car. Statement 5 follows statement 3, because statement 5 provides further details about the attack and places Mr. Montauk in a vulnerable position. Statement 4 is next, as Mrs. Hunter shot the man who was attacking her and then called 911 to report it. Finally, Officer Martin would only know that the gun was registered to Mr. Hunter if he checked the registration after Mrs. Hunter reported the shooting. Therefore, statement 2 is last.

Remember: The sentences in the answer options provided for you won't contain all the details in the incident report. Many events, such as Mrs. Hunter's shooting of Mr. Montauk in the previous example, may not be listed as options. You'll have to fill in the holes with inferred information and work around that information to determine the chronology of the events.

Officer Zelinka completed an incident report following a burglary of a local business. The following five sentences were removed from the body of the report in no particular order:

1. Police matched one set of fingerprints to Mr. Johnson's son, Carl.

2. Mr. Johnson arrived at Johnson & Sons Bait and Tackle at 8:55 a.m. and discovered that he'd been robbed.

3. Police apprehended Carl Johnson on Highway 51 with two lures in his passenger seat worth $100 each.

4. Mr. Johnson refused to pay his son's bail for two full days after the incident.

5. Crime-scene investigators lifted two sets of prints from the windowsill in Mr. Johnson's office.

---

2. Which of the following represents the correct order in which these events would appear in Officer Zelinka's police report?

   A. 4, 2, 5, 1, 3
   B. 2, 5, 1, 3, 4
   C. 5, 1, 2, 3, 4
   D. 3, 2, 4, 1, 5

The correct answer is **B.** Officer Zelinka's report should begin with statement 2, in which Mr. Johnson arrived at his shop in the morning and discovered that he'd been robbed. After calling the police, crime scene investigators arrive at Mr. Johnson's shop and dust for fingerprints, statement 5. Statement 1 follows statement 5, because they match the discovered fingerprints to Carl Johnson. Next is statement 3, the apprehension of Carl on Highway 51 with evidence of the burglary in his car. Finally, statement 4 indicates that Carl is thrown in jail for his crime and his father is angry.

Practice

Directions (1–10): Answer these questions solely on the basis of the information provided.

Questions 1 and 2 refer to the following information.

In class, recruit officers learn that at some point in the future, they may be responsible for receiving found property. Found property can be an item discovered by someone on the street, at work or school, or in a public building. The person who found the property brings it to the police station, hoping that the person who lost it will eventually call to claim it. These items aren't necessarily pieces of evidence to any crimes, but they still should be logged and documented. Recruit officers are told to follow these steps when processing found property:

1. Record the following information: the name of the person who turned in the property, the place where the person found the property, a description of the property, and the current location of the property in the police station.
2. Write a report in which the above information is included.
3. Tag the property.
4. Write on the tag the report number, your badge number, your name, and the date and time the property was turned in to the department.
5. Place the property in the property room and turn in your report.

1. The class is then given the following scenario: Officer Kraft is working at the main desk when a woman enters the police department. The woman tells Kraft that she found a man's wallet in the parking lot behind her office building. She didn't recognize the name on the driver's license as an employee at her office, so she decided to turn in the wallet to the police. Officer Kraft asks for the woman's name and the exact location of the parking lot. What should he do next?

    A. Put the wallet in the property room.
    B. Look up the owner's name in the phone book and call him.
    C. Write a found property report using the information from the woman.
    D. Tag the wallet and write his name, the woman's name, and his badge number on the tag.

2. The class is given a second scenario: Officer Montana is working at the main desk when a man comes in with a set of keys. He says the keys are not his, places them on the desk, and turns to leave the station. What should Officer Montana do?

    A. Tag the keys and write his name and badge number on the tag.
    B. Write a found property report that states an unidentified man turned in the keys.
    C. Place the keys in the property room with a note saying when the keys were turned in.
    D. Call the man back to the desk and ask for his name and the location where he found the keys.

Question 3 refers to the following information.

Officer Taylor completed an incident report following a driving while intoxicated (DWI) traffic offense. The following five sentences were removed from the body of the report in no particular order:

1. He submitted to the breathalyzer test.
2. At 11:38 p.m., I pulled over the driver of a 1993 Chrysler LeBaron traveling at excessive speeds and swerving erratically.
3. Mr. Malloy claimed he had only one drink that night.
4. Vehicle owner James Malloy of 303 Venice Ave. had an outstanding warrant for assault and battery.
5. Mr. Malloy registered a blood alcohol level of 0.22 percent.

  3. Which of the following represents the correct order in which these events would appear in Officer Taylor's police report?

    A. 2, 4, 3, 1, 5
    B. 4, 3, 1, 5, 2
    C. 3, 1, 5, 2, 4
    D. 5, 4, 2, 3, 1

Question 4 refers to the following information.

Officer Harmon completed an incident report following a car theft. The following five sentences were removed from the body of the report in no particular order:

1. Mr. White is the owner of a black sedan, license plate FAV 4568.
2. Mr. White left his house at 6:30 a.m. and noticed his car was no longer in front of his house.
3. Police discovered pieces of Mr. White's car during a raid of a chop shop near the bay two days later.
4. Four cars on Mr. White's block have been stolen over the past three weeks.
5. Mrs. Bomber, a neighbor, stated that she thought she heard a car start in the middle of the night.

  4. Which of the following represents the correct order in which these events would appear in Officer Harmon's police report?

    A. 5, 2, 1, 3, 4
    B. 4, 5, 1, 2, 3
    C. 2, 1, 5, 4, 3
    D. 2, 1, 3, 4, 5

Questions 5 and 6 refer to the following information.

A handful of the calls that police officers in Ohio respond to are false alarms. Many times, uninformed employees or customers at local shops or stores accidentally trigger these alarms. Even certain weather conditions can set off a car alarm, holdup alarm, or burglary alarm. In class, recruit officers at an academy close to Cincinnati learn what to do when responding to an alarm that may have accidentally been triggered. These steps include:

1. Approach the scene with caution.
2. Investigate the cause of the alarm.
3. If proven false, request that the alarm company cancel the alarm.
4. Complete Form 315, which is an Alarm Response Report.

5. Recruit officers are then presented with the following scenario: A team of officers responds to a burglary alarm at a local business. When they arrive, the lights in the store are all on, but they find no signs of forced entry. As they approach, they look for any evidence that may lead them to believe someone is inside the building. What should they do next?

   A.   Call the alarm company and ask them to shut off the alarm.
   B.   Announce that the scene is safe since no one is around.
   C.   Enter the building and attempt to locate what set off the alarm.
   D.   Gather the information needed to fill out Form 315.

6. The instructor then presents his class with an additional scenario: A silent alarm at a local government office has been tripped and the response team knows that the suspect is still inside the building. In fact, they can see him in one of the windows as they pull onto the scene without activating their lights and sirens. Leaving their cruisers, they rush into the building and catch the suspect in the act of copying confidential files from a computer. Which step did the response team skip?

   A.   Approach the scene with caution.
   B.   Investigate the cause of the alarm.
   C.   Request the cancellation of the alarm.
   D.   Complete Form 315.

Question 7 refers to the following information.

Officer Monroe completed an incident report following a theft at a grocery store. The following five sentences were removed from the body of the report in no particular order:

1. The police arrive at the grocery store and request security footage.
2. A woman carrying a seemingly heavy purse and a bulking backpack left the grocery store at 1:03 p.m.
3. An unidentified woman entered the grocery store at 12:42 p.m. carrying a backpack and a large purse.
4. A customer tells the store manager that a woman with a backpack placed packaged meat in her purse.
5. The manager uses the PA system to announce a Code 99.

7. Which of the following alternatives represents the correct order in which these events would appear in Officer Monroe's police report?

   A.   1, 5, 3, 4, 2
   B.   3, 4, 5, 2, 1
   C.   3, 5, 4, 1, 2
   D.   2, 1, 5, 3, 4

Question 8 refers to the following information.

Officer Milton completed an incident report following a report of a missing child. The following five sentences were removed from the body of the report in no particular order:

1. Timmy arrived home at 5:30 p.m. with a handful of flowers for his mother.
2. Billy, a friend of Timmy's, told police that Timmy had a surprise planned but didn't know the details.
3. Timmy, a 9-year-old boy, typically arrives home from school at 3:20 p.m.
4. At 4:30 p.m., Timmy's mother, Mrs. Frost, called 911.
5. Police cruisers traveled up and down the streets Mrs. Frost noted as Timmy's route home from school.

8. Which of the following alternatives represents the correct order in which these events would appear in Officer Milton's police report?

   A. 4, 3, 5, 2, 1
   B. 3, 4, 2, 5, 1
   C. 4, 5, 3, 2, 1
   D. 5, 2, 1, 3, 4

Questions 9 and 10 refer to the following information.

In class, recruits learn the correct and incorrect ways to respond to an aircraft crash. These incidents involve the crash of an aircraft that is taking off, landing, or in flight that results in an injury to anyone on board or on the ground. The crash also may cause significant damage to the body of the aircraft. At the scene of this type of accident, the affected district officer in charge should immediately assume command and complete the following critical tasks:

1. Take command of the operation.
2. Label the kill, or hot, zone.
3. Label an inner perimeter, or warm zone.
4. Label an outer perimeter, or cold zone.
5. Establish a command post.
6. Identify a staging area.
7. Make a list of additional resources that are required.

9. The class of recruits is then presented with the following scenario: Officer Suarez is appointed district officer in charge at the scene of an aircraft crash. A private plane has fallen from the sky and crashed alongside a stretch of highway. Officer Suarez and her team have already taken control of the operation and have clearly established the perimeters of the hot, warm, and cold zones. They are currently setting up a staging area. Which critical step did they skip?

   A. identifying an inner and outer perimeter
   B. exercising command over the entire operation
   C. establishing a command post
   D. requesting additional resources for the operation

10. The class is then presented with another scenario: A small plane has fallen from the sky outside a residential area. There appears to be minimal damage to the plane, but the engine is smoking and jet fuel is leaking onto the ground. Officer Williams has been appointed district officer in charge and has taken command of the situation. What should he do first?

   A. Establish a command post.
   B. Label an outer perimeter.
   C. Set up a warm zone.
   D. Identify the kill zone.

Answers

1. **C** After Officer Kraft collects the necessary information from the woman with the wallet, he should write a found property report using the information from the woman. This report will include who turned in the wallet, where it was found, when it was found, and where Officer Kraft is holding it.

2. **D** The first thing Officer Montana needs to do is call the man back to the desk and ask for his name and where he found the keys. Then he has to write a found property report, tag the keys, fill out the tag, and place the keys in the property room. He shouldn't allow the man to leave without first trying to get the necessary information to complete his property report.

3. **A** The officer's report begins with statement 2, which is suggested by the nature of the statement. The next statement, statement 4, indicates that the officer has run the vehicle's plates to find out who the owner is and if he has any warrants. This is followed by statement 3, in which the driver of the vehicle answers the officer after being asked if he has been drinking. Statement 1 then indicates that the driver agrees to take a breathalyzer test, the results of which are reported in statement 5.

4. **C** The first sentence to appear in Officer Harmon's police report should be statement 2, which describes the discovery of the missing car. You can assume that Mr. White then called the police to report that his vehicle was stolen. Once the police arrive, they ask Mr. White to provide specific details about his car and question the neighbors to see if anyone heard or saw anything. This would mean that statements 1 and 5 are next. While speaking to neighbors, the police discover that Mr. White's vehicle is not the only one that's been stolen within the past three weeks, statement 4. Statement 5 would come at the end of the police report because this event occurred after the others.

5. **C** The officers in question are in the process of carefully approaching the scene. They know an alarm has been tripped, and they suspected that someone may be inside the building, but what they've witnessed so far doesn't indicate a burglary. Their next step should be to enter the building and attempt to locate what set off the alarm.

6. **A** The response team did not approach the scene with caution, as they should have. Rushing into the building broke protocol and put the entire team in danger.

7. **B** The first sentence that should appear in Officer Monroe's incident report is statement 3, which describes an unidentified woman entering the grocery store with a backpack and a purse. After the woman is spotted stealing meat by customers in statement 4, the manager of the grocery store notifies the employees that a theft is in progress by announcing a Code 99, statement 5. The police are most likely called, but, as described in statement 2, the woman leaves the store with the meat. When the police finally arrive, statement 5 says that they ask to see security footage of the theft.

8. **A** The first sentence in Officer Milton's incident report should be statement 4, which describes the beginning of the incident. Then statement 3 would be included in the report, because this is the reason Mrs. Frost gave as to why she thought Timmy was missing. Next, statements 5 and 2 would appear in the report because these are the actions police took to search for Timmy. Finally, statement 1 would end the report, because it describes Timmy coming home with a surprise for his mother.

9. **C** Officer Suarez's crew never set about establishing a command post. This should happen before they set up the staging area, but after identifying the zones and perimeters around the crash site.

10. **D** The first thing Officer Williams needs to do is identify the kill zone. The kill zone, or hot zone, is the area closest to the event. People stationed in this area have the highest risk of being injured, because explosions may occur. Once the hot zone has been labeled, the warm and cold zones should be identified. Then Officer Williams can establish a command post.

C. Interpersonal and Public Relations

A few questions on the police officer exam are designed to test your ability to work with others. These questions may be about working one-on-one with your partner, your supervisor, or even suspects. They also may be about interacting professionally and responsibly with members of the public.

You'll recognize interpersonal and public-relations questions on the written exam because many of them involve discussions between two officers, an officer and his or her superior, or an officer and a member of the public. You'll often be asked to think like the officer in the scenario and choose the correct and most appropriate response or action.

1. Interpersonal Relations

The term *interpersonal relations* simply refers to your interactions with other people, particularly other police officers. Your relationship with other officers is extremely important, because these are the people you'll expect to help you stay safe in dangerous situations. If you don't trust and respect your fellow officers, they may not trust or respect you in return. This distrust can cause communication problems and can turn a routine operation into a life-threatening event. As a police officer, one of your main priorities should always be to represent and protect the men and women of your department.

Your ability to feel dedication, respect, and trust toward other officers in a department will be tested through judgment and problem-solving questions about interpersonal relations. These questions present you with scenarios in which members of your department or even suspects of crimes depend on you to solve a problem. Some questions may even place you in a predicament that allows you to show that you're able to depend on others or follow the orders of others. Even though you're taught at the academy that you should always take responsibility for your own words and actions, it's important to realize that you should never be afraid to ask for help or advice if you need it.

Although many interpersonal-relations questions may present you with scenarios in which you must work alongside your partner, others may test your ability to respect your superiors. For example, when responding to an emergency, you should always follow the directions given to you by your lieutenant, captain, or chief, regardless of whether you agree with him or her. If you'd like to discuss an issue with one of your superiors, be sure to do it respectfully and privately.

When answering these judgment and problem-solving questions, remember that you should always be honest and show respect to those around you. Now, try the following examples. Imagine yourself in the situation and choose the most appropriate response from the options provided.

Examples:

---

1. Despite a recent injury to his knee, Officer Lincoln insists on responding to calls. Lincoln's captain tells him that he can't respond to any emergencies until he sees a doctor and his knee properly heals. When a call comes in minutes after their conversation ends, Lincoln grabs his coat. He feels he is healthy enough to go with the others. What should he do?

   A. Ask the chief if he can go.
   B. Put on his coat and jump in his cruiser.
   C. Stay at the station while everyone else responds.
   D. Beg the captain to allow him to respond to the emergency.

The correct answer is **C**. If Officer Lincoln responded to the emergency, he would not only be defying his superior's orders, but he'd also be putting everyone at the scene in danger. If his knee is injured, he may not be able to perform to the best of his abilities, thus hindering the performance of the entire squad. Instead, Officer Lincoln should stay at the station while everyone else responds to the emergency.

---

2. While questioning a suspect, Detective Miles watches her partner grow red with irritation. The suspect refuses to speak about his role in an armed robbery, but Detective Miles's partner is convinced that the suspect was an accomplice. Her partner swears at the suspect and then walks around the table and leans in close to the suspect's ear. Detective Miles has never seen her partner strike a suspect before, but she wonders if she should fear for the suspect's safety. What should she do?

   A. Wait to see what her partner's next move will be.
   B. Request that her partner pour her a cup of coffee.
   C. Ask her partner to step away from the suspect and calm down.
   D. Allow her partner to do what he must to get a confession out of the suspect.

The correct answer is **A**. Detective Miles should wait to see what her partner's next move will be before she takes any action. It's possible that her partner is putting on an act, trying to scare the suspect into confessing. He may be in complete control of his actions and may never lay a hand on the suspect. Because this possibility exists, choices B and C are incorrect. Out of respect for her partner, she should trust that he won't act in ways that would jeopardize their case or the interview. Asking him to pour her some coffee would also be demeaning and may possibly embarrass her partner. Choice D is also incorrect because even though her partner has some freedom, Detective Miles is obligated to intervene if the interview becomes violent.

2. Public Relations

Whether they're on the scene of an emergency or eating at a local diner with friends, police officers should always show respect to civilians. Police officers' relationships to members of the public are important because people need to know they can depend on their local police departments. All civilians, regardless of age, need to trust their local police officers. Children often look up to police officers as mentors or role models. They need to understand that if they're ever in trouble, they can seek out a police officer for help, protection, or even advice.

As a police officer, you may not have the answer or solution to every civilian's problem, but you should still be polite and patient when you respond—even if you don't have an answer or can't legally perform the task or favor they're asking of you. This relationship between a department's police officers and the citizens of the town or city it services is called *public relations.*

Judgment and problem-solving public-relations questions normally include a short passage that describes a situation involving a police officer and a member of the public. Typically, the civilian asks the police officer a question, and you have to choose the answer to the question that follows rules and procedures while simultaneously showing the most concern for the civilian's safety and feelings.

You can't really study for public-relations questions that appear on the police officer exam because they test your ability to communicate and reason with people. Depend on your common sense to answer these questions, but keep in mind that the best answer will include keeping everyone involved safe. If an answer is going to put someone in danger, it's most likely incorrect. If a civilian is angry with your response, but everyone is safe and you've selected an answer that follows general department protocol, then the civilian's anger is acceptable.

Remember: Thoroughly read every passage and answer option, especially when dealing with public-relations questions. At first, many answers may seem correct, but upon closer inspection, you may notice that one shows a civilian more respect while another may put a fellow officer in danger.

Try the following judgment questions about public relations. Be sure to select the answer that keeps everyone safe.

Examples:

1. You're at a party when a friend from high school approaches you. Minutes after he finds out that you're a police officer, he tells you about a parking ticket he received recently. He says he wasn't parked illegally and asks if there's any way you can do something about the ticket so he doesn't have to pay it. How should you respond?

    A.   Tell him you can't help him because there's a reason he got the ticket in the first place.
    B.   Tell him that you'll look into it during your next shift, but don't make any promises.
    C.   Tell him there's nothing you can do for him because you didn't issue the ticket.
    D.   Tell him to bring you the ticket and you'll make sure he doesn't have to pay it.

The correct answer is **C.** You should tell him there's nothing you can do for him because you didn't issue the ticket. This response explains why you can't help your friend without making him frustrated or making him think you'll attempt to nullify the ticket. Choice D is incorrect because you can't legally erase his ticket, and choice A is incorrect because it might make your friend angry. Choice B is also incorrect because it will make your friend assume that there's a chance that all officers can "take care" of these issues when it's against protocol to do so. If you chose choice B, thinking that you could simply tell him that you'll look into it and then not do so later, this is incorrect because it's a lie. Law enforcement should always be honest with civilians.

2. During a holiday parade, your local police department carries a banner and throws candy to the children. An older man approaches you on a street corner once the parade is over and claims that you've just wasted his tax dollars. He says that police should be spending time patrolling the streets for criminals and protecting the city's youth, not marching in a parade. How should you respond?

   A. Walk away from the man without responding.
   B. Ask him to further explain why he feels that way.
   C. Remind him that he is wasting your time by talking to you.
   D. Tell him that if he doesn't like parades, he should've stayed home.

The correct answer is **B.** You should ask him to further explain why he feels that way. The best thing to do in this situation is show an interest in the man's thoughts and beliefs. Once he justifies why he feels the way he does, he may be more respectful because you were patient with him. He might then listen to you when you explain that your presence in the parade is good public relations for the department and shows children that police officers are good people who are always around if they need help. Choices A, C, and D are incorrect because these responses are disrespectful and inappropriate.

Practice

Directions (1–10): Answer these questions solely on the basis of the information provided.

1. You're interrogating a suspect. Which of the following approaches would *not* be an appropriate way to encourage the suspect to talk?

   A. Listen to the suspect carefully and intently.
   B. Assure the suspect that his alleged crime is not that big of a deal.
   C. Make the suspect feel as though you care for him.
   D. Tell the suspect that you can understand and appreciate his situation.

2. Your department has recently hired a handful of new part-time recruits. When they arrive, you notice one of the new recruits incorrectly loading his firearm. What should you do?

   A. Wait for a supervisor to catch him and teach him the correct way.
   B. Tell him to stop and show him the correct way to load the gun.
   C. Nothing because he should already know how to load a weapon.
   D. Ask one of the other officers to show him what he's doing wrong.

3. On your day off, you take the time to do some work on your front lawn. As you start the lawnmower, you notice a little girl walking toward you. As she moves closer, you recognize her from a class at the elementary school where you've spoken a few times. She's standing at the edge of your lawn, crying. What should you do?

   A. Tell her to wait on your porch while you finish cutting the grass.
   B. Ask her to go home and tell her parents what's bothering her.
   C. Shut off your mower and ask her why she's crying.
   D. Take her to the police station so she can talk to a social worker.

4. Over the past few weeks, you and your partner have been assigned to perform five stakeouts. About an hour or two into the stakeouts, your partner has been excusing himself and coming back about an hour later. He says he's been walking to the closest restaurant and using the bathroom, but you're sure he's up to something else. The chief has asked you to stake out a building on the outskirts of town. What should you say?

   A. Tell the chief you'll do it only if he'll talk to your partner about his disappearing acts.
   B. Tell the chief you won't do it because you feel like you're working by yourself.
   C. Tell the chief you'll go and then ask your partner to be honest with you.
   D. Tell the chief you'll go and follow your partner when he leaves the car.

5. After almost every shift, you get something to eat with your partner at the diner across from the police station. You've become close with the servers and the owner; they know what you're going to order before you even pick up the menu. Recently, the owner of the diner passed away. As the day of his funeral nears, the owner's wife asks you to speak during services. What should you do?

   A. Tell her yes, you'd be honored.
   B. Tell her no, you barely knew the owner.
   C. Tell her no, the department doesn't allow one person to represent the entire squad.
   D. Tell her yes, but you'll have to check with your superiors before you speak in public.

6. You live in a neighborhood that's seen a bit of drug activity lately, so the captain decided to issue patrols for the area. On your days off, you like to sit on your porch and read the newspaper. Over the past two weeks, you've noticed the same cruiser go by the house at the same time each day. You recognize the driver as one of the new members of the squad, and you know the officer should vary the times of his patrol. What should you do?

   A. Nothing because it's not your problem when you're not on duty.
   B. Tell the captain that the recruit isn't varying his routes.
   C. Suggest to the recruit that he change the times of his patrol routes.
   D. Volunteer to patrol the neighborhood since you know it best.

7. While you're working the front desk at the police station, an older woman comes in and tells you that the man who lives next door to her is too loud. She says that he works out in his garage at 5:30 p.m. every day and is constantly dropping weights and yelling. She wants you to issue him a citation. What should you do?

   A. Tell her there's nothing you can do because the man is not violating any ordinances.
   B. Go home with her and listen to the man to determine if he's a true disturbance.
   C. Write out a civil citation for a $250 fine and ask her to give it to her neighbor.
   D. Suggest that she speak to her neighbor and ask him not to yell loudly.

8. As you finish your last incident report for the day, the captain approaches your desk with a handful of papers. She says the papers are your partner's incident reports and she can't read them. Since you've been with your partner for over three years now, the captain thinks you can read his writing and asks you to type them before you leave. What should you do?

   A. Ask her if you can type the reports in the morning.
   B. Tell her that the work is your partner's responsibility and you won't do it.
   C. Take the files and complete the task before you leave.
   D. Call your partner and ask him to come back in to finish his work.

9. You're the first to arrive on scene at a car accident. As you're assessing the situation, an ambulance arrives. An EMT gets out of the vehicle and asks you to step aside so he can assess the conditions of the victims. What should you do?

   A. Ignore him and continue assessing the scene.
   B. Shove the EMT worker out of the way and continue working.
   C. Suggest that you work together to control the situation.
   D. Talk to the EMT's superior about his attitude.

10. You're investigating a missing-person case. A newly hired detective asks you for your research notes, so she can become more familiar with the case. Afterward, you find out she presented the information you gathered as her own findings to the police chief. What should you do?

   A. Confront her about it and ask her not to do it again.
   B. Start spreading rumors about the detective.
   C. Nothing because the detective has higher rank than you do.
   D. Threaten to hurt her if she doesn't tell your supervisor the truth.

Answers

1. **B** You should not assure the suspect that his alleged crime is not that big of a deal. This can minimize the significance of the suspect's alleged crime and cause him or her to feel less guilt. If the suspect stops feeling guilty, he or she may become less cooperative and willing to answer questions.

2. **B** Although this new recruit is not technically your responsibility, he is still one of the members of your department, and you should be concerned about his safety. When you notice that he's incorrectly loading his firearm, you should tell him to stop and show him the correct way to load the gun. Ignoring the issue could endanger the new recruit and anyone near him at a future scene.

3. **C** Even though it's your day off, you should still help those in need. You're a police officer regardless of whether you're wearing your uniform at the time of an emergency or complicated situation. You should shut off your mower and ask her why she's crying. She has obviously recognized you from class, just as you've recognized her, and knows she can trust you with her problems. You shouldn't take her to the police station because you currently don't have a reason to do so.

4. **C** You should tell the chief you'll go and then ask your partner to be honest with you. You should take this action because it shows respect to both your superior and your partner. If you were to tell the chief that your partner has been disappearing during his shifts, he may be in trouble with the department. Since you don't know where he's going, you should ask him about his actions. If he

continues to lie to you, then you should inform him that you're going to tell your superior. Never operate behind anyone's back; this breaks trust and hurts the team dynamic.

5. **A** You should tell her yes, you'd be honored. As a devoted diner customer and someone who grew close to the owner and the staff, you have plenty of nice things you can say about the owner at the service. Since you'll be speaking positively about a citizen of the town, your superiors won't have an issue with your participation.

6. **C** You should suggest to the recruit that he change up his patrol routes. If he travels the same route every day, people— including criminals—are going to notice. They're going to be able to predict when he'll be around and will be sure to steer clear of illegal activities during those times. You shouldn't go to the captain unless you tell the recruit to change his route and he fails to do so.

7. **D** You should suggest that she speak to her neighbor and ask him not to yell loudly. Since the neighbor works out before most people sleep at night, he's not disturbing anyone's quality of life.

8. **C** You should take the files and complete the task before you leave. You should always respect authority; therefore, you should complete any tasks your superior asks of you without hesitation. You can mention the incident to your partner the next day, but don't call him back into the office to complete paperwork. Choice A is incorrect because you shouldn't try to bargain with your superior.

9. **C** You should suggest that you work together to control the situation. Because the lives of others may be at stake at an accident scene, you should try to work together. You should not ignore the EMT's orders or get into a physical confrontation with him. The EMT's action doesn't require you to talk to the EMT's supervisor.

10. **A** You should confront her about it and ask her not to do it again. You should give her the chance to explain why she presented your work as her own. If this doesn't rectify the situation, you should talk to your supervisor. You should not spread rumors about the detective or threaten to harm her.

D. Deductive and Inductive Reasoning

Deductive and inductive reasoning are two methods of logic used to arrive at a conclusion. On the police officer exam, you'll be asked to read either a definition or deductive-reasoning passage and then use the information you're given to answer the questions that follow. You'll also be asked to read an inductive-reasoning passage or table and use the information to reach a conclusion and answer the question.

1. Deductive Reasoning

Deductive reasoning is a method of logic in which you apply general rules to a specific situation. The police officer exam includes two types of deductive-reasoning questions. The first type asks you to read a definition or a set of definitions and then choose the situation that best fits the definition or definitions provided. The second type asks you to read a passage that contains specific information that you'll use to answer the questions that follow. These types of questions aren't much different than the reading comprehension passages in Chapter V. Everything you need to answer the questions is found in the definitions or passages. Don't forget: You can refer back to the definitions or passages when answering these types of questions.

Consider this statement: "All fish can swim." Your child has a goldfish named Goldie. Goldie is a type of fish and lives in a bowl of water. You can use deductive reasoning to draw this conclusion: "Goldie can swim." You use something general (all fish) to come to a conclusion about something specific (Goldie).

Try a few of the type of deductive-reasoning questions you may see on the police officer exam.

Tip: You can find the answers to deductive-reasoning questions right in the passage. Read the question and look back to the passage to find the correct answer.

Examples:

The New York City Police Department and the city government recently revised some of the existing citywide parking regulations to cut down on parking offenses and update parts of the former parking code that were obsolete. The following are a few of the new or updated ordinances from the new parking code as instituted by the department and the government.

1. All vehicles parked on the street must be no more than 6 inches from the curb.
2. No vehicles may be parked less than 4 feet from an intersection.
3. Commercial delivery trucks may remain double-parked for deliveries for no more than 15 minutes.
4. Vehicles may not remain in a Limited-Time Parking Zone for more than 25 minutes.
5. Median parking is allowed in only designated Median Parking Zones.
6. Vehicles may be parked in Green Zones only between 5 a.m. and 5 p.m.
7. Taxis may occupy a particular parking spot for no more than 30 minutes at a time.
8. Parking in White Zones is restricted to emergency vehicles at all times.

---

1. Based on the information provided, which of the following vehicles is in violation of the city's new parking code?
   A. a sedan parked in a Green Zone for 45 minutes at 2:43 p.m.
   B. a flower delivery truck parked in a designated Median Parking Zone for 32 minutes
   C. a taxi parked 3.5 feet from an intersection in a Limited Time Parking Zone for 14 minutes
   D. a pickup truck parked 4 inches from the curb in a Green Zone

---

The correct answer is **C**. Based on the passage, the only vehicle currently in violation of the new parking code is the taxi parked 3.5 feet from an intersection in a Limited Time Parking Zone for 14 minutes. Although the taxi has not incurred any time violations, it's parked too near the intersection. According to the parking code, the taxi should not be parked any closer than 4 feet from the intersection.

An individual commits a **violation** when he or she knowingly or unknowingly breaks or does not follow the laws.

Sometimes a police officer writes a **citation,** which may or may not include a monetary fine or some other punishment, for an individual who breaks the law.

Sometimes a police officer **arrests** an individual or takes him or her into police control for breaking the law.

When a convicted individual has his or her sentence suspended and is given freedom under the supervision of another official, this individual is given **probation.**

2. Which of the following is an example of a violation?

   A. When Mary Kane gets in her vehicle, she notices a police officer placed a parking ticket on the windshield while she was gone.

   B. Desiree Philips knows that her driver's license is expired, but she still drives her vehicle on a daily basis.

   C. Rodney Arnone serves 4 months of a 12-month sentence, and he now reports to a parole officer every week.

   D. After a domestic violence dispute, Roberto Diaz is handcuffed and placed into a police cruiser by Officer Martirano.

The correct answer is **B.** Desiree is committing a violation because she knows that her license is expired, but she continues to drive. Choice A is an example of a citation, choice C is an example of probation, and choice D is an example of an arrest.

2. Inductive Reasoning

Inductive-reasoning questions are similar to deductive-reasoning questions, but the answers to these questions are not always found directly in the text. You have to use the information you're given to come to a conclusion about something so you can answer a question about it. Instead of applying a generalization, you need to infer something about the information you're given. The police officer exam includes two types of inductive-reasoning questions. The first type asks you to read a passage and come to a conclusion using the information in the passage. The second type provides you with a table containing information from which you must draw a conclusion to answer the question.

Think of inductive reasoning like this: Casts are applied to broken limbs. If your co-worker comes to work one day with a cast on her arm, you can use inductive reasoning to assume your co-worker broke the bone in her arm.

Tip: You must use the information from the passage or table to come to a logical conclusion to answer these types of questions.

Try a few inductive-reasoning questions. Remember to draw a conclusion about the information you're given to help you answer the questions.

Examples:

An instructor informs his class of recruit officers that they will be observing a roadblock this upcoming weekend. The instructor tells his class that approximately 1 percent of all drivers that pass through a roadblock are typically under the influence of drugs or alcohol, although exceptions apply during holiday seasons and weekends of major sporting events such as the Super Bowl. He then explains the guidelines for constructing a roadblock:

   1. Select a location that allows approaching motorists to see that all cars will be stopped.

   2. Staff the location with required personnel including uniformed officials to perform the initial stop, officers to perform sobriety tests, and a command observation officer.

   3. Stop all motorists that pass through the roadblock.

4. Briefly question drivers not suspected of being under the influence. If a driver is suspected of drinking, have them pull to the side of the road for a sobriety test.

5. Take down the roadblock after approximately two hours.

---

1. Using the information provided, you may infer that police officers take down roadblocks after only two hours of operation because:

   A. Only 1 percent of drivers are typically arrested so police officers become bored at checkpoints and start performing sobriety checks on everyone.

   B. After about an hour, word spreads about the location of the roadblock and drivers who have been drinking know to avoid the area.

   C. Police departments are normally understaffed; therefore, police officers have various responsibilities and duties to complete and can't spend all night at a checkpoint.

   D. Police officers' assistance is often needed on calls in the middle of the night that are more important than drunk driving.

The correct answer is **B**. As mentioned in the passage, every car that passes through the roadblock is stopped and every driver is questioned, regardless of whether the police are suspicious of him or her. After an hour or so, word spreads about the location of the roadblock and drivers who have been drinking know to avoid the area; therefore, there is no longer a point in staffing a roadblock in that particular area.

New recruit officers are learning about traffic and moving violations in the state of Pennsylvania. They receive a handout containing the following information:

Vehicle Code	Description of Violation	Points
3112	Failure to stop at a red light	3
3323	Failing to stop at a stop sign	3
3341	Failure to comply with train crossing gate	4 (and 30-day suspension)
3345	Failure to stop for a school bus with lights on	5 (and 60-day suspension)
3362	Exceeding the speed limit	2 to 5
3542	Failure to yield at a crosswalk	2

---

2. After reviewing the table, it would be most correct for an officer to conclude that:

   A. A driver cited for failing to yield to a pedestrian crossing the street will lose his or her license for 30 days.

   B. A driver cited for exceeding the speed limit will receive a warning from the police officer.

   C. A driver cited for not complying with a train crossing gate will incur two points on his or her driving record.

   D. A driver cited for passing a school bus with red lights flashing will lose his or her license.

The correct answer is **D**. By using the information in the table, you can infer that if a driver fails to stop for a bus with its lights flashing, he or she will receive 5 points on his or her driving record and lose his or her license. So, you can assume that a driver stopped for passing a school bus with red lights flashing will lose his or her license.

Practice

Questions 1 through 3 refer to the following information.

In an effort to keep drivers and pedestrians safe, the Atlas Police Department is enforcing new parking regulations during declared snow emergencies. Violators of these new parking regulations are subject to fines ranging from $45 to $250 and they'll have their vehicles towed. During a declared snow emergency, residents of Atlas should follow these new parking regulations:

- Do not park on streets with signs saying TOW-ZONE: SNOW EMERGENCY.
- Cars parked in driveways should be completely in the driveway and should not extend onto the sidewalk or street.
- Disabled cars on the roadway must be removed as soon as possible.
- Refrain from parking less than 15 feet from an intersection.
- Refrain from parking more than 1 foot from curbs.
- Resident parking stickers must be visible within 12 hours after the end of the snowstorm.
- Remove "space-savers" in shoveled parking spaces within eight hours after the end of the snowstorm.

1. According to the passage, after a snowstorm, residents' parking stickers must be visible within:

   A. 1 hour
   B. 8 hours
   C. 12 hours
   D. 15 hours

2. According to the passage, during a snow emergency, residents should:

   A. Park their vehicles no less than 2 feet from a curb.
   B. Disregard signs saying TOW-ZONE: SNOW EMERGENCY.
   C. Leave their disabled cars in the roadway until the snow passes.
   D. Remove "space-savers" no more than eight hours after the snow ends.

3. According to the passage, violators will be:

   A. given a warning
   B. arrested
   C. fined
   D. put on probation

Questions 4 and 5 refer to the following definitions.

> **Assailant:** An individual who assaults or attacks another individual
>
> **Intruder:** An individual who enters a home or business illegally
>
> **Burglar:** An intruder who steals items from the home or business
>
> **Convict:** An individual who is either found guilty of committing a crime or is serving a sentence for a crime

4. Which of the following is an example of an assailant?

   A. A jury found Boris Manuel guilty of raping an elderly woman.
   B. Melissa Borat scanned the office before taking a laptop computer and fleeing.
   C. Art Frank let himself into his neighbor's house and used the telephone.
   D. During questioning, Donald McNamara smacked the detective.

5. Which of the following is an example of an intruder?

   A. Geoffrey and his friends snuck into the movie theater.
   B. The woman was sentenced to 15 years for killing her husband.
   C. Thomas slipped a pack of gum into his pocket while the clerk was busy.
   D. Jennifer walked up to a woman and pushed her to the ground.

Questions 6 through 8 refer to the following information.

The city of Bellville recently revised some of its existing citywide recycling regulations. The following are a few of the new or updated ordinances as instituted by the city's supervisor of streets and sanitation:

1. All bottles, jars, and cans should be rinsed and cleaned.
2. Plastic products should be crushed.
3. Broken glass will not be accepted.
4. Labels do not have to be removed.
5. Bottle and jar tops will not be accepted.
6. Newspapers and magazines will be accepted only if bundled with string or placed in a brown paper bag.
7. The following items will not be accepted and should be placed with trash: aerosol spray cans, aluminum foil, ceramics, cereal boxes, hazardous materials, miscellaneous cardboard, motor oil bottles, paint cans, pizza boxes, tissue boxes, and telephone books.
8. Items must be placed in a city-provided recycling container and placed 2 feet from the curb no earlier than 4 p.m. on the day before pickup.

6. Using the information provided, which of the following items can you infer is accepted for recycling?

   A. a cardboard box from a television set
   B. a Styrofoam takeout container
   C. a broken light bulb
   D. a stack of magazines tied with twine

7. Using the information provided, which of the following is the best example of a person who is acting in accordance with Bellville's recycling regulations?

   A. Mr. Williams removes the labels from the jars he's recycling.
   B. Mr. Vicmoore places his items at the curb at 6 p.m. the night before pickup.
   C. Ms. Fernando places her recyclable items in a brown paper bag.
   D. Mrs. Hellmann forgets to rinse her soda bottles before recycling them.

8. According to the information listed, why can you infer that a broken glass container is not an acceptable item for recycling?

    A. Workers picking up recyclables can be injured by broken glass.
    B. Broken glass should be placed with trash.
    C. Broken glass containers cannot be rinsed.
    D. Lids cannot be removed from broken glass containers.

Questions 9 and 10 refer to the following information.

New police officer recruits are learning about the frequency of traffic citations at busy intersections in a particular city. To understand how the presence of a decoy police vehicle affects the number of traffic violations issued per week, the class is given the following information:

Intersection	Citations	Decoy Car
Rock and Parsonage streets	8	Yes
Luzerne Street and Bennett Avenue	34	No
Main Street and Brandenburg Lane	12	Yes
Fort Place and Monroe Avenue	19	No
Meyer and Lavelle streets	4	Yes
Bulford Street and Union Avenue	21	No

9. Based on the information in the table, the recruits could correctly assume that the presence of a decoy police vehicle:

    A. results in fewer citations
    B. causes more citations
    C. is effective only at intersections
    D. doesn't affect the number of citations

10. Based on the information in the table, the recruits could correctly assume that the presence of a decoy police vehicle at:

    A. Luzerne Street and Bennett Avenue will result in fewer citations
    B. Meyer and Lavelle streets does not currently affect the number of citations
    C. Fort Place and Monroe Avenue will not affect the number of citations
    D. Bulford Street and Union Avenue will result in more citations

Answers

1. **C** According to the passage, residents' parking stickers must be visible within 12 hours after the end of a snowstorm.

2. **D** According to the passage, residents should remove "space-savers" no more than eight hours after the snow ends.

3. **C** According to the passage, violators of the Atlas snow ordinance will be fined.

4. **D** *During questioning, Donald McNamara smacked the detective* is an example of someone acting as an assailant. Since Donald assaulted the detective, Donald is an assailant. Choice A is an example of a convict, choice B is an example of a burglar, and choice C is an example of an intruder.

5. **A** *Geoffrey and his friends snuck into the movie theater* is an example of an intruder. Because the boys entered a business illegally, they're intruders. Choice B is an example of a convict, choice C is an example of a burglar, and choice D is an example of an assailant.

6. **D** According to the recycling regulations, a stack of magazines tied with twine is accepted for recycling. The other choices are not acceptable items for recycling.

7. **B** According to the information, you can infer that Mr. Vicmoore is in accordance with the recycling regulations because he places his items at the curb after 4 p.m. on the day before pickup.

8. **A** According to the information, you can infer that a broken glass container is not accepted because workers picking up recyclables can be injured by broken glass.

9. **A** According to the information provided in the table, the recruits can determine that the presence of a decoy police vehicle results in fewer citations. The information in the table clearly indicates that the presence of a decoy police vehicle reduces the number of citations issued at intersections.

10. **A** According to the information provided in the table, the recruits can determine that the presence of a decoy police vehicle at Luzerne Street and Bennett Avenue will result in fewer citations. The information in the table clearly indicates that the presence of a decoy police vehicle reduces the number of citations issued at intersections, so an intersection with a high amount of citations—such as Luzerne Street and Bennett Avenue—would benefit from a decoy vehicle at this intersection.

IX. Full-Length Practice Test with Answer Explanations

Answer Sheet

Section 1

1 Ⓐ Ⓑ Ⓒ	21 Ⓐ Ⓑ Ⓒ Ⓓ
2 Ⓐ Ⓑ Ⓒ	22 Ⓐ Ⓑ Ⓒ Ⓓ
3 Ⓐ Ⓑ	23 Ⓐ Ⓑ Ⓒ Ⓓ
4 Ⓐ Ⓑ Ⓒ	24 Ⓐ Ⓑ Ⓒ Ⓓ
5 Ⓐ Ⓑ Ⓒ	25 Ⓐ Ⓑ Ⓒ Ⓓ
6 Ⓐ Ⓑ Ⓒ Ⓓ	26 Ⓐ Ⓑ Ⓒ Ⓓ
7 Ⓐ Ⓑ Ⓒ Ⓓ	27 Ⓐ Ⓑ Ⓒ Ⓓ
8 Ⓐ Ⓑ Ⓒ Ⓓ	28 Ⓐ Ⓑ Ⓒ Ⓓ
9 Ⓐ Ⓑ Ⓒ Ⓓ	29 Ⓐ Ⓑ Ⓒ Ⓓ
10 Ⓐ Ⓑ Ⓒ Ⓓ	30 Ⓐ Ⓑ Ⓒ Ⓓ
11 Ⓐ Ⓑ Ⓒ Ⓓ	31 Ⓐ Ⓑ Ⓒ Ⓓ
12 Ⓐ Ⓑ Ⓒ Ⓓ	32 Ⓐ Ⓑ Ⓒ Ⓓ
13 Ⓐ Ⓑ Ⓒ Ⓓ	33 Ⓐ Ⓑ Ⓒ Ⓓ
14 Ⓐ Ⓑ Ⓒ Ⓓ	34 Ⓐ Ⓑ Ⓒ Ⓓ
15 Ⓐ Ⓑ	35 Ⓐ Ⓑ
16 Ⓐ Ⓑ	36 Ⓐ Ⓑ Ⓒ Ⓓ
17 Ⓐ Ⓑ	37 Ⓐ Ⓑ Ⓒ Ⓓ
18 Ⓐ Ⓑ	38 Ⓐ Ⓑ Ⓒ Ⓓ
19 Ⓐ Ⓑ Ⓒ Ⓓ	39 Ⓐ Ⓑ Ⓒ Ⓓ
20 Ⓐ Ⓑ Ⓒ Ⓓ	40 Ⓐ Ⓑ Ⓒ Ⓓ

41. _____   46. _____

42. _____   47. _____

43. _____   48. _____

44. _____   49. _____

45. _____   50. _____

Section 2

1	Ⓐ	Ⓑ	Ⓒ	Ⓓ	**26**	Ⓐ	Ⓑ	Ⓒ	Ⓓ
2	Ⓐ	Ⓑ	Ⓒ	Ⓓ	**27**	Ⓐ	Ⓑ	Ⓒ	Ⓓ
3	Ⓐ	Ⓑ	Ⓒ	Ⓓ	**28**	Ⓐ	Ⓑ	Ⓒ	Ⓓ
4	Ⓐ	Ⓑ	Ⓒ	Ⓓ	**29**	Ⓐ	Ⓑ	Ⓒ	Ⓓ
5	Ⓐ	Ⓑ	Ⓒ	Ⓓ	**30**	Ⓐ	Ⓑ	Ⓒ	Ⓓ
6	Ⓐ	Ⓑ	Ⓒ	Ⓓ	**31**	Ⓐ	Ⓑ	Ⓒ	Ⓓ
7	Ⓐ	Ⓑ	Ⓒ	Ⓓ	**32**	Ⓐ	Ⓑ	Ⓒ	Ⓓ
8	Ⓐ	Ⓑ	Ⓒ	Ⓓ	**33**	Ⓐ	Ⓑ	Ⓒ	Ⓓ
9	Ⓐ	Ⓑ	Ⓒ	Ⓓ	**34**	Ⓐ	Ⓑ	Ⓒ	Ⓓ
10	Ⓐ	Ⓑ	Ⓒ	Ⓓ	**35**	Ⓐ	Ⓑ	Ⓒ	Ⓓ
11	Ⓐ	Ⓑ	Ⓒ	Ⓓ	**36**	Ⓐ	Ⓑ	Ⓒ	Ⓓ
12	Ⓐ	Ⓑ	Ⓒ	Ⓓ	**37**	Ⓐ	Ⓑ	Ⓒ	Ⓓ
13	Ⓐ	Ⓑ	Ⓒ	Ⓓ	**38**	Ⓐ	Ⓑ	Ⓒ	Ⓓ
14	Ⓐ	Ⓑ	Ⓒ	Ⓓ	**39**	Ⓐ	Ⓑ	Ⓒ	Ⓓ
15	Ⓐ	Ⓑ	Ⓒ	Ⓓ	**40**	Ⓐ	Ⓑ	Ⓒ	Ⓓ
16	Ⓐ	Ⓑ	Ⓒ	Ⓓ	**41**	Ⓐ	Ⓑ	Ⓒ	Ⓓ
17	Ⓐ	Ⓑ	Ⓒ	Ⓓ	**42**	Ⓐ	Ⓑ	Ⓒ	Ⓓ
18	Ⓐ	Ⓑ	Ⓒ	Ⓓ	**43**	Ⓐ	Ⓑ	Ⓒ	Ⓓ
19	Ⓐ	Ⓑ	Ⓒ	Ⓓ	**44**	Ⓐ	Ⓑ	Ⓒ	Ⓓ
20	Ⓐ	Ⓑ	Ⓒ	Ⓓ	**45**	Ⓐ	Ⓑ	Ⓒ	Ⓓ
21	Ⓐ	Ⓑ	Ⓒ	Ⓓ	**46**	Ⓐ	Ⓑ	Ⓒ	Ⓓ
22	Ⓐ	Ⓑ	Ⓒ	Ⓓ	**47**	Ⓐ	Ⓑ	Ⓒ	Ⓓ
23	Ⓐ	Ⓑ	Ⓒ	Ⓓ	**48**	Ⓐ	Ⓑ	Ⓒ	Ⓓ
24	Ⓐ	Ⓑ	Ⓒ	Ⓓ	**49**	Ⓐ	Ⓑ	Ⓒ	Ⓓ
25	Ⓐ	Ⓑ	Ⓒ	Ⓓ	**50**	Ⓐ	Ⓑ	Ⓒ	Ⓓ

CUT HERE

Section 3

1	Ⓐ Ⓑ Ⓒ Ⓓ	26	Ⓐ Ⓑ Ⓒ Ⓓ
2	Ⓐ Ⓑ Ⓒ Ⓓ	27	Ⓐ Ⓑ Ⓒ Ⓓ
3	Ⓐ Ⓑ Ⓒ Ⓓ	28	Ⓐ Ⓑ Ⓒ Ⓓ
4	Ⓐ Ⓑ Ⓒ Ⓓ	29	Ⓐ Ⓑ Ⓒ Ⓓ
5	Ⓐ Ⓑ Ⓒ Ⓓ	30	Ⓐ Ⓑ Ⓒ Ⓓ
6	Ⓐ Ⓑ Ⓒ Ⓓ	31	Ⓐ Ⓑ Ⓒ Ⓓ
7	Ⓐ Ⓑ Ⓒ Ⓓ	32	Ⓐ Ⓑ Ⓒ Ⓓ
8	Ⓐ Ⓑ Ⓒ Ⓓ	33	Ⓐ Ⓑ Ⓒ Ⓓ
9	Ⓐ Ⓑ Ⓒ Ⓓ	34	Ⓐ Ⓑ Ⓒ Ⓓ
10	Ⓐ Ⓑ Ⓒ Ⓓ	35	Ⓐ Ⓑ Ⓒ Ⓓ
11	Ⓐ Ⓑ Ⓒ Ⓓ	36	Ⓐ Ⓑ Ⓒ Ⓓ
12	Ⓐ Ⓑ Ⓒ Ⓓ	37	Ⓐ Ⓑ Ⓒ Ⓓ
13	Ⓐ Ⓑ Ⓒ Ⓓ	38	Ⓐ Ⓑ Ⓒ Ⓓ
14	Ⓐ Ⓑ Ⓒ Ⓓ	39	Ⓐ Ⓑ Ⓒ Ⓓ
15	Ⓐ Ⓑ Ⓒ Ⓓ	40	Ⓐ Ⓑ Ⓒ Ⓓ
16	Ⓐ Ⓑ Ⓒ Ⓓ	41	Ⓐ Ⓑ Ⓒ Ⓓ
17	Ⓐ Ⓑ Ⓒ Ⓓ	42	Ⓐ Ⓑ Ⓒ Ⓓ
18	Ⓐ Ⓑ Ⓒ Ⓓ	43	Ⓐ Ⓑ Ⓒ Ⓓ
19	Ⓐ Ⓑ Ⓒ Ⓓ	44	Ⓐ Ⓑ Ⓒ Ⓓ
20	Ⓐ Ⓑ Ⓒ Ⓓ	45	Ⓐ Ⓑ Ⓒ Ⓓ
21	Ⓐ Ⓑ Ⓒ Ⓓ	46	Ⓐ Ⓑ Ⓒ Ⓓ
22	Ⓐ Ⓑ Ⓒ Ⓓ	47	Ⓐ Ⓑ Ⓒ Ⓓ
23	Ⓐ Ⓑ Ⓒ Ⓓ	48	Ⓐ Ⓑ Ⓒ Ⓓ
24	Ⓐ Ⓑ Ⓒ Ⓓ	49	Ⓐ Ⓑ Ⓒ Ⓓ
25	Ⓐ Ⓑ Ⓒ Ⓓ	50	Ⓐ Ⓑ Ⓒ Ⓓ

Section 4

1 Ⓐ Ⓑ Ⓒ Ⓓ	26 Ⓐ Ⓑ Ⓒ Ⓓ
2 Ⓐ Ⓑ Ⓒ Ⓓ	27 Ⓐ Ⓑ Ⓒ Ⓓ
3 Ⓐ Ⓑ Ⓒ Ⓓ	28 Ⓐ Ⓑ Ⓒ Ⓓ
4 Ⓐ Ⓑ Ⓒ Ⓓ	29 Ⓐ Ⓑ Ⓒ Ⓓ
5 Ⓐ Ⓑ Ⓒ Ⓓ	30 Ⓐ Ⓑ Ⓒ Ⓓ
6 Ⓐ Ⓑ Ⓒ Ⓓ	31 Ⓐ Ⓑ Ⓒ Ⓓ
7 Ⓐ Ⓑ Ⓒ Ⓓ	32 Ⓐ Ⓑ Ⓒ Ⓓ
8 Ⓐ Ⓑ Ⓒ Ⓓ	33 Ⓐ Ⓑ Ⓒ Ⓓ
9 Ⓐ Ⓑ Ⓒ Ⓓ	34 Ⓐ Ⓑ Ⓒ Ⓓ
10 Ⓐ Ⓑ Ⓒ Ⓓ	35 Ⓐ Ⓑ Ⓒ Ⓓ
11 Ⓐ Ⓑ Ⓒ Ⓓ	36 Ⓐ Ⓑ Ⓒ Ⓓ
12 Ⓐ Ⓑ Ⓒ Ⓓ	37 Ⓐ Ⓑ Ⓒ Ⓓ
13 Ⓐ Ⓑ Ⓒ Ⓓ	38 Ⓐ Ⓑ Ⓒ Ⓓ
14 Ⓐ Ⓑ Ⓒ Ⓓ	39 Ⓐ Ⓑ Ⓒ Ⓓ
15 Ⓐ Ⓑ Ⓒ Ⓓ	40 Ⓐ Ⓑ Ⓒ Ⓓ
16 Ⓐ Ⓑ Ⓒ Ⓓ	41 Ⓐ Ⓑ Ⓒ Ⓓ
17 Ⓐ Ⓑ Ⓒ Ⓓ	42 Ⓐ Ⓑ Ⓒ Ⓓ
18 Ⓐ Ⓑ Ⓒ Ⓓ	43 Ⓐ Ⓑ Ⓒ Ⓓ
19 Ⓐ Ⓑ Ⓒ Ⓓ	44 Ⓐ Ⓑ Ⓒ Ⓓ
20 Ⓐ Ⓑ Ⓒ Ⓓ	45 Ⓐ Ⓑ Ⓒ Ⓓ
21 Ⓐ Ⓑ Ⓒ Ⓓ	46 Ⓐ Ⓑ Ⓒ Ⓓ
22 Ⓐ Ⓑ Ⓒ Ⓓ	47 Ⓐ Ⓑ Ⓒ Ⓓ
23 Ⓐ Ⓑ Ⓒ Ⓓ	48 Ⓐ Ⓑ Ⓒ Ⓓ
24 Ⓐ Ⓑ Ⓒ Ⓓ	49 Ⓐ Ⓑ Ⓒ Ⓓ
25 Ⓐ Ⓑ Ⓒ Ⓓ	50 Ⓐ Ⓑ Ⓒ Ⓓ

CUT HERE

Section 1: Verbal

Time: 50 minutes

50 questions

Directions (1–6): Select the best answer choice for each sentence.

1. My partner yelled, "The suspect is over
   _____."
   - **A.** their
   - **B.** there
   - **C.** they're

2. The officer asked his supervisor _____ type
   up the incident report for him.
   - **A.** two
   - **B.** too
   - **C.** to

3. Officer Lightner and _____ assisted the par-
   ents in the search for their missing child.
   - **A.** me
   - **B.** I

4. One of the _____ walked up behind the
   unsuspecting woman and demanded money.
   - **A.** assailant's
   - **B.** assailants'
   - **C.** assailants

5. After he arrested the burglar, the officer
   placed his handcuffs on the _____ wrists.
   - **A.** suspects
   - **B.** suspect's
   - **C.** suspects'

6. The missing child was last seen wearing a pair
   of _____, an aqua T-shirt, and navy sneakers.
   - **A.** khakis
   - **B.** khakis'
   - **C.** khaki's

Directions (7–12): Select the word that is spelled incorrectly in each sentence.

7. The buisness owner explained to the officers
   that the assailant approached her from
   behind and placed his hand over her mouth.
   - **A.** buisness
   - **B.** explained
   - **C.** assailant
   - **D.** approached

8. The suspect is ackused of assaulting an
   elderly man at the intersection of Dennison
   and Cartwright.
   - **A.** suspect
   - **B.** ackused
   - **C.** elderly
   - **D.** intersection

9. The suspect is described as a white male with black hair, wearing light trowsers and a dark tunic.

   A. suspect
   B. described
   C. trowsers
   D. tunic

10. On the burgulary report, Officer Jamison noted that an X-ray machine and computer were stolen from the physician's office.

   A. burgulary
   B. noted
   C. machine
   D. physician's

11. The elderly woman recounted the events that took place on the night when she was approached and subsequently assalted by a male suspect wearing a black ski mask.

   A. elderly
   B. subsequently
   C. approached
   D. assalted

12. The driver of the Honda Accord failed to maneuver around the baricade and swerved into a fire hydrant.

   A. failed
   B. maneuver
   C. baricade
   D. hydrant

Directions (13): Choose the word or words that reflect an error in capitalization.

13. J. Edgar Hoover was the first director of the federal bureau of investigation (FBI) of the United States.

   A. J. Edgar Hoover
   B. director
   C. federal bureau of investigation
   D. United States

Directions (14): Choose the sentence that corrects the error(s) in punctuation.

14. Officers Renald, Vasquez, and Popky were called to the scene: of a home invasion early Monday morning.

   A. Officers Renald; Vasquez; and Popky were called to the scene of a home invasion, early Monday morning.
   B. Officers Renald, Vasquez, and Popky were called to the scene of a home invasion; early Monday morning.
   C. Officers Renald; Vasquez and Popky were called to the scene of a home invasion early Monday morning.
   D. Officers Renald, Vasquez, and Popky were called to the scene of a home invasion early Monday morning.

Directions (15–18): Answer these questions solely on the basis of the following incident report.

INCIDENT REPORT — POLICE DEPARTMENT			
1. ADDRESS OF INCIDENT	2. OFFENSE	3. CODE	4. DATE
5. NAME OF VICTIM: INDIVIDUAL OR BUSINESS		6. ADDRESS	PHONE
T. ASSIGNED OFFICERS/BADGE NUMBERS	8. AGE OF VICTIM	9. RACE OF VICTIM	10. VICTIM'S DATE OF BIRTH
11. NAME OF SUSPECT		12. ADDRESS	

13. AGE	14. RACE	15. SEX	16. DATE OF BIRTH	17. HEIGHT	18. WEIGHT
19. HAIR	20. EYES	21. PHYSICAL DESCRIPTION			

22. CHARGES

23. ITEM	24. BRAND	25. SERIAL NUMBER	26. VALUE
27. ITEM	28. BRAND	29. SERIAL NUMBER	30. VALUE
31. ITEM	32. BRAND	33. SERIAL NUMBER	34. VALUE

35. _____
SIGNATURE OF OFFICER/BADGE NUMBER

Maxine Manard, owner of Cupcakes Bakery at 42 Washington Ave., called police headquarters at 5:35 a.m. on Tuesday, March 2, to report that her bakery had been burglarized. Officers Artie Millard and Francesca Lee arrived at the business at 5:55 a.m. to investigate the incident. Mrs. Manard reported that the front door was damaged, the front window was broken, and $48 in cash was missing from the cash register. The bakery's phone number is 998-2211. Mrs. Manard's home phone number is 998-7893.

15. The incident report can be fully completed based on the information in the paragraph.

A. True
B. False

16. The incident was reported on March 4.

A. True
B. False

Rita Hoffman, owner of a home located at 77 School Rd., called police headquarters at 7:35 a.m. to report a home invasion during the early morning of Monday, January 9. Officers Bertrand Moyer and Gina Tillman arrived at the residence at 7:41 a.m. to investigate the incident. Ms. Hoffman reported that she awoke to the sound of smashing glass coming from downstairs. After she heard the noise, she said she put on her robe and slowly made her way downstairs to investigate. From the middle of the stairs, she was able to see that her front door was open and shards of glass were on the floor. Ms. Hoffman said she went back upstairs and called 911. The operator stayed on the phone until police arrived on scene. Ms. Hoffman determined that her late husband's stamp collection was taken from the hutch in her dining room and a pearl necklace was removed from the kitchen table. No other items were removed from the residence.

17. The incident report can be fully completed based on the information in the paragraph.

   A. True
   B. False

18. A stamp collection and pearl necklace were the only items taken from the residence.

   A. True
   B. False

Directions (19–24): Select the answer choice that best explains the sentences.

After responding to a robbery call, Officer Miller returns to the station and writes up an incident report. It contains the following two sentences:

   I. The victim was walking her dog south on Orange Lane when she was approached by an unknown assailant.
   II. After the assailant demanding the victim give him cash, the victim's dog will chase the assailant north on Orange Lane.

19. Which of the following best describes the above sentences?

   A. Only sentence I is grammatically correct.
   B. Only sentence II is grammatically correct.
   C. Neither sentence I nor sentence II is grammatically correct.
   D. Both sentence I and sentence II are grammatically correct.

After responding to a robbery call, Officer Kelly returns to the station and writes up an incident report. It contains the following two sentences:

   I. As the victim had stepped away from the ATM, an unknown assailant produced a gun and ordered them to stay still and keep quiet and hand over the money.
   II. After the victim handed over $300, the assailant fled the scene.

20. Which of the following best describes the above sentences?

   A. Only sentence I is grammatically correct.
   B. Only sentence II is grammatically correct.
   C. Neither sentence I nor sentence II is grammatically correct.
   D. Both sentence I and sentence II are grammatically correct.

Captain Pierce is reviewing an incident report, which contains the following two sentences:

I. Paul Davis, of 22 Chalmers Dr., was pull over after his vehicle was seen swerving erratically.

II. After failing several field sobriety tests Mr. Davis arrested and charged with driving under the influence.

21. Which of the following best describes the above sentences?

A. Only sentence I is grammatically correct.

B. Only sentence II is grammatically correct.

C. Neither sentence I nor sentence II is grammatically correct.

D. Both sentence I and sentence II are grammatically correct.

Officer Walden has written a special report about the rise in crime in his community. As he reviews the report, he finds the following two sentences:

I. Over the past two years, the city of Garnet has seen a dramatic increase in drug-related crimes.

II. The police department needs funding to hire more police officers help patrol our streets.

22. Which of the following best describes the above sentences?

A. Only sentence I is grammatically correct.

B. Only sentence II is grammatically correct.

C. Neither sentence I nor sentence II is grammatically correct.

D. Both sentence I and sentence II are grammatically correct.

Sergeant Fernandez is filling out an incident report, which contains the following two sentences:

I. The victim told police that $50 were stolen from his unlocked car was outside his residence on 40 Slocum St.

II. The victim said he knows who took the money, but he won't give the officer a name.

23. Which of the following best describes the above sentences?

A. Only sentence I is grammatically correct.

B. Only sentence II is grammatically correct.

C. Neither sentence I nor sentence II is grammatically correct.

D. Both sentence I and sentence II are grammatically correct.

Officer Clerico is preparing a statement, which contains the following two sentences:

I. As I stepped in to break up the fight, one of the man punched me in the face.

II. I noticed that the men sitting directly behind me were involved in a altercation.

24. Which of the following best describes the above sentences?

A. Only sentence I is grammatically correct.

B. Only sentence II is grammatically correct.

C. Neither sentence I nor sentence II is grammatically correct.

D. Both sentence I and sentence II are grammatically correct.

Directions (25–27): Answer the following questions solely on the basis of the information provided.

While on patrol, Officer Devers responded to a domestic-abuse call. The following details were recorded at the scene:

> Place of crime: 34 Pine St.
>
> Time of crime: 11:42 p.m.
>
> Victim: Margarita Lopez
>
> Crime: Assault
>
> Suspect: Eppi Lopez

25. Officer Devers must complete a report of the crime. Which of the following expresses the above information most clearly, accurately, and completely?

    A. At 34 Pine St., at 11:42 p.m., Margarita Lopez was assaulted by Eppi Lopez.

    B. Margarita Lopez was assaulted by Eppi Lopez at 34 Pine St. at 11:42 p.m.

    C. At 11:42 p.m., Eppi Lopez, at 34 Pine St., assaulted Margarita Lopez.

    D. Margarita Lopez, at 34 Pine St. at 11:42 p.m., was assaulted by her husband.

While on patrol, Officer Raneri responded to an assault. The following details were recorded at the scene:

> Place of crime: 98 Curtis Lane
>
> Time of crime: 12:54 a.m.
>
> Victim: William Bearde
>
> Crime: Assault
>
> Suspect: James Braden

26. Officer Raneri must complete a report of the crime. Which of the following expresses the above information most clearly, accurately, and completely?

    A. At 12:54 a.m., William Bearde was assaulted by James Braden at 98 Curtis Lane.

    B. William Bearde was assaulted at 98 Curtis Lane at 12:54 a.m.

    C. William Bearde and James Braden were involved in an assault at 12:54 a.m.

    D. At 98 Curtis Lane, at 12:54 a.m., James Braden assaulted someone.

While on patrol, Officer Morales responded to a traffic accident. The following details were recorded at the scene:

Place of accident: Intersection of Benedict Street and News Lane

Time of accident: 2:20 p.m.

Vehicle involved: 2010 Ford Fiesta

Driver: Patrick Lampert

Damage: The vehicle struck a guardrail after the driver swerved to miss a child, causing a large dent in the rear driver's side door.

27. Officer Morales must complete a report of the incident. Which of the following expresses the above information most clearly, accurately, and completely?

   A. Driving a 2010 Ford Fiesta, Patrick Lampert, at the intersection of Benedict Street and News Lane struck a guardrail, causing a dent in the rear driver's side door at 2:20 p.m.

   B. A 2010 Ford Fiesta driven by Patrick Lampert struck a guardrail at the intersection of Benedict Street and News Lane at 2:20 p.m., causing a dent in the rear driver's side door.

   C. At 2:20 p.m., Patrick Lampert was driving a 2010 Ford Fiesta at the intersection of Benedict Street and News Lane, where he struck a guardrail, causing a dent in the rear driver's side door.

   D. Patrick Lampert was the driver of a 2010 Ford Fiesta. At 2:20 p.m., Lampert hit a guardrail at the intersection of Benedict Street and News Lane. There is a dent in the rear driver's side door.

Directions (28–29): Answer the following questions solely on the basis of the definitions provided.

Question 28 refers to the following definitions.

A **sergeant** is a police officer who oversees an entire shift in small departments, or part of a precinct or detective squad in large departments.

A **detective**'s main job is to investigate crimes. He or she usually wears plain clothes instead of a uniform.

A **lieutenant** is responsible for supervising two or more sergeants. He or she is usually in charge of overseeing an entire shift of police officers or detective squad in large police departments or entire precincts in small police departments.

The job of a **captain** is to supervise or oversee an entire police station or a division of the police station.

28. Which of the following best describes a detective?

   A. This person is responsible for assigning police coverage to communities within Springfield.
   B. This person is responsible for overseeing the Springfield Police Department.
   C. This person is responsible for reporting crimes to the mayor of Springfield.
   D. This person is responsible for investigating crimes in Springfield.

Question 29 refers to the following definitions.

Abuse: The physical maltreatment of an individual by another individual

Assault: A physical or verbal attack on an individual

Harassment: Any verbal or physical conduct that is uninvited and unwelcome

29. Which of the following best describes an incident of assault?

   A. Mary was crossing the street when a mailman accidentally hit her with his truck.
   B. Jorge was waiting at the bus stop and heard a woman yelling for help.
   C. Walter was walking home from work and a man punched him in the face.
   D. The doctor questioned the bruises on Gerianne's legs.

Directions (30–39): Answer these questions solely on the basis of the passages provided.

Questions 30 through 33 refer to the following passage.

On August 4, 2010, Officer Armand and Officer Jendrewski arrived at 133 N. Main St., Apt. 4B, at 5:06 p.m., in response to a domestic-abuse report by Ms. Velopez. The officers announced themselves and Ms. Velopez opened the door. She was bleeding above her left eye and holding an ice pack on her head. She explained that her boyfriend, Manuel Rodriguez, came home from work at 4:30 p.m. He is usually home by 4 p.m., but he stopped to visit his buddies at a bar. He was intoxicated and started screaming at her because he didn't like what she had prepared for dinner. She told officers that she tried to reason with him, but he wouldn't listen. She said they both began screaming. Ms. Velopez said she became frightened and grabbed the telephone, but Mr. Rodriguez pulled the telephone from her hand and then hit her in the head with it. She said she screamed and then he pummeled her in the eye before fleeing their apartment. She gave the officers a description of her boyfriend. He is a 31-year-old Hispanic who is about 5'10" tall and weighs 160 pounds. He has straight black hair and was wearing a red T-shirt and black jeans at the time of the incident. She also gave the officers a list of places he may have gone, which includes his mother's home, a local bar, and a bowling alley.

As the officers prepared to leave, Ms. Velopez told them that she did not want to press charges against Mr. Rodriguez. She did not offer any further explanation.

30. Which of the following is true of Mr. Rodriguez?

A. He works at the bowling alley.
B. He is African American.
C. He was wearing a red T-shirt.
D. He is married to Ms. Velopez.

31. At what time did Mr. Rodriguez arrive home?

A. 4 p.m.
B. 4:30 p.m.
C. 5:02 p.m.
D. 5:06 p.m.

32. All the following are places Mr. Rodriguez hangs out except:

A. the bowling alley
B. his mother's home
C. a local bar
D. the park

33. Which of these words could best replace the word *pummeled* in the following sentence:

She said she screamed and then he pummeled her in the eye before fleeing their apartment.

A. ravished
B. walloped
C. raised
D. confronted

Questions 34 through 37 refer to the following passage.

On July 22, 2010, Officer Kennedy and Officer Milan arrived at 81 Blueberry Lane, Apt. 1A, at 6:38 p.m., in response to a burglary reported by Mr. Fellmoore. The officers were greeted by Mr. and Mrs. Fellmoore. Mr. Fellmoore told the officers that he left for work at a local law firm at 8:30 a.m. He dropped off his wife at her job at the library on his way to the office. A co-worker gave Mrs. Fellmoore a ride home at 6 p.m. Mr. Fellmoore arrived home at 5:50 p.m. and found the door to the apartment open. He went inside and found that the apartment had been ransacked. No one was inside, but the place was a mess. Every drawer and cupboard was opened. Dishes were broken, couch cushions were slashed, and planters were overturned. The couple's lockbox, which resembles a black briefcase, was taken from the coat closet along with Mrs. Fellmoore's diamond bracelet, which was on the dining room table. The lockbox contained their passports, birth certificates, Social Security cards, $5,000 in cash, and plane tickets for their upcoming trip to Aruba. While Officer Milan interviewed the Fellmoores, Officer Kennedy visited the two other apartments on the floor.

Ms. Hammond, age 27, lives in Apt. 1C, located directly across the hall from the elevator. Although Ms. Hammond works from home, she told Officer Kennedy that she wears headphones while she works and did not hear anything strange all day.

Officer Kennedy knocked on the door of Apt. 1B and was greeted by Mr. Miles, 57, who was home sick from work. He told Officer Kennedy that he was trying to sleep when he heard what sounded like glass shattering. He said he peered out his door but didn't see anything. A few minutes later, he heard more sounds in the hallway and opened the door again. He saw two men hurrying down the hall carrying what appeared to be a briefcase. He said he thought nothing of it because many businessmen live in the building. He said one of the men was wearing a dark suit. The man had a black fedora on his head, and sunglasses covered his eyes. He appeared to be in his 40s and looked to be about 6'3" tall, weighing about 220 pounds. The other man, who was carrying the briefcase, was also wearing a dark suit. He had gray hair and dark eyes. He appeared to be in his 50s. He was 5'8" tall and weighed about 300 pounds.

Officer Kennedy hurried back to the Fellmoores' apartment to tell Officer Milan what he learned from Mr. Miles. The officers then returned to the police station to complete their crime report.

34. Which of the following is true of Mrs. Fellmoore?

   A. She doesn't know how to drive.
   B. She works in a library.
   C. She is Mr. Fellmoore's sister.
   D. She was planning a trip to Mexico.

35. The lockbox was located in Mr. and Mrs. Fellmoores' coat closet.

   A. True
   B. False

36. At what time did Officers Kennedy and Milan arrive at the scene?

   A. 5:50 p.m.
   B. 6 p.m.
   C. 6:30 p.m.
   D. 6:38 p.m.

37. From the context of the following sentence, what is a *fedora?*

   The man had a black fedora on his head and sunglasses covered his eyes.

   A. a toupee
   B. a scarf
   C. a jacket
   D. a hat

Questions 38 and 39 refer to the following passage.

On May 1, 2010, Officer Emily Meeker and Officer Pamela Vega arrived at 55 Packer Ave., Apt. 1C, at 7:52 p.m., in response to a burglary reported by Mrs. Dolman. They were greeted on the scene by Mr. and Mrs. Dolman. Mrs. Dolman told the officers that she and her husband arrived home from the grocery store around 7:40 p.m. to find the lock on their door broken. They entered their residence, and everything seemed to be in place. Nothing was taken. The only damage was to the lock on the door.

While Officer Meeker interviewed the Dolmans, Officer Vega visited the other apartments on the floor to see if any of the neighbors heard or saw anything suspicious.

Mr. Kennywood, age 22, lives in Apt. 2C, which is located down the hall from the Dolmans' apartment. He told Officer Vega that he had just arrived home from work and didn't hear or notice anything strange in the building.

Officer Vega knocked on the door to Apt. 3C, but there was no answer. She returned to the Dolmans' apartment to report her findings to her partner. After taking statements from Mr. and Mrs. Dolman, Officer Meeker and Officer Vega returned to the police station to complete their crime report.

38. Which of the following is true of Mr. Kennywood?

    A. He works from home.
    B. He lives down the hall from the Dolmans.
    C. He was out at the grocery store at the time of the incident.
    D. He is 42 years old.

39. At what time did the police officers arrive at the residence?

    A. 7:35 p.m.
    B. 7:42 p.m.
    C. 7:45 p.m.
    D. 7:52 p.m.

Directions (40–50): Answer the following questions solely on the basis of the corresponding incident reports.

Questions 40 through 45 refer to the following incident report.

INCIDENT REPORT –– POLICE DEPARTMENT

1. ADDRESS OF INCIDENT	2. OFFENSE	3. CODE	4. DATE
1942 Washington Dr.	Assault	H2-1515	12/17

5. NAME OF VICTIM: INDIVIDUAL OR BUSINESS	6. ADDRESS	PHONE
Frederick Mancini	1942 Washington Dr.	555-3355

7. ASSIGNED OFFICERS/BADGE NUMBERS	8. AGE OF VICTIM	9. RACE OF VICTIM	10. VICTIM'S DATE OF BIRTH
Maureen Rigby #669	22	Black	02/14/1988

11. NAME OF SUSPECT	12. ADDRESS
Michael Dillon	12 Broadview Rd.

13. AGE	14. RACE	15. SEX	16. DATE OF BIRTH	17. HEIGHT	18. WEIGHT
21	White	Male	1/29	6' 2"	250

19. HAIR	20. EYES	21. PHYSICAL DESCRIPTION
Blond	Blue	Wearing khakis and a red hooded sweatshirt

22. CHARGES
Assault

23. ITEM	24. BRAND	25. SERIAL NUMBER	26. VALUE

27. ITEM	28. BRAND	29. SERIAL NUMBER	30. VALUE

31. ITEM	32. BRAND	33. SERIAL NUMBER	34. VALUE

35. *Maureen Rigby #669*
SIGNATURE OF OFFICER/BADGE NUMBER

40. Where did the incident take place?

_____

41. What is the name of the victim?

_____

42. What is the name of the suspect?

_____

43. What is the suspect's address?

_____

44. What is the offense?

_____

45. What is the hair color of the suspect?

_____

Questions 46 through 50 refer to the following incident report.

INCIDENT REPORT -- POLICE DEPARTMENT			
1. ADDRESS OF INCIDENT 4156 Germania Ave.	**2. OFFENSE** Burglary	**3. CODE** G4-9685	**4. DATE** 09/19

5. NAME OF VICTIM: INDIVIDUAL OR BUSINESS Candy Jenkins, owner of Candy's Confections	**6. ADDRESS** 4156 Germania Ave.	**PHONE** 555-4649

7. ASSIGNED OFFICERS/BADGE NUMBERS Juan Fernandez #3558	**8. AGE OF VICTIM** 35	**9. RACE OF VICTIM** White	**10. VICTIM'S DATE OF BIRTH** 05/01/15

11. NAME OF SUSPECT Lila Jenkins	**12. ADDRESS** 44 N. Main St.

13. AGE 35	**14. RACE** White	**15. SEX** Female	**16. DATE OF BIRTH** 05/01/15	**17. HEIGHT** 5' 1"	**18. WEIGHT** 115

19. HAIR Brown	**20. EYES** Green	**21. PHYSICAL DESCRIPTION** Wearing black jeans and a black hooded sweatshirt

22. CHARGES Burglary			

23. ITEM Cash	**24. BRAND**	**25. SERIAL NUMBER**	**26. VALUE** $600
27. ITEM Miscellaneous items	**28. BRAND**	**29. SERIAL NUMBER**	**30. VALUE** $450
31. ITEM	**32. BRAND**	**33. SERIAL NUMBER**	**34. VALUE**

35. *Juan Fernandez #3558*
SIGNATURE OF OFFICER/BADGE NUMBER

46. What is the total value of the items?

_____

47. What is the name of the victim?

_____

48. What is the suspect's address?

_____

49. What is the victim's address?

_____

50. What is the height of the suspect?

_____

IF YOU FINISH BEFORE TIME IS CALLED, CHECK YOUR WORK ON THIS SECTION ONLY. DO NOT WORK ON ANY OTHER SECTION IN THE TEST.

Section 2: Memorization and Visualization

Time: 50 minutes

50 questions

Directions (1–50): Answer the following questions solely on the basis of the corresponding passage and/or visual aid.

Questions 1 through 5 refer to the following photograph. Study the photograph for ten minutes; then cover the photograph and answer the questions based on your memory.

1. How many steps are there in the stairwell?

   A. 8
   B. 9
   C. 10
   D. 11

2. What is the address printed on the awning?

   A. 17 East 9th Street
   B. 9 East 17th Street
   C. 9 West 17th Street
   D. 17 West 9th Street

3. What is the phone number printed on the awning?

   A. 242-2111
   B. 242-2777
   C. 224-2777
   D. 277-4222

4. How many windows are above the awning?

   A. 1
   B. 2
   C. 3
   D. 4

5. What is piled on the sidewalk in front of the building?

   A. garbage
   B. cardboard
   C. plastic recycling
   D. books

Question 6 refers to the following passage.

Officer Evanko was dispatched to a shooting on Randolph Avenue. When he arrived on the scene, witnesses told the officer that after shooting the victim, the suspect headed north on Randolph Avenue for about three blocks before turning right at Province Street. Another witness at that intersection told Evanko that the suspect then ran two more blocks before turning left at McCoy Avenue. A final witness on McCoy Avenue reported seeing the suspect turn left into an alley.

6. Which direction was the suspect headed when last seen?

   A. north
   B. south
   C. east
   D. west

Question 7 refers to the following passage.

While speaking with the owner of a vehicle that has just been stolen, you are told that the suspect was seen driving south. The car owner saw the suspect turn left and then right before he lost sight of the suspect.

7. According to the information you received, you would be most correct if you reported that the suspect was last seen traveling:

   A. north
   B. south
   C. east
   D. west

Question 8 refers to the following passage.

While questioning a crime victim, you're told that the suspect grabbed the victim's purse as he was walking by her on a crowded street. The suspect headed north and the victim chased the suspect as he made two left-hand turns and then got into a vehicle that turned right.

8. According to the information in the passage, you would be most correct if you reported that the suspect was last seen traveling:

   A. north
   B. south
   C. east
   D. west

9. You're on a routine patrol when you walk past these buildings:

As you turn the corner, your view of the buildings changes. Which of the following most accurately represents your view from the back of the buildings?

A.

B.

C.

D.

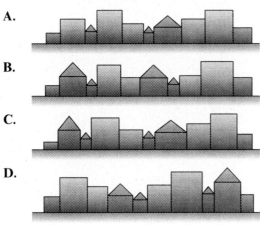

Question 10 refers to the following passage.

Officer Chang responds to the scene of a motor vehicle accident on Riviena Avenue and State Street. The woman driving vehicle 1 tells the officer that she was traveling east on Riviena Avenue when vehicle 2, traveling north on State Street, failed to stop at a stop sign and continued through the intersection. Vehicle 2 hit vehicle 1 in the intersection. Vehicle 1 was then struck from behind by vehicle 3.

10. Which diagram is most consistent with the driver's statement?

A.

B.

C.

D.

Questions 11 through 14 refer to the following map. The flow of traffic is indicated by the arrows. You must follow the flow of traffic.

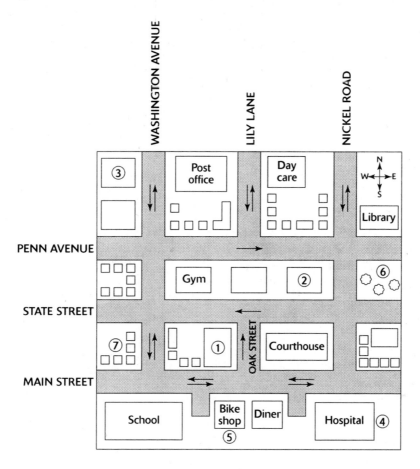

11. What is the quickest route from point 4 to the day care?

    A. north on Nickel Road, west on Penn Avenue, north on Lily Lane

    B. north on Nickel Road, west on State Street, north on Washington Avenue, east on Penn Avenue, north on Lily Lane

    C. west on Main Street, north on Washington Avenue, east on Penn Avenue, north on Lily Lane

    D. west on Main Street, north on Oak Street, east on State Street, north on Nickel Road, west on Penn Avenue, north on Lily Lane

12. While patrolling the park at point 6, you're called to an emergency at the home on the corner of Washington Avenue and Main Street. You parked your patrol car at the northern-most entrance of the park. Which of the following is the quickest route from point 6 to point 7?

    A. west on Penn Avenue, south on Washington Avenue

    B. south on Nickel Road, west on State Street, south on Washington Avenue

    C. south on Nickel Road, west on State Street, south on Oak Street, west on Main Street

    D. east on Penn Avenue, south on Washington Avenue, west on Main Street

13. You're at the entrance of the courthouse, facing south, when you hear a woman scream. You look across the street to your right and see a woman struggling to pull a purse away from a man in jeans. You run to her just as the man yanks one last time at the purse and runs away. You run after the thief, following him north one block before he takes a left and then a right. Tired, you radio for backup. In which direction is the perp is heading?

A. north
B. south
C. east
D. west

14. Starting at the post office, if you travel south on Lily Lane, east on Penn Avenue, south on Nickel Road, west on State Street, and south on Washington Avenue, which of the following buildings will you face?

A. the bike shop
B. the diner
C. the library
D. the school

15. You're on a routine patrol when you walk past these buildings:

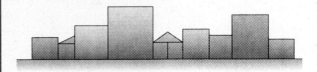

As you turn the corner, your view of the buildings changes. Which of the following most accurately represents your view from the back of the buildings?

A.

B.

C.

D.

Questions 16 through 19 refer to the following map. The flow of traffic is indicated by the arrows. You must follow the flow of traffic.

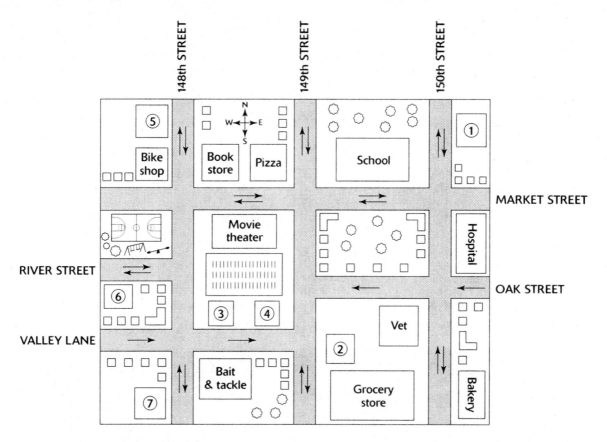

16. From the parking lot behind points 3 and 4, what is the quickest route to the bakery?

   A.   east on Oak Street, south on 150th Street

   B.   north on 148th Street, east on Market Street, south on 150th Street

   C.   north on 149th Street, east on Market Street, south on 150th Street

   D.   east on Valley Lane, north on 149th Street, east on Market Street, south on 150th Street

17. While at the grocery store, you receive a call to respond to an emergency at point 7. You pull out of the east entrance of the grocery store. What is the best route to point 7?

   A.   west on Valley Lane, south on 148th Street

   B.   north on 149th Street, west on Market Street, south on 148th Street

   C.   north on 150th Street, west on Oak Street, south on 149th Street, west on Valley Lane, south on 148th Street

   D.   north on 150th Street, west on Market Street, south on 148th Street

18. Starting at point 5, you travel south, passing through one intersection, and then make a right. What is your nearest point?

    A. the movie-theater parking lot
    B. the playground next to the soccer field
    C. the bait-and-tackle shop
    D. the bookstore

19. Starting at point 2, you travel north on 149th Street, west on Market Street, south on 148th Street, east on Valley Lane, north on 149th Street, and then make two right-hand turns. What is your nearest point?

    A. the hospital
    B. the bakery
    C. the movie theater
    D. the pizza shop

Question 20 refers to the following passage.

While responding to the scene of a purse snatching, you're told by the victim that a male suspect knocked her to the ground, took her purse, and then continued running south. She got up and tried to chase him but couldn't keep up with the assailant. The victim followed the suspect as he made a left, a right, another right, and then a left.

20. According to the information provided by the victim, you would be most correct if you reported that the suspect was last seen traveling:

    A. east
    B. west
    C. north
    D. south

Questions 21 through 23 refer to the following photograph. Study the photograph for ten minutes; then cover the photograph and answer the questions based on your memory.

21. Which of the following directions does the arrow painted on the ground face?

   A. northeast
   B. southeast
   C. northwest
   D. southwest

22. What type of business can you assume is in the photograph?

   A. library
   B. police department
   C. fire department
   D. ambulance association

23. How many people are in the photograph?

   A. 2
   B. 3
   C. 4
   D. 5

Questions 24 through 26 refers to the following photograph. Study the photograph for ten minutes; then cover the photograph and answer the questions based on your memory.

24. How many people are in the photograph?

    A. 2

    B. 3

    C. 5

    D. 6

25. What is the woman on the left-hand side of the photograph wearing?

    A. glasses

    B. a hat

    C. a scarf

    D. mittens

26. How many chandeliers are visible in the photograph?

    A. 1

    B. 2

    C. 3

    D. 4

27. You're on a routine patrol when you walk past these buildings:

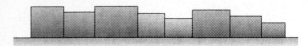

As you turn the corner, your view of the buildings changes. Which of the following most accurately represents your view from the back of the buildings?

    A.

    B.

    C.

    D.

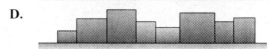

Questions 28 through 31 refer to the following map. The flow of traffic is indicated by the arrows. You must follow the flow of traffic.

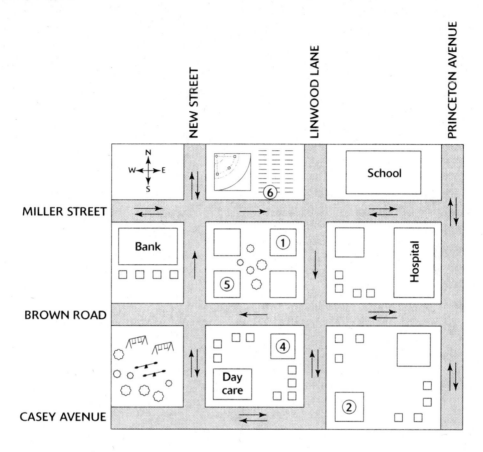

28. If you're at point 4 and must travel to point 1, in which direction must you travel first?

A. north
B. south
C. east
D. west

29. After transporting a suspect in a crime to the hospital, you're instructed to respond to a mugging at point 6, the parking lot beside the baseball field. Which of the following is the quickest route from the hospital to the baseball field?

A. north on Princeton Avenue, west on Miller Street

B. north on Princeton Avenue, east on Miller Street

C. south on Princeton Avenue, west on Brown Road, north on New Street, east on Miller Street

D. south on Princeton Avenue, west on Brown Road, north on Linwood Lane, west on Miller Street

269

30. Starting at the day care, if you travel north on New Street, east on Miller Street, south on Linwood Lane, and then make a right, which point is on your left-hand side?

   A. point 2
   B. point 3
   C. point 4
   D. point 5

31. After patrolling the park across the street from the day care, you get in your patrol car and head east on Casey Avenue, deciding to patrol your surrounding area. At the second intersection, you make a left. You then make a right, three left turns, and two right turns. What is on your left-hand side?

   A. the bank
   B. the hospital
   C. the school
   D. the baseball field

Question 32 refers to the following passage.

When Officer Mahoney responds to a robbery, the victim tells him that an unidentified man with a knife demanded his MP3 player and ran away. The victim said the suspect ran off in an eastward direction before turning right. A witness said the suspect turned right again a few blocks later.

32. According to the information provided, Officer Mahoney would be most accurate if he reported that the suspect was last seen traveling:

   A. east
   B. west
   C. north
   D. south

Questions 33 through 36 refer to the following map. The flow of traffic is indicated by the arrows. You must follow the flow of traffic.

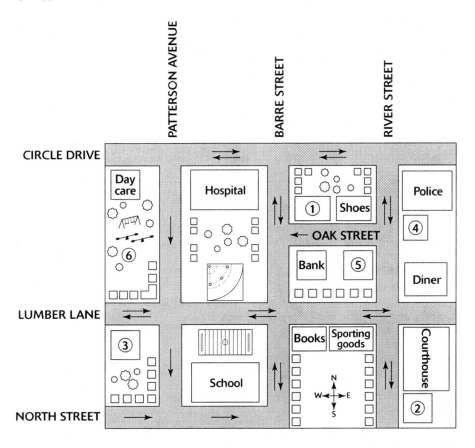

33. After a stop at the local school for a short lecture on stranger danger, you're called to a burglary at the shoe store. Which of the following is the quickest route from the school to the shoe store?

   A. north on Barre Street, east on Oak Street, north on River Street
   B. north on Barre Street, east on Lumber Lane, north on River Street
   C. north on Barre Street, east on Circle Drive, south on River Street
   D. north on Barre Street, west on Circle Drive, south on River Street

34. Once you've completed a walk-through of the park at point 6, you get in your patrol car and decide to drive around the area for a while, keeping an eye out for suspicious activity. You travel south on Patterson Avenue, west on North Street, north on Barre Street, and east on Lumber Lane. At the next intersection, which of the following buildings will you see on your right-hand side?

   A. the bank
   B. the football field
   C. the sporting-goods store
   D. the hospital

35. If you left the northernmost entrance of the police station and traveled west for two blocks, south for one block, east for two blocks, and then turned right, you would be closest to:

    A. point 1
    B. point 2
    C. point 3
    D. point 4

36. While at the day care, you receive a call to respond to a burglary at the bank. Which of the following is the most direct route from the day care to the bank?

    A. north on Patterson Avenue, east on Circle Drive, south on Barre Street, east on Oak Street

    B. north on Patterson Avenue, east on Circle Drive, south on River Street, west on Oak Street

    C. south on Patterson Avenue, east on Lumber Lane, north on Barre Street, east on Oak Street

    D. south on Patterson Avenue, east on Lumber Lane, north on River Street, west on Oak Street

Questions 37 through 40 refer to the following photograph. Study the photograph for ten minutes; then cover the photograph and answer the questions based on your memory.

37. Which of the following items is the woman in the photograph *not* wearing?

    A. a purse
    B. jeans
    C. shoes
    D. a sweater

38. The woman in the photograph is walking a dog. In proximity to the woman, where is the dog located?

    A. ahead of her to her right
    B. ahead of her to her left
    C. behind her to her right
    D. behind her to her left

39. What are the letters printed on the sign hung vertically on the right-hand side of this photograph?

    A. area
    B. anna
    C. aina
    D. anea

40. Which two letters of the car's license plate are visible in the lower-left corner of this photograph?

    A. PX
    B. RV
    C. BM
    D. EY

41. You're on a routine patrol when you walk past these buildings:

As you turn the corner, your view of the buildings changes. Which of the following most accurately represents your view from the back of the buildings?

A.

B.

C.

D.

Questions 42 through 45 refer to the following map. The flow of traffic is indicated by the arrows. You must follow the flow of traffic.

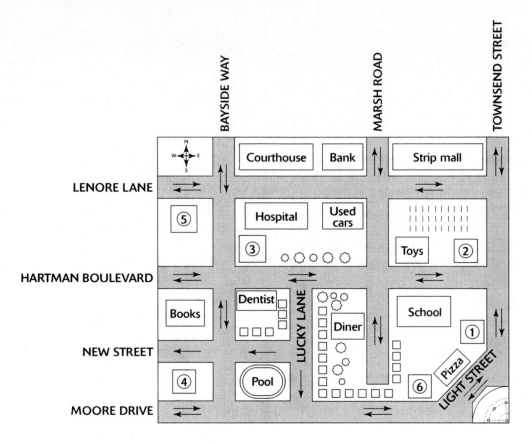

42. While on patrol in the parking lot across the street from the strip mall, you receive a call to respond to an emergency at the local public pool. Which of the following is the most direct route from the strip mall to the pool?

   A. west on Lenore Lane, south on Bayside Way, east on New Street, north on Lucky Lane

   B. south on Marsh Road, west on Hartman Boulevard, south on Lucky Lane, west on New Street

   C. south on Townsend Street, southwest on Light Street, west on Moore Drive, north on Lucky Lane, west on New Street

   D. south on Townsend Street, southwest on Light Street, west on Moore Drive, north on Bayside Way, east on New Street

43. At the diner, you receive a call that you must provide police escort to a celebrity who is signing autographs at the baseball field. The celebrity needs to get to point 5. Which of the following routes allows you to meet the celebrity at the baseball field and lead his car to point 5 in the least amount of time?

   A. south on Marsh Road, west on Moore Drive, northeast on Light Street, north on Townsend Street, west on Lenore Lane
   B. north on Marsh Road, east on Hartman Boulevard, south on Townsend Street, southwest on Light Street, west on Moore Drive, north on Bayside Way
   C. north on Marsh Road, west on Hartman Boulevard, south on Lucky Lane, east on Moore Drive, northeast on Light Street, north on Townsend Street, west on Lenore Lane
   D. north on Marsh Road, east on Hartman Boulevard, south on Townsend Street, southwest on Light Street, west on Moore Drive, north on Lucky Lane, west on Hartman Boulevard, north on Bayside Way

44. From the toy store, if you traveled east on Hartman Boulevard, made two left turns, turned left at the nearest intersection and then right, it would be most accurate to say that you would now be traveling:

   A. north
   B. south
   C. east
   D. west

45. Starting at point 4, if you traveled north on Bayside Way, east on Lenore Lane, south on Marsh Road, east on Hartman Boulevard, and south on Townsend Street, you would be closest to:

   A. point 1
   B. point 3
   C. point 5
   D. point 6

Question 46 refers to the following passage.

Officer Bradley is called to the scene of an arson at a restaurant. The owner said one of his kitchen workers intentionally started a grease fire and fled. Another employee said he saw the suspect heading south before making a right. Another witness stated that she then saw the suspect turn right again. A third witness saw the suspect turn left.

46. According to the information provided, Officer Bradley would be most accurate if he reported that the suspect was last seen traveling:

   A. east
   B. west
   C. north
   D. south

Questions 47 through 50 refer to the following photograph. Study the photograph for ten minutes; then cover the photograph and answer the questions based on your memory.

47. How many people are riding the escalator in this photograph?

    A. 2
    B. 3
    C. 4
    D. 5

48. There are four visible trash cans/recycling bins in this photograph. Three are against the concrete structure with the trees in the center of the photograph. Where is the fourth trash can located?

    A. at the base of the escalator
    B. in the center of the food court
    C. in front of the jewelry stand
    D. next to the cabinet with the coffee advertisement

49. Which of the following appears in the photograph of the food court?

A. a skateboard
B. a stroller
C. a shopping cart
D. a "wet floor" sign

50. How many tables are visible in this photograph?

A. 6
B. 8
C. 10
D. 12

IF YOU FINISH BEFORE TIME IS CALLED, CHECK YOUR WORK ON THIS SECTION ONLY. DO NOT WORK ON ANY OTHER SECTION IN THE TEST.

Section 3: Mathematics

Time: 50 minutes

50 questions

Directions (1–50): Answer these questions based solely on the information provided.

Questions 1 and 2 refer to the following information.

In the past five months, crime rates have both increased and decreased. In April, 35 incidents of domestic violence were reported. In September, 50 incidents of domestic violence were reported. In the spring, only 6 home burglaries were reported. In September, 12 people reported that their homes had been broken into. In April there were 5 reported arsons while September only saw 2.

1. How many assaults, burglaries, and arsons were reported in September?

    A. 37
    B. 52
    C. 64
    D. 110

2. By what percentage did the reports of domestic violence increase from April to September?

    A. 43%
    B. 55%
    C. 65%
    D. 70%

3. The number of arrests Officer Marks made each week for the past 12 weeks was 6, 5, 8, 4, 6, 8, 5, 14, 3, 7, 3, and 6. What is the average number of arrests she made per month?

    A. 15
    B. 25
    C. 30
    D. 35

4. Find the perimeter of the object shown below.

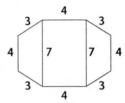

    A. 14
    B. 28
    C. 34
    D. 41

Questions 5 and 6 refer to the following information.

In preparing a report on a burglary in an electronics store, Officer Boots listed the following stolen items and their values.

> 3 desktop monitors: $200 each
> 4 MP3 players: $120 each
> 2 laptops: $550 each
> Cash: $2,500
> TOTAL: $4,680

5. What is the total value of the stolen items except for one of the laptops?

    A. $3,260
    B. $3,380
    C. $3,580
    D. $4,130

6. While attempting to organize the shop the following morning, the owner finds that the burglars stole only 3 MP3 players, but they took another laptop that had been on hold for a customer behind the registers. What is the new total value of the stolen items?

   A. $4,130
   B. $4,250
   C. $4,375
   D. $5,110

7. The closest convenience store and the police station are approximately 6 miles apart. If Officer McGrane made five trips to the convenience store this week, how many miles in all did he travel?

   A. 30 miles
   B. 40 miles
   C. 50 miles
   D. 60 miles

8. Find the radius of the circle shown below using the formula $D = 2r$.

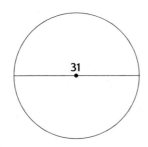

   A. 12
   B. 15.5
   C. 18
   D. 21.5

9. During a search and seizure, a police unit discovers 40 guns. After processing the weapons at the station, they're told that the homeowners had owner's permits for 60% of the weapons seized. How many guns did the homeowners *not* have permits for?

   A. 12
   B. 16
   C. 20
   D. 24

10. While responding to a burglary at a coffee and tea shop, the owner of the shop tells Officer Michaels that the thieves stole 50 containers of the owner's most expensive brew. The owner estimates that the total value of the stolen items is approximately $3,200. What is the value of an individual container of coffee?

    A. $46
    B. $52
    C. $64
    D. $78

Questions 11 and 12 refer to the following information.

In preparing a report on a burglary of a winery, Officer Little listed the following stolen items and their values:

   Cash: $675
   Cheese and meats: $250
   Grapes: $2,400
   Wine-making supplies: $950
   Wine: $15,000
   TOTAL: $19,275

11. What is the total value of the stolen items except for the wine?

    A. $3,600
    B. $4,025
    C. $4,275
    D. $7,050

12. The winery owner finds six cases of wine she originally thought were stolen, but realizes that two bushels more of grapes are missing. The wine is valued at $950 and the grapes are worth $2,200. What is the new total value of the stolen items?

   A. $14,475
   B. $16,250
   C. $20,525
   D. $21,475

13. The closest dry cleaner is approximately 8 miles away from the police station. If Lieutenant Brady made 11 trips to the dry cleaner in the past month, how many total miles did he travel?

   A. 76 miles
   B. 88 miles
   C. 142 miles
   D. 176 miles

Questions 14 and 15 refer to the following information.

   In the past six months, crime rates have increased in the town of Lenox. In November, 4 murders were reported and 12 were reported in April. In November, local businesses reported 6 arsons. In April, local businesses reported 15 arsons. In November, 19 gang-related incidents were reported, while April had 28.

14. By what percentage did the reports of gang-related incidents increase from November to April?

   A. 47%
   B. 55%
   C. 68%
   D. 72%

15. How many murders, arsons, and gang-related incidents were reported in November?

   A. 25
   B. 29
   C. 55
   D. 84

16. Sergeant Wolfe worked 9 surveillance shifts over the past 2 weeks. They lasted 5 hours, 9 hours, 9 hours, 11 hours, 14 hours, 6 hours, 8 hours, 4 hours, and 10 hours. What is the average length of time he spent working surveillance each shift? Round to the nearest whole number.

   A. 5 hours
   B. 6 hours
   C. 8 hours
   D. 9 hours

17. The number of arrests Officer Jin made each week for the past four months was 4, 6, 9, 12, 6, 7, 4, 17, 13, 2, 5, 18, 9, 5, 14, and 1. What is the average number of arrests she made per week? Round to the nearest whole number.

   A. 6
   B. 8
   C. 11
   D. 16

18. Find the width of the room shown below using the formula $A = lw$.

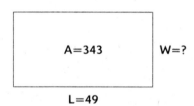

   A. 7
   B. 9
   C. 14
   D. 18

19. Solve: $990.99 - 44.77 \times 0.66 + 111$. Round to the nearest hundredth.

   A. 487.36
   B. 999.42
   C. 1,062.54
   D. 1,072.44

20. Find the diameter of the circle shown below using the formula $D = 2r$.

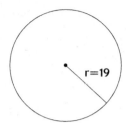

r=19

A. 9.5
B. 38
C. 145
D. 361

Question 21 refers to the following information.

Officer Franklin completes an incident report following a robbery at a department store. He lists the following stolen items and their values:

Shoes: $120
Sweaters: $200
Perfumes: $750
Pants: $95
Accessories: $84

21. What is the total value of all the stolen items?

A. $1,248
B. $1,249
C. $1,250
D. $1,251

22. While on patrol, Officer Sanders normally drives his squad car about 225 miles per week, or about 45 miles per day. This week, however, his squad car was at the garage for two days. How many miles did Sanders drive in his car this week?

A. 130 miles
B. 135 miles
C. 140 miles
D. 145 miles

23. Officer McMahon normally drives his squad car about 360 miles per week. In an average five-day week, about how many miles does he drive in a day?

A. 60
B. 72
C. 73
D. 90

Question 24 refers to the following information.

Following a robbery of a pawn shop, Officer Hunter prepares an incident report and records the following stolen items and their values:

8 gold rings: $750 each
3 DVD players: $175 each
6 bracelets: $300 each
2 paintings: $400 each

24. What is the total value of the stolen bracelets?

A. $1,500
B. $1,800
C. $2,100
D. $2,400

25. Your police department typically issues traffic citations to about 120 motorists per week. About 40% of these citations are for speeding. About how many speeding citations are issued per week?

A. 44
B. 46
C. 48
D. 50

26. Officer Freemont usually works the 11 p.m. to 7 a.m. shift five days per week. He is asked by his supervisor to report for duty at 10:30 p.m. each day this week. At the end of the week, how many hours of overtime will Officer Freemont have worked?

 A. 1 hour, 30 minutes
 B. 2 hours
 C. 2 hours, 30 minutes
 D. 3 hours

27. The number of arrests Sergeant Bombulie made each week for the past eight weeks was 8, 9, 2, 19, 7, 4, 11, and 2. What is the average number of arrests he made per month?

 A. 19
 B. 24
 C. 31
 D. 62

Questions 28 and 29 refer to the following information.

In the past 12 months, crime rates have both increased and decreased. In January 2009, 42 burglaries were reported. In January 2010, 60 burglaries were reported. In January 2009, 4 trespassing incidents were reported, while January 2010 saw only 1. In January 2009, 15 gang-related incidents were reported. In January 2010, there were 39 gang-related incidents.

28. How many burglaries, trespassing incidents, and gang-related incidents were reported in January 2009?

 A. 52
 B. 61
 C. 75
 D. 136

29. By what percentage did the reports of burglary increase from January 2009 to January 2010?

 A. 43%
 B. 65%
 C. 77%
 D. 80%

Questions 30 and 31 refer to the following information.

In preparing a report on a burglary in a specialty sandwich shop, Officer Naughton listed the following stolen items and their values:

 6 cases of flavored coffee: $100 each = $600
 4 sandwich presses: $175 each = $700
 12 blocks gourmet cheese: $145 each = $1,740
 Cash: $1,900
 TOTAL: $4,940

30. What is the total value of the stolen items except for two of the sandwich presses?

 A. $4,190
 B. $4,240
 C. $4,590
 D. $4,765

31. While cleaning up the mess left behind by the burglars, the owner realizes that only ten blocks of gourmet cheese were taken. What is the new total value of the stolen items?

 A. $4,300
 B. $4,650
 C. $4,745
 D. $4,795

32. Officer Jennings usually works the 3 p.m. to 11 p.m. shift five days per week. She is asked by her supervisor to report for duty on Monday at 12:45 p.m. for a special training program. If she works her entire shift on Monday, how many hours of overtime will Officer Jennings have worked?

   A. 2 hours
   B. 2 hours, 15 minutes
   C. 2 hours, 30 minutes
   D. 3 hours

33. The closest coffee shop and the police station are approximately 3 miles apart. If Sergeant Fu made four trips to the coffee shop this week, how many miles in all did he travel?

   A. 12 miles
   B. 18 miles
   C. 24 miles
   D. 48 miles

34. Find the diameter of the circle shown below using the formula $D = 2r$.

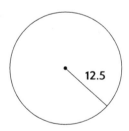

   A. 12.5
   B. 25
   C. 37.5
   D. 50

35. While responding to a burglary at an electronics store, the owner of the shop tells Officer Drew the thieves stole 19 touch-screen cellphones. The owner estimates that the total value of the stolen items is approximately $4,275. What is the value of each individual touch-screen cellphone?

   A. $225
   B. $245
   C. $295
   D. $325

36. Officer Warner worked eight surveillance shifts over the past two weeks. They lasted 9 hours, 8 hours, 5 hours, 14 hours, 2 hours, 7 hours, 4 hours, and 1 hour. What is the average length of time she spent working surveillance each shift? Round to the nearest whole number.

   A. 6 hours
   B. 7 hours
   C. 9 hours
   D. 10 hours

37. The number of arrests Officer Farley made each week for the past three months was 4, 5, 6, 14, 9, 8, 15, 6, 7, 18, 1, and 2. What is the average number of arrests she made per week? Round to the nearest whole number.

   A. 4
   B. 6
   C. 8
   D. 12

38. $55.77 - 989.42 \times 0.12 + 289$. Round to the nearest hundredth.

   A. 112.54
   B. 226.04
   C. 275.96
   D. 387.01

39. Find the area of the room shown below using the formula $A = lw$.

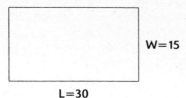

W=15

L=30

    A.   30
    B.   150
    C.   375
    D.   450

40. Your police department typically issues parking citations to about 400 vehicles a month. About 5% of these citations are never paid. About how many parking citations are delinquent per month?

    A.   20
    B.   30
    C.   40
    D.   50

41. The courthouse and the police station are approximately 3.5 miles apart. If Lieutenant Quinn made nine trips to the courthouse in the past month, how many total miles did he travel?

    A.   24.5 miles
    B.   43 miles
    C.   63 miles
    D.   82.5 miles

Questions 42 and 43 refer to the following information.

Officer Moody completes an incident report following a robbery at a skate shop. He lists the following stolen items and their values:

    Shoes: $325
    Skateboards: $250
    Jackets: $130
    Hats: $55
    Accessories: $80

42. What is the total value of all the stolen items?

    A. $740
    B. $840
    C. $890
    D. $920

43. While cleaning up the mess left behind by the burglars, the owner of the skate shop realizes that only four, not five, pairs of shoes were stolen. What is the new total value of the stolen items, if each pair of shoes has the same value?

    A. $725
    B. $775
    C. $805
    D. $865

44. Your police department typically issues parking tickets to about 85 motorists per week. About 30% of these citations are for double parking. About how many parking tickets are issued for double parking per week?

    A.   25.5
    B.   37.5
    C.   49.5
    D.   59.5

45. Officer Greene usually works the 1 p.m. to 9 p.m. shift five days per week. She is asked by her supervisor to report for duty on Monday and Tuesday at 11:15 a.m. for a special training program. If she works her entire shifts on Monday and Tuesday, how many hours of overtime will Officer Jennings have worked?

A. 3 hours
B. 3 hours, 15 minutes
C. 3 hours, 30 minutes
D. 3 hours, 45 minutes

46. Find the area of the rectangle shown below using the formula $A = lw$.

10 ⎡⎢⎣   ⎤⎥⎦
                    45

A. 400
B. 450
C. 500
D. 550

47. Solve: $8.26 - 0.42 + 3.41 \times 2.17$. Round to the nearest hundredth.

A. 12.48
B. 13.42
C. 15.24
D. 24.41

48. Sergeant Bush worked eight surveillance shifts over the past 2 weeks. They lasted 6 hours, 12 hours, 4 hours, 8 hours, 5 hours, 7 hours, 8 hours, and 2 hours. What is the average length of time he spent working surveillance each week? Round to the nearest whole number.

A. 6.5 hours
B. 12 hours
C. 21.5 hours
D. 26 hours

49. During a raid, a police unit discovers 28 illegal weapons. After processing the weapons at the station, they are told that 70% of the weapons were loaded and ready for use upon the squad's arrival. How many guns were loaded when the police arrived at the warehouse?

A. 10
B. 15
C. 20
D. 25

50. The number of arrests Officer Marquee made each week for the past 12 weeks was 4, 1, 7, 2, 9, 8, 0, 5, 7, 2, 2, and 7. What is the average number of arrests she made per week?

A. 3.5 arrests
B. 4 arrests
C. 4.5 arrests
D. 5 arrests

IF YOU FINISH BEFORE TIME IS CALLED, CHECK YOUR WORK ON THIS SECTION ONLY. DO NOT WORK ON ANY OTHER SECTION IN THE TEST.

STOP

Section 4: Judgment and Problem Solving

Time: 50 minutes

50 questions

Directions (1–50): Answer these questions based solely on the information provided.

Questions 1 and 2 refer to the following definition.

Robbery: The act of removing or attempting to remove a piece of property from its owner's possession by use of force, intimidation, or threat of violence

1. According to the definition, which one of the following is the best example of robbery?

   A. Mike has too many beers at the bar and sticks the pretzel bowl in his bag to take home with him.

   B. Lucy sneaks into her parents' room, goes in the sock drawer, and takes $100 to buy a new bathing suit.

   C. Emilio approaches a woman at an ATM, presses a knife to her throat, and demands her to withdraw $1,000.

   D. Julie lags behind when her friends run downstairs, and she snatches a bottle of nail polish off her best friend's desk.

2. According to the definition, which one of the following is *not* an example of robbery?

   A. When Ramona goes to the copy machine, someone steals her cellphone off the desk in her office.

   B. During recess, Mikey is approached by a bully who says he'll punch Mikey if he doesn't give him $5.

   C. After parking his car in the garage, Raphael is shoved to the ground and a man in a ski mask demands his keys.

   D. While Tiffany is out jogging, a man approaches her, yanks her MP3 player from her armband, and runs away.

Question 3 refers to the following information.

The State of Delaware's Animal Regulation ordinances state that the ordinance is designed to protect both people and animals, wild and domestic, from abuse and maltreatment. Stated in Section 24-12 of this ordinance, titled "Proper and Humane Care of Animals Required," are requirements that all Delaware residents must meet or they will be penalized. Requirements include:

1. Owners of animals should never fail to provide food, water, and shelter for their animals.

2. Owners should never neglect, beat, torment, overwork, or cruelly treat animals in their care. They should never force an animal to fight another animal.

3. Owners should never abandon their animals.

4. Owners should never use their animals as payment or incentive to enter a business agreement, contest, or any type of competition.

5. If any Delaware resident hits an animal with his or her car, he or she should stop the vehicle immediately, attempt to contact the animal's owner, and report the incident to county officials.

6. Delaware residents should never place poison in an area where it may be consumed by any animals.

3. According to the information provided, which of the following is the best example of an owner who is violating Section 24-12 of Delaware's Animal Regulation ordinance?

   A. Rebecca is going away for the weekend and has asked her neighbors to watch and feed her two cats.
   B. George works two jobs and sometimes forgets to feed his dog between shifts; however, he always puts food out for his dog before he goes to sleep at night.
   C. José plays five rounds of the same carnival game and wins two goldfish, which he takes home as a present for his two daughters.
   D. Francine is sick of the neighbor's dog digging up her flowers, so she puts poison along the perimeter of her garden and hopes that the smell will keep the dog away.

Questions 4 and 5 refer to the following information.

Police departments frequently engage in undercover operations to prevent crimes. Some crimes, however, are better prevented with the presence of uniformed officers.

4. Which of the following scenarios would best be addressed with uniformed officers?

   A. investigating a suspected pedophile
   B. breaking up a prostitution ring
   C. operating a drug sting
   D. directing traffic before and after a sporting event

5. Which of the following scenarios would best be addressed with undercover officers?

   A. providing security at a public event
   B. escorting a celebrity
   C. arresting men who attempt to hire prostitutes
   D. preventing auto theft

Question 6 refers to the following information.

Officers studying the law are learning about the frequency of traffic accidents. To understand how the presence of a four-way stop sign affects the number of accidents that may take place at intersections per year, the class receives a handout containing the following information:

Intersection	Accidents (2007)	Stop Sign
1st and Oak streets	18	No
134th and Broad streets	8	Yes
Willow Avenue and Lark Lane	24	No
4th Street and Ocean Boulevard	6	Yes
7th Street and Tropics Lane	10	Yes

6. After reviewing the table, it would be most correct for an officer to conclude that the presence of four-way stop signs:

   A. results in more accidents
   B. results in fewer accidents
   C. does not affect the number of accidents
   D. is necessary at all intersections

7. You and your partner respond to an attempted robbery and, during the course of the pursuit and apprehension of the suspect, your partner does not provide you with adequate support and backup. How should you deal with this problem?

   A. Discuss the issue with your partner personally.
   B. Report the issue to your supervisor.
   C. File a formal complaint and ask for a new partner.
   D. Refuse to offer your partner any future support.

8. Officer Daniels is arresting a wealthy 63-year-old man who is suspected of committing securities fraud. Based on the nature of the crime and the suspect's assurances that he does not intend to resist arrest, the officer opts not to apply handcuffs. Which of the following is true?

   A. This is a bad policy because the officer should maintain the public's perception of his authority.
   B. This is a good policy because the suspect is already under control and cooperative.
   C. This is a good policy because the suspect's crime is nonviolent.
   D. This is a bad policy because an unrestrained suspect presents a threat to the officer.

Questions 9 and 10 refer to the following information.

Lieutenant Pollack is trying to reduce crime in his precinct. He is reviewing the following crime reports and the schedule from the last month:

Date	Day	Crime	Time	Location
10/2	Friday	Arson	9:02 p.m.	100 block of 8th Street
10/8	Thursday	Vandalism	5:09 p.m.	1300 block of 19th Avenue
10/10	Saturday	Burglary	3:23 a.m.	500 block of 13th Avenue
10/11	Sunday	Burglary	11:43 p.m.	700 block of 13th Avenue
10/16	Friday	Arson	3:39 p.m.	900 block of 43rd Street
10/21	Wednesday	Burglary	6:21 a.m.	2400 block of 96th Street
10/29	Thursday	Vandalism	12:02 a.m.	3300 block of 47th Avenue
10/29	Thursday	Burglary	7:25 p.m.	600 block of 19th Avenue

Shift	Schedule
Tour I	7 a.m.–3 p.m.
Tour II	3 p.m.–11 p.m.
Tour III	11 p.m.–7 a.m.

9. If Lieutenant Pollack wants to assign extra police officers to reduce the number of burglaries and vandalism incidents, which of the following would most likely achieve that goal?

A. Assign a Tour III to patrol 13th Avenue on the weekends and a Tour II to patrol 19th Avenue on Thursdays.

B. Assign a Tour I to patrol 19th Avenue on Saturdays and a Tour III to patrol 8th Street on Fridays.

C. Assign a Tour II to patrol 8th Street on Fridays and a Tour II to patrol 43rd Street on Fridays.

D. Assign a Tour III to patrol 19th Avenue on Thursdays and a Tour II to patrol 13th Avenue on the weekends.

10. If Lieutenant Pollack wants to assign extra police officers to reduce the number of arsons, which of the following would most likely achieve that goal?

A. Assign a Tour I and a Tour III to patrol 43rd Street on Fridays.

B. Assign a Tour II and a Tour III to patrol 8th Street on Fridays.

C. Assign a Tour II to patrol 43rd Street and 8th Street on Fridays.

D. Assign a Tour II to patrol 8th Street and 43rd Street on Thursdays.

Question 11 refers to the following information.

Serious injuries or other medical emergencies may sometimes necessitate a change in normal procedures. If a suspect is seriously hurt or otherwise in need of emergency medical assistance, you should postpone arresting him or her and call for medical help.

11. Which of the following scenarios would indicate the need for emergency medical care?

A. A man breaks his left thumb during a pursuit.

B. A man caught in an act of arson suffers minor burns.

C. A woman suffers a small puncture wound from a kitchen knife.

D. A man is found unconscious in a park with an empty pill bottle next to him.

12. All police officers wear badges. Which of the following is the most important reason for this practice?

A. Badges identify the wearer as a police officer.

B. Badges suggest authority and control.

C. Badges can intimidate criminals.

D. Badges make officers look more professional.

Question 13 refers to the following definition.

Receiving or concealing stolen property in the first degree: Knowingly receiving or holding stolen property with the intention of depriving the lawful owner of its use or using the property for personal gain; property value must exceed $1,500.

13. Based on the definition, which of following is the most accurate example of receiving or concealing stolen property in the first degree?

A. Peter's friend steals a $500 stereo system, and Peter agrees to hold it for him for a while.

B. Doug steals a car from a parking lot and stores it in a remote garage until police interest in the case has waned.

C. Micah finds an envelope on the ground with $350 in it. His neighbor's name is printed on the envelope.

D. Jewelry store proprietor LaBron willingly accepts $5,200 worth of stolen gemstones that his friend has acquired for him.

14. While on patrol in a small community of town houses, Officer Bradley notices a fire at the rear of one row of town houses. What should the officer do next in this situation?

   A. Run to each town house in the row and tell the residents to evacuate their homes.
   B. Attempt to extinguish the fire himself.
   C. Call the fire department and use his car's PA system to notify residents.
   D. Attempt to determine the cause of the fire.

Question 15 refers to the following information.

Officer Jones completed an incident report following a theft. The following five sentences were removed from the body of the report in no particular order:

   1. Ms. Turner left the cash drawer slightly open and later removed $200.
   2. After being dispatched, I located and arrested Ms. Turner seven blocks away from the store.
   3. Department store clerk Samantha Turner checked out a customer.
   4. Witnesses stated that Ms. Turner fled the store and headed south on Dodsworth Avenue.
   5. Store security witnessed Ms. Turner's actions via a security camera but was unable to apprehend her.

15. Which of the following alternatives represents the correct chronological order of events?

   A. 2, 4, 3, 1, 5
   B. 3, 1, 5, 4, 2
   C. 3, 5, 1, 2, 4
   D. 1, 4, 2, 3, 5

16. Police Officer Ericson is dispatched to a home robbery in progress. When he arrives on the scene, the suspect runs out the back door of the residence. As the officer gives pursuit, the suspect attempts to jump over a tall, wooden fence and breaks his leg in the process. With the suspect now secured, how should the officer proceed?

   A. Place the suspect under arrest and transport him to the police precinct.
   B. Contact his immediate supervisor for further instructions.
   C. Call for an ambulance because the suspect needs emergency medical care.
   D. Release the suspect for fear that he may accuse him of police brutality.

Question 17 refers to the following information.

A group of police-officer recruits are learning about unusual circumstances they may come across in the field. One topic their instructor covers is what to do in the event that you find a downed power line. The instructor says that in this situation, a police officer's main goal is to secure the scene and inform the utility company of the issue. The instructor highlights the following procedural guidelines:

   1. Approach and assess the scene carefully.
   2. Take note of signs like arcing or sparking, which would indicate that the wire is still live.
   3. Do not attempt to touch or move the wire for any reason.
   4. Secure the scene, making sure that any bystanders remain at a safe distance.
   5. Contact the utility company and maintain scene security until repairs are made and safety is restored.

17. Recruit officers are then presented with the following scenario: An officer is patrolling a residential neighborhood after a severe thunderstorm when he finds a downed power line lying across the road. He cautiously approaches the wire and assesses the scene. He does not see any arcing or sparking. What should he do next?

    A. Move the wire off the road since it does not appear to be live.

    B. Contact the utility company.

    C. Avoid touching the wire and secure the scene.

    D. Call his supervisor for further instructions.

18. Today is the city's annual St. Patrick's Day parade and you have been assigned to traffic control at a normally busy intersection. While the festivities are in progress, an ambulance with flashing lights and sirens approaches your intersection. How should you proceed?

    A. Tell the ambulance driver that he'll need to take a different route.

    B. Seek guidance from your immediate supervisor.

    C. Tell the ambulance driver to cross the street at an intersection the parade has not yet reached.

    D. Stop the parade momentarily and allow the ambulance to cross the street.

Question 19 refers to the following information.

Northridge City Police Chief Charles Johnson calls for a department-wide meeting of all officers to discuss plans for a major upcoming construction project in the city. A new, state-of-the-art conference center is going to be built in the busy downtown district. With construction set to begin in under a month, the police department must organize a plan for traffic control and public safety during the project. Johnson highlights the following priority concerns that the plan must address:

- **New traffic patterns:** Because the project will disrupt the normal traffic patterns in the immediate vicinity, the police department will have to work with the local government to design and implement temporary traffic patterns to be used while construction is in progress.

- **Enforcement:** Because the new traffic patterns being implemented during construction will be unfamiliar to the public, Johnson urges his officers to be very careful about enforcing traffic laws in the construction zone. He says that drivers may be likely to become easily frustrated or confused and should be treated with restraint and understanding. Johnson also makes it clear, however, that all existing traffic laws must be obeyed and enforced.

- **Construction safety:** Johnson says that the police department will be monitoring the construction project at all times in order to ensure that the various parties involved are observing the proper safety protocols and are themselves obeying all traffic laws.

- **Public safety:** Finally, Johnson tells his officers that they will be patrolling the construction zone and the surrounding vicinity regularly to ensure that no bystanders attempt to enter the construction site or in any way violate safety protocols involving the project.

19. Which of the following would most accurately describe Police Chief Johnson's primary goal concerning the upcoming construction project?

    A. ensuring that construction companies follow all regulations

    B. maintaining public safety and security

    C. keeping the city's traffic flow moving smoothly

    D. using the new traffic patterns to issue citations

20. You're dispatched to investigate a report of a drunken man walking around a residential neighborhood with an obviously visible firearm. When you reach the scene, you find a suspicious-looking man wearing a long coat standing in the middle of the street. How should you proceed?

    A. Arrest the man immediately and take him to your police headquarters.
    B. Question the complainant about the identity of the man with the firearm.
    C. Shoot the man in the road, as he presents a serious threat to the public.
    D. Tell the complainant that the man is harmless and should be ignored.

21. Investigation of which of the following cases would prove most difficult for law-enforcement officials?

    A. credit-card fraud
    B. domestic abuse
    C. drug trafficking
    D. grand theft auto

Question 22 refers to the following definition.

Aggravated assault: Attacking a person with the intent to cause severe bodily injury

22. Which of following is the most accurate example of aggravated assault?

    A. Peter Black attempts to rob a minimart, but the clerk is uncooperative, so he stabs the clerk multiple times.
    B. Floyd Samson walks into his home to find a burglar trying to steal his stereo. He produces a gun and shoots the man.
    C. Gang leader Randall Wright finds out that one of his subordinates has been talking about him to members of a rival gang. As punishment, he goes to the man's home and beats him with a lead pipe.
    D. Michelle Brown learns that her husband has been having an affair with his secretary. Enraged, she goes to the woman's home to confront her. An argument ensues and Michelle attacks the woman with a knife.

23. Officer Chang is on patrol when a visibly upset man approaches him and complains that a man selling watches on the street just sold him a fake watch. He wants Chang to arrest the man and get his money back. How should he proceed?

    A. Immediately arrest the man who is selling watches on the street.
    B. Confront the seller and tell him if he doesn't return the money, he will be arrested.
    C. Tell the complainant that the situation is a civil manner and there is nothing you can do.
    D. Question the seller and determine if any further action is required.

Question 24 refers to the following information.

Police Officer Patterson completed an incident report following an arrest for concealing stolen property in the third degree. The following five sentences were removed from the body of the report in no particular order:

1. A suspect identified as Frank Thompson was seen on a security video stealing a DVD player worth $130 from the loading dock of an electronics retailer.
2. Mr. Thompson was arrested and charged with theft.
3. Mr. Hutton was arrested and charged with concealing stolen property.
4. Mr. Thompson told interrogators what he did with the stolen DVD player.
5. Mr. Thompson took the stolen DVD player to the residence of Patrick Hutton, who knowingly agreed to conceal it.

24. Which of the following alternatives represents the correct chronological order of events?

    A. 1, 5, 3, 2, 4
    B. 2, 3, 1, 5, 2
    C. 3, 1, 5, 2, 4
    D. 1, 5, 2, 4, 3

25. Police Officer Clifton is on the scene of a crime and he is communicating with his precinct over the radio in his squad car. While talking, he is sure to speak clearly and make his statements brief and precise. What is the most important reason for the use of this radio communication technique?

    A. It makes messages easier to understand and reduces the risk of miscommunication.
    B. It prevents busy communication lines from being constantly tied up.
    C. It makes you sound more professional when you're speaking in front of civilians.
    D. It helps the department save money on airtime expenses.

Questions 26 and 27 refer to the following definitions.

Larceny: The act of taking cash, property, or valuable item from its rightful owner with the intent to permanently deprive the owner of the value of the stolen item

Robbery: The act of removing or attempting to remove a piece of property from its owner's possession by use of force, intimidation, or threat of violence

Embezzlement: The theft of any money or property carried out by any individual who is trusted with or responsible for the assets.

26. Based on the definitions provided, which of the following is the best example of larceny?

    A. Carl approaches a man running through the park, pulls a gun, and orders the man to hand over his wallet.
    B. Phyllis, who works at the checkout of a grocery store, takes a few dollars out of her register at the end of her shift.
    C. Antoine sees a clearly intoxicated man stumbling through the alley; she hits him and takes his wallet.
    D. When the man in the next cubicle at work goes to the restroom, Frank takes his cellphone from his desk.

27. Based on the definitions provided, which of the following would be the best example of embezzlement?

    A. When Rose, the office secretary, takes the day's company deposit to the bank on her way home, she takes out $100 to keep for herself.

    B. Rodger enters a convenience store with a shotgun and orders the clerk to give him all the money in the register.

    C. Laura is walking down the street when an unknown man knocks her to the ground and takes her purse.

    D. George is a maintenance man at a gym. While he is working in the locker room, he finds a wallet in someone's gym bag and takes $50 from it.

Question 28 refers to the following information.

The town of Loganburg, Ohio, recently passed a new curfew ordinance. This ordinance is designed to prevent criminal acts from being committed against or by young people through the establishment of a code of regulations concerning the whereabouts of minors during certain hours. The ordinance contains the following provisions:

1. All individuals considered minors—that is, under 18 years of age—must be within private residences between the hours of 12 a.m. and 5 a.m.

2. Curfew for minors under 13 years of age will extend from 10 p.m. and 6 a.m.

3. Minors accompanied by a parent or legal guardian are exempted from the curfew.

4. A minor in violation of the curfew may be exempted in the event of an emergency.

5. Parents or legal guardians who knowingly allow violation of the curfew will be held responsible.

28. According to the information provided, which of the following is the best example of an individual in violation of the curfew?

    A. Joey, 14 years old, is delivering newspapers at 5:15 a.m.

    B. Samantha, 11 years old, is at a sleepover at her friend's house at 1:30 a.m.

    C. Elizabeth, 8 years old, is walking down the street with her aunt at 10:25 p.m.

    D. Tom, 12 years old, and his older brother are standing on the sidewalk after having been in a car accident at 11:10 p.m.

Question 29 refers to the following information.

Officer O'Leary completed an incident report following a robbery. The following five sentences were removed from the body of the report in no particular order:

1. Mr. Murphy handed over his MP3 player and the suspect fled.

2. I apprehended the suspect and placed him under arrest.

3. Kevin Murphy was jogging in Grove Park when he was approached by an unidentified man.

4. Mr. Murphy noticed me walking past the pond ahead of the suspect and alerted me.

5. The suspect produced a small pistol and ordered Mr. Murphy to give him his MP3 player.

29. Which of the following alternatives represents the correct chronological order of events?

    A. 3, 5, 1, 4, 2
    B. 3, 1, 4, 5, 2
    C. 2, 4, 1, 5, 3
    D. 3, 5, 1, 4, 2

Question 30 refers to the following information.

Officer Walter Daniels is on patrol in his police cruiser at 2:35 a.m. when he is called to respond to a home robbery in progress. He heads to the scene but turns off his lights and sirens. When he arrives, he approaches the front of the home, noticing that a small window alongside the door has been broken. He opens the door through the window and enters the home. Once inside, he hears movement upstairs. He walks to the second story of the house and finds the suspect trying to break into a safe in the master bedroom. The suspect sees him and tries to flee. After a brief struggle, the suspect makes it out of the bedroom but, with Officer Daniels in close pursuit, falls down the stairs and suffers a head laceration. Officer Daniels places the man under arrest and transports him to the precinct for booking.

30. Using the information provided, you may infer that Officer Daniels immediately arrests the suspect once he is subdued because:

   A. He has already escaped capture once, so the officer isn't going to take any chances.
   B. The suspect's crime is serious enough to warrant the officer to overlook the suspect's injury.
   C. His injury is not severe, so immediate arrest is more important than seeking medical attention.
   D. It's too late at night to call for medical assistance, and the suspect will have to wait until morning.

Question 31 refers to the following information.

New police recruits studying the law are learning about the frequency of speeding citations on highways and interstates. To understand how the presence of a decoy police vehicle affects the number of speeding violations issued on local highways and interstates per week, the class is given a handout containing the following chart:

Highway or Interstate	Speeding Citations	Decoy Car
Interstate 81	9	Yes
Interstate 66	23	No
Highway 15	17	No
Interstate 95	12	Yes
Highway 55	5	Yes
Highway 222	19	No

31. Based on the information in the chart, the recruits could correctly assume that the presense of a decoy police vehicle:

   A. results in more speeding citations
   B. results in fewer speeding citations
   C. doesn't affect speeding citations
   D. is effective only on interstates

32. Two months ago, you were assigned a new partner. On several occasions since that time, your partner has failed to provide you with adequate backup in the field. You've spoken with him about this problem several times, but he has failed to improve. What should you do next?

   A. Continue to discuss the problem with your partner, but take no further action.
   B. Notify your supervisor and tell him or her about the issue.
   C. Get back at him by refusing him any future support when he needs it.
   D. Have some of your fellow officers talk to him for you.

33. Officer Tunney is arresting a well-known political figure who has been charged with corruption. The suspect asks to not be placed in handcuffs for his transport to the precinct because of media presence. Since he's been very cooperative and nonviolent, Tunney decides not to restrain him. This decision would be considered:

   A. good policy, because the suspect is cooperative and noncombative

   B. bad policy, because the officer is making the department seem soft on crime

   C. good policy, because of the nature of the suspect's crime and his public persona

   D. bad policy, because all suspects must be restrained for safety and security purposes

Questions 34 and 35 refer to the following information.

Police Chief Ray Bernardi is trying to reduce crime in his precinct. He is reviewing the following crime reports and the schedule from the last month:

Date	Day	Crime	Time	Location
3/8	Monday	Auto Theft	11:38 p.m.	1400 block of 7th Street
3/10	Wednesday	Burglary	6:43 p.m.	600 block of 19th Avenue
3/12	Friday	Arson	3:23 a.m.	2500 block of 6th Avenue
3/13	Saturday	Vandalism	11:43 p.m.	300 block of 17th Avenue
3/16	Tuesday	Arson	3:39 p.m.	1900 block of 52nd Street
3/17	Wednesday	Burglary	3:16 p.m.	2000 block of 84th Street
3/23	Tuesday	Auto theft	12:02 a.m.	1500 block of 8th Street
3/31	Wednesday	Burglary	12:45 a.m.	800 block of 9th Avenue

Shift	Schedule
Tour I	7 a.m.–3 p.m.
Tour II	3 p.m.–11 p.m.
Tour III	11 p.m.–7 a.m.

34. If Chief Bernardi wants to assign extra police officers to reduce the number of burglaries, which of the following would most likely achieve that goal?

    A. Assign a Tour II to patrol 9th Avenue and a Tour I to patrol 19th Avenue and 84th Street on Wednesdays.

    B. Assign a Tour III to patrol 7th Street on Mondays and 8th Street on Tuesdays.

    C. Assign a Tour III to patrol 9th Avenue and a Tour II to patrol 19th Avenue and 84th Street on Wednesdays.

    D. Assign a Tour I to patrol 52nd Street on Fridays and a Tour III to patrol 6th Avenue on Saturdays.

35. If Chief Bernardi wants to assign extra police officers to reduce the number of auto thefts, which of the following would most likely achieve that goal?

    A. Assign a Tour III to patrol 7th Street on Mondays and 8th Street on Tuesdays.

    B. Assign a Tour III to patrol 6th Avenue on Fridays and a Tour II to patrol 84th Street on Wednesdays.

    C. Assign a Tour I to patrol 7th Street on Mondays and 8th Street on Tuesdays.

    D. Assign a Tour II to patrol 19th Avenue on Wednesdays and 52nd Street on Tuesdays.

36. While you're interrogating a suspect, you tell him that his alleged crime is not that big of a deal, hoping that this will encourage him to confess. This strategy would be considered:

    A. good policy, because the suspect will believe that his punishment will be mild, so he'll be more cooperative

    B. bad policy, because this will make the suspect feel less guilty and, in turn, less willing to cooperate

    C. good policy, because this will make the suspect more relaxed and willing to cooperate

    D. bad policy, because the suspect will take this as disrespect and become less cooperative

37. Which of the following parts of a police officer's uniform functions as the primary means of identifying the wearer as a police officer?

    A. police hat
    B. badge
    C. uniform patches
    D. handcuffs

Question 38 refers to the following definition.

> **Voluntary manslaughter:** Intentionally killing another person without premeditation; usually the result of sudden extreme emotional or mental stress

38. Based on the definition provided, which of the following is the most accurate example of voluntary manslaughter?

   A. Steve receives a text message from his wife that reveals that she's been having an affair with his friend Paul. Steve is furious and plans to kill Paul. That night, Steve finds Paul outside his favorite bar and beats him to death with a baseball bat.

   B. Matt and Mike rob a bank and get away with thousands of dollars. Afterward, Matt feels exhilarated, but Mike is remorseful and says that he his going to turn himself in. Knowing that this means that he'll get caught too, Matt becomes infuriated and abruptly shoots Mike, killing him.

   C. Frank has just spent the night drinking at a bar. He's very intoxicated, but he insists on driving home. Along the way, he swerves into oncoming traffic and hits another car head-on. Frank has only minor injuries, but the other driver is killed.

   D. Omar enters a convenience store carrying a shotgun. He approaches the clerk and demands all the money in the register. The clerk trips a silent alarm and tries to stall. Omar grows frustrated and angry. Suddenly, he sees a man running toward him out of the corner of his eye. He spins around and shoots the man, killing him instantly.

39. Officer Roland is on patrol in his district when he finds a tree that has fallen down and broken a power line, which is now lying across the road. On examination, the power line does not appear to be live. Officer Roland's next step should be to:

   A. Secure the scene and contact the electric utility company.

   B. Remove the downed wire from the roadway himself.

   C. File the appropriate report and continue on his patrol.

   D. Move the downed wire with a stick or tree branch.

Question 40 refers to the following information.

Officer Marella completed an incident report following a carjacking. The following five sentences were removed from the body of the report in no particular order:

1. Crain contacted police, and I arrived on the scene.

2. Robert Crain was driving a silver 2009 Mercedes Benz, license plate number 2R1914, on Plaza Boulevard when he stopped at a traffic light.

3. The suspect entered the car and sped away.

4. As Crain waited to proceed, an unidentified man approached the driver's window pointing a gun.

5. The suspect ordered Crain to get out of his car and Crain complied.

40. Which of the following alternatives represents the correct chronological order of events?

   A. 1, 2, 4, 5, 3
   B. 2, 4, 5, 3, 1
   C. 2, 4, 5, 1, 3
   D. 1, 3, 5, 4, 2

Question 41 refers to the following information.

A class of police officer recruits is learning about what to do when responding to a motor-vehicle accident. Police officers encounter motor-vehicle accidents on a daily basis and must understand how to handle such calls. Accident scenes can be very dangerous, and victims may require immediate medical intervention. When responding to motor-vehicle accidents, officers should follow these procedures:

1. Cautiously approach and assess the scene.
2. Make sure to look for dangers such as fire or leaking fluids.
3. Assess the condition of any victims and check for injuries.
4. If injuries are present, call for emergency medical support.
5. If no injuries are present, question the parties involved and determine the circumstances of the accident.
6. Make any necessary arrests and prepare an accident report.

41. Recruit officers are then presented with the following scenario: An officer responds to a car accident in which a tractor-trailer has collided with a car on a highway. The officer arrives on-scene and finds a badly damaged car and a tractor-trailer with relatively little damage to its right side. He sees no indications of active danger. He approaches the car and sees that the driver is seriously injured. What should he do next?

    A. Call for emergency medical support.
    B. Arrest the tractor-trailer driver.
    C. Question both drivers about the accident.
    D. Treat the car driver's injuries.

42. Sergeant Stevens is assigned to oversee police security at a diplomatic conference in the city. During the event, he receives a phone call from an unidentified man who claims to have placed a bomb in the building. How should he proceed?

    A. Attempt to locate and disarm the bomb.
    B. Make an emergency announcement to evacuate.
    C. Call the bomb squad and begin an orderly evacuation.
    D. Try to track the caller's location and have him arrested.

43. Officer Neri is assigned to traffic control during the city's annual Columbus Day parade. While the parade is in progress, a fire truck with its lights and sirens on approaches Neri's intersection. Neri temporarily stops the parade and lets the truck pass through the intersection. Neri's decision would be considered:

    A. bad policy, because the parade should not have been interrupted
    B. good policy, because the fire truck was en route to an emergency
    C. good policy, because the passing truck was entertaining for the crowd
    D. bad policy, because the interruption distracted the parade viewers

Question 44 refers to the following information.

Officer Leo Charles is on patrol in his district when he is dispatched to the scene of an alleged assault at a local bar. When Officer Charles arrives at the bar, he enters the building cautiously, observing the scene and looking for any potential dangers. He finds two groups of men, one of which is surrounding a man who has blood on his shirt and appears to be injured. The other group is surrounding a man who is clearly intoxicated and appears visibly upset. The patrons identify this man as the suspect. After ascertaining that the victim has only minor injuries, he interviews the alleged victim and gets his side of the story. The officer then interviews the alleged suspect, as well as other bystanders, and develops a sense of what happened during the incident. Once he is satisfied that an arrest is in order, he takes the suspect into custody and transports him to the precinct for booking.

44. Officer Charles's primary objective in responding to the incident would be to:

A. Take the suspect into custody as quickly as possible.
B. Get all the pertinent information he will need for his report.
C. Efficiently assess the scene and make an arrest, if warranted.
D. Evacuate all patrons and order the bar closed for the night.

45. Officer Logan receives a call to investigate an alleged indecent exposure at a nearby park. A woman called police and reported that a man was exposing himself to children in the park. When Logan arrives on the scene, he sees a man in a long coat sitting on a park bench. What should the officer do first?

A. Find the complainant and ask her to identify the man she reported.
B. Immediately place the man sitting on the park bench under arrest for indecent exposure.
C. Disable the man with a stun gun, as he presents an immediate risk to the safety of others.
D. Ignore the man and state in your report that you found nothing out of the ordinary.

46. Investigation of which of the following cases would prove most difficult for law-enforcement officials?

A. sexual assault
B. child abuse
C. embezzlement
D. securities fraud

Question 47 refers to the following definitions.

Assault/battery: Attempting to strike or actually striking another individual or threatening another with harm

Aggravated assault: A more serious form of assault, usually involving a weapon

47. Based on the definitions provided, which of following is the most accurate example of assault/battery?

   A. A fellow driver cuts off Jeff Jameson on the highway, so Jameson forces him off the road and attacks him with a tire iron, fracturing his skull.
   B. Nick DiScala is at a baseball game when the man next to him accidentally spills a beer on him. Nick stands up and punches the man in the face.
   C. Paul Jones and another man get into an argument at a bar. Paul pulls out a switchblade knife and cuts the other man's arm.
   D. Phil Harrison gets into an altercation with another man at a biker rally. The two exchange heated words before Phil hits the other man over the head with a beer bottle.

48. While on patrol in the shopping district, Officer Goldman is approached by an obviously irate man. The man claims that he just bought a CD from a merchant down the block, but he discovered that it was a bootleg CD when he opened the case to play it in his car. He demands that Goldman arrest the merchant and get his money back. At this point, Goldman should:

   A. Inform the complainant that he cannot assist him because it is a civil matter.
   B. Locate the merchant and immediately place him under arrest.
   C. Interview the merchant and determine the best course of action.
   D. Order the merchant to return the man's money, but don't arrest him.

Question 49 refers to the following information.

Officer Ross completed an incident report following an arrest for driving while intoxicated (DWI) and drug possession. The following five sentences were removed from the body of the report in no particular order:

1. I asked Mr. Cole to step out of the vehicle; when he did so, I found a bag of cocaine on which he'd been sitting.
2. I placed Mr. Cole under arrest and charged him with DWI and drug possession.
3. When I approached the vehicle, Mr. Cole appeared intoxicated, as his eyes were bloodshot and he had some sort of white substance on his face and clothing.
4. I witnessed a silver Cadillac Escalade speeding and swerving erratically and pulled over the driver.
5. The vehicle was registered to Miguel Cole of 52 Vintage Rd., Haverford.

49. Which of the following alternatives represents the correct chronological order of events?

   A. 4, 5, 3, 2, 1
   B. 2, 1, 3, 5, 4
   C. 5, 4, 3, 1, 2
   D. 4, 5, 3, 1, 2

50. Officer Kaufman is on the scene of a crime and he's using the radio in his squad car to communicate with the precinct. While he's on the radio, he speaks in long sentences and uses several minutes of airtime. This method of radio communication would be considered:

    A. good policy, because it delivers important information to the precinct all in one long conversation, rather than several segmented comments

    B. bad policy, because it takes up too much valuable time

    C. bad policy, because it ties up communication lines shared by multiple agencies

    D. good policy, because it makes radio communication more personable

IF YOU FINISH BEFORE TIME IS CALLED, CHECK YOUR WORK ON THIS SECTION ONLY. DO NOT WORK ON ANY OTHER SECTION IN THE TEST.

Answer Key

Section 1: Verbal

1. B	14. D	27. B	40. 1942 Washington Dr.
2. C	15. B	28. D	41. Frederick Mancini
3. B	16. B	29. C	42. Michael Dillon
4. C	17. B	30. C	43. 12 Broadview Rd.
5. B	18. A	31. B	44. Assault
6. A	19. A	32. D	45. Blond
7. A	20. B	33. B	46. $1,050
8. B	21. C	34. B	47. Candy Jenkins
9. C	22. A	35. A	48. 44 N. Main St.
10. A	23. B	36. D	49. 4756 Germania Ave.
11. D	24. C	37. D	50. 5'1".
12. C	25. B	38. B	
13. C	26. A	39. D	

Section 2: Memory and Visualization

1. B	14. D	27. B	40. B
2. B	15. A	28. D	41. C
3. B	16. C	29. C	42. B
4. C	17. D	30. C	43. B
5. B	18. B	31. A	44. D
6. D	19. B	32. B	45. A
7. B	20. D	33. B	46. B
8. D	21. D	34. C	47. B
9. C	22. D	35. B	48. A
10. A	23. D	36. D	49. B
11. C	24. A	37. D	50. B
12. B	25. B	38. B	
13. A	26. B	39. C	

Section 3: Mathematics

1. C	14. A	27. C	40. A
2. A	15. B	28. B	41. C
3. B	16. C	29. A	42. B
4. B	17. B	30. C	43. B
5. D	18. A	31. B	44. A
6. D	19. D	32. B	45. C
7. D	20. B	33. C	46. B
8. B	21. B	34. B	47. C
9. B	22. B	35. A	48. D
10. C	23. B	36. A	49. C
11. C	24. B	37. C	50. C
12. C	25. C	38. B	
13. D	26. C	39. D	

Section 4: Judgment and Problem Solving

1. C	14. C	27. A	40. B
2. A	15. B	28. C	41. A
3. D	16. C	29. A	42. C
4. D	17. C	30. C	43. B
5. C	18. D	31. B	44. C
6. B	19. B	32. B	45. A
7. A	20. B	33. D	46. B
8. D	21. B	34. C	47. B
9. A	22. C	35. A	48. C
10. C	23. D	36. B	49. D
11. D	24. D	37. B	50. C
12. A	25. B	38. B	
13. D	26. D	39. A	

Answer Explanations

Section 1: Verbal

1. **B** The correct answer is choice B, *there,* which is an adverb used to show placement. Choice A, *their,* is a possessive pronoun, and choice C, *they're,* is a contraction for *they are.* Both are homophones for the correct answer, *there.*

2. **C** The correct answer is choice C, *to,* which is used as part of an infinitive with the present tense of the verb *type* in this sentence. *Two* is an adjective used to describe more than one and *too* is an adverb, which means "also." Both are homophones for the correct answer, *to.*

3. **B** The correct answer is choice B, *I.* The pronoun *I* is correct because it refers to the subject *(Officer Lightner and I)* performing the action *(assisted).*

4. **C** The correct answer is choice C, *assailants,* which is a plural noun. The singular possessive noun *assailant's* and the plural possessive noun *assailants'* are incorrect.

5. **B** The correct answer is choice B, *suspect's,* because it's a singular possessive noun. *Suspects'* is a plural possessive noun and *suspects* is a plural noun.

6. **A** The correct answer is choice A, *khakis,* because it's a plural noun. *Khakis'* is a plural possessive noun and *khaki's* is a singular possessive noun.

7. **A** Choice A, *buisness,* is spelled incorrectly. The correct spelling is *business.*

8. **B** Choice B, *ackused,* is spelled incorrectly. The correct spelling is *accused.*

9. **C** Choice C, *trowsers,* is spelled incorrectly. The correct spelling is *trousers.*

10. **A** Choice A, *burgulary,* is spelled incorrectly. The correct spelling is *burglary.*

11. **D** Choice B, *assalted,* is spelled incorrectly. The correct spelling is *assaulted.*

12. **C** Choice C, *baricade,* is spelled incorrectly. The correct spelling is *barricade.*

13. **C** The *federal bureau of investigation* is a proper noun and should be capitalized.

14. **D** This choice correctly omits the colon. A colon is used after an independent clause that is before a list.

15. **B** Based on the information in the paragraph, the incident report cannot be fully completed, so the answer is false. To complete the incident report, the officers need additional information such as the victim's date of birth, the name of the suspect, and the charges filed.

16. **B** The paragraph states that the incident occurred on March 2, so the answer is false.

17. **B** Based on the information in the paragraph, the incident report cannot be fully completed, so the answer is false. To complete the incident report, the officers need additional information such as the victim's date of birth and telephone number and the name of the suspect.

18. **A** The paragraph states that a stamp collection and pearl necklace were the only items taken from the residence, so the answer is true.

19. **A** Sentence I is correct, but sentence II uses incorrect verb tenses. The sentence should be written in the past tense: *After the assailant demanded the victim give him cash, the victim's dog chased the assailant north on Orange Lane.*

20. **B** Sentence II is correct, but sentence I contains errors. The verb tense is incorrect and the pronoun and antecedent do not agree. The sentence should read: *As the victim stepped away from the ATM, an unknown assailant produced a gun and ordered him to stay still, keep quiet, and hand over the money.*

21. **C** Both sentence I and sentence II contain errors. Sentence I contains the incorrect verb tense. The verb *pull* should be replaced with the past tense *(pulled).* Sentence II needs a comma placed after the participial phrase *After failing several field sobriety tests.*

22. **A** Sentence I is correct, but sentence II requires the preposition *to* to make sense.

23. **B** Sentence II is correct, but sentence I is incorrect because the subject of the sentence, *$50,* is singular, so the singular verb *was* should be used. The sentence is also missing the word *which* between the words *car* and *was. Which* should be preceded by a comma.

24. **C** Sentence I is incorrect because the singular word *man* should be replaced with the plural *men.* Sentence II contains an incorrect article. The article *a* should be replaced with the article *an* because it comes before a word that begins with a vowel *(altercation).*

25. **B** This answer provides all the necessary information in a clear and concise statement. The other answers either are confusing or do not provide all the necessary information.

26. **A** This answer provides all the necessary information in a short, easy-to-read statement. Choices B, C, and D do not provide all the necessary information.

27. **B** This answer provides a clear and accurate summary of the incident. It uses simple wording to help the reader understand exactly what happened. The other answers provide accurate information but are written in such a way that they could confuse the reader.

28. **D** Since a detective's main job is to investigate crimes, choice D is correct.

29. **C** Since an assault is a physical or verbal attack on an individual, choice C is an example of an assault.

30. **C** According to the passage, Mr. Rodriguez is a Hispanic male whom Ms. Velopez identified as her boyfriend. However, he was wearing a red T-shirt.

31. **B** According to the passage, Mr. Rodriguez arrived home at 4:30 p.m. He typically gets home at 4 p.m., but he stopped for a drink first.

32. **D** The victim gave the officers a list of places Mr. Rodriguez frequents, but the park was not included on the list.

33. **B** The word *pummeled* means "to beat." The word that is closest to this meaning is *walloped,* which means "to hit or beat."

34. **B** According to the passage, Mrs. Fellmoore is Mr. Fellmoore's wife. Her car is in the shop and they're planning a trip to Aruba. However, she works in a library.

35. **A** According to the passage, the Fellmoores kept their lockbox in the coat closet.

36. **D** The officers arrived on the scene at 6:38 p.m.

37. **D** A fedora is a type of hat.

38. **B** According to the passage, Mr. Kennywood is a 22-year-old man and he lives down the hall from the Dolmans.

39. **D** According to the passage, the police officers arrived at the residence at 7:52 p.m.

40. **1942 Washington Dr.**

41. **Frederick Mancini.**

42. **Michael Dillon.**

43. **12 Broadview Rd.**

44. **Assault.**

45. **Blond.**

46. **$1,050.**

47. **Candy Jenkins.**

48. **44 N. Main St.**

49. **4756 Germania Ave.**

50. **5'1".**

Section 2: Memory and Visualization

1. **B** There are nine steps in the stairwell in the photograph.

2. **B** The correct address on the awning is 9 East 17th Street.

3. **B** The correct phone number printed on the awning is 242-2777.

4. **C** There are three windows above the awning in the photograph.

5. **B** There is cardboard piled on the sidewalk in the photograph.

6. **D** Based on the information Officer Evanko receives from the first witnesses, he can deduce that the suspect was headed north the last time he was seen. After running north three blocks on Randolph Avenue, the suspect turned right onto Province Street, heading east. After turning left at McCoy Avenue, the suspect was again heading north. The suspect's final turn, a left into an alley off McCoy Avenue, indicates the suspect was last seen traveling west.

7. **B** If the owner of the car watched the suspect travel south and then saw him make a left and then a right, it would be most accurate to report that the suspect was last seen traveling south.

8. **D** If the crime victim chased the suspect north and made two lefts and then watched the suspect get into a vehicle that turned right, it would be most accurate to report that the suspect was last seen traveling west.

9. **C** Your view from the back should be the opposite of your view from the front. All the buildings should be in the same order; none of the roofs should be switched on any of the buildings, and none of the buildings should move from their original locations. Choice C is correct because it shows the street in the correct, reversed order.

10. **A** Choice A is correct. This diagram correctly shows the directions in which the vehicles were traveling. While choice B may look correct, vehicle 2 is traveling south in this diagram, not north as indicated in the passage.

11. **C** The quickest route from point 4, the hospital, to the day care is west on Main Street, north on Washington Avenue, east on Penn Avenue, and north on Lily Lane. Traveling west on Penn Avenue is illegal because it's a one-way street traveling east.

12. **B** The quickest route from point 6, the park, to the houses at point 7 is south on Nickel Road, west on State Street, and south on Washington Avenue.

13. **A** You would be correct to report that the perpetrator was last seen traveling north. From your view at the southernmost entrance of the courthouse, you saw a purse snatching happen outside of point 1. You followed the thief north on Oak Street, west on State Street, and then called for help when he ran north on Washington Avenue.

14. **D** Starting at the post office, if you traveled south on Lily Lane, east on Penn Avenue, south on Nickel Road, west on State Street, and south on Washington Avenue, you would end up at the school.

15. **A** Your view from the back should be the opposite of your view from the front. All the buildings should be in the same order; none of the roofs should be switched on any of the buildings, and none of the buildings should move from their original locations. Choice A is correct because it shows the street in the correct, reversed order.

16. **C** From the parking lot behind points 3 and 4, the quickest route to the bakery is north on 149th Street, east on Market Street, and south on 150th Street. You can't travel east on Oak Street because Oak Street is a one-way street traveling west.

17. **D** If you must exit the grocery store to the east, then the best route to point 7 is north on 150th Street, west on Market Street, and south on 148th Street. If you exited the parking lot to the west, you would use 149th Street instead of 150th Street.

18. **B** Starting at point 5, if you travel south on 148th Street and pass through one intersection before making a right-hand turn, your nearest point would be the playground next to the soccer field. When traveling south, your right-hand turns would be in the direction of west instead of east; therefore, you wouldn't turn into the parking lot.

19. **B** Starting at point 2, if you travel north on 149th Street, west on Market Street, south on 148th Street, east on Valley Lane, north on 149th Street, and then make two right-hand turns, you would be near the bakery.

20. **D** After traveling south, making a left (east), a right (south), another right (west), and a left, it would be most correct if you reported that the suspect was last seen traveling south.

21. **D** According to the photograph, the arrow painted on the ground is facing southwest.

22. **D** Because there is an ambulance in the picture and the word *ambulance* is painted on the building, you can assume the building is an ambulance association.

23. **D** There are five people in this photograph. Three people are standing to the left of the ambulance and two people are standing to the right near the cars.

24. **A** There are two people in this photograph. There is a woman on the left side of the photograph and another woman is walking down the hall.

25. **B** The woman on the left side of the photograph is wearing glasses. She is not wearing a hat or a scarf. Her hands are not visible, so you can't determine if she is wearing mittens.

26. **B** There are three chandeliers visible in this photograph.

27. **B** Your view from the back should be the opposite of your view from the front. All the buildings should be in the same order; none of the roofs should be switched on any of the buildings, and none of the buildings should move from their original locations. Choice B is correct because it shows the street in the correct, reversed order.

28. **D** If you're at point 4 and you need to travel to point 1, you must travel west on Brown Road first. Then you have to travel north on New Street and east on Miller Street. You can't travel east on Brown Road or north on Linwood Lane because these streets are one-way streets traveling west and south, respectively.

29. **C** From the hospital to point 6, the parking lot beside the baseball field, the quickest route to travel is south on Princeton Avenue, west on Brown Road, north on New Street, and east on Miller Street. You can't travel west on the block of Miller Street where the baseball field is located; therefore, choices A and D are incorrect. Choice D is also incorrect because you can't travel north on that particular block of Linwood Lane. Choice B is incorrect because the baseball field is located west of the hospital, not east.

30. **C** Starting at the day care, if you travel north on New Street, east on Miller Street, south on Linwood Lane, and then make a right, you would be traveling west on Brown Road and point 4 would be on your left. When you're traveling south and you make a right, you're always traveling west.

31. **A** After traveling east on Casey Avenue, you make a left at the second intersection of Casey Avenue and Brown Road. You're now traveling north. Then you make a right onto Brown Road and travel west. You then make three left turns, meaning you travel north on Princeton Avenue, west on Miller Street, and south on Linwood Lane. You then make two right turns, which take you west on Brown Road and north on New Street. The building on your left is the bank.

32. **B** The suspect was last seen headed west. After first running to the east and turning right, the suspect is headed south. When he makes his second right turn, he's headed west.

33. **B** The quickest route from the school to the shoe store would be to travel north on Barre Street, east on Lumber Lane, and north on River Street. Choice C will also get you to the shoe store, but it'll take you a bit longer since the store is located on the southern side of the block. Choice A is incorrect because Oak Street is a one-way street traveling west.

34. **C** From the park, if you travel south on Patterson Avenue, west on North Street, north on Barre Street, and east on Lumber Lane, you'll end up at the intersection of Lumber Lane and River Street. On your right, you'll see the sporting-goods store.

35. **B** If you left the northernmost entrance of the police station and traveled west for two blocks on Circle Drive, south for one block on Patterson Avenue, east for two blocks on Lumber Lane, and then turned right (south) onto River Street, you would be closest to point 2.

36. **D** The most direct route from the day care to the bank would be to travel south on Patterson Avenue, east on Lumber Lane, north on River Street, and west on Oak Street. Choices A, B, and C are incorrect because Patterson Avenue is a one-way street traveling south and Oak Street is a one-way street traveling west.

37. **D** The woman in the photograph is wearing jeans, shoes, and a purse, but she isn't wearing a sweater. Her arms, back, and shoulders are bare.

38. **B** The woman is holding the dog's leash in her left hand and it's walking a few steps ahead of her; therefore, in proximity to the woman, the dog is walking ahead of her and to her left.

39. **C** The sign on the side of the building reads aina. There is a circle around the in and the sign is hung so that the word runs up and down rather than right to left.

40. **B** The two letters of the car's license plate that are visible in this photograph are *RV*. The car is in the lower-left side of this photograph. The woman is walking away from it.

41. **C** Your view from the back should be the opposite of your view from the front. All the buildings should be in the same order; none of the roofs should be switched on any of the buildings, and none of the buildings should move from their original locations. Choice C is correct because it shows the street in the correct, reversed order.

42. **B** The most direct route from the strip mall to the public pool is to travel south on Marsh Road, west on Hartman Boulevard, south on Lucky Lane, and west on New Street. Choices A, B, and C are incorrect because Lucky Lane is a one-way road traveling south and New Street is a one-way road traveling west.

43. **B** The quickest, most direct route from the diner to the baseball field to point 5 is to travel north on Marsh Road, east on Hartman Boulevard, south on Townsend Street, southwest on Light Street, west on Moore Drive, and north on Bayside Way.

44. **D** From the toy store, if you traveled east on Hartman Boulevard, made two left turns (north, then west), turned left at the nearest intersection (south) and then right (left), it would be most accurate to say that you're now traveling west.

45. **A** Starting at point 4, if you traveled north on Bayside Way, east on Lenore Lane, south on Marsh Road, east on Hartman Boulevard, and south on Townsend Street, you would be closest to point 1.

46. **B** The suspect was last seen headed west. After first running to the south and turning right, the suspect is headed west. When he makes his second right turn, he's headed north. After making a final left, the suspect is again headed west.

47. **B** There are three people riding the escalator in the photograph: two men and a woman.

48. **A** The fourth trash can/recycling bin is located at the base of the escalator. Specifically, if you were to step onto the escalator that goes to the floor above you, the bin would be to your right.

49. **B** Skateboards, shopping carts, and wet floor signs aren't visible in this photograph; however, there is a stroller in the middle of this image. In fact, two strollers are visible in this picture. The other one is to the right of the photograph, in front of the jewelry stand.

50. **B** There are eight tables visible in this photograph. Although the man toward the base of the escalator may be sitting at a table, it's not actually visible in the image.

Section 3: Mathematics

1. **C** There were 64 assaults, burglaries, and arsons reported during the month of September: 50 + 12 + 2 = 64.

2. **A** Reports of domestic violence increased 70% from April to September: 50 − 35 = 15, 15 ÷ 35 = 0.43 and 0.43 × 100 = 43%.

3. **B** The average number of arrests Officer Marks made each month is 25: 6 + 5 + 8 + 4 + 6 + 8 + 5 + 14 + 3 + 7 + 3 + 6 = 75 and 75 arrests ÷ 3 months = 25 arrests per month.

4. **B** The perimeter of the object is 28. The perimeter is the measurement of the outside of the object; therefore, you do not need to figure in either of the sevens (7) in the middle of the diagram. Instead, just add 3 + 4 + 3 + 4 + 3 + 4 + 3 + 4 = 28.

5. **D** The total value of the stolen items except for one of the laptops is $4,680 − $550 = $4,130.

6. **D** The new total value of the stolen items is $5,110: $4,680 − $120 = $4,560 and $4,560 + $550 = $5,110.

7. **D** If Officer McGrane made five trips to a convenience store 6 miles away this week, then he drove 60 miles total. Since he drove there and back, each trip was 12 miles: 12 × 5 = 60 miles.

8. **B** The radius of a circle is exactly half its diameter. The diameter of the figure shown is 31: 31 ÷ 2 = 15.5.

9. **B** The homeowners did not have permits for 16 of their guns: 60% = 0.60, 40 × 0.60 = 24, and 40 − 24 = 16.

10. **C** The value of one container of coffee is $64: $3,200 ÷ 50 = $64.

11. **C** The total value of the items except for the wine is $4,275. Subtract the wine from the total amount: $19,275 − $15,000 = $4,275.

12. **C** The new total value of the stolen items is $20,525. Subtract $950 from the total for the found cases of wine and add the missing grapes to the total: $19,275 − $950 = $18,325. Then $18,325 + $2,200 = $20,525.

13. **D** If Lieutenant Brady made 11 trips to the dry cleaner 8 miles away in the past month, then he drove 176 miles total. Since he drove there and back, each trip was 16 miles: 16 × 11 = 176 miles.

14. **A** Reports of gang-related incidents increased by 47%. Subtract 28 − 19 = 9; 9 ÷ 19 = 0.4737 = 47.37%.

15. **B** There were 29 murders, arsons, and gang-related incidents reported during the month of January: 4 + 6 + 19 = 29.

16. **C** He worked an average of 8 hours per surveillance shift. Add the number of hours worked over the past two weeks and divide by the number of shifts: 5 + 9 + 9 + 11 + 14 + 6 + 8 + 4 + 10 = 76, and 76 ÷ 9 = 8.44, which rounds to 8 hours.

17. **B** Officer Jin made an average of 8 arrests each week. Add the number of arrests each week and then divide by the number of weeks: 4 + 6 + 9 + 12 + 6 + 7 + 4 + 17 + 13 + 2 + 5 + 18 + 9 + 5 + 14 + 1 = 132 and 132 ÷ 16 = 8.25, which rounds to 8.

18. **A** The width of the room shown is 7. Using the formula: $A = lw$, 343 = 49w. Divide each side by 49 to get 7 = w.

19. **D** To solve this problem, follow the order of operations. First, multiply 44.77 × 0.66, then subtract the product from 990.99 and then add 111; 990.99 − 29.5482 + 111 = 1,072.4418. Rounded to the nearest hundredth, the answer is 1,072.44, so choice D is correct.

20. **B** The diameter of the circle shown is 38. The diameter of a circle is two times the radius ($D = 2r$), so if $r = 19$, then $D = 2 \times 19 = 38$.

21. **B** The total value of the stolen items is $1,249: $120 + $ 200 + $750 + $95 + $84 = $1,249.

22. **B** Officer Sanders drove only 135 miles in his car this week: 225 miles – (45 × 2) = 135 miles.

23. **B** Officer McMahon normally drives his squad car about 72 miles per day: 360 miles ÷ 5 days = 72 miles.

24. **B** The total value of the stolen bracelets was $1,800: 6 bracelets × $300 = $1,800.

25. **C** About 48 speeding citations are issued per week: 40% = 0.40 and 120 citations × 0.40 = 48.

26. **C** If Officer Freemont works an additional 30 minutes each day for 5 days, he will have worked 2 hours, 30 minutes of overtime for the week. Multiply the number of minutes of overtime worked each day by the number of days: 30 × 5 = 150 minutes. Divide that number (150) by the number of minutes in an hour (60): 150 ÷ 60 = 2.5 hours or 2 hours and 30 minutes.

27. **C** The average number of arrests Sergeant Bombulie made each month is 31: 8 + 9 + 2 + 19 + 7 + 4 + 11 + 2 = 62 and 62 arrests ÷ 2 months = 31 arrests per month.

28. **B** There were 61 burglaries, trespassing incidents, and gang-related incidents reported in January 2009: 42 + 4 + 15 = 61.

29. **A** Reports of burglary increased 43% from January 2009 to January 2010: 60 – 42 =18. Then 18 ÷ 42 = 0.428. Round that to 0.43, and 0.43 × 100 = 43%.

30. **C** The total value of the stolen items except for two of the sandwich presses is $4,590: $175 + $175 = $350 and $4,940 – $350 = $4,590.

31. **B** The new total value of the stolen items is $4,650: $145 + $145 = $290 and $4,940 – $290 = $4,650.

32. **B** If Officer Jennings reports to work at 12:45 p.m. Monday instead of 3 p.m., she will have worked 2 hours, 15 minutes of overtime.

33. **C** If Sergeant Fu made four trips to a coffee shop 3 miles away this week, then he drove 24 miles total. Since he drove there and back, each trip was about 6 miles: 6 × 4 = 24 miles.

34. **B** The diameter of a circle is twice the size of its radius. The radius of the figure shown is 12.5, so 12.5 × 2 = 25.

35. **A** The value of one touch-screen cellphone is $225: $4,275 ÷ 19 = $225.

36. **A** She worked an average of six hours per surveillance shift. Add the number of hours worked over the past two weeks and divide by the number of shifts: 9 + 8 + 5 + 14 + 2 + 7 + 4 + 1 = 50 and 50 ÷ 8 = 6.25, which rounds to 6 hours.

37. **C** Officer Farley made an average of eight arrests each week. Add the number of arrests each week and then divide by the number of weeks: 4 + 5 + 6 + 14 + 9 + 8 + 15 + 6 + 7 + 18 + 1 + 2 = 95 and 95 ÷ 12 = 7.92, which rounds to 8.

38. **B** To solve this problem, follow the order of operations. First, multiply 989.42 × 0.12, then subtract the product from 55.77, and then add 289: 55.77 – 118.7304 + 289 = 226.0396. Rounded to the nearest hundredth and the answer is 226.04, so choice B is correct.

39. **D** The area of the room shown is 450. Using the formula: $A = lw$, $A = 30 \times 15$, so $A = 450$.

40. **A** About 20 parking citations are delinquent per month: 5% = 0.05 and 400 citations × 0.05 = 20.

41. **C** Lieutenant Quinn traveled a total of 63 miles between the courthouse and the police station in the past month. To solve, add $3.5 + 3.5 = 7$ miles. This is the total distance he traveled to the courthouse and back on each trip. Then, multiply $7 \times 9 = 63$.

42. **B** The total value of the stolen items is $840. To solve, add $325 + \$250 + \$130 + \$55 + \$80 = \$840$.

43. **B** The new total value of the stolen items is $775. To solve, divide the total value of the shoes that were stolen by how many pairs the owner initially reported stolen: $\$325 \div 5 = \$65$. Then subtract the price of one pair of shoes from the original total: $\$840 - \$65 = \$775$.

44. **A** Police officers in your department issue a total of 25.5 parking citations for double parking each week. To solve, multiply the total number of parking citations by the percentage of those issued for double parking: $30\% = 0.30$ and $85 \times 0.30 = 25.5$.

45. **C** Officer Greene worked a total of 3 hours and 30 minutes of overtime this week. Her supervisor asked her to come in at 11:15 a.m. instead of 1 p.m. This is 1 hour and 45 minutes earlier than normal. Since she has to come in 1 hour and 45 minutes earlier on two days, multiply and then divide: 1 hour = 60 minutes, so $60 + 45 = 105$ minutes; $105 \times 2 = 210$, $210 \div 60 = 3.5$, and 3.5 = 3 hours, 30 minutes.

46. **B** The area of the rectangle shown is 450. Using the formula, $A = 10 \times 45 = 450$.

47. **C** To solve this problem, follow the order of operations. First, multiply 3.41×2.17. Then, subtract and add: $8.26 - 0.42 + 7.3997 = 15.2397$, which rounds to 15.24.

48. **D** Sergeant Bush spent an average of 26 hours working surveillance shifts each week. To solve, add the amount of time he spent working each day, and then divide by the number of weeks: $6 + 12 + 4 + 8 + 5 + 7 + 8 + 2 = 52$ and $52 \div 2 = 26$.

49. **C** Of the guns seized in the raid, 20 of them were loaded when the police arrived on the scene. To solve, multiply the total number of weapons seized by the percent of weapons loaded: $28 \times 0.70 = 19.6$. Rounded to the nearest whole number, $19.6 = 20$.

50. **C** Officer Marquee made an average of 4.5 arrests each week. To solve, add the number of arrests and divide by the number of weeks: $4 + 1 + 7 + 2 + 9 + 8 + 0 + 5 + 7 + 2 + 2 + 7 = 54$ and $54 \div 12 = 4.5$.

Section 4: Judgment and Problem Solving

1. **C** Since robbery requires both force and the victim's physical presence, choice C is correct. Choices A, B, and D are examples of burglary, which does not require the victim's presence or the use of force, threats, or intimidation.

2. **A** Ramona is the victim of a burglary, not a robbery, because she was not present when the crime occurred. She was also not threatened, intimidated, or forced to hand over her possessions.

3. **D** The State of Delaware's Animal Regulation ordinance states that Delaware residents should never place poison in an area where it may be consumed by animals; therefore, choice D is correct. The ordinance goes on to state that only police officers, game wardens, and Animal Control officers are allowed to set poison.

4. **D** Uniformed officers would be most appropriate for directing traffic before and after a sporting event. Motorists should be able to identify and recognize police officers attempting to control the heavy traffic that occurs around the time of a sporting event. The other choices would be more suitable for undercover officers.

5. **C** Undercover officers would be most useful when arresting men who attempt to hire prostitutes. In most cases, these operations are conducted by an undercover officer posing as a prostitute. The other choices would be more suitable for uniformed officers.

6. **B** According to the information provided in the chart, officers may conclude that the presence of four-way stop signs results in fewer accidents. The intersections that have stop signs appear to have been the location of fewer traffic accidents than those that do not have four-way stop signs.

7. **A** In the event of any problems between you and your partner, you should first discuss the issue with your partner personally. Choices B and C should be considered only in cases where this problem has become a frequent occurrence. Choice D is not acceptable under any circumstances.

8. **D** All suspects should be handcuffed because an unrestrained suspect presents a threat to the officer. If the suspect is not restrained, he or she may cause injury to the officer or potentially escape custody.

9. **A** According to the chart, burglaries and vandalism incidents occur most frequently during late night and early morning on the weekends and during the early morning and evening on Wednesdays and Thursdays. To reduce the number of burglaries and vandalism incidents, Lieutenant Pollack should assign a Tour III to patrol 13th Avenue on the weekends and assign a Tour II to patrol 19th Avenue on Thursdays.

10. **C** To reduce the number of arsons, Lieutenant Pollack should assign a Tour II to patrol 43rd Street and 8th Street on Fridays, which is where and when the arsons are occurring.

11. **D** In the event that a man is found unconscious in a park with an empty pill bottle next to him, you should immediately call for medical assistance, as the suspect has likely taken an overdose of medication. The other options would not require immediate medical assistance.

12. **A** The most important reason that police officers wear badges is because badges identify the wearer as a police officer. While the badge does contribute to an officer's professional appearance, this function is secondary to identification. The other choices are incorrect.

13. **D** Although both choices A and D would qualify as cases of receiving or concealing stolen property, the property in question in choice A is not valuable enough to carry a first-degree charge. Since the property in question in choice D is worth more than $1,500, this crime would carry a first-degree charge.

14. **C** The officer should immediately call the fire department and use his squad car's PA system to notify residents. Extinguishing the fire and determining the cause should be left to the professionals from the fire department. Using the squad car's PA system to alert the town house residents of the need for evacuation would be much quicker and more efficient than running to each town house separately.

15. **B** The officer's report would begin with statement 3, which introduces the suspect and the location where the crime was committed. Next, statement 1 indicates that after the suspect completed the transaction with the customer, she left the cash box slightly ajar so she could reopen it and take some money. Statement 5 then documents that the store's own security force was aware of the incident and attempted to intervene. When security then called the police, they were able to use eyewitness accounts to inform police which direction the suspect was headed in, as implied in statement 4. This information subsequently led to her being found and arrested by the officer, as per statement 2.

16. **C** In this scenario, the officer should immediately call for an ambulance because the suspect needs emergency medical care. When a suspect is seriously injured, ensuring that he or she receives proper emergency medical care is more important than immediate arrest.

17. **C** The officer's next step at this point would be to avoid touching the wire and secure the scene. Although he or she will want to contact the utility company soon, this should occur only after the scene has been secured. There is no need to contact a supervisor in this scenario. Whether it is live or not, you should never touch a downed wire.

18. **D** The medical emergency should take precedence over all other matters, so you should stop the parade momentarily and allow the ambulance to cross the street. The other choices would all cause an unnecessary and potentially dangerous delay in the patient's transport to a medical facility.

19. **B** Chief Johnson's primary goal during the project is maintaining public safety. New traffic patterns, enforcement methods, and various safety protocols are all designed to ensure that public safety is properly maintained throughout the course of the construction project.

20. **B** The first action you should take upon your arrival at the scene would be to gather as much information about the situation as possible. It's only with this information that you can take the appropriate actions to ensure public safety and secure the scene. Choices A, C, and D all assume that the man in the street is the suspect and you don't yet know that. In addition, choice D is incorrect because the suspect is obviously a danger to the public. Choice B is the only option that will allow you to properly identify the suspect and handle the situation appropriately, so that is the correct answer.

21. **B** The most difficult case to investigate among the choices would be domestic abuse. This type of crime generally occurs inside private residences and requires police intervention into family matters. The personal emotions of those involved may hamper the investigation. When such cases involve children, the lines between corporal punishment and abuse may be difficult to determine.

22. **C** Randall Wright's assault on a fellow gang member is the only scenario that would constitute aggravated assault. He went to the man's home with the clear intent of causing serious injury.

23. **D** In the event of disputes of this manner, you should always get both sides of the story from the parties involved and make an informed decision on what, if any, actions you should take, so choice D is correct.

24. **D** The officer's report would begin with the theft of the DVD player from the electronics store by Mr. Thompson. This would be followed by Mr. Thompson bringing the DVD player to Mr. Hutton's home and their subsequent agreement. The later arrest of Mr. Thompson and his admission during interrogation would be next. Finally, the report would conclude with the arrest of Mr. Hutton.

25. **B** The most important reason that an officer should speak clearly and make his or her statements brief and precise is because it prevents busy communication lines from being constantly tied up. Radio networks are commonly used by multiple agencies, and long messages and conversations can tie up communications for everyone trying to use the system.

26. **D** Frank steals an item that belongs to his co-worker without using force or the threat of force, so he didn't commit a robbery. Since the cellphone didn't belong to the company, this wouldn't be a case of embezzlement.

27. **A** An example of embezzlement is choice A. In this scenario, Rose has stolen company funds that she is responsible for, which would qualify as embezzlement. She does not use force or the threat of force to acquire the funds, so this couldn't be considered a robbery. Rose couldn't be charged with larceny, because the funds belonged to the company, not a private individual.

28. **C** A curfew violation occurs when Elizabeth, 8 years old, is walking back to her parent's home with her aunt at 10:25 p.m. In this scenario, Elizabeth is outside her home after curfew and is not accompanied by a parent or legal guardian. The curfew has not been violated in any of the other choices.

29. **A** Officer O'Leary's report would begin with Mr. Murphy being approached by the unidentified man while jogging in the park, followed by the suspect's demand for his MP3 player after pulling out a gun. The report would then continue with the suspect fleeing and Murphy alerting O'Leary. The report would conclude with the suspect's capture and arrest.

30. **C** Officer Daniels opts to immediately arrest and transport the suspect because his injury is not severe, so immediate arrest is more important than seeking medical attention. Officers should delay arrest only in the event of a serious injury that requires immediate medical attention.

31. **B** According to the information provided in the chart, the recruits can determine that the presence of a decoy police vehicle results in fewer speeding citations. The information in the chart clearly indicates that the presence of a decoy police vehicle reduces the number of speeding citations issued on both highways and interstates.

32. **B** Discussing the matter any further with your partner would be unlikely to help, as he hasn't responded to any previous discussions. You should seek intervention from a superior, rather than any other officers, because this situation is potentially dangerous and should be formally addressed. Refusing to support your partner would be unacceptable under any circumstance.

33. **D** The officer's decision would be considered bad policy, because all suspects must be restrained for safety and security purposes. Unrestrained suspects present danger to officers and other people with whom they come in contact. Regardless of the nature of the suspect's crime or their personal status, he or she must be properly restrained prior to transport.

34. **C** According to the chart, burglaries most frequently occur during the late night/early morning and in the afternoon on Wednesdays. To reduce the number of burglaries, Chief Bernardi should assign a Tour III to patrol 9th Avenue and a Tour II to patrol 19th Avenue and 84th Street on Wednesdays.

35. **A** To reduce the number of auto thefts, Chief Bernardi should assign a Tour III to patrol 7th Street on Mondays and 8th Street on Tuesdays, which is where and when the auto thefts are taking place.

36. **B** Telling a suspect under interrogation that his crime is not that big of a deal would be bad policy, because this will make the suspect feel less guilty and, in turn, less willing to cooperate.

37. **B** The part of a police officer's uniform that is meant as the primary means of identifying the wearer as a police officer is the badge. Uniform patches also serve as forms of identification but are secondary to the badge. The other choices are incorrect.

38. **B** Because Matt abruptly shoots and kills Mike without premeditation in a moment of extreme emotion, choice B is the best example of voluntary manslaughter. Choice A would be considered first-degree murder because the act was intentional and premeditated. Choice C would be an example of involuntary manslaughter, since the act was unintentional and resulting from Frank driving while intoxicated. Choice D would be considered second-degree murder because Omar killed the man without thought while in the process of robbing the convenience store.

39. **A** Officer Roland should first secure the scene and contact the electric utility company. This situation is potentially dangerous, and the officer's primary responsibility is to inform the utility company of the problem and maintain security at the scene until they arrive. At no time should the officer attempt to move the wire himself in any way or leave the scene before the appropriate support arrives.

40. **B** Officer Marella's report would begin with Mr. Crain's initial whereabouts and a description of the car he was driving. It would then continue with the suspect approaching the car and ordering Crain to exit. This would be followed by the suspect entering the vehicle and driving away. The report would conclude with Officer Marella's arrival on scene.

41. **A** At this point, the officer should immediately call for emergency medical support, due to injuries suffered by the driver of the car. The driver of the car is not likely to be able to answer any questions at this time, and the officer doesn't have any reason to arrest the driver of the tractor-trailer yet. The officer should not attempt to treat the driver's injuries; this should be left to medical professionals.

42. **C** When Sergeant Stevens receives the bomb threat, he should immediately call the bomb squad and begin an orderly evacuation. Only trained members of the bomb squad should attempt to defuse bombs. Making an emergency announcement for everyone to evacuate would likely incite panic and only exacerbate the problem. Although finding and arresting the suspect is important, Sergeant Stevens's first priority would be to secure the scene at the conference.

43. **B** Officer Neri's decision would be considered good policy, because the fire truck was en route to an emergency. Any emergency vehicle should be allowed to pass through an intersection when responding to an emergency, as time is of the essence and any delay could be life threatening.

44. **C** Officer Charles's primary objective in responding to the incident would be to efficiently assess the scene and make an arrest, if warranted. None of the other choices accurately reflects the officer's responsibilities in this scenario.

45. **A** When the officer first arrives on the scene he should find the complainant and ask her to identify the man she reported. Even if he may look suspicious, the officer doesn't yet know if the man on the bench is the suspect, so he shouldn't arrest him before he finds out if the man in question is the suspect. Unless the suspect tries to flee, there would be no cause to disable him in any way. The officer should not leave the scene until he is sure the suspect is no longer present and he has spoken to all witnesses.

46. **B** The most difficult case to investigate among the choices would be child abuse. Any form of domestic abuse is difficult to investigate because of the emotional nature of the crime and the need for police intervention into private family issues. Child abuse may be particularly difficult to investigate because you may need to differentiate between abuse and corporal punishment.

47. **B** Nick DiScala's attack on the man who spilled beer on him would qualify as assault/battery because Nick struck the man, but didn't cause serious injury. In choices A, C, and D, the suspects used weapons to attack their victims, which would lead to a charge of aggravated assault.

48. **C** Officer Goldman should interview the merchant and determine the best course of action. Before taking any other action, it is imperative that the officer investigate the situation fully, speaking with everyone involved. Once he has a solid understanding of the incident, Goldman can then determine and carry out the appropriate measures.

49. **D** The officer's report would begin with him spotting the vehicle driven erratically and pulling over the driver. It would then continue with the officer running the car's license plate number to determine ownership. This would be followed by the officer's approach to the vehicle and description of the driver's condition. Next, the report would move on to the suspect exiting the car and the officer finding the bag of cocaine. Finally, the report would conclude with the officer arresting and charging the suspect.

50. **C** Officer Kaufman's method of radio communication would be considered bad policy, because it ties up communication lines shared by multiple agencies. Officers should always speak clearly and briefly while using radio communication, to take up as little airtime as possible. This helps to ensure that all agencies using the radio communication network have ample airtime with which to communicate.

The Oral Board Interview

The oral board interview for police officer candidates is not a typical job interview. In most interviews, you meet with your future boss one-on-one, discuss your résumé, and answer a few questions that show you understand the requirements of the job.

During the interview, you appear before a board of police officers and civil service professionals prepared to discuss information about your physical abilities, written abilities, and sometimes polygraph results. The board also may have information about you that has been gathered from background checks and interviews with your references.

Similar to the written police officer exam, you can study or prepare for the oral board interview. You can do some research, learn what to expect during the interview, and present yourself in such a way that, upon stepping into the room, the board will know you're serious about moving on to the police academy and a career in law enforcement.

One way to prove to others that you're the best candidate for the job is to tell them just that. During the oral interview, you have the opportunity to explain that you have the skills and enthusiasm necessary to become a successful police officer. As long as you remain honest and confident (but not egotistical), you'll do just fine.

What to Expect from the Interview

Expect to see figures such as the chief of police, police captains, and local politicians, alongside civil service workers, psychologists, and other professionals, on your oral board. Members of the board will ask you questions based on your résumé, background investigation, written exam, physical exam, and even your personal history statement (see Appendix D).

> **Tip:** Be sure to review the information on your résumé and personal history statement before the day of your interview, because many of the questions you'll have to answer will come from these documents. The board will compare your oral answers with the information in these documents and will ask you about any discrepancies that exist between your answers.

Some police departments conduct structured interviews, in which the interviewers ask all candidates the same questions in the same order. Members of the board have scoring guidelines, or what are considered to be the best responses to the questions. They use these guidelines to analyze your responses. Other department interviews are unstructured and more conversational; they may last for an indefinite amount of time and may include various types of questions.

Here are a few question types you should expect the board members to ask:

- **Icebreaker questions:** Board members use icebreaker questions to get you talking. Answers to these questions serve as an introduction to the board. These questions are typically from information you supply in your résumé and your personal history statement. They should be fairly straightforward and may ask you about your employment history, your educational background, a hobby such as reading or hunting, and so on. They also may include common interview questions such as, "Why do you want to become a police officer?"

- **Situational or scenario-based questions:** For these questions, the board members typically create a situation or scenario related to police work and then ask you to explain how you'd handle it. Because you don't yet have any formal police training, you won't be expected to know the exact protocol for these situations, but you'll have to show that you understand that everyone needs to be safe and your actions must be ethical.

  For example, the interviewers may ask how you'd handle a situation involving public drunkenness or domestic violence. You may be asked to act out your response with another officer. This is called role-playing, and it's something you'll have to do at the police academy many times.

- **Probing questions:** These questions may be about your professional or personal background. At first, it may be unclear to you why the board members want to know the answers to these questions. For example, in your personal history statement, you say that you've never been involved in any drug activity. The background investigation, however, reveals an arrest for possession of marijuana. Wanting to know why this information differs, a board member may ask whether you've ever been arrested for drug possession. She already knows the answer, but she wants to see if you'll respond honestly.

  Do you say "no" and stick to your original story? If you do, the interviewers may push further or may simply label you as a liar. It's better to confess to the arrest and offer an honest explanation: "I was actually arrested for possession of marijuana when I was 17. It was such a long time ago, though, and I wasn't charged because I was able to prove that the drugs weren't mine, so sometimes I forget that it even happened. I quickly realized that hanging out with people who do drugs is dangerous, and ever since, I've stayed away from any areas that may involve drug activity."

- **Ethics questions:** Like most questions during the oral interview, ethics questions test your honesty and integrity. These are similar to scenario-based questions, as board members will describe situations that test your morals and values.

  For example, what would you do if you saw a fellow officer planting evidence at a crime scene? Would you report him? Would you pull him aside and talk privately? When answering ethics questions, honesty is always the best policy, regardless of whether you feel as though your answer is "right" or "wrong."

- **Open-ended questions:** You can't answer open-ended questions with a simple "yes" or "no." These questions allow you to express your personality and share learning experiences with the board. As you respond, the interviewers consider both your response and the way you communicate your thoughts.

  Interviewers can ask a variety of open-ended questions on just about any subject. You may hear "What do you think of drugs and alcohol in the workplace or at home?" or "What are your biggest fears?" These questions may be related to a hobby you listed in a document, a question you answered on the written exam, or even about your thoughts related to police work thus far. They may ask you to define your strengths and weaknesses. Or they may simply say, "Tell us about yourself."

- **Personal questions:** In most job interviews, interviewers are not allowed to ask potential employees personal questions about certain topics such as marital status, religion, and so on. In the oral board interview to become a police officer, however, all details of your life can be discussed. Board members are instructed not to allow these details to bias their opinions of you, however.

Remember: Answer every question honestly. Not only do members of the oral interview board want you to tell them the truth, but they expect you to be honest with them. If they can't trust you in a private interview setting, how can a victim or a fellow police officer trust you with his life during an emergency?

How to Respond to Interview Questions

Members of the oral interview board will expect not only honesty, but also insight into the way you think and feel. One of the most common mistakes candidates make in these settings is to try to tell the board what the candidate thinks the board wants to hear. The board knows when answers aren't sincere; they interview candidates all the time and they're able to identify answers that are impersonal or insincere.

Don't be afraid to tell the board what *you* think and how *you* feel about a particular situation. Don't worry about whether your answer may be "right" or "wrong." Just focus on putting the truth out there for them to evaluate.

Another thing to keep in mind during the oral board interview is to stand behind your answers, even if the interviewers attempt to badger you out of them. They do this to test your dedication, commitment, and personal strength. They may present you with a tough situation, such as, "Suppose you're approached at a party by a friend or family member who recently got a speeding ticket. She tells you she can't afford to pay the ticket and the rent for her apartment in the same month. She begs you to take care of the ticket for her. What do you do?" The answer is simple: You tell her no, regardless of whether she's your best friend, sister, wife, or even mother.

As you answer the oral board's questions, don't let the members' lack of emotion discourage you. They're instructed to show little emotion, so they may not laugh when you make a joke or smile when you tell a funny story. Don't let this lack of emotion stop you from giving honest, personal answers.

Tip: Listen carefully to what you're asked. Before answering, make sure you fully understand the question and give it thought and consideration. If you need the board to clarify something, ask. It's better to ask for clarification than to misinterpret the question and provide an incorrect, unrelated answer. Keep in mind, however, that during structured interviews, the interviewers probably won't be allowed to rephrase or reinterpret the question for you. Instead, they may simply repeat the question and that's it.

When you finish the interview, don't talk about it with your friends or other candidates who may be taking part in the process after you. Sharing the types of questions you were asked, the way you answered them, and anything else you noticed may result in your elimination from the entire process. This information is confidential. The police department may need to throw out the entire interview format if information about the interview questions is leaked. Plus, you're hurting yourself by giving your friends an advantage over you—they'll know what to expect from the board before they set foot in the room.

How to Present Yourself to the Board

In the oral board interview, you'll be judged not just on your answers to the interview questions, but on how you present yourself. The adage "You can't judge a book by its cover" may be running through your mind right now, but it doesn't apply here. Your appearance and behavior both play a large role in the result of your interview.

Something as simple as the time you arrive for your interview can affect the entire interview itself. If you're early and the interview starts on time, you'll make a better impression than if you get lost on the way there; rush to the interview site; and appear before a panel flustered, sweaty, and out of breath.

To avoid being late, make sure you know the exact date, time, and location of your interview a few days before it actually happens. If you're not sure how long it will take you to travel to the site or if don't know how to get to the location, do a practice drive to the site using the type of transportation (car, bus, bike, taxi) you'll use the day of the interview. This way, you'll know exactly where you're going and how long it'll take you. If you need or want to, you can even go a bit further and enter the building to locate the room or office where you'll interview.

On the day of the interview, arrive 10 to 15 minutes before your scheduled interview time. *Remember:* Arriving late is unprofessional. No one wants to put his life in the hands of a police officer who is repeatedly late for important events or meetings. Because you want to be a police officer, you should follow the rule "Early is on time, and on time is late."

When you arrive at the interview site, be professional and polite to the receptionists, security guards, and anyone else you may encounter in the parking lot of the building, the lobby of the building, or the waiting room. The oral board may ask these men and women to offer their opinions of you, so you need to make a good impression.

Before you even set foot in the interview room, your behavior and appearance have been documented or observed, but the moment you actually enter the room is when you have to turn your charm on full power and start impressing your judges.

The first things that the members of the oral board will notice are nonverbal cues such as your eye contact, posture, and handshake. For example, if you walk into the room with your head held high and your back straight, and you look your interviewers in the eye and offer a firm handshake, the board will assume that you're confident and ready to face challenges that come your way. They may think you're well mannered, professional, and personable. On the other hand, if you enter the room with your eyes glued to the floor and your shoulders slumped, your interviewers may assume that you're not confident. As a police officer responsible for protecting your own life and the lives of many others, you need to believe in yourself and work through the pressure and stress you may feel in emergencies or other dangerous situations.

Before you even begin speaking, your attire will tell the board members a lot about you. In case you haven't noticed by now, police departments are military-like organizations. They like structure, uniformity, and precision in everything—including dress. Members of the military and paramilitary organizations like police departments typically appear neat and orderly: Their hair is clean and well groomed, their uniforms are pressed, and they've place their pins and badges in exactly the right spot. As a police officer—and even as a recruit at the academy—you'll be expected to present yourself in a clean and organized way, so why not get ahead of the game and show the interview board that you're ready for the challenge by dressing professionally and appropriately for your oral interview?

What does dressing professionally for this interview entail? It definitely means that you shouldn't show up in torn jeans and a hooded sweatshirt with stains down the front. It also means that you should consider wearing a business suit or even a pair of pressed dress pants or a skirt with a dress shirt. Men should consider wearing a tie. Women should try not to accessorize too much. Shine your shoes and comb or style your hair. This all seems menial, but putting effort into your appearance shows that you're putting even more of an effort into getting the job and may help your interviewers take you seriously from the moment you enter the room.

Aside from your attire, your interviewers also will grade you on your behavior during the interview, so keep a cool head. Take deep breaths, sit straight in your chair, try not to fidget, and speak clearly. Whether you're introducing yourself or answering a personal question, you should make an effort to keep your voice clear and steady—don't shout, but don't mumble or whisper, either.

If you feel nervous during the interview, that's okay, but don't let your nerves ruin the opportunity for you. When the nerves kick in, you may be inclined to talk faster than you typically would. When you speak quickly, you may slur your words together or even stutter. This makes it difficult for the interviewers to decipher what you've said. They may ask you to repeat yourself or they may misunderstand your answer in its entirety, thus resulting in a lower grade or fewer points on their rating sheets.

To avoid this confusion, take a deep breath before answering the question and think about what you want to say. This should help you avoid tripping over your words or even providing details that aren't necessarily related to what they've asked you. Members of the oral interview board will be impressed when the answers to your questions are organized and well spoken.

It's important to find a balance between taking your time and rushing to answer the interviewers' questions. You want to take a few seconds to collect your thoughts, but you need to make sure that you don't sit in silence for too long. A few seconds should be more than enough to determine what you want to say and begin speaking. Be sure to answer the questions concisely and completely. If you're confused by a question, calmly ask the interviewer to clarify. If you're frustrated with an answer you've given, don't sweat it. Showing this frustration or anger will only cause your judges to dock more points from their rating sheets.

You know that your answers should be honest, complete, concise, and spoken clearly, but they also should be polite. Members of the oral interview board don't only pay attention to the content of your answers; they also listen for the way in which you present your answers. When answering questions, be sure to respond with "Yes, ma'am" and "No, sir" instead of "Yeah," "Yep," "Nope," and "Nah." If you don't understand a question, don't say "Huh?" Instead, say something similar to "I'm not sure I understand the question. Will you please repeat it?" Politely answering the interviewers' questions shows that you understand that you should always respect your authorities and superiors. This is crucial to a police officer's career.

Remember: Listen carefully and don't allow yourself to daydream or your mind to wander. Listen intently to what the interviewers have to say and respond appropriately. Candidates often become nervous during these interviews and may misinterpret questions, answer questions they haven't been asked, or repeat the same response for nearly every question. If you don't understand a question, or if you miss the first half of a question or comment because you weren't paying attention, ask the interviewer if she can repeat the question.

Although what you say and how you say it are the most important things to keep in mind during your oral board interview, remember that your body language speaks volumes about you as well. Interviewers with backgrounds in police work and psychiatry will be able to read every move you make, so be sure to remain aware of what your body is doing during the interview. These behaviors may lead interviewers to believe you're bored, unconfident, or unaware of your presence around people. During the oral interview, try not to:

- Slouch in your chair.
- Bounce your feet or knees.
- Wring your hands.
- Scratch or rub your body.
- Touch your hair.
- Drum your fingers.
- Play with your pen.
- Pick or bite your nails.
- Tug at your clothing.
- Rest your chin in your hand.
- Avoid eye contact.
- Sniffle.
- Sigh.
- Yawn.

In addition, don't have gum in your mouth during your interview, and turn off your cellphone and leave it in your pocket or purse.

Tip: Ideal candidates dress professionally and appear friendly and confident in their abilities to be police officers. They show an interest in police work; answer the board's questions honestly, accurately, and concisely; and are well mannered. They sit up straight in their chairs, make eye contact with the board members, and keep their hands relaxed in their laps. Behave appropriately—don't let your first impression be your last.

At the end of the interview, the interviewers may ask you if you have anything to add or if you have any questions about the process. If you think you have qualities they've yet to discover that will help you get the job, this is your time to share. This is one of your last opportunities to stress that you're the right person for the job, so make sure to close the interview on a high note. Try choosing two or three good qualities or characteristics about yourself and say something similar to, "I just want you to know that I'm a dedicated individual and I enjoy working with others to solve problems. I look forward to being part of the department."

All interviews should begin and end with a firm handshake and a smile. Thank the board for meeting with you and leave the room with your head held high. Say goodbye to the receptionists, tell the security guards to enjoy the rest of their day, and then let it all out. Smile, laugh, or simply try to relax. At this point, it's out of your hands. Your interview board will decide if you get to continue or if you should be eliminated as a candidate.

How to Prepare for the Oral Board Interview

Now that you know what the oral board interview entails, we're going to help you prepare for it. You already know your dress should be professional and neat and you should arrive early, but there are plenty of other tips and tricks to acing the oral interview.

You can't exactly *study* for the interview, because you don't know which questions your interview board will actually ask, but you can (and should) still spend some time preparing for it. The interview is your chance to show the panel that you're the best candidate for the job. You want the board to know that you'll be a dedicated, reliable, honest, and enthusiastic member of their department. For this reason, you should spend time preparing for this opportunity.

As you already know, the panel of interviewers for your oral board interview will most likely consist of a number of people. Because you'll have to speak in front of a group at the interview, you should practice speaking in front of a group of people. Even if you consider yourself to be a good public speaker, you can benefit from practice.

To practice, you might consider holding a mock interview or two. Ask your friends or family members to act as your panel. Have them create questions similar to the ones discussed in "What to Expect from the Interview," earlier in this appendix. These questions will most likely be similar to those your panel will ask, so this will give you a chance to prepare exactly what you would say in case the interviewers ask you similar questions.

Mock interviews also help you identify and change bad habits that you might not even realize you have. You may not know that you tend to wring your hands, touch your hair, or drum your fingers. Your friends or family members will notice these habits during the interview and point them out to you. After you identify any bad habits, you can change them so that you avoid sending nonverbal cues to your oral interview board that may make them believe you're bored, unnecessarily worrisome, or not confident in yourself.

Your friends and family members can also tell you whether you say words and phrases such as *um* or *like* while you speak. They also can pick out moments when you should say "yes" instead of "yeah" and "no" instead of "nah" or "nope."

Once you have all this information, you'll know exactly what you need to work on for the interview. You'll be able to make a conscious effort to stop using *um* and *like,* to keep your knees from bouncing, and to keep your hands out of your hair. You'll be able to teach yourself to slow the speed at which you speak and to properly enunciate your words.

If you're not comfortable asking your friends or family members for help, reach out to a fellow candidate and ask if you can practice with him. Someone who is experiencing the same process as you may be even more helpful because that person understands what you're going through and may have additional information to offer.

> **Tip: If no one's available to practice with you, you can always stand or sit in front of a mirror and practice. The mirror won't lie. You'll easily be able to catch any awkward or repetitive movements. If you're worried about repeating words, stuttering, or mumbling, record yourself answering a few questions and play it back. Listening to the recording will help you identify and fix any problem areas you have in your speech.**

Another way to prepare yourself for the interview process is to contact your local police department and see if you can volunteer your time with them. Ask if they'll allow you to come down to the station and speak with a few officers, help at the front desk, or even accompany them on a few patrol routes. If you get such an opportunity, talk to the police officers and detectives to gain insight into their jobs. Members of the oral interview board will most likely ask you scenario-based questions that place you in an officer's shoes, so if you can, find out how they would respond in certain situations.

When spending time with career police officers, ask them questions such as:

- What is a typical day like for you?
- Why did you become a police officer?
- What challenges have you faced as a police officer?
- What is the most rewarding aspect of being a police officer?
- What advice do you have for people like me who are interested in law enforcement?

Although first-hand interviews with officers will teach you about the work they do, you can learn other information about law enforcement in books and magazines and on the Internet. You can read about the history of police work in the United States, crime trends and rates, technological advances that have improved law enforcement, and so on. Every bit of information will help you prepare.

Another way to prepare for your interview is to learn about the town, city, or region in which you'd like to be a police officer. Find out as much as you can about the area where you'd be working if the department decided to hire you. Research the most popular restaurants and annual community events in the area. You'll impress your panel if you show that you have an understanding of the city and the citizens you want to serve.

The most important thing you can do to prepare for your oral board interview, however, is to know yourself. Understand your own moral code and values and be sure of where you stand on sensitive issues. Know what you like to do with your spare time and why you enjoy those activities. Have some personal stories prepared in case they ask you for more details about the time you studied abroad in Ireland or the road trip you took last summer with your father. These stories will help showcase your personality and your ability to talk about topics unrelated to police work.

Be sure to review your job application, résumé, and personal history statement before you go to your interview. You should know these documents like the back of your hand. These papers speak for you before you get to speak for yourself, so your interview board will be familiar with them before you walk into the room. If there are discrepancies between your statement and your résumé, know why. If you had a three-month break in employment last year, be able to explain why you didn't work during that time period. If you never went to college because of financial difficulties or family issues, but you want to someday earn a degree, be sure to explain that during the interview as well. You should be able to answer any questions about your educational or work history during the interview.

Remember: The more you prepare for the oral board interview, the more comfortable you'll feel in the interview setting. Dress professionally, act appropriately, speak clearly, and give the best interview you can. Take the time to prepare and be sure to let the board know that you're the best candidate for the job.

The Medical and Psychological Evaluations

The process of becoming a police officer can be compared to a long and winding road with a lot of stops along the way. These "stops" include the police officer exam, the physical ability test, and the oral interview. The final two stops along the road to becoming a police officer are the medical and psychological evaluations. These evaluations are vitally important because they ensure that you and all the other candidates are ready for active duty as a police officer.

For candidates to be allowed into the academy, they must prove that their bodies and minds are ready for the challenging training and work that lie ahead. Police work is demanding. It demands you to perform physically and mentally exhausting tasks such as chasing suspects, directing traffic, testifying in court, and collecting evidence. If your body or mind isn't up for these challenges, you could put your life and the lives of others in danger.

In this section, we take a close look at the medical evaluation and the psychological evaluation. Unlike the police officer exam or physical ability test, you can't study or prepare for these evaluations. You can't control your medical background or your genetics, but you can and should know what to expect.

The Medical Evaluation

The medical evaluation is similar to a detailed physical exam performed by your family doctor. During the medical evaluation, the doctor will not only examine your body, but also ask you about your personal medical history and possibly your family's medical history. Because you'll be answering questions about your medical history, it's a good idea to write down any important information about your health, including medications you're allergic to, surgeries you've undergone, and immunizations you've had. You also may write down information about any serious illnesses that occurred in your family.

> Tip: Don't lie to the physician during the medical evaluation. Generally, the truth will eventually come to light, and you could be disqualified from the application process or even be removed from your position on the police force. The rules that police forces have about medical requirements are to ensure the safety of all the officers and the public. If you lie about your medical conditions to get on the force, you're putting your safety, your fellow officers' safety, and the public's safety at risk.

Once the doctor has gathered your medical history, he'll record your weight, height, temperature, and blood pressure. This is important because many police departments have strict height, weight, and body-fat percentage standards, which you must meet to be eligible to continue in the hiring process. You must be able to perform essential tasks, such as chasing a suspect, without your weight affecting your ability to do so. Next, the physician will examine your eyes, ears, nose, and mouth, and check your heart and lungs for any potential problems.

After the basic examination is complete, the doctor will perform a more detailed medical evaluation to determine if you're healthy enough to work as a police officer. Because you can't prevent or control certain medical diseases or conditions—especially those that run in your family—you shouldn't get too worked up about this part of the evaluation. Not all medical conditions will disqualify you from becoming a police officer, but some more serious conditions may. It all depends on the specific department's standards.

Tip: Every police department has its own set of medical standards. Contact the specific police department for more information regarding its medical standards. Learning this information early can help you from being surprised later in the hiring process.

In the following sections, we explain some of the more specific tests and procedures that a physician may perform during the medical evaluation.

Eyes

Having good vision is very important for a police officer. You need to be able to see at near and far distances so you can perform the everyday responsibilities of a police officer, including reading license-plate numbers and house numbers, identifying suspects, and so on. Some eye conditions can be corrected, but others, such as color blindness, can prevent an individual from becoming a police officer. Police officers must be able to decipher colors to identify suspects, vehicles, and more, so being colorblind will generally disqualify potential law-enforcement candidates.

Along with testing your ability to see colors and your peripheral vision, the physician will test your ability to see distances. Many people have experienced eye exams in which they look at a chart of numbers and letters and are asked to read the smallest line of print they can. During the medical evaluation, you'll undergo the same type of eye exam. If you wear corrective lenses or glasses, you may be tested with the corrective lenses and without the corrective lenses. Some departments allow officers to wear corrective lenses, while others insist that officers have good vision without corrective lenses.

Ears

Because officers must be alert and aware of their surroundings, it makes sense that they must have the ability to hear well. A police officer needs to be able to hear sirens, gunshots, radio dispatches, and normal conversations. During the medical evaluation, the physician will conduct a hearing test and look into both of your ears to check for any conditions such as infection or deformity.

An audiometer and headphones will be used to measure how well you can hear different-pitched tones and sounds. Some hearing loss—depending on the severity—may not disqualify you from becoming a police officer. These standards vary at various departments, so be sure to check with the department you're applying to.

Heart and Lungs

During the medical evaluation, the physician will also monitor your heart and lungs. She'll listen to your heart and lungs, take your pulse rate, and check your blood pressure. These simple tests are used to determine if any heart or lung conditions exist and whether they require further tests, such as a chest x-ray, an electrocardiogram, or a cardiac stress test.

Range of Motion and Reflexes

Police officers have to perform many physical tasks on the job. Running, climbing, crawling, and lifting all can be part of a police officer's daily duties. Because officers may be required to complete physical tasks, they should be able to bend, stretch, and move with ease. The physician performing the medical evaluation will most likely ask you to touch your toes and bend in various ways so he can make sure your range of motion and reflexes are adequate for the job. Candidates whose reflexes or ranges of motion are inadequate may be disqualified. The physician also may look for disorders of your musculoskeletal system, such as arthritis, fractures, dislocations, or a muscle strains.

Drug Use

During the medical evaluation, you'll most likely be required to give blood and urine samples so the physician can test for diseases and for drug use. Having illegal drugs in your system will most likely disqualify you from a position in any police force. Officers who are in charge of upholding the law can't be compromised by breaking the law through taking illegal drugs. If the physician detects legal drugs in your system, you'll be required to verify that you have prescriptions for those drugs. Because you know you want to be a part of law enforcement, you should never take illegal drugs and be sure not to abuse legal drugs.

Other Diseases, Illnesses, and Conditions

As you already know, you should be prepared to give blood and urine samples during the medical evaluation. The blood and urine samples can tell the physician if you have any number of diseases that could hinder your performance as a police officer. You may be tested for diseases such as diabetes, HIV/AIDS, anemia, glandular disorders (such as hypothyroidism or Addison's disease), and more.

In addition to taking blood and urine samples, the physician will review your medical records and take note of diseases such as epilepsy, gastrointestinal disorders, and heart disease. During the physical part of the evaluation, the doctor will check for problems such as hernias. Men undergoing the medical evaluation may be checked for diseases of the prostate and testicles. Women may be tested for pregnancy and uterine diseases.

> Tip: Because the physician conducting your medical evaluation will take blood and urine samples for testing, you most likely will not know the results of the evaluation for a few weeks. It's important to remain patient throughout the process. Your patience and determination will help prove you're ready to become a police officer.

The Psychological Evaluation

Some law-enforcement organizations do psychological evaluations only in certain circumstances. For example, candidates who've had any problems with the law in the past can expect to undergo psychological evaluations. Other organizations require all candidates to undergo these evaluations. Just hearing the term *psychological evaluation* can make some candidates nervous, but you actually have nothing to worry about.

This evaluation is designed to examine how well you perform in stressful situations and to test your mental stability. The information from the psychological evaluation is used by police departments to help them determine if you're the right fit for the job. It also shows them the personality traits you possess, such as your leadership skills, honesty, and ability to work as part of a team.

The psychological evaluation usually consists of a personality test that may be followed by a session with a psychologist or psychiatrist. As with the medical evaluation, this varies from department to department.

Tip: Be truthful. Answer each question during the psychological examination honestly, and don't choose answers based on what you think the psychologist wants to hear. If you lie and the psychologist knows that you're being dishonest, it could reflect badly on you as a candidate.

The Personality Test

You can't study for the personality test, but you can be prepared. As long as you answer the questions honestly, you should have no problem with this portion of the psychological evaluation. The test usually contains several hundred questions and takes a few hours to complete. Check with the department before the test, so you know how long the test will take.

The personality test contains questions that are designed to evaluate your attitude, interests, and motivation for wanting to become a police officer. The following is a list of the kinds of questions that may be asked on the personality test:

- Do you enjoy speaking in front of groups?
- Do you pay attention to details?
- Are you relaxed most of the time?
- Do you often forget to put things back in their proper places?
- Do you enjoy being isolated?
- Do you get stressed easily?
- Are you interested in people?
- Do you feel comfortable around people?
- Are you usually prepared?

The personality test will ask about these and other personality traits by presenting a statement such as, "I prefer working in a team." Then you state whether you think the statement fits your personality. Some of these questions may be in a true/false format, so you'll answer *true* if the statement fits your personality, and you'll answer *false* if the statement doesn't fit your personality. Other questions may ask you to use a scale system to rate how much you agree or disagree with the statement. This scale will most likely include the choices *strongly agree, agree, neither agree nor disagree, disagree,* and *strongly disagree.* If you very much prefer to work in a team, you should answer *strongly agree,* but if you very much prefer to work by yourself, you should answer *strongly disagree.*

When answering either type of question, make sure you state how you really feel about these statements or how you would typically react in certain situations. Don't stress out about these questions or spend too much time analyzing any one question. Go with your first choice, and trust your gut instinct. Many police forces give these tests because they can help identify which candidates are best for the job. Law-enforcement jobs are critical in society, so it's important that all the people working in these jobs are right for their positions. As long as you answer the questions honestly, you'll do well on this portion of the evaluation.

The Psychologist Interview

Just like the personality test, not all departments require you to interview with a professional psychologist or psychiatrist. But some do, so that's why you should prepare for it. You shouldn't feel nervous because the psychologist won't make you lie on a couch or pick your brain to reveal your deepest, darkest secrets. The psychologist will ask questions related to your education, work experience, relationships, and interests. She may ask questions about your application, personal history statement, or personality questionnaire, or ask you how you would handle a hypothetical situation. The psychologist may also delve into problems you may have had in your past—especially if these problems were revealed during the background check. As long as you're honest and open and accept responsibility for your past actions, you shouldn't necessarily be disqualified from the hiring process.

The following are a few examples of the types of questions the psychologist may ask:

- What types of activities do you like to do in your spare time?
- Why did you leave your last job?
- How did you become interested in police work?
- How would you react to a situation that left you permanently injured?
- What type of student were you in high school or college?
- What would you do if you saw a person drop a $100 bill on the ground?
- What are you afraid of?
- Do you prefer to work alone or in a group setting?
- How do you react to criticism?
- How would you describe yourself?

Your answers, along with the way you respond to these questions, help the psychologist learn more about you and help her determine if you have the mental and emotional stability to handle the stress that comes with being a police officer.

Tip: You can't study for the psychological interview, but as long as you relax and answer the questions honestly, you shouldn't have any problems with the interview process.

Police officers are tasked with responding to life-threatening situations and making critical decisions in mere seconds. Because of the stresses and responsibilities of the job, it's important that only the candidates with the proper attitudes and personalities get the job. Both the interview with the psychologist and the personality test will help ensure that all the candidates are ready for what will be expected of them at the academy and during their careers.

The Physical Ability Test

Becoming a police officer is a process that takes dedication, commitment, and hard work. As you go through the process of becoming a police officer, you'll prepare by filling out paperwork, studying, and practicing speaking in front of others. Another way to prepare to become a police officer is to exercise. Police departments usually require applicants to complete a physical ability test, sometimes also known as the physical agility test or the fitness test, to prove that they're ready for the physical challenges of being a police officer.

Although officers spend a lot of time patrolling and completing paperwork, they also have to run, jump, climb, and crawl when it's necessary. Police officers are expected to be in excellent physical condition, and the physical ability test ensures that only physically fit candidates move on in the hiring process.

Even though the physical ability test will test your physical ability, you won't be expected to be in the same physical shape as cadets who are about to graduate from the academy. In the academy, you'll undergo rigorous physical training that will help you meet the challenges of your job.

As you probably realize by now, all police departments have different eligibility requirements for their candidates. The same is true about the physical ability test. Each department has a specific physical ability test with different events and regulations. Some versions of the physical ability test focus on traditional fitness skills, such as running and doing basic exercises like sit-ups, push-ups, or pull-ups. Other versions of the physical ability test may require recruits to perform physical tasks that are directly related to common police work, such as vehicle exits and the trigger pull. Some departments use a test that combines elements of both basic formats. Although the physical ability test varies from department to department, this appendix provides you with an overview of the most commonly used events on physical ability tests.

Introduction to the Physical Ability Test

Aside from getting yourself into reasonable physical shape, the best way to prepare for the physical ability test is to learn as much about it as possible. Before you try to take the test, spend some time researching it. Learn about why it's used, the required exercise skills you may need to develop, and the common events that are part of most versions of the physical ability test.

You might also try to learn more about the specifics of the physical ability test you'll be taking by seeking information at the police department you're attempting to enter. You may be able to find some information on your physical ability test online. Try visiting the police department's Web site for information about the events included in that department's physical ability test. You also can contact the local municipal office or police department; personnel at the department should be able to offer you the information you need or direct you to someone else who can.

Before you attend your physical ability test, you should have a good idea of what to expect. Be sure you know the answers to the following questions before you attend the test:

- What events will be included on the physical ability test?
- How is each of the events scored?

- What requirements must I meet for each event on the physical ability test?
- Do I have more than one opportunity to pass a particular event?
- Where will the test be given? Will it be administered inside or outside?
- How should I dress for the physical ability test?
- Is there a training program in which I can participate? If so, when and where will it be held, how can I apply, and how much does it cost? If there isn't a training program, are there any department suggestions for preparing for the test?

Researching the physical ability test prior to the day of the test can go a long way toward improving your chances of success. Knowing exactly what you'll be expected to do will help you to focus your training and build your confidence.

Tip: Some police departments have different requirements for male and female candidates, and some departments have the same requirements regardless of gender. Be sure you understand the requirements you have to meet before you attend the physical ability test.

What the Test Is

The physical ability test is part of the multiple-step selection process for prospective police officers that includes a series of tests, evaluations, and interviews designed to determine whether an applicant is eligible and qualified to become a police officer. The physical ability test is the portion of this selection process that measures the physical abilities of applicants through various physical exercises and events. The exact order of the elements in the selection process and the placement of the physical ability test within the process vary based on the requirements mandated by the state and the department itself. Because the physical ability test can be extremely physically demanding at times, applicants may be required to submit to a physical examination before being allowed to take the test. Those applicants who successfully complete the physical ability test then become eligible to move on to the next portion of the selection process.

Remember: The specific events that make up the physical ability test vary, and they're usually determined by the state in which the test is being administered or by the officials in charge of the police department. Sometimes, the makeup of the physical ability test is influenced by the municipality or area the department serves. This means that, outside the governmental requirements that they must follow, each police department is generally free to design its own physical ability test and choose which physical skills it wants its police officer candidates to demonstrate. The important thing to remember is that, wherever you're taking the test, you have to endure a highly challenging physical examination in order to have a chance at becoming a police officer.

The Skills You Need

Regardless of what specific events are included in the physical ability test you take, most forms of the test will be centered on the same basic set of physical skills:

- **Aerobic endurance and power:** Aerobic endurance and power exercises are designed to push your cardiovascular system to its limits. These exercises quickly raise your heart rate and dramatically increase the flow of blood throughout your body. An aerobic power workout forces you to breathe harder, which increases your oxygen intake. This makes your heart start pumping faster in order to meet your body's high demand for oxygenated blood. The more physically fit you are, the longer you'll likely be able to sustain such a workout. Specific examples of exercises that will help you improve your aerobic power include swimming, cycling, and long-distance runs or walks.

- **Anaerobic power:** Anaerobic power exercises have the same basic effect on your body as aerobic power exercises, but they work a bit differently. Where aerobic power exercises are long lasting and generally involve a steady level of physical effort, anaerobic power exercises consist of short bursts of extremely high-intensity effort. During these exercises, your body's demand for oxygen will often surpass its supply. Short-distance sprinting and weight lifting are examples of anaerobic power exercises.

- **Strength:** Strength exercises are all about muscular power. If you're asked to perform some sort of strength exercise on the physical ability test, the exam administrators will be looking to test your muscular force abilities. Weight lifting and resistance training are examples of strength exercises.

- **Muscle endurance:** Muscle endurance exercises are simple, repetitive movements that force you to use a certain group of muscles over and over again for a long period. Different types of endurance exercises each target specific muscle groups. For example, sit-ups target your abdominal muscles and push-ups target the chest, arm, and back muscles.

- **Flexibility:** Flexibility exercises are based on your ability to stretch your muscles. Your flexibility may be tested through activities such as climbing, crawling, or bending. Simply reaching for an object from various positions would be an example of a less strenuous flexibility exercise.

- **Agility:** Agility exercises are designed to test your coordination. These exercises often require you to perform quick movements or rapidly change directions. Some examples of agility exercises include climbing stairs and hurdling obstacles.

These skills are critical for police officers, and developing these skills is a very important part of preparing for the physical ability test.

The Events

The individual events of the physical ability test are determined by the state, local municipality, or police department. Many times, all three of these sources play a role in the development of a specific physical ability test. In this section, we outline some of the most common physical ability test events.

Dash or Sprint

Some police departments require candidates to complete a dash or a sprint as part of the physical ability test. Many departments that include this type of event require candidates to run 300 meters as quickly as they can. If a dash is part of your physical ability test, you'll be timed while you run. The time requirements will vary by department, but if you're completing a 300-meter dash, you'll most likely have to complete it in less than 80 seconds.

Tip: A 300-meter dash covers approximately three-fourths of one lap of a standard track.

Run

A running test is included in many physical ability tests, and the 1½-mile run is one of the most common running tests. By including a 1½-mile run, test administrators may judge your aerobic power. Because officers in the field frequently pursue fleeing suspects, candidates must be able to run long distances. If your physical ability test includes a 1½-mile run, it will most likely be timed. Although different departments have different required times, you'll most likely be expected to complete the run in less than 19 minutes.

If a 1½-mile run will be part of your physical ability test, be sure to warm up before you run. If you start the run cold, you risk injury and disqualification. Take a five-minute cool-down walk after the event.

The administrator will tell you your time as soon as you cross the finish line.

Vertical Jump

In the normal course of their duties, police officers occasionally find themselves in situations where they must climb walls or fences or jump over various obstacles. These actions require explosive leg power. The vertical jump is specifically designed to demonstrate your explosive leg power.

Police departments often use the Vertec vertical-jump testing device for this event. This apparatus is an adjustable vertical pole with lines called *vanes* on one side. The test administrator adjusts the testing device according to your height so that you can just barely touch the lowest vane when standing normally with one arm raised.

Keep the following tips in mind when taking this test:

- The distance you should stand away from the device will probably be marked. If it isn't, remember that either your right or left foot should be no more than 12 inches from the device. Also, remember that you may not move the foot nearest to the device before the jump begins.
- Jump as high as you possibly can and reach upward at all times.
- As you reach your maximum height, lightly tap the Vertec vanes to make them move. This indicates the height of your jump for the test administrator.
- You'll be allowed three jumps. Only your highest score will be counted.

Obviously, your goal in this event is to jump as high as you possibly can, but about 13½ inches is usually the lowest acceptable height.

Modified Squat Thrust

This challenging event will likely push you to your limits while testing your stamina, coordination, and agility. This may be one of the most difficult portions of the physical ability test. To perform the modified squat thrust, follow these steps:

1. **Lie chest-down on the floor mat beside the 3-foot-high rail vault.**
2. **Quickly stand and vault yourself over the rail to the floor mat on the opposite side.**
3. **When you reach the opposite side, touch your back to the floor mat, and then stand.**
4. **Repeat this exercise until both your back and your chest have touched the floor mat five times.**

Because this is a timed event, you need to complete your squat thrusts as quickly as possible. On most tests, the maximum acceptable time is 60 seconds.

Warning: If you grab the rail during the modified squat thrust, you may be given a penalty in the form of time added to your score.

Push-ups

Push-ups are one of the exercises you'll likely have to complete on the physical ability test, as well as at the police academy. Some push-up tests are timed and others are untimed. Generally, if your push-up test is timed, it will be one minute long. Although doing as many push-ups as you can during the time allotted is important, you should pay close attention to your form while doing the push-ups. If you complete a push-up incorrectly, the test administrator won't count that push-up toward your total. You can tire quickly if you have to do more work because your form was incorrect.

Here's the correct method for doing a push-up:

1. **Put your hands on the ground, keeping them shoulder-width apart with your fingers facing forward.**
2. **Starting from the "up" position, lock your elbows, and straighten your back.**
3. **Lower your body until your chest is only a few inches from the ground. (During the physical ability test, you may have to touch your chest to an object on the ground.)**
4. **Resume the "up" position with only your hands and toes touching the ground.**

Sit-ups

Sit-ups are another type of exercise that is common on many physical ability tests. Sit-ups test your abdominal muscle endurance. Some departments require candidates to complete a certain number of sit-ups in a specific amount of time. Other departments require candidates to complete a certain number of sit-ups without a time limit. Many of the events in physical ability tests require you to complete the exercise using a specific, proper form.

To properly execute a sit-up:

1. **Lie on your back, bend your knees, and keep your feet flat on the ground.**
2. **Lock your fingers behind your head and ask a friend to hold your feet on the ground or use a heavy object to keep them stationary. (At the time of the physical ability test, another candidate will most likely hold your feet in place.)**
3. **Sit up and touch your elbows to your knees.**
4. **Recline backward and touch your shoulder blades to the ground.**

When you're completing sit-ups, your hips should remain on the floor the entire time. If your hips rise from the floor when you're completing one of your sit-ups, that repetition won't be counted toward your total. Keeping the correct form is vital in order to pass the physical ability test.

Tip: Some departments may increase the difficulty of the testing by requiring you to wear a weighted vest or belt during all or some of the events. Officers must carry heavy gear while they're on duty, and wearing a vest or belt that simulates the weight helps determine which candidates are best suited for the job.

Pull-ups

Pull-ups are included on physical ability tests to test your upper-body strength and muscle endurance. Pull-ups are physically demanding, and police departments are usually strict about the form a candidate uses to complete the exercise. Most pull-up tests are untimed, but you have to complete a certain number of pull-ups without stopping in order to pass.

Bike Peddling

Bike peddling is a required event on some physical ability tests because it tests candidates' leg power and endurance. To pass this section of the physical ability test, you'll likely have to pedal a stationary bike as quickly as you can for a set amount of time (for example, two minutes). This event is generally rated by the speed you keep while you pedal.

Weight Lifting

Weight lifting is included on some physical ability tests because it tests muscle endurance. Police academies require cadets to lift weights at the academy, so you'll be ahead of the game if you practice weight lifting for your physical ability test. Generally, candidates have to lift a percentage of their body weight or a set number of pounds—whichever is smaller.

Stair Climb or Stair Climb with Window Entry

These two tests are used to test your strength, endurance, and flexibility. During the stair climb, you'll be expected to run as quickly as you can up and down flights of stairs. This test is timed, and you'll have to move quickly to pass.

The stair climb with window entry is similar to the stair climb, but you'll have to climb through a window frame at the top of the stairs after you've finished running. This event is also timed.

Obstacle Courses

Some police departments include obstacle courses in the physical ability test. These courses can include a number of different challenges such as fences and stairs to climb and cones to run around. Typically, obstacle courses are timed, and you have to finish all the required steps in order to pass. Often, candidates will be allowed to have a practice run through the obstacle course before they officially perform the course for the physical ability test. If you're given an opportunity to go through the course, you should take it. Understanding the course will help you pass this part of the physical ability test.

Vehicle Exit

Physical ability tests sometimes include a vehicle-exit event so police departments can test candidates on how quickly they can exit a vehicle. Although exiting a vehicle is something most people do on a regular basis, candidates performing vehicle exits as part of their physical ability tests must exit within seconds. Generally, when you perform this test, you'll be sitting in the front seat of a squad car with your seatbelt buckled and the door open.

Trigger Pull

Because police officers are expected to be able to hold and fire a weapon, some physical ability tests require candidates to complete a trigger-pull test. The exact requirements of the trigger pull can vary widely on different versions of the physical ability test. For many of these tests, you have to raise an inoperative weapon and quickly pull the trigger a certain number of times using both hands. Other tests require candidates to hold a weapon with their arms extended for a certain period of time; in this type of test, you may not even have to pull the weapon's trigger.

Weight Drag

Some physical ability tests require candidates to perform weight drags because officers sometimes have to lift or drag people to safety. Most of these tests require candidates to drag a weighted dummy or bag for a certain distance. For the most basic dummy drag, you'll be required to simply drag a dummy over a given distance in a short amount of time. In more challenging dummy drags, you may be asked to first remove the dummy from a structure or a car before dragging it the required distance.

An Exercise Guide

When you're trying to get yourself into shape, physical activity is the name of the game. This doesn't necessarily mean hitting the gym every day, however. You can start simply by walking, running, or doing any type of exercise. One great way to build and maintain your condition is to play sports. Team sports such as football, baseball, basketball, or soccer may provide excellent strength, stamina, and cardiovascular training. If you aren't into team sports, you can try individual activities such as bicycling, hiking, jogging, and rowing—all of which can make considerable contributions toward your physical fitness. You also may try enrolling in a fitness class. Organized programs that feature activities such as aerobics, calisthenics, or yoga can be beneficial and are usually led by well-trained professionals who can offer guidance and other training ideas. Classes that involve hand-to-hand combat, such as martial arts or kickboxing, can serve the dual purpose of increasing your fitness level and introducing you to the concepts of self-defense, which are often very useful for police officers.

If you want to take your training to the next level, exercise programs are a great way to get in shape in anticipation of the physical ability test. Either on your own or with the help of a fitness professional, you can create an entire training program to get your body into shape and ready for the physical challenge that awaits you in the physical ability test. An exercise program can combine elements of various kinds of physical activities like weight lifting, aerobics, and endurance exercises and offer you a well-rounded training regimen that is sure to improve your physical fitness.

Remember: Before you begin an exercise program, ensure that the program you choose is right for you and that you know how to proceed wisely and safely. Your personal health and safety should always be your number-one concern.

The following is a brief guide designed to help you make the most of your training and avoid unnecessary injuries.

Tip: Some police departments require candidates going to the police academy to prove that they're still physically prepared to be a police officer by completing the physical ability test upon arrival at the academy. Even after you've passed your physical ability test, stay in shape and exercise regularly so you can perform well once you reach the academy.

Get the Green Light from Your Doctor

The first thing you should do before attempting to start any type of training program is to make sure that you're healthy enough to engage in strenuous physical activity. Make an appointment with your doctor and get a physical examination. Your doctor can tell you if you have any preexisting conditions that may make working out dangerous for your health. Know what your body can handle before you start working out.

Choose the Right Program

Once you know that you're fit enough for exercise, you need to choose a program that's right for you. If you're new to exercise, don't try to start an advanced training program right off the bat. Not only will this approach fail, but it will also likely lead to injury. Your body probably won't be ready for anything too difficult in the beginning, so start slowly and work your way toward more advanced exercises.

Most doctors and fitness experts recommend working out at least three times a week. To prepare for a physical test like the physical ability test, you should try to work out at least five times a week. This may seem like a lot, but it will pay off.

Remember: The physical ability test is a very basic physical exam. You won't be expected to be as fit as an actual police officer is. You'll receive that level of training if you pass the physical ability test, make it through the rest of the selection process, and enroll in a police academy. To start, you just want to ensure that you're in good enough shape to endure the physical events of the physical ability test.

Warm Up

Before you start any workout, you should always take at least a few minutes to warm up. If your body has been at rest for a long period, your muscles will likely be stiff and your circulation level may be low. If you start an intense workout in this shape, you could be risking injuries such as pulled muscles and strained ligaments or tendons.

To prevent possible injuries, always start your workouts with some simple stretching exercises. Stretching can loosen up your muscles and get your blood flowing properly. This can help to prevent injuries and ensure a more successful workout. Stretching also can help improve your flexibility, increase your range of motion, and alleviate stress.

Remember: You can't pass the physical ability test if you get hurt during training, so always warm up before your workouts.

Cool Down

By the time you finish your workout, your body will be in overdrive. Ending your workout abruptly can lead to injuries, so end your exercise session slowly and progressively. This will gently lower your heart rate and allow your muscles to begin relaxing.

When you've completed the main portion of your workout, do some more simple stretching exercises or take a light walk. This will help cool down your muscles and return your body to its normal state. Cool-down exercises not only help to prevent injuries, but also increase the effectiveness of your workout, so taking your time and ending your workout gradually will be of great physical benefit.

Eat a Healthy Diet

Maintaining a healthy diet can be difficult. You may not necessarily have to go on a diet, but you should pay closer attention to what you're eating. Try to eat healthier foods in reasonable portions. Avoid too much junk food or foods with too much fat. Try to eat on a regular schedule and reduce the amount of snacking you do throughout the day.

Remember: If you don't control your diet, your exercise sessions won't be as productive as they could be. Exercise and diet go hand in hand, and physical fitness is dependent upon both factors.

Nix Bad Habits

Bad habits such as smoking and excessive drinking can take a toll on your health and physical fitness. If you're a smoker, try to stop now. Once you're in the police academy, you won't be able to smoke or drink. Talk to your doctor if you feel you need help ending these habits.

Get Enough Rest and Sleep

You need to get plenty of rest to stay in shape. A good, strenuous workout can take a toll on your body. Rest allows your muscles to relax, heal, and grow. If you don't give your body adequate time to rest, you could be at risk for an injury. Make sure you take time to rest between workouts and other activities and give your body a chance to regenerate.

Also, be sure you're getting enough sleep. The body needs sleep to function properly. Getting a good night's sleep is like recharging your batteries. If you don't charge yourself all the way, you'll run out of energy, possibly when you need it the most. Aim for at least eight hours of sleep a night. This will help to ensure that you have enough energy to get you through the day.

Stay Motivated

Staying motivated and on track is vital if you want to pass your physical ability test. To help you stay on track, ask a family member or friend to work out with you and help you monitor you progress. You can ask your partner to work out with you and cheer you on when you get tired. You can also ask someone to time you while you run, hold your feet while you do sit-ups, or count the number of push-ups you've done. Having someone to support you while you train can make a world of difference.

> **Tip: If you know the requirements of your physical ability test before you go, you should try to meet and even surpass those standards during your workouts. Use a journal to track your workout schedule and to track how close you are to meeting the physical ability test requirements.**

Don't get discouraged if you don't see immediate results. It'll take time, but you'll get there. Don't give up!

Test-Day Reminders

The best way you can prepare yourself to take the physical ability test is to stay strong, both physically and mentally. It's very important to get in shape and stay positive because you'll need your mind and body to be at their best when you start the test. Mentally, you should build your confidence by remembering your goals and believing in yourself. Physically, you should exercise often; eat healthy, balanced meals on a regular basis; and get plenty of sleep.

In the last few days before the test, you may want to reduce the length and intensity of your workout sessions so your body is well rested. The day before and the morning of the test, you should eat only light meals so that you don't feel full or get sick during testing. Some applicants choose not to eat anything at all for a few hours prior to the test for this reason.

When your test day finally arrives, make sure that you're prepared with everything you need:

- **Proper attire:** If your physical ability test has a standard dress code, you'll know exactly what kind of clothing to wear or to avoid. If there is no set dress code, you'll have to decide what to wear on your own. Opt for simple, casual clothes, and comfortable athletic shoes or sneakers.

  If your test will be conducted outdoors, keep the current weather conditions in mind. On hot summer days, you'll likely want to wear shorts and a light T-shirt to prevent yourself from overheating. On colder days, you may want to wear sweatpants and a sweatshirt. Dressing in layers is often a wise choice—this way, you can remove an article of clothing if you get too warm.

- **Water, juice, or a sports drink:** Though you may choose not to eat anything before the test, you must drink plenty of fluids. Staying hydrated throughout the test is key to operating at your peak performance level. Drinking lots of water or juice will keep you hydrated during the test. A sports drink will also replenish your body's supply of carbohydrates and electrolytes. Avoid caffeinated beverages or energy drinks—these may leave you feeling jittery or cause your metabolism to crash in the middle of the test.

- **Paperwork:** Often, you'll be required to fill out various forms in advance. Remember to bring these important forms with you on test day. Without them, you may not be allowed to participate.

  Some physical ability tests also require you to present a doctor's note certifying that you're physically qualified to take the test. If this is the case with your physical ability test and you show up without your doctor's permission, you'll likely be denied permission to test.

- **Identification:** You may be asked to bring some form of photo identification, such as a valid driver's license or a passport. Keep these items on you or in an easy-to-reach place.

- **Payment:** Many departments charge applicants a fee to take the physical ability test, so you'll need to be prepared to pay the fee. The price will be determined by the department, but most are around $25 to $50. In many cases, a check or money order is the preferred method of payment, but check beforehand to make sure.

The Personal History Statement

The ideal police officer candidate has an immaculate record, is the picture of health, and can easily handle the challenges that law-enforcement officers face every day. Of course, very few candidates meet these high standards. It may be impossible to find an ideal candidate, but police departments are looking for the best person for the job. One tool that police departments use to assess candidates is the personal history statement. Candidates fill out this document after passing the police officer exam and submit their statements with a formal job application.

The personal history statement requires you to list details about your past. Background investigators will then verify every detail of this statement for accuracy. You'll be notified if something doesn't check out, and investigators may interview you to clear up any discrepancies. This is why it's important to include all relevant details when answering questions on the personal history statement. What you reveal—or don't reveal—affects the department's decision to hire you.

Tip: Don't lie or embellish your answers on the personal history statement. The police department checks out everything you include in this statement, so it's best to be honest.

The personal history statement asks for a lot of information, so you should start gathering the necessary data and documents as soon as you learn the results of your police officer exam. Keep in mind that many departments have deadlines for submissions, so you must organize your records quickly.

The personal history statement varies from department to department, but candidates are usually asked to include the following information:

- General information, including your name, address, date of birth, telephone numbers, and driver's license number
- Physical description, including your height, weight, hair color, eye color, and any identifying marks, such as scars or tattoos
- Information about any arrests, jail time, and lawsuits
- Traffic-record information, including accidents and tickets
- Military-service information
- Information about your family members
- Educational background
- Work skills and employment history, including every job you've ever worked (whether part-time, full-time, or volunteer), and the names and contact information of your current and previous supervisors or managers
- Residential information, including previous addresses, names and contact information of your current and previous landlords or property managers, and names and contact information of your current or previous neighbors
- Driving history, possibly including every traffic violation you've received in the past five years (speeding tickets, driving violations, parking violations, and so on)

- Financial information, including all outstanding debts
- Club or association memberships
- Awards or accomplishments
- Your signature
- A recent photograph of yourself
- Names of personal and/or professional references (friends, neighbors, or employers who can verify information about you and provide the investigator with an unbiased opinion of your personality, work ethic, or character), as well as their current contact information

Tip: Family members, such as siblings and parents, should not be included as references. Make sure you trust your references—after all, the information these people provide could determine whether you get the job. Always include updated contact information for your references.

Remember to include all relevant information in your personal history statement. Some departments only require you to include information from the past decade, while others ask for details from your childhood. If you can't remember the address of that apartment you lived in five years ago or the name of your high school principal, ask friends and relatives for assistance.

You'll also need to include copies of several important documents, such as your birth certificate and Social Security card, with your personal history statement. If you don't have these documents or aren't sure where they are, you may need to apply for new ones.

Tip: It may take up to six weeks to receive replacements of birth certificates or Social Security cards.

The following is a list of documents you may need to submit copies of with your completed personal history statement:

- Birth certificate
- Social Security card
- DD Form 214 (veterans only)
- Naturalization papers (if applicable)
- High school diploma or equivalent
- High school transcripts
- College transcripts
- Driver's license
- Driving record (available from your local department of motor vehicles)
- Credit report
- Selective Service card
- Marriage certificate or divorce papers

Keep in mind that some departments require original copies of these documents, while others require only a photocopy. In some cases, a department may ask that certain documents, such as your driving record or college transcripts, be sent directly to them from the issuing institution. Contact the police department to find out the proper procedure for filing these documents.